GEM
CUTTING

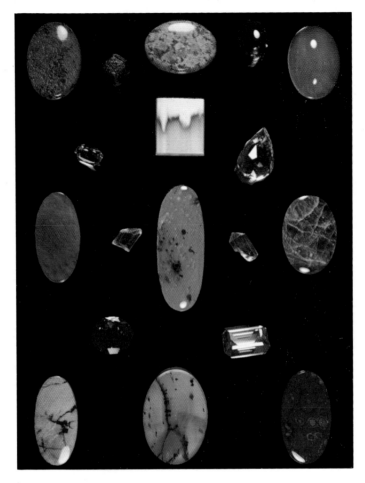

GEMSTONES CUT AND POLISHED BY THE AUTHOR
WITH SOME IN THE ROUGH
(From Left to Right)

Top Row
LAZULITE—North Groton, N. H.; ALMANDINE GARNET
CRYSTAL—near Dallas, Ga.; UNAKITE—Rose River, Va.;
AMETHYST—Four Peaks, Arizona; ROSE QUARTZ—Brazil.

Second Row
TOPAZ—Mason County, Texas; OPALIZED WOOD—State
of Washington; AQUAMARINE, pendant—Brazil.

Third Row
CALIFORNITE—Siskiyou County, Calif.; APATITE CRYS-
TAL—Durango, Mexico; WILLIAMSITE—Line Pits, Pa.;
APATITE CRYSTAL—Mexico; SODALITE—Ontario,
Canada.

Fourth Row
Two Brazilian CITRINES, faceted.

Bottom Row
RHODONITE—Butte, Mont.; MONTANA AGATE—Montana;
ORBICULAR JASPER—Morgan Hill, Calif.

SECOND EDITION

GEM CUTTING

A LAPIDARY'S MANUAL

JOHN SINKANKAS

Captain, U. S. Navy (Ret.)
Certified Gemologist
American Gem Society

 VAN NOSTRAND REINHOLD COMPANY

NEW YORK   CINCINNATI   TORONTO   LONDON   MELBOURNE

Van Nostrand Reinhold Company Regional Offices:
New York   Cincinnati   Chicago   Millbrae   Dallas

Van Nostrand Reinhold Company International Offices:
London   Toronto   Melbourne

Published by Van Nostrand Reinhold Company
450 West 33rd Street, New York, N.Y. 10001

Published simultaneously in Canada by
Van Nostrand Reinhold Ltd.

16 15 14

TO THE LATE

Dr. W. F. Foshag

Whose unfailing encouragement
and practical assistance
made this book possible

Preface to First Edition

T HE CUTTING of gems by amateurs is not new; before 1800 complete instructions, and sometimes equipment, were obtainable by anyone who cared to get them. In this respect, amateur gem cutting is blessed with many more years of tradition than some of our more recent hobbies, such as photography. In spite of earlier beginnings, only during the last two decades have serious attempts been made to give gem cutting popularity and place its methods, raw materials, and equipment within the reach of all.

A number of books have been written on how to cut gems, but such rapid strides have been made in the hobby that an up-to-date treatment is considered worthwhile showing the basic steps with regard to modern equipment. Older techniques and those seldom used are given second place, the greatest emphasis being placed on those phases which have proved to be the most widely enjoyed.

For the first time in print, a large list of minerals which may be used by the amateur is given, along with the essential details on their treatment. It is hoped that both the beginner and those more advanced will make use of this list to widen their acquaintance with the many fascinating members of the Mineral Kingdom. Some of these are rare; others so common that they have been customarily ignored because of their very abundance. The finding of such materials is a source of great pleasure, and the uncovering of their hidden beauty by cutting is keenly gratifying.

The author wishes to acknowledge the enormous debt owed to Dr. William F. Foshag of the U.S. National Museum who, along with his colleagues, Dr. George F. Switzer and Mr. James H. Benn, threw open the extensive collections of that institution for inspection and study. Not enough can be said of these kindly public servants who so faithfully discharge the mission of the Smithsonian Institute, of which they are part, "For the Increase and Diffusion of Knowledge Among Men." Grateful acknowledgment is also given to the many commercial concerns whose excellent photographs grace the pages of this book. Those which are not individually credited, including the colored frontispiece, have been carefully prepared by Messrs. Joseph and Frank Delaney of Arlington, Va., under the direction of the author. Finally, the author wishes humbly to acknowledge the constant encouragement, advice, and active preparation of written material by his wife, Marjorie, she is truly a partner.

JOHN SINKANKAS

San Diego, Calif.
July, 1955

Preface to Second Edition

SCIENCE IS FLOODING the world with new ideas and inventions which affect every part of our lives, even our spare-time pursuits. The gem cutting hobby has also seen its share of changes and no book, including this one, can hope to stay up to date indefinitely unless it is revised to keep pace.

The greatest stress is still placed on cabochon and facet work which remain the most popular forms of cutting. However, other methods and projects are coming to the fore and these are given far more space because of their increasing importance. For example, finishing gems by tumbling is fully treated since it is now used to produce enormous quantities of inexpensive stones. Similarly, as more amateurs try carving, mosaic work, and other forms of lapidary work, it becomes important to explain the tools and methods used for these. In addition, the text of this revision is sprinkled with countless new ideas and techniques which developed since the first edition was written. Because of these changes it has been necessary to entirely rewrite the text. This second edition is therefore a completely new book.

Among other major changes are many new illustrations which replace older ones or supplement them. Finally, the very important section on the description and treatment of gemstones has been enlarged to take in more species and to accommodate more recent information on those previously included.

Since a revision also provides an opportunity to eliminate parts proven to be of little lasting value, a word or two on what has been done along this line is in order. Soon after the first edition appeared, it was discovered that lists of clubs, dealers, and manufacturers speedily got out of date, and by leading readers into fruitless correspondence with defunct clubs and businesses, caused more harm than good. These lists no longer appear. Their value, even temporarily, is questionable in view of the more recent and far better lists which appear every year in the April issue of *Lapidary Journal* called the *Rockhound Buyers Guide*. Readers are urged to obtain the latest issue of the *Guide* to get this information.

Other deletions are a chapter on collecting gemstones and portions of another on the origin of gemstones. Both topics are covered completely in the author's *Gemstones and Minerals—How and Where to Find Them*, and therefore are no longer included here. Similarly, details on gemstone localities in North America have been eliminated or reduced because much better information is available in the author's *Gemstones of North America*.

J.S.

Acknowledgments

THE GREATEST DEBT I owe for much of the information in this book is to the host of inventive amateur gem cutters who thought of ideas to make gem cutting better in some way, and then proceeded to test these ideas and to publish their results in our fine gem cutting journals. By making room for these articles, the editors of the journals are to be congratulated.

Among amateur gem cutters, I acknowledge a special debt to Griffin Grant Waite of Toronto, Ontario, whom I consider to be the dean of amateur cutters. His series of excellent articles in the *Lapidary Journal* some years ago excited my interest in cutting the rare and unusual gemstones, and particularly those so soft or cleavable that completion becomes a severe test of skill. Since then, I have kept up our correspondence and exchange of ideas, and I think, have gained much more from it than he has.

For lending photographs and supplying helpful information, I wish to thank the many manufacturers and dealers whose names appear on the photographs supplied by them. Excellent photographs were also furnished from the files of the *Lapidary Journal* through the courtesy of Hugh Leiper. Others were supplied by Herbert Walters of Treasure Crafts, Ramona, California, who, with his partner, Elbert McMacken, graciously allowed me to spend many hours in their shops gathering material for the chapter on tumbling. This chapter was reviewed by Elbert McMacken. Ideas on carving methods were similarly gained from George Ashley of Pala, California. Photographs were obtained from the Smithsonian Institution, Don L. Spaulding, Hazel Finnell, Frank Hewlett, Dr. Ing. Walther Fischer of Stuttgart, Germany, and from Paul A. Broste, R. S. Harvill, Betty Campbell, Sheu-Tse Koo, Jim Carnahan, Ed and Leola Wertz, George Ashley, and H. H. Cox, Jr.

Lastly I wish to express my gratitude for the unstinting assistance given by my wife, Marjorie, and my daughter, Sharon, in reading the manuscript, suggesting many helpful changes, and typing the final draft.

JOHN SINKANKAS

San Diego, California

Contents

CONTENTS

List of Illustrations

Gemstones – The Raw Material of the Lapidary

1

N O ONE knows how long ago man developed a love for gems. Every civilization unearthed by archeologists shows that its members prized certain colorful minerals for personal ornamentation, or sometimes, as in the case of the jade of the Chinese, held some as sacred. The cutter and carver of gem materials enjoyed special privileges because only he knew the secrets of the stones entrusted to his care, and, seemingly by magic, could shape them to his will despite the fact that they were supremely harder than the finest metals. The ancient Greeks, and after them, the Latins, gave to us *lapidary*, from *lapis*, or stone, as the name of the artisan who carves, shapes, or engraves precious stones or gems. For hundreds of years the art of the lapidary was a secretive one and only in the last few decades has it become known, to the point where anyone at all can learn how to fashion the raw material—gemstones—into gems, carvings, and many other objects of ornament.

Before we go further, it is a good idea to define *gemstone*, since it is not always to a mineral that one is referring. Originally, most

raw materials used for gems came from the rocks and minerals in the earth's crust, but in a few favored places in the world, primitive man discovered beautiful pearls within oysters, and in certain sedimentary formations, amber and jet, and because of their beauty and value, they too were classed as gemstones. Later, such materials as tortoise shell, pearl shell, coral, and a number of types of ivory were added to the list, and in most modern books on gemology, these are described and discussed along with mineral gemstones.

■ MINERAL GEMSTONES

About 150 years ago, Arthur Aikin, Secretary to the Geological Society of Great Britain, wrote a small mineralogy in which he listed about 250 minerals which were well-recognized at the time. By the close of the nineteenth century, the list had grown to about 750 species; today it is nearly 2,000. Despite the rapid rise in the number of minerals recognized as separate species, there are still only about a hundred which provide gems from suitable pieces of rough; of these, only about twenty-five are known to the layman. The mineral species furnishing the principal gemstones of greatest value, or the classical *precious* stones, are:

Diamond
Corundum (ruby and sapphire)
Beryl (emerald, aquamarine, etc.)

Chrysoberyl (alexandrite, catseye, etc.)
Opal (white and black)

The following species furnish important gemstones, or those regularly handled in the gem and jewelry trade:

Feldspar Group (moonstone, amazonite, etc.)
Garnet Group
Jadeite
Nephrite
Olivine (peridot)
Quartz (amethyst, citrine, chalcedony, etc.)

Spinel
Topaz
Tourmaline
Turquois
Zircon

At this point it is wise to distinguish between certain gemstones which are composed of several minerals, and hence are more like *rocks*, geologically speaking, than single mineral species. Prominent among such are *marbles*, which though usually composed of a single species, in this instance, calcite, occur in such quantity that they are classed as rocks rather than as large masses of a single mineral. Other rock-like gemstones are serpentine, lapis lazuli, various granites, and other stones which may or may not be good enough to use in jewelry but are frequently carved or cut into *ornamental* objects, often of large size. The following list of gemstones of lesser importance includes both mineral species and rock types, the latter designated by the letter R:

Calcite (R)
Fluorite
Gypsum (R)
Hematite
Idocrase (R)
Lapis lazuli (R)
Malachite
Obsidian (R)
Pyrite
Rhodonite

Scapolite
Serpentine (R)
Sinhalite
Smithsonite
Sodalite
Spodumene
Steatite (R)
Thomsonite
Variscite
Zoisite

The following gemstones are so rare, or for some reason unsuited for use in jewelry, that they are seldom seen outside collections:

Amblygonite
Anatase
Andalusite
Apatite
Apophyllite
Axinite
Azurite
Benitoite
Beryllonite
Brazilianite
Brookite
Cassiterite
Danburite
Datolite
Diopside
Dioptase
Enstatite
Epidote
Euclase
Fibrolite

Hambergite
Hemimorphite
Iolite
Kornerupine
Kyanite
Lazulite
Phenakite
Pollucite
Prehnite
Pumpellyite (chlorastrolite)
Rhodizite
Rhodochrosite
Rutile
Sphalerite
Sphene
Staurolite
Tektite
Willemite
Zincite

■ THE QUALITIES OF GEMSTONES

What qualities distinguish gemstones from ordinary rocks and minerals? Why are certain of them prized, and others scorned? There is no doubt that the most important quality is *beauty*, for without it, a mineral or rock will not be prized, regardless of what else it has. Gemstones are therefore attractive to the eye, primarily because of vivid coloration, often enhanced by clever cutting, but also because of intriguing patterns, inclusions, or some other characteristic which lifts them above the ordinary. Beauty is evident in the strong coloration of red ruby, blue sapphire and green emerald, but it is also visible in the patterns of agate, in the spangles of aventurine, and in the gleaming coppery needles of rutilated quartz.

Since gems are meant to be worn, they are liable to be rubbed, chipped, or knocked against hard objects. It is important that they resist this treatment, or be *durable*. The importance of this quality soon proves itself in gems set in rings or bracelets. Those which are strong and hard, like diamond, ruby, sapphire, and chrysoberyl, will sparkle and gleam with undiminished luster after years of wear have worn the gold or platinum of the settings to the point where stones may be lost unless the settings are repaired. On the other hand, durability is not all important. Consider opal as an example: this gemstone is brittle and soft, and, when worn in rings, soon develops a frosted surface from rubbing and knocking unless its wearer is extremely careful. Obviously it is not nearly so durable as diamond and sapphire, but its beauty is so overwhelmingly great that its softness is tolerated. However, as a general rule, principal and important gemstones are noted for the fact that they are harder and tougher than many other minerals which may be considered as candidates for gemstone rank.

Because of the great rise in amateur gem cutting in the last few decades, many minerals which do not qualify as genuine gemstones because they lack durability, are nevertheless cut as curiosities, and others are cut because they are so soft or fragile that the difficulties, like an unscaled mountain to a mountain climber, present a challenge which cannot be ignored. Many such "gemstones" are listed in Chapter 19, and are included not to swell the list of classical gemstones, but because they offer a strong challenge to the cutter who is interested in going beyond mastery of ordinary kinds.

The last important quality of most gemstones is that of *rarity*. This is not really a quality of the gemstone but a way of thinking by the persons who are interested in gems. It is human nature to prize the rare, and no amount of reasoning will nullify the fact that between two objects of equal beauty, it is likely that the rarer one will be prized more highly. Thus, synthetic gems, or even ordinary glass imitations, can be made as beautiful or even more beautiful than natural gems, yet the vast majority of persons when acquainted with the facts will choose the natural gems. In such cases, rarity is not the only issue; many connoisseurs undoubtedly feel that the natural stones formed by mysterious and wonderful processes within the rocky heart of the earth, are really preferable on that account.

■ GEMSTONE CRYSTALS

Most gem rough is found as crystals or parts of crystals, as shown in Figures 1, 2 and 3. To see crystals close at hand, it is only necessary to sprinkle some grains of salt or sugar on a piece of paper and examine them

Fig. 1 Gemstone crystals. *Top.* Clear colorless quartz (rock crystal) from Arkansas. *Bottom.* Amethyst quartz from Pennsylvania. (Courtesy Smithsonian Institution)

under a magnifying glass. Each grain of salt will look like a small cube while each sugar grain will look like a miniature tablet with a sharp roof-shaped dome on each end. If the crystals are nearly perfect, all faces will be flat and will twinkle with reflected light. These are the typical crystal forms of these substances, salt actually being a mineral while sugar is a vegetable substance.

Practically all minerals show some kind of crystal faces if they had the chance to grow under the right conditions in nature, and, in many instances, when gem rough is bought, part or all of the crystal faces may be seen. The flat faces seen on crystals do not just happen to be there, they appear only when the inner arrangement of atoms follows a definite pattern, and actually they tell much about the geom-

Fig. 2 Don L. Spaulding of Omaha, Nebraska looks on as gem miners in the famed Mogok District of Burma, wash gem-bearing gravels. The concentrates are washed carefully in open-weave baskets to remove all soil and waste material. Gems settle due to their greater weight. At bottom are rough gemstones typical of this area—sapphire, ruby, zircon, spinel, tourmaline, quartz, and others. (Courtesy Don L. Spaulding)

etry of the arrangement. In fact, many years ago before mineralogists used x-rays to prove that the atoms inside crystals were regularly spaced, this fact was suspected from the way the outside planes of a crystal were arranged, as shown so well in the beryl specimen of Figure 3. The regular spacing of atoms inside crystals also causes many differences in their properties, including such things as color, hardness, ease of splitting, and many others, which the lapidary must take into account when he cuts them.

■ AMORPHOUS GEMSTONES

When minerals or rocks do not have the regular internal arrangement of atoms as in crystals, they are called *amorphous*. This word is taken from the Greek and means "no form." Because there is no pattern to amorphous materials, the atoms are jumbled together in small groups like the particles in a pile of sand. There is no tendency to take shape, and consequently crystals are never seen. Ordinary glass is a good example of an amorphous material, and among gemstones, opal and obsidian. Amorphous minerals, rocks, and other substances, tend to break in curved shell-like surfaces as shown in Figure 4. There are very few amorphous gemstones; the majority are crystalline although this isn't always easy to tell, especially in gemstones such as jade where many very small crystals are grown together in apparently solid stone.

■ GEMSTONES FOR DIFFERENT PURPOSES

Clear crystals are used most often for cutting *faceted* gems. This is the form of cutting seen in engagement ring diamonds, and consists of covering the entire stone with many small flat faces or *facets*. Certain patterns are used as well as certain angles because these take advantage of the optical properties of the gemstone and make the finished gem far more brilliant than would be possible otherwise. More will be said later in the book about how faceted gems are designed and cut.

Fig. 3 Beryl gems and crystals from the collections of the Smithsonian. A magnificent group of aquamarine crystals (*top*), clearly displaying the hexagonal form, is shown growing from a base of feldspar crystals, black tourmaline, and mica. *Lower left,* a fine dark green crystal of emerald set in a wooden base. In the foreground are aquamarine, morganite, and other beryl gems. The large oval aquamarine in the center is over 500 carats in weight and was cut for the Smithsonian by the author. (Courtesy Smithsonian Institution)

Not all clear crystals are cut with facets; some which contain beautiful inclusions such as slender needles of rutile or tourmaline, may be cut in flat form or in rounded loaf-like forms known as *cabochons.* Of course, if a gemstone is opaque, there is not much point in cutting it with facets since not enough light can pass through it to make the sparkling reflections we prize so much in faceted gems. There are many beautiful gemstones which are therefore

Fig. 4 Fracture piece of obsidian (*top*), and small nodules of obsidian in perlite, the so-called "Apache tears" (*bottom*). (Courtesy Smithsonian Institution)

cut in cabochon form, among them the star gems such as star ruby and sapphire, the catseye gems such as chrysoberyl (Figure 77), the gems which show blue or silvery lights as moonstones, and many others which for color or some special effect are cut without facets. The color plate at the front of the book shows examples of both faceted gems and cabochons. Figure 3 shows faceted beryl gems.

Although the forms of cutting just described make up the majority of finished gems, other forms are used for ornamental objects. For example, in carvings, blocks of massive gemstone or large single crystals are used, while in mosaic work, table-top work, inlay, etc., blocks of suitable material are sliced and the thin slabs polished either separately or after they have been fitted together. There are many kinds of lapidary projects, and for each, specially suited rough must be used.

■ HOW ROUGH IS SOLD

Rough material for cabochons is usually sold by the pound, but sometimes by the ounce, the gram, or even the carat. To give an idea of carat and gram weights, a 1 carat cut diamond is about ¼ inch across while a piece of quartz of about the size of a small pea also weighs about a carat. A gram is 5 carats and is the standard weight used for selling faceting materials. Expensive cabochon materials sold by the ounce or gram are lapis lazuli, turquois, chrysoprase, tourmaline, beryl, topaz, etc. Rough catseye chrysoberyl and star sapphires, to name a few, are often sold by the carat.

Prices of rough vary according to the beauty of the material, its scarcity, the presence or absence of flaws, the color, and the size of the gem which the piece is expected to cut. Red tourmaline, for example, can be bought for as little as $.60 per gram for flawed cabochon material, to as high as $15.00 per gram for fine facet-grade material. Rock crystal, citrine, and smoky quartz, are seldom over about $.10 per gram and yet make fine, brilliant gems. Amethyst in medium violet hues is also cheap, but fine quality pieces of large size sell for $1.00 or more per gram.

Cabochon rough prices also vary but, for the most part, average about $.75 to $2.50 per pound. Most dealers would like to sell at even lower prices, but because of mailing and packaging costs a minimum price must be set. Slabs and blanks for cutting cabochons are also sold with prices somewhat higher than for ordinary rough because of the cost of sawing and because only a few good slabs may come out of a large piece of rough. A typical shop catering to amateur cutters is shown in Figure 5. All sorts of inexpensive material is kept in bins, and the buyer may pick his own for so much a pound.

Rough gems come in from all over the world, but the chief sources of supply for the amateurs are: America for its agates, jaspers, sodalite, labradorite, nephrite, and turquois; Brazil, which furnishes most of our faceting material; Australia for opals, and Africa for its

Fig. 5 San Fernando Valley Gem Company's stock bins filled with agates, jaspers, petrified woods, and other inexpensive gem materials for amateur use. Such shops are popular "prospecting" grounds for the amateur cutter who browses and picks out the rough which suits his fancy. (Courtesy San Fernando Valley Gem Co., Van Nuys, California)

malachite and tigereye. Generally it is difficult to buy from miners unless one is present in the field. Consequently, a dealer in the country producing the gemstone will buy up lots of the stone from the miners, sort it into grades, and sell it to importers in the United States. When an importer brings in rough, it is in large lots, in barrels or in boxes. It is carefully graded and the price of each grade determined from how much salable material remains after sorting. Considerable judgment must be used to place prices at levels that will assure a fair profit and at the same time, result in ready sales. Figure 6 is a view of the interior of a gemstone shop in New York City, and shows material being unpacked and graded.

Many dealers send "approval selections," that is, a parcel is sent from which the buyer chooses and returns the rest. In this way he gets exactly what he wants and in a price range that he can afford. It is better than ordering material blindly, and avoids disappointments.

Fig. 6 Inside the A. G. Parser display and sales rooms in New York City. Bins hold pound material while expensive rough materials are in cases to the right. Crystal specimens may be seen on top of the cabinets and on the table in the foreground. (Courtesy A. G. Parser, Inc.)

2 | *How To Get Started*

■ **AMATEUR CLUBS AND SOCIETIES**

In 1930 there were only several thousand amateur lapidaries in all of the United States and Canada, and practically none abroad. Only one popular magazine, *Rocks and Minerals,* founded in 1926, served amateur gem cutters, as well as amateur mineralogists. As more and more enthusiasts were gathered into the fold, particularly in the western United States, two new publications were founded. The first, in 1933, was the *Mineralogist,* a magazine which proved popular to lapidaries and earth science enthusiasts in the Pacific Northwest. The second, a slim bulletin entitled *Mineral Notes and News,* entered the field in 1937, later changing into a formal magazine in 1951, and still later changing its title to *Gems and Minerals,* in 1953.

World War II slowed growth of the lapidary hobby because of restrictions placed on travel and upon materials necessary to make hobby equipment. But in 1946, *Earth Science Digest* magazine began publication to serve interests of amateurs in the Midwest, later changing its name to *Earth Science.* The following year, the tremendous promise of the lapidary hobby inspired the publication of the *Lapidary Journal,* devoted to gem cutting, jewelry making and related interests. Also during the postwar period, articles on field trips for gemstones and minerals, as well as a section on lapidary work appeared regularly in *Desert Magazine.* Including *Desert Magazine* among the others, which cater almost entirely to amateur earth science interests, it is estimated that a total of over one hundred thousand individuals, libraries, and other organizations subscribe to these magazines. Of this total, at least seventy-five thousand subscribe because of their lapidary interests. In addition, there are over four hundred amateur earth science organizations in the United States and Canada, of which it is safe to say that the overwhelming percentage of members are primarily interested in gem cutting and allied arts. Although exact figures are lacking, the author concludes that there are about three hundred thousand hobbyists actively participating in some phase of the lapidary arts.

The idea of cutting and polishing gems is frightening at first because it seems impossible to gain the necessary skill. However, much of the skill which formerly came only after years of practice, is now no longer needed because machines and devices designed specially for the amateur are readily available. Actually the hobby is easy, even the cutting of faceted gems is mastered every day by persons who never dreamed that they could turn out gems fine enough to be set in jewelry!

■ **HELP FROM OTHERS**

The best way to learn a "how-to-do-it" hobby is to watch someone else. Looking over the shoulder of an expert is worth thousands of words of description, but finding an expert is sometimes a problem, since the lapidary hobby, though still growing, is not as well known as it should be. A good introduction to the hobby, and the least expensive, is to learn about clubs in your vicinity and join one. A list of hundreds in all parts of the United States and in many portions of Canada, is given every year in the special April issue of the *Lapidary Journal* called the "Lapidary Journal Rockhound Buyers Guide," and you should get a copy or consult one at your local library. This magazine, as well as others in the amateur field, is listed in Appendix 4 at the end of the book. You may be pleasantly surprised to find that an active group is close enough to visit during a meeting night. Amateur gem cutters are a friendly group, so don't worry about needing an invitation. Go in at meeting time and introduce yourself to an officer of the organization and tell him you are interested. That is all the introduction you need.

If there is no club, don't fail to check schools and colleges. Often high schools teach cutting as part of manual training courses, and the instructors are glad to show you around the shop and point out the various items of equipment as well as samples of the students' work. Colleges and universities may have workshops but of a different kind. They are mainly interested in cutting and polishing of mineral specimens in connection with courses in mineralogy, geology, and mining. Nevertheless, many of the methods are the same and the same equipment is used. Even if the schools have no cutting facilities, they are acquainted with lapidary work and may be able to tell you of any local person who is doing cutting.

Another way to get started in the hobby is to see if a local industry provides facilities for gem cutting. Many large firms now recognize the need for organizing the spare time activities of their employees and are more than glad to lend a helping hand. Adult education programs are still another way of learning about the hobby efficiently and inexpensively. A typical adult education class is shown in Figure 7.

Fig. 7 Adult Education Class in lapidary work sponsored by the Ferndale, Michigan, Board of Education. Facilities and equipment furnished by Brad's Rock Shop of Ferndale. The members of this group are cutting and polishing cabochons. (Courtesy Brad's Rock Shop, Ferndale, Michigan)

To appreciate the material you are going to work with, it pays to visit institutions with outstanding collections of gemstones and

Fig. 8 A heavily-attended gem show at Phoenix, Arizona in 1961 sponsored by the Maricopa Lapidary Society and the Mineralogical Society of Arizona. Shows like these provide places for amateurs to show their work and the competition and enthusiasm are both high! (Hazell Finnell photo, Maricopa Lapidary Society)

lapidary work. Such museums are also listed in the April issue of *Lapidary Journal*. For deeper study into special phases of gem cutting and gemology, a list of books and magazines is given in Appendix 4. A magazine subscription is necessary because in addition to articles on lapidary work, it is here that dealers and manufacturers advertise their wares and it is from them that you obtain catalogs of the equipment you will use and the rough gemstones you will cut. A magazine also gives news about local societies, announcements of the large and exciting club conventions and shows, such as the one illustrated in Figure 8, and other odds and ends of useful information. Each magazine and book is described in Appendix 4 to help you decide which to get. Since magazines reflect news and developments in areas having most subscribers, many amateurs subscribe to several to keep abreast of the hobby both at home and elsewhere in the country.

■ HOW MUCH EQUIPMENT DO YOU NEED?

Questions always raised by the beginner are, "What do I need to start," and "How little can I spend and still get by until I decide that I really like the hobby and want to go on?" The answers are simple—you can start with nothing except a few dollars or spend hundreds right away; it depends entirely upon you. *Gems and Minerals* magazine once tried to see what a "minimum cost" outfit for polishing cabochons could be bought for and came up with a figure of a little over $14.00. This was not a professionally made outfit, but one whose parts were bought separately and assembled by the beginner, with scrap wood and metal used wherever possible. You can get by inexpensively of course, but with better and more versatile equipment you can do more types of work and save time. However, the best equipment cannot buy skill, or good honest craftsmanship; these you must provide yourself.

The choosing of specific pieces of equipment is easier and safer if you get the advice of someone experienced in the hobby. Such a person has actually worked with the equipment and has talked to others who may have different types and compared notes. If nothing else, he can tell you whether or not he likes the machinery he is using. As mentioned before, the best place to find such an expert is your local club on meeting night. Usually it is only a matter of a brief conversation before a club member tells you the names of the more experienced members, or of the club instructor in charge of lapidary instruction. Although most gem cutting tools are based on a few simple designs, there is considerable variation in quality as well as cost. In general, one gets exactly what one pays for in terms of good design, long life, trouble-free operation, and high quality materials.

Aside from dollars and cents, there are other important things to consider before buying equipment. Suppose, for example, that you are an apartment dweller. The noise that will be tolerated by the neighbors, not to speak of the landlord, is going to be limited. Next, apartments are not generally large. Taking these factors into consideration, the equipment that an apartment dweller selects must be quiet and small. On the other hand, if you live in a house where basement, garage, barn, or other workshop space can be used, you can spread out, make benches, install almost any amount of equipment, and otherwise do it up in full style. The space available is always a determining factor in selection of equipment.

■ HOW TO SAVE ON EQUIPMENT

There are many ways in which substitute equipment can be used, not to mention the savings made possible by collecting your own rough gem material. This latter aspect, which has become very important to many field-tripping amateurs is covered fully in the author's *Gemstones and Minerals—How and Where to Find Them,* as described in Appendix 4.

The resourceful beginner lowers cost on machines by using electric motors from old washing machines, refrigerators, etc. Secondhand and junk dealers also have motors that cost but a fraction of new ones. This is only one way of saving money, many others are suggested in the chapters which follow.

Recognizing that most amateurs cannot make ball-bearing arbors, shafts, laps, saw parts, and other items of machinery, a few lapidary equipment manufacturers make components specially for the economy-minded amateur. From such parts are made excellent trim and slabbing saws, grinding and polishing arbors and other devices which would cost more if bought ready to use. You should not assume, however, that making your own equipment is always a good idea. You must balance your own skill against that needed to turn out a really good machine. There is nothing worse than a rickety, inaccurate machine which is always going wrong and which, even when running right, turns out poor work at best. There is no doubt that many amateurs have neither the skill nor the time to make substitutes, and they should choose from the manufactured units which are offered in a wide price range.

Many beginners and even advanced amateurs solve equipment problems by sharing jointly owned units or using club equipment. A number of societies throughout the country follow this scheme, especially in large cities where the proportion of apartment residents is high. When everyone contributes to the purchase of a complete, good quality outfit, only a little expense is borne by any one member. However, in spite of the availability of club equipment, most people prefer the convenience of privately owned units.

Another way to avoid the initial expense of equipment is to enroll in a night school craft course in gem cutting. If you are in an area where local schools give such instruction, it is an excellent method of acquainting yourself with the hobby and finding out if you are going to like it enough to invest money of your own. Some persons enroll in night school classes not so much to receive instruction, but to be able to use items of equipment which they cannot afford or for which they have no room at home.

■ SETTING UP SHOP

Let us assume that you decide to get your own equipment—what is needed to set up a workshop? First, you should know from the size of the equipment how much space is needed and can plan where it should be put with regard to available floor space. Then you must provide current for lights and electric motors, and also a water supply to the grinding wheels and some way of taking away the waste water.

Too much cannot be said about proper lights for the working area. For shaping and polishing work the author uses a reflector flood-type bulb of 150 watts in a gooseneck lamp and swiveled to shine upon the operation being done at the time. The distance from the front of the bulb to the point of work is about 2 feet. For trim sawing and slab sawing, such close, strong light is not required. For faceting, which is even more close in its nature than other types of work, a 100-watt bulb is used in a gooseneck lamp with the hood of the lamp shading the eyes. Most small mistakes made in the last stages of gem cutting can be traced to the lack of good lighting—the amateur simply could not see what he was doing!

In a shop with complete cutting equipment it is likely that two or more motors will be used. If they run at the same time with all the shop lights, there will be considerable current drain. In such a case, the hobbyist must check the size of the electrical leads going into his shop for current-carrying capacity. Most often, however, little trouble occurs because only the exceptional shop will have such a wide variety of equipment. Several warning signs

appear whenever the load on the lines becomes great. If a motor is turned on and the lights dim for several seconds, the wiring is too small in size to take the current. If the lights merely flick to dim and immediately resume their former brightness, there is no need to worry; this is the normal reaction of any electrical circuit when a heavy load is suddenly applied.

Within the house itself, good construction practice calls for one circuit in the kitchen designed to take very heavy loads, such as refrigerator, washing machine, toaster, etc. If convenient, it is best to connect the lapidary machinery to one of the kitchen outlets, being certain first that not all appliances are in operation—a fuse may blow as a result of adding the load of the motor to the others. Most small gem cutting units, however, have only one motor to run and they may be safely plugged in to any baseboard outlet regardless of where it is located. Just remember: do not turn on every light and appliance whenever you decide to do some grinding.

Noise in the workshop is annoying to those who have to live with it and it reduces efficiency. The most helpful and simplest precaution is to insulate the equipment from noise. A small unit set on a table will send its vibrations into the table top and down the legs to the floor. Both the table top and the surface on which it is resting will drum loudly. To eliminate this, put pads of sponge rubber or felt under the base of the unit. Pads of cloth or squares of Celotex will also do, although sponge rubber or sponge plastic is best. Pads need to be about ¼ to ½ inch thick.

Professionally made machines can be bought with their own stands but often this additional cost can be saved and extra space obtained by making your own work benches. All benches should be stout and strong, preferably with 4-inch by 4-inch legs, 2-inch by 6-inch tops, and bracing to suit. Secondhand furniture stores are treasure houses of suitable tables or benches, and it pays to look into them before deciding to build your own. One of the best work tables of all, is an old fashioned oak library table because most were made very strongly of stout wood. Since they are now out of style, they may sometimes be bought cheaply.

Gemstones cannot be ground without water, so ways and means of supplying water to the machinery must be considered. Compact units are often equipped with a trough directly under the wheels. Water is poured into the trough, while the unit is running, until the wheels just begin to pick it up and are moist enough to allow grinding without burning the stone. Too much water results in heavy spray. Other units place sponges under the wheels to provide water. Still others supply water spray or drip attachments. The best is the kind that directs a forcible spray onto the grinding face of the wheel. A valve located close at hand allows the spray to be regulated. In still another type of unit, a built-in pump is used to pick up water from the sump beneath the wheels and deliver it to where it is needed. Most shops, however, take water from the household supply and feed it to the grinders through suitable small-diameter tubing. Where water cannot be piped in, it can be fed to the wheels from an overhead can or tank. Some amateurs use one gallon glass jars or tin cans; others use larger tanks made from discarded metal drums. If much work is to be done, it pays to use as large a container as practicable because the consumption of water will be well above just a few gallons. Such a reservoir can be filled with a garden hose and avoids the annoying interruptions caused by running out of water in the middle of work. Still another scheme is to use a 5-gallon can of heavy metal

to act as a sump and to which is attached a small electrically driven pump. When the can is filled with water, the pump circulates the water to the grinding wheels. From the wheels, it drops back via a hose to the can and is recirculated. This scheme uses the same water over and over and, at the same time, permits grit to settle in the can. When enough grit accumulates in the bottom, it is taken out and thrown away.

The placement of equipment is of considerable importance, due to the danger of dust and dirt falling on polishing equipment. It is wise to carry on messy operations, such as grinding and sanding, as far away from the polishing unit as possible. In compact type units where all operations are done on the same machine, this is impossible. Nevertheless, if separate accessories are used, they should be stored on shelves with protective covers to keep them clean. One of the best coverings is newspaper—it can be thrown away when removed, taking with it all the dirt that has accumulated. Special care should be given to storing polishing buffs and laps.

Dirt is trapped under fingernails and upon the skin, especially after grinding or using loose abrasives. If a sink is not available, a bucket of water should be kept handy to scrub the hands and forearms. A small, stiff-bristle brush is recommended for fingernails. Cleanliness in gem cutting is more than a virtue, it is a necessity; nothing is more annoying than to bring a stone almost to a perfect polish and then have it scratch because a loose bit of grit fell on the polishing buff.

3 | *Sawing*

Just as a tree is of little use to the carpenter unless it is sawed into usable sections, most gem rough is of little use to the cutter unless it is sectioned into pieces small enough to be cut further by other lapidary processes. For this purpose, the amateur cutter uses several types of diamond saw blades, each mounted in appropriate machinery, depending on how large the rough is and exactly what must be done to it. The largest blades are used for slicing rough into slabs or blocks, somewhat smaller blades for slabbing and trimming of small pieces of rough, while the smallest blades are used for sectioning valuable material, in order to waste as little as possible.

Most beginners seeing the modern lapidary saw at work are amazed that it can cut through stone. When the blade stops spinning, they cannot resist feeling its edge for the sharp "teeth" which they are sure must be there. They are even more amazed to feel nothing but a slight grittiness, if they can detect that. It takes much explaining to convince them that the thin disk of steel is not doing the cutting, but that the very small particles of diamond in the edge, which they cannot see or feel, are actually the "teeth." Yet this is all there is to the diamond saw blade—a thin steel disk and some crushed diamond imbedded along its edge. Behind it is a long history of development, and of many trials and experiments before makers produced blades good enough and cheap enough to be within reach of the amateur. It is one of the advances which makes it possible for lapidary work to be the hobby of many thousands instead of the profession of a few hundred.

Before diamond saws were perfected, it was customary to use abrasives such as emery and silicon carbide to "charge" the steel blades. Such abrasives could not be imbedded in the blade itself and had to be supplied to the edge in the form of a thin paste or mud. As the soft steel disk turned, the grit particles were caught and swept against the stone, gradually grinding a channel somewhat larger than the thickness of the blade. This slow, messy, and tedious process, called "mud sawing," is seldom used by amateurs today but is returning to favor for some special operations which will be dis-

15

cussed later in this chapter. For the present, the diamond saw and how it is made will be discussed.

■ DIAMOND POWDER FOR SAWS

The use of diamond powder is very old, in fact, diamond was used as an abrasive long before it was found how to polish this supremely hard mineral. Today, most stone-cutting saws the amateur cutter is likely to use are charged with diamond powder. Very large saws, such as those used for cutting large blocks of stone for masonry and monuments, still employ loose grit, although many are switching to diamond blades because they cut so much faster. Diamond powder is also used in many other applications besides sawing, as can be seen in Figure 9.

Fig. 9 A variety of diamond tools used in industrial applications. The thin disk in the background is a sintered-rim saw blade and could be used for slicing gemstones. The tools to the left are used for grinding, while those in the right center are special tools in which individual diamond crystals are set in holders. (Courtesy Norton Company and General Electric Company)

Diamond is the hardest known substance and it is this property which makes it so valuable for cutting other minerals, even such very hard ones as sapphire and chrysoberyl. Gem quality diamonds, like those in engagement rings, are the purest form but split too easily to be used for cutting. Furthermore, they are too expensive. The impure forms, known as "bort" or "carbonado," are the most useful for abrasive purposes because they are tougher and therefore last longer. Crushed and sorted into different sizes, diamond powder is sold by the carat by lapidary supply houses for a variety of purposes from grinding to polishing. The new synthetic diamond powder is equally satisfactory for all lapidary uses.

■ DIAMOND POWDER SIZES

There are two ways of designating powder size: *mesh* size and *micron* size. Mesh sizes are based on sifting powder through fine screens with specified numbers of wires or threads to the inch. Thus a "100-mesh" grit is powder which passes through a screen of 100 meshes to the inch but cannot pass through the next smaller screen. The greater the number of meshes, the finer the powder. In the micron system, the size of particles is given in *microns* which are units of measurement where one micron is equal to one thousandth of a millimeter. In lapidary work, diamond grits are usually specified by the mesh size method, or simply as a numbered "grit" which means the same.

The following are some commonly used diamond grits:

Charging large saws	50–100	mesh
Charging small saws	120–250	mesh
Coarse cutting laps	400–600	mesh
Fine cutting laps	800–1200	mesh
Polishing laps	3200–6400	mesh

■ DIAMOND SAWS

Diamond saws differ from mud saws in one vital respect—the abrasive is locked in the blade instead of being loose. No recharging is necessary and when the blade is worn out it is thrown away. There are several ways of imbedding diamond in the blade edge, the type of blade taking its name from the method used. The blades are usually of soft steel, although small blades are often of bronze or copper. Blades as small as 4 inches in diameter are used for sectioning valuable materials, 8-inch diameter for trimming, up to several feet in diameter for slabbing.

■ NOTCH-RIM BLADES

For the majority of amateur work, the mild steel blade is most popular. It comes in a variety of sizes and thicknesses and with light, medium, or heavy charges of diamond powder. It is also the least expensive. The method of charging is to slot the entire outside edge with "notches" and to fill these with powdered metal in which diamond particles are uniformly sprinkled. The edge is rolled to close the notches and to thicken it slightly so that the blade cuts its own clearance. Then the blade is heated to fuse the powdered metal around the diamond particles. This is followed by straightening and truing. The use of a powdered metal insert is often omitted for small blades and diamond powder alone put into the notches.

Notch-rim blades are made with notches vertical to the edge, as shown in Figure 10, or with notches slanted to the edge. The first type is designed to run in either direction but some of the latter type should be run only in the direction specified by their manufacturers, although many amateurs reverse them when necessary and do not notice any appreciable difference in efficiency. In any event, it is beneficial to be able to reverse blades because no matter how carefully they are used, one edge tends to get more wear than the other and this leads to cuts which drift to one side. By reversing the blades from time to time, wear is evenly distributed and greater accuracy is obtained.

Fig. 10 Typical notched-rim diamond saw blade. In this type the notches are at right angles to the periphery of the blade and therefore this blade can be run in either direction. "Spacer" washers are provided at the arbor hole to accommodate different size shafting. (Courtesy Highland Park Manufacturing Company, South Pasadena, California)

■ SINTERED-RIM BLADES

In another process, diamond powder is mixed with metal powder and compressed into a thin hoop. This is heat treated, or *sintered,* until the particles fuse together. The hoop is then soldered to the metal disk and forms what is called the sintered-rim saw. A variation of this method is called the segmented sintered-rim saw and is illustrated in Figure 11. The sintered sections are made and applied separately instead of all at once. The gaps between segments allow stone dust to be cleaned out and the saw to work more efficiently. Both notch-rim and sintered-rim blades are used extensively but the notch-rim is generally preferred because it is cheaper and less likely to be damaged in use. However, the sintered-rim blades are smoother in action, last a long time with careful use, and for certain operations, are definitely superior. Sintered-rim blades may be spun in either direction al-

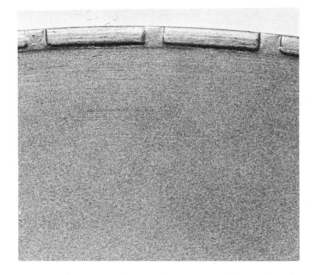

Fig. 11 Magnified section of a sintered-rim type blade. Sintered segments are attached in curved strips on either side of the disk. Other sintered-rim blades are fitted with continuous strips of sintered material. (Courtesy Highland Park Manufacturing Company, South Pasadena, California)

though they should be reversed from time to time for the reasons given before.

The cutting action of all diamond saws is the same. When the stone is fed to the blade, it scrapes off the metal until a particle of diamond is exposed; at this instant the saw begins to cut. As more diamond is exposed, performance is improved and the saw is then said to be "broken in."

■ SAW MACHINERY

A stone-cutting saw does not differ greatly in principle from a woodworking saw and about the same arrangements can be seen in one as in the other. The essentials are a shaft or arbor of steel upon which to mount the blade, a pulley and vee belt arrangement to connect the shaft with a source of power, usually an electric motor, and finally, a platform or carriage upon which to rest the material being sawed. In the case of stone saws, it is also necessary to provide a tank of cooling liquid in which the blade dips while running. This is needed to cool the blade and wash out

the rock dust. Thus a diamond saw is basically a simple piece of machinery. The essential parts are shown in Figures 12 and 13.

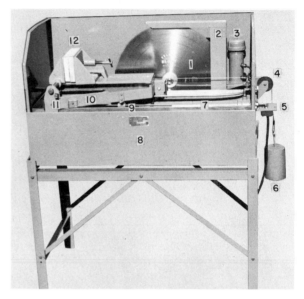

Fig. 12 The Great Western slabbing saw showing essential parts. 1. Saw blade and arbor accommodating blades up to 18 inches in diameter. 2. Splash hood. 3. Hydraulic fluid reservoir. 4. Weight-feed wire and pulley. 5. Motor switch. 6. Weight. 7. Hydraulic retarding cylinder. 8. Coolant tank. 9. Adjustable motor switch cut-off. 10. Carriage. 11. Cross-feed screw (crank not shown). 12. Rock clamp. (Courtesy Great Western Lapidary Equipment, Chula Vista, California)

Although a stone-cutting saw works like a wood-cutting saw, it is important to realize that special techniques must be used because minerals are much harder than wood. A diamond saw working properly can cut through soft minerals at the rate of an inch or so in five minutes, harder and tougher minerals taking somewhat longer. However, a woodworking saw can slice through the same distance in wood in seconds. Since diamond blades are narrower and many times more expensive, they must be used with much more care to prevent jamming, binding, or bending. It is therefore necessary that any lapidary saw be made with more attention to accuracy.

Experience shows that it is impractical to saw rough stones by hand if the size is over

■ **SHAFTS AND BEARINGS**

several inches. Most rough is seldom flat and cannot be placed securely on a saw table. For this reason, some sort of clamp must be used to hold the rough gemstone so firmly that twisting or wobbling is impossible. The clamp is attached to a carriage which slides along a track toward the saw blade. It is fed slowly and accurately so that contact with the blade is gentle. Clamp assemblies are standard equipment on slabbing saws as shown in Figures 12 and 13.

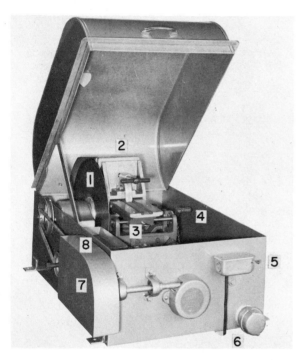

Fig. 13 Highland Park slabbing saw with mechanical feed. 1. Saw blade and arbor. 2. Rock clamp. 3. Carriage. 4. Cross-feed crank. 5. Power cut-off switch box. 6. Coolant tank drain. 7. Automatic mechanical feed mechanism. 8. Slab-catching tray. (Courtesy Highland Park Manufacturing Co., South Pasadena, California)

In review, the essentials of a lapidary saw are a shaft upon which to mount the blade, a power drive arrangement to rotate the blade, a carriage with rock clamp, and a tank which holds the coolant and supports the machinery. Each of these will be described in detail to show how they work and to assist you in making your own if you so desire.

Saw blades must be mounted on steel shafts sufficiently thick to remain rigid and accurate under the stresses imposed. Small blades up to 8 inches in diameter may be used successfully on ½-inch shafts, although ⅝-inch shafts are preferred. For diameters up to 16 inches, shafts should be ¾ to 1 inch thick. Smaller sizes are acceptable at the blade end of the shaft if the remainder is of proper thickness. Blades are mounted with flanges on each side to insure stiffness and true running. Thin blades need flanges larger in proportion than for thick blades. Use 3-inch diameter flanges for 4½-inch blade; 1½- to 2-inch flanges for 8-inch steel blade and 3- to 3½-inch flanges for 12- to 16-inch blades. In special cases, such as sawing thin slots with great accuracy, flanges may extend to within ½ inch of the blade edge.

The saw shaft must rest in bearings which permit easy yet accurate spinning. Ball bearings are strongest and should be used if possible. They remain accurate after many hours of use and thus insure straight cuts and maximum useful life from the blade. Some saws use sleeve bearings which are tubes of steel lined with soft, anti-friction metals. However, sleeve bearings go "out of round" very easily if much force is applied to the ends of shafts supported by them and this results in a wobbling shaft and loss of accuracy. For these reasons, most saws now provide ball bearings only.

Most bearings require lubrication, especially sleeve bearings where the thin film of grease keeps the shaft centered and prevents friction. Because frequent lubrication is a bothersome chore, several types of bearings are available which dispense with lubrication entirely or require it only occasionally. Certain ball bearings are made with the grease "sealed" in and need no further attention. Sealed bearings are also protected from stray grit, which can be disastrous once it gets inside. Another trouble-free bearing uses a porous bronze sleeve to support the shaft. The bronze is soaked with oil which provides lubrication for many days.

Whatever kind of shafting or bearings are

obtained with cutting equipment, remember that the shafting must be stiff enough not to whip or bend, and the bearings must allow accurate running. If these conditions are met, cutting operations will proceed efficiently.

■ THE SAW CARRIAGE

Next in importance to the blade and shaft assembly is the carriage and clamp arrangement for holding and feeding the stone into the blade. Modern machines are fitted with stout carriages and clamps so that pieces of rough, from as small as several inches to as large as a foot in length, can be handled with ease and precision. Although metal jaws are employed for strength, it is usual to line their inner surfaces with pieces of hardwood, the resiliency of the wood giving a much better grip on the stone. The carriage slides forward on guide bars adjusted to provide movement parallel to the saw blade. In Figure 12, the carriage (10) rolls on small ball bearings on two parallel steel bars. In Figure 13, the carriage moves forward on a slide bar and a screw bar, the latter driving the carriage forward. The most important requirement of any slabbing saw is that the carriage slide or roll exactly parallel to the saw blade. If it does not, the saw will rub and bind when large stones are being cut.

■ CARRIAGE FEEDS

The simplest type is the "swinging arm" feed used in the Covington saw, shown in Figure 14. There is one bearing at the top of the arm which acts as a hinge and permits the arm to swing downward into the blade. This arrangement is fed into the blade by a small wire attached to a weight or it can be pushed by hand. Almost as simple is the straight weight-feed saw in which the sliding carriage is fed into the saw by a wire looped over a pulley and attached to a weight in the back of the machine. The operator starts the saw, then feeds the carriage by hand to start the cut. When the cut is about ½ inch deep, or

Fig. 14 Covington No. 106 portable combination slabbing and trimming saw. The unit is shown ready to slice a large nodule of rough material. The cord shown at the right leads to a weight which draws the stone into the blade during sawing. A conversion kit changes the saw into a trim saw. (Courtesy Covington Engineering Corporation, Redlands, California)

even deeper, he allows the weight to pull the carriage. The amount of weight varies with the size of the rough.

There are some disadvantages to weight-feeds, which should be explained. Since most rough is irregular in outline, the cross-section varies, some places being thick, others quite thin. Thus in thicker spots, the weight should be heavier while in thinner spots it should be lighter, yet this is not easy to adjust unless one pays constant attention to the machine. If a fairly heavy weight is used, thin sections will place a great deal more pressure on the blade and cause it to wear very rapidly. If the weight is selected to avoid this, the cutting in thick spots will be far too slow. Another disadvantage with a weight feed is that as the cut nears its end, the cross-section suddenly narrows and the blade races through the cut. It is at this time that the last bit of material often breaks off, leaving a jagged piece of rough in the path of the blade. The blade then tends to "ride over" this protuberance, and in doing so, is severely bent and "dished." A final disadvantage is the fact that a blade running slightly out of round tends to become more and more lopsided. Eventually the "bumping" becomes so bad that further sawing is useless and the blade must be thrown away, probably with much good diamond still left in it. On the credit side, however, straight weight feed saws are considerably less expensive because complicated machinery is left out and if the operator is aware of the disadvantages described above, he can use his saw with care and obtain excellent results.

There are several ways of propelling the carriage mechanically, the most common being by screw feed or regulated weight feed. The screw feed uses a long threaded shaft which passes through the carriage or is attached to it by the equivalent of a threaded nut. As the saw spins, the threaded shaft is slowly turned, propelling the carriage forward. Some machines allow varying the threaded shaft speed and hence the rate of feed. Very large sections, or exceptionally tough materials like chalcedony or jade, call for slowest feeds while soft materials like calcite onyx or serpentine may be fed faster. A valuable feature on some mechanical feed saws is a slipping clutch designed to prevent jamming the stone into the blade, in the event that it is not cutting as fast as the carriage propels it.

The regulated weight feed is used in the Great Western saw, shown in Figure 12. The heavy carriage rolls on small ball bearings and is pulled along by a wire looped over a pulley (4) and attached to the heavy weight (6). The speed of travel is regulated by a hydraulic cylinder (7), and this in turn is regulated by a small valve shown just below the pulley. When the valve is shut, the hydraulic fluid in the cylinder cannot flow and the carriage is prevented from moving. However, when the valve is opened slightly, the carriage begins to roll

slowly toward the saw blade. If the valve is opened more, the rate of feed is increased. The most important feature of this clever arrangement is that the carriage *cannot* go any faster than the speed regulated by turning the valve. This allows thin sections of stone to be cut without placing damaging pressures on the saw blade and yet allows thick sections to feel the full force of the weight. The screw feed is shown in the Highland Park saw in Figure 13.

■ **ROCK CLAMPS**

Most saw carriages provide cross-feeds which enable the operator to take off several slices of stone before the rock has to be shifted in the clamp. However, great care must be taken in clamping stones to prevent them from slipping during cutting and damaging the blade. Many beginners using a slabbing saw for the first time, are tempted to place only the very end of the stone in the clamp so as to get as many slices as possible before reclamping. Unless the stone is clamped very securely, it may shift and twist the saw blade, sometimes resulting in irreparable damage. Accurate clamps make it possible to cut slabs as thin as $\frac{1}{16}$ inch or blocks up to 4 inches in thickness.

■ **COOLANTS**

All saws need a liquid bath through which the blades must run. Considerable heat is generated during sawing and this heat, as well as the stone dust created by the abrasive action, must be carried away from the cut. Friction of blade against stone is also considerable and the cooling liquid acts like a lubricant. The liquids used are known as *coolants* even though this is not their sole purpose. The most popular and generally most satisfactory coolants are light, almost colorless oils known as "white" oils or "flushing" oils, used extensively in automobile repair shops. They are not ordinarily kept in stock at service stations and must be ordered specially. Another coolant which is very popular, although objectionably smelly, is kerosene to which is added ordinary automobile oil in the ratio of 1 or 2 parts of oil to 10 parts of kerosene. Some users prefer more oil but the author has found that only a little gives very satisfactory results. Diesel oil has been used for sawing but is also very smelly. Transformer oil has been used but differs little from the flushing oil previously described.

Water solutions of soluble oil are used in machine shops for cutting metals and have been recommended for stone sawing. However, they tend to lose their oil to certain porous minerals and become less efficient and also to rust saw parts, no matter how carefully the saw is cleaned and wiped dry. For these reasons, many saw makers strongly recommend against their use or the use of plain water.

Permanent car radiator anti-freeze of the diethylene glycol class has been used as a coolant, reportedly with good results. It evaporates slowly, is incombustible, and has practically no odor. However, it is water soluble, highly penetrating, and expensive, and in the author's opinion, offers no real advantages over petroleum coolants.

When sawing, it is a good idea to keep a bucket filled with strong detergent solution handy to put the slabs in after wiping off excess oil. If sawing many slabs, a box of sawdust is also useful for absorbing excess oil, but it represents a fire hazard. Rags used for wiping oil must not be stored in closed containers because they are likely to catch fire through spontaneous combustion. Coolant oils are penetrating and the sooner they are wiped off, the less likely the gem material is to be stained. Some porous materials such as variscite and turquois absorb oil so rapidly that it is advisable to soak them in water for several days ahead of time before sawing. The water fills the pores and prevents the oil from penetrating. Another trick is to spray the rough with acrylic resin, but this does not prevent the oil from creeping in through the face of the slab although it may help other areas.

The fine particles of rock dust which form sludge on the bottom of the tank must eventu-ally be cleaned out. When the time comes to do this, do not operate the saw for several days, to let the sludge settle. Carefully dip up or siphon off the clear coolant on top and save. The thin sludge left can be poured into a stout paper bag propped up on a block of wood in a can and left to settle for several weeks. The clear coolant which oozes from the paper bag is saved and re-used, while the sludge in the bag is discarded. Thoroughly clean the tank, pour back the clean oil and add more to bring the coolant up to the proper level. In general, only ¼ to ½ inch of the bottom of the saw blade should dip into the coolant.

■ COOLANT TANKS

In most slabbing saws, the tank serves not only to hold the coolant but to support the saw assembly and carriage. In such cases, the tank is usually made of heavy galvanized iron sheet welded together at the joints. In other types, the tank is merely a liner made of thin sheet metal resting in a wooden box, which, in turn, supports all of the machinery. It is highly important that this supporting box or tank be as rigid as possible, because it supports the carriage and the saw blade and keeps them in alignment.

Whether homemade or purchased, every saw should rest squarely and firmly on its supports. Placing cushions of felt or sponge rubber under the corners will do much to reduce noise and vibration. Most manufacturers sell stands for their slabbing saws but satisfactory substitutes can be made from two-by-four lumber.

■ SPLASH HOODS

While the saw is running, the oil picked up by the blade is splashed over the rock, the carriage, and anything else in the way. For this reason, a hood is needed to catch the spray and return it to the tank. Hoods are available in metal and in plastic, the latter more expensive. If one wants to watch the saw in action, a plastic hood is a good idea but definitely a luxury. A metal hood can have a plastic window installed in it, but the task of working the plastic to shape and fastening it to the hood with a leakproof joint is considerable.

■ CUT OFF SWITCHES

To allow for unattended operation, many slabbing saws are fitted with automatic cut off switches which turn off the motor when the saw carriage has reached a certain point of travel, as selected beforehand. In the Great Western saw shown in Figure 12, a sliding rod adjustable to the size of the rough contacts a push plate which, in turn, flips off the motor switch. Other arrangements are used in different saws, as in the Highland Park unit in Figure 13 where an adjustable length chain flips off the electrical switch when the carriage has gone far enough. The amateur can convert his switching arrangement to automatic very easily. The simplest way is to attach a flexible wire cable of small diameter to the saw carriage and pass it through a small hole in the side of the saw and over a small pulley or bearing block to an ordinary chain-pull type light socket in which the electrical cord to the motor is plugged. A strong piece of twine with loops on it connects the cable to the chain pull. The carriage is run forward to where it should shut off and the wire is hooked to the proper loop in the cord. The carriage is returned to start the cut and the power turned on. When the carriage travels to the end of the cut, it pulls the chain-pull on the socket and shuts off the power.

■ CONVERTIBLE SAWS

A recent development in saw making is to provide accessories to a basic saw by which it can be converted from a slabbing saw to a trim saw, or the other way around. An excellent convertible unit is shown in Figure 15, and illustrates how a slabbing saw can be changed to a trim saw by removing the large blade and carriage assembly and substituting a smaller blade and table top. The saw shown in Figure 14 also changes to a trim saw, while

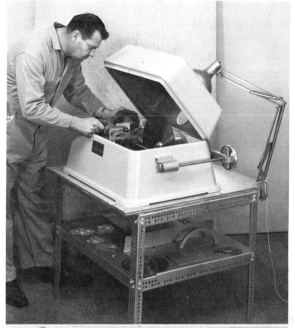

Fig. 15 *Top.* The Hillquist F10–14 slabbing-trimming saw in operation as a slabbing unit. The agate nodule shown is being adjusted in the clamp prior to engaging the automatic feed device. *Bottom.* The same unit converted to a trim saw. A slab of agate is now being sawn into smaller sections. Note the accessories on the shelf of the stand which make it possible to convert this unit from one type of saw into another. For slabbing, the saw uses a 14-inch blade; for trimming, a 10-inch blade is used. (Courtesy Lapidary Equipment Company, Inc., Seattle, Washington)

the basic trim saw shown in Figure 20 converts to a slabbing saw by providing a clamp arrangement to hold rough. The clamp slides in a track at the right of the table and can be moved after each cut to take another slice.

■ HOMEMADE SLABBING SAWS

Figure 16 shows a simple homemade saw which is not difficult to make. The diagram gives the essential features of construction leaving out dimensions, since these vary according to the size blade used. The heart of any slabbing saw is the arbor for the blade and the carriage for feeding the stone into the saw. The box for the coolant tank supports both parts and must be rigid to keep them in alignment when the saw is running.

The coolant tank should be made from ⅛-inch galvanized iron welded together at the joints. However, tanks have been made from hardwood planks or ¾-inch plywood lined with metal sheeting soldered at the joints. If well made, these are almost as good as heavy metal tanks.

After the tank is made, the arbor is fitted to the side with bolts and lock washers. If wood is used, large washers must be put under the bolts to keep the wood from crushing and the bolts from loosening. The rock clamp is simple to make since it is a piece of 2- by 4-inch lumber with an ordinary door hinge at one end. A piece of hardwood fastened with long bolts and butterfly nuts clamps the stone. Since

the hinge cannot move, it is necessary to re-clamp the rock each time for a new cut. However, if a piece of pipe is placed across the front of the tank, and the arm fastened to a sleeve which slides along the pipe, a series of slabs can be cut without reclamping. Great accuracy is not possible with this arrangement but with a little practice, good slabs can be produced.

The remaining items are a ¼-hp motor, vee belt, and a splash hood to trap spray. The back side of the spray hood can be made of any kind of sheet metal and the sides and front can be covered with canvas strips which can be raised to inspect sawing. The entire assembly, tank and motor, should be fastened to a common surface with pads of sponge rubber or felt under the box and motor to cut down noise and vibration.

A far better slabbing saw can be made with the parts shown in Figure 17. These are made accurately and can be bought separately or as a kit. The cross-bars are meant to be fastened to the front and back inner walls of the coolant tank and must be installed accurately to insure that they are aligned at right angles to the arbor. This is necessary to prevent the saw blade from wandering off and jamming.

■ OPERATING THE SLABBING SAW

If you purchased a slabbing saw, all instructions furnished by the manu-facturer should be read carefully. A stout table

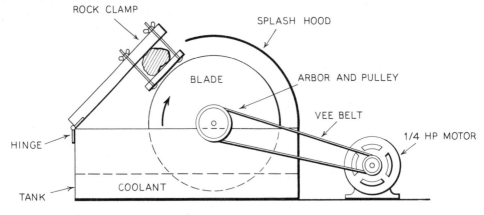

Fig. 16 Homemade slabbing saw.

Fig. 17 Slabbing saw parts sold separately to amateurs who want to make their own. These parts are the heart of a good machine and cannot be made easily by the average amateur. (Courtesy The Ducketts, Medford, Oregon)

or stand should be available and the saw set securely in place. Install the blade on the end of the shaft. Tighten in place carefully and spin it by hand to see that all moving parts are free. Next pour in coolant until the lower edge of the blade is submerged about ¼ inch. Do not use more as it will only splash and leak.

For slabbing saws of 16 to 18 inches in diameter, a ⅛ hp, heavy-duty motor is best, but others as low as ¼ hp will do if the stone is not fed into the blade at too fast a rate. In any case, the manufacturer will specify the motor to be used and his advice should be followed if possible. The use of too weak a motor results in overheating and decreases the efficiency of sawing. Most motors are made to run at speeds of 1,725 to 1,750 rpm for ordinary purposes, or at speeds of 3,450 or 3,500 rpm whenever a higher rpm is needed. The lower speeds are most useful in gem cutting; however, higher

speeds may be used if the motor pulley size is reduced or the saw pulley size increased, or a combination of both.

Some saws have platforms or other means for mounting driving motors; others do not and the purchaser must provide his own. Remember that the motor and saw must be mounted securely to a common surface so that neither will "creep" and cause the pulleys to be misaligned or the driving belt to slacken. Some amateurs construct a stout table of lumber using 4- by 4-inch stock for the legs, 2- by 6-inch, for the top, and 2- by 4-inch bracing. Special stands are also available but at extra cost.

The size of the table top is determined by placing the saw and motor on a cleared section of the workshop floor and adjusting each in relation to the other until both pulleys are exactly in line. It is best to place the motor toward the rear. Slip on the vee belt for the exact position that the motor will occupy when the sawing outfit is complete. The distances may now be measured. Add at least 6 inches to each dimension to give space for adjusting the position of the motor as well as to provide space for other tools and equipment.

There are two ways of mounting the motor to the table: (1) holes are drilled under each corner of the motor base plate for receiving the hold-down bolts; or (2) (preferred) the motor is attached to a piece of hardwood board which, in turn, can be slid back and forth to create tension on the belt. In the first method, a pair of holes is drilled in the table below each corner of the motor base plate and the intervening wood sawed out to provide slots at least 3 inches long. The slots permit adjustment of the motor position. In the second method, similar slots are cut in the front and back of the motor baseboard, which is made at least 4 inches longer on each end for this purpose. The object of both methods is to provide means for installing and replacing belts and for taking up the slack which inevitably develops in the belt after the machine has been run for some time. Wide washers should be used with the hold-down bolts to prevent the wood of the table top from being crushed. Wing nuts may be installed on the bolts to permit easy loosening whenever required. In aligning the motor, it is essential that both pulleys be as nearly in line as possible; even small deviations result in belt slippage and rapid wear.

The saw chassis is fastened to the table top with small attachment lugs. If these are not available, a pair of small wooden blocks can be screwed to the table top at each corner of the saw. To prevent excessive vibration and "drumming," slip pieces of sponge rubber or felt under each corner of the saw as well as under the motor.

■ SAW SPEEDS

One large manufacturer of saw blades and sawing equipment recommends that diamond-saw rim speeds range from 2,000 to 2,500 surface feet per minute for agate, to as high as 6,000 to 8,000 surface feet per minute for marble (calcite). The amateur seldom deals with gemstones as soft as calcite; but agate, and gemstones similar in hardness, are often cut and polished. Accordingly, most saws are set to run at lower speeds, the range from 2,000 to 3,000 surface feet per minute being most useful. Since the speed of the saw rim will vary directly with its diameter, it is necessary to determine the proper combination of pulleys on the motor and arbor shaft to give the desired figure. Suppose that your saw is equipped with a 14-inch diameter blade. What will be the pulley combination required to give a surface speed at the rim of about 2,000 feet per minute? To find the answer, turn to Appendix 1 at the back of the book and look in the table entitled "Table of Rim Speeds for Saws and Wheels." Under the column labeled "2,000," run down until you find the figure "545" opposite "14," the diameter of the blade in inches. The figure 545 is the rpm at which the saw arbor must turn in order to give a surface speed, at the rim, of 2,000 feet per minute.

Next, turn to the table preceding entitled "RPM Obtained by Using Various Pulley Combinations," and find in the table a figure which nearly corresponds to 545. Above this figure will be found the size of the arbor pulley, and to the left will be found the size of the motor pulley. Note that, although the *exact* figure of 545 cannot be found, several can which are close enough for all practical purposes, for example, 515 for a 3-inch and 9-inch pulley combination, 530 for a 2¾-inch and 8-inch combination, 540 for a 2½-inch and 7-inch combination, and 560 for a 2¼-inch and 6-inch pulley combination. This flexibility permits you to use a wide variety of pulleys, possibly even some which you already have in the shop.

■ CLAMPING THE STONE

Most gemstones, such as agate and jasper, occur in rounded nodules or masses. Great care must be taken in clamping stones of this shape to prevent slippage during cutting. Blades are ruined by the shifting of a piece of rough in the clamp, causing binding of the blade, overheating, and sometimes bending or breaking of the rim. Of great value in clamping troublesome shapes are small chips and bits of soft wood which can be inserted around the stone to provide additional points of support. It is *always* worthwhile to take a little extra time and trouble at this stage. Once the stone is in place, test its firmness by twisting it with the hands in a deliberate attempt to move it; if it does, it is not fastened properly and *must be reclamped.*

Try to visualize what you want to get out of the rough. If you want slabs, be sure to clamp the stone out far enough so that a number of cuts can be made before the stone has to be reshifted. Inasmuch as it is difficult to line up the stone so that the next cut is parallel to the first, it is best to get as many cuts as you can from one clamping as this automatically insures slices with parallel sides. Extremely irregular or long and narrow specimens often require a trimming cut in order to make them fit in the clamp. Each piece of rough has to be studied to determine the best way to saw it. The extra time spent may mean the difference between a good yield of slabs or a poor one.

■ FEEDING

All that remains now is to start feeding the stone into the saw for the actual cutting operation. If your saw has a mechanical feed, run the carriage up so that the rough is just short of the blade; set the feed speed on low, lower the hood, and start the motor. In a moment or two you will hear a metallic ringing noise as the blade begins to cut into the rock. Continue cutting for a few moments, stop the motor and examine progress. Check the alignment of the cut with the blade to see that the blade isn't binding or that the stone hasn't shifted. If all looks well, start the motor again and continue sawing. If the rough is of small cross section, this is a good time to shift

to a higher rate of feed; however, if it is of large size, a lower rate of feed is proper.

It is advisable to start the feed at the very slow rate because much rough is jagged and sharp, and jamming it quickly into the blade may result in severe damage. This is particularly true of weight-feed saws. Most skilled cutters use only the pressure of the fingers to start the cut or they push the stone into the blade with a small stick. The saw cuts past the jagged spot in a minute or two, at which time weights are added in proportion to the size of the stone.

Avoid starting a cut on a sloping surface. The blade tends to veer off to one side, obviously much out of alignment. If the cut is continued, the blade will jam in the sides of the slot and become dished. This is another reason why the slowest rate of feed should be used at the start—it gives the blade a chance to cut a small square-edged shelf in the stone which allows it to continue accurately. It is *essential* that this be done. Figure 18 shows how the

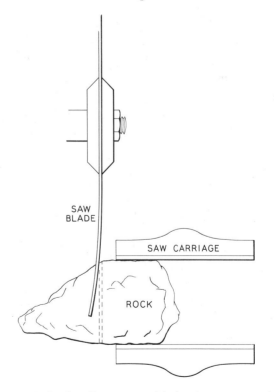

Fig. 18 "Dishing" in a saw blade. A poor start has caused the blade to cut a curved path. Dotted line shows path that blade should have taken.

starting of a saw cut on a sloping surface causes swerving of the blade. If a saw blade becomes dished, it seldom runs accurately unless repaired.

■ FINISHING A CUT

As the blade reaches the end of a cut, it is again important to avoid letting too much pressure develop on the blade. When the slab finally breaks off, it has a nasty habit of leaving behind a sharp projection which can seriously gouge or dish the blade. Many experts stop the saw just short of completing the cut and break off the slab with their fingers. This is not so necessary when using a mechanical-feed saw but it is always a good idea. The steps in slabbing are shown in Figure 19.

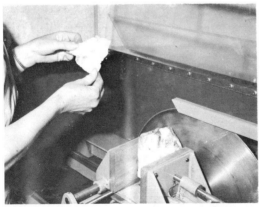

Fig. 19 Steps in slabbing. *Upper left.* Clamping stone preparatory to slicing on the Great Western saw. *Upper right.* Saw blade shown part way through the rock. *Lower left.* The first slice has just been taken off and is being examined. Note carriage is past saw blade leading edge. *Lower right.* Carriage returned for another slice and crossfeed being operated to move stone over. Four turns of the crossfeed crank yield a slab 3/16 inch in thickness. (Courtesy Great Western Lapidary Equipment Company, Chula Vista, California)

■ SAW GLAZING

Some minerals clog or "glaze" saw blades and cause considerable difficulty. Among these are nephrite, malachite, jadeite, and idocrase. Sometimes the mineral deposits a coating on the blade while the mineral itself develops a polish at the bottom of the cut instead of being ground away as it should be. In any case, sawing is slowed, overheating occurs, and blades warp or jam. To help prevent this, adjust the rate of carriage feed to its slowest speed since this allows the diamond particles to cut cleanly. If glazing persists, touch the edge of the blade from time to time with a piece of brick while it is spinning. Brick cleans the blade and uncovers the diamond particles. Sometimes the trouble lies in the fact that the coolant is too thick and lubricates the saw cut too well to allow good cutting action. In this case, some coolant should be dipped out and plain kerosene substituted. In other instances, the trouble is due to trying to saw too large a cross-section. If the blade is almost completely buried in a long cut, its edge bears on far more surface and the individual diamond teeth are unable to "sink in." There is no cure for this except to avoid cutting sections that are too large for the blade. If a large section is to be cut, find someone with a larger saw and arrange to have him cut it for you.

■ TRIM SAWS

Another type of saw used extensively is a smaller and less complicated version of the slabbing saw. Used for sectioning and trimming slabs and small bits of rough, it is popularly called a "trim saw." The principal features are a strong metal tank supporting the saw arbor, and a table of metal through which projects the upper part of the saw blade. Above the blade is a small hood of metal or plastic which prevents oil spray from being thrown on the operator. The essentials of a trim saw are shown in Figure 20 where an unusually complete and versatile unit is illustrated.

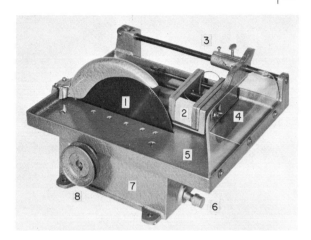

Fig. 20 Highland Park trim saw with slabbing feed. 1. Saw blade. 2. Rock clamp which can be swung out of the way for hand feeding. 3. Weight feed slide and hook. Wire passes over pulley shown at upper left corner. 4. Plastic splash hood at front. 5. Coolant tank top and table. 6. Drain. 7. Coolant tank and arbor support. 8. Pulley for belt to motor. (Courtesy Highland Park Manufacturing Co., South Pasadena, California)

■ OPERATING THE TRIM SAW

Procedures for setting up trim saws follow those specified for slabbing saws, but the operation is different because the work is fed and guided by hand. The trim saw is used for minor sawing jobs such as cutting out blanks for cabochons, slicing small bits of rough, and trimming fragments of faceting rough. In general, all operations are simple, but a few precautions must be observed.

Slabs leaving the slabbing saw usually have small projections at the point where they were broken off and these must be removed before the slab can lie flat. An ordinary pair of pliers can be used for this purpose.

To saw a slab, place flat on the saw table, being sure that no chips of rough are underneath. Hold it down with firm pressure and slide *very* slowly toward the blade. The position of the hands is shown in Figure 21 and also in Figure 15. Initial contact must be very gentle, because the knifelike edge of the slab can gouge the soft steel of the blade and wear it very quickly. Continue feeding at a very slow rate until the blade is well past the edge;

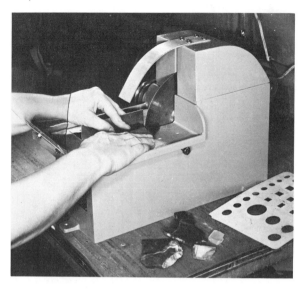

Fig. 21 Position of hands during trim sawing. The slab is held flat upon the saw table and fed into the blade with steady forward motion. (Courtesy Brad's Rock Shop, Ferndale, Michigan)

then move the slab forward at a slightly faster rate. How fast to feed is a question that can be answered only from experience. Gemstones vary in hardness and toughness, and it is not practical to tell what the reaction of each is going to be. However, there are a few warning signs that appear whenever the rate of feed is excessive. A shower of sparks at the point of contact is one sign; the drying out of the slab at the point of cutting, along with the presence of dry dust, is another. If either of these warning signals appear, slow up the rate of feed.

It is difficult, at first, to saw accurately along a line inscribed on a slab, and some experience is needed to do it well. Once a cut has started, do not attempt to correct its direction by twisting the slab sideways. This will certainly change the direction but will also cause the blade to wear badly along its edges. Since the blade must be thicker at the cutting edge to cut its own clearance, wearing of the edge will cause the blade to bind.

Starting a cut on a sloping slab edge has the same disadvantages noted in a similar situation for the large saws. Again the proper procedure is to start the cut very gently until the blade

is well past the edge of the slab and has no further tendency to wander off to one side.

Guide lines should always be drawn on slabs to aid in accurate sawing. A line drawn with a bit of aluminum wire is satisfactory in most cases, but sometimes it cannot be seen well under the coolant spray. In this event, ordinary colored pencils may be better, especially if the color is in sharp contrast to that of the slab.

■ TRIM SAWING SMALL BITS OF ROUGH

Sawing slabs is easy because the slab lies perfectly flat on the saw table. In the case of irregular bits of rough, such as pebbles and broken fragments, great care must be taken to prevent them from tilting and "grabbing" the blade. Smooth pebbles are particularly troublesome because they tend to roll. They saw easily at the start but as the cut deepens, any slight twisting immediately results in great friction on the blade and the pebble will be plucked from the fingers. It is here that damage occurs because the pebble may twist the blade or even break the edge. Sintred-rim blades may lose large rim sections this way and be completely ruined, while notch-rim blades will be useless for further sawing until the blade is taken off and hammered flat.

There are several ways to reduce the danger of grabbing. An excellent way, especially for round pebbles, is to flatten one side on a grinding wheel. The flat spot serves to keep the pebble steady while being sawed. Another simple method is to dop or cement a troublesome piece of rough on the end of a piece of lumber. After the cement is hard, the stone can be sliced easily either on the slabbing saw or fed by hand in a trim saw. A good cement is a generous dab of water glass which is allowed to harden thoroughly. It is removed later by soaking in warm water. Much stronger cements are the epoxy resins, which many cutters use for this purpose.

Recognizing the difficulties involved in sawing small pieces of rough, some manufacturers provide small clamps for their trim saws such as shown in Figure 20. A clever device for holding rounded end-sections of nodules which are sliced on larger saws is also available. The round section or "heel" as it is commonly called, is slipped into the recesses on each side of a special clamp and the screw tightened. The entire assembly is either placed in a large saw for further slabbing or cut on the trim saw.

A device for sawing slabs at angles is shown in Figure 22. It is a small three-legged

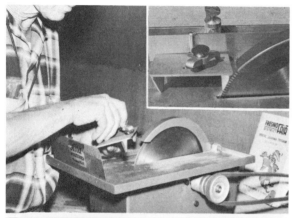

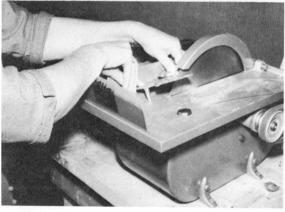

Fig. 22 Trim sawing bevels on slabs. *Top.* Clamping slab section. *Bottom.* Feeding slab into the trim saw blade. *Inset.* The clamping device. (Courtesy Alta Industries, Fresno, California)

metal table with a clamp on top. The slab is placed in the jaws of the clamp and tightened with the hand screw. The angle is changed by means of the screw in the back, which by turning raises or lowers the back edge. With this device it is possible to cut squares, rec-

tangles, and other geometrical figures with accurately sloping sides, or, in the case of cutting blanks which will later be used for cabochons, to provide a slope which can be followed later when the shape is being accurately ground.

■ **TRIM SAW SPEEDS**

The same rim speeds recommended for slabbing saws are used in trim sawing except when using very thin blades meant for slicing faceting rough. The latter are treated in Chapter 13 along with instructions for their use.

■ **HOMEMADE TRIM SAWS**

A homemade saw needs care in construction at only one place—the table. To be satisfactory, it must be made of metal, at least ⅛-inch thick, to provide a solid backing for any slab being sawed. Flimsy tables result in severe vibration and chattering which wears the blade and harms the gemstone. Thinner metal can be used but must be backed with ⅝-inch plywood to provide the necessary stiffness. Figure 23 shows a schematic drawing of a homemade trim saw as seen from the rear. The table can be hinged at the front or back but the solid metal part must be just in front of the saw blade. Figure 24 shows an excellent home designed and home made saw in use.

Splashing of coolant is a problem with trim saws and unless it is solved, much coolant will find its way to the clothing of the operator and to the floor. A small metal guard must be placed over the top of the saw and, preferably, another of plastic just in front at the edge of the table, as shown in Figure 21. This takes care of spray from the blade. The table also turns up around the edges and holes are bored in the top to let the coolant drain back into the tank. Splashing also occurs underneath and must be considered in making the saw because coolant will leak out from under the table edge. The upper edge of the tank should therefore be covered with thin strips of neoprene rubber,

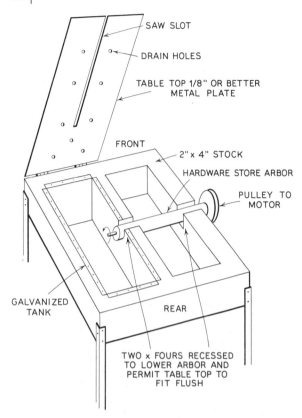

SAW SLOT

DRAIN HOLES

TABLE TOP 1/8" OR BETTER
METAL PLATE

FRONT

2" x 4" STOCK

HARDWARE STORE ARBOR

PULLEY TO
MOTOR

GALVANIZED
TANK

REAR

TWO x FOURS RECESSED
TO LOWER ARBOR AND
PERMIT TABLE TOP TO
FIT FLUSH

Fig. 23 Homemade trim saw.

cork, or some other oil-proof soft material. When the table is lowered, it will rest on the rubber strips and seal the tank.

The coolant tank should be fitted with a drain, since it is awkward to clean out rock dust and chips of stone from within the narrow space without removing the coolant. A convenient drain is a piece of pipe screwed into the tank, or, if the liner is sheet metal, a cylinder of sheet metal soldered to the bottom. Attach a piece of garden hose and bring its end up to table level and suspend from a hook. As long as the hose opening is higher than the level of coolant, no leaking will occur.

■ MUD SAWS

Mud saws have some advantages over diamond saws. First, they are very cheap because the blades and loose grits cost very little as compared to diamond blades. Second, they can be made in very large sizes

for slicing massive pieces of rough, which, if cut on diamond blades, would involve great blade expense. However, if cutting time is a factor, then the advantages may be lost since mud saws take much longer to cut than diamond saws.

Mud Saw Types. There are three types of mud saw blades in use, (1) circular saw blades, (2) straight blades, and (3) wire blades. Straight blades can be divided further into hack-saw types where the motion is back-and-forth, as in ordinary hand sawing, and band saws where a narrow ribbon of metal runs over rollers in a vertical plane. Jig saws, that is those which run a band of metal up and down, are not used, although there seems to be no reason why they cannot be. In all types, the loose silicon carbide grit is applied to the blade or wire as a wet slurry, and drawn into the cut and rubbed against the stone by the metal band or wire, thus deepening the cut until the stone is sectioned. Circular blades leave a flat smooth surface which is sometimes of better quality than that produced by a diamond saw. On the other hand, band saw blades often leave wavy surfaces, depending on the width of the blade. A wavy surface also results from the use of hack saw blades but if the blade is wide enough, the surface will be flat. The worst surfaces are left by the wire saw since any slight lateral movement of the machine which runs the wire back and forth results in wandering.

The Chinese Circular Mud Saw. The ancient genius of the Chinese solved the problem of the circular mud saw long before anyone else, and despite the availability of modern diamond saw machinery, they still use their ancient, tried-and-true model, as shown in Figure 25. This machine looks rickety and the idea of cutting anything on it seems impossible but when one sees an artist working on this machine, and notes how quickly and accurately he can slice through the toughest jade, one begins to feel respect. The author saw such artists using this machine in Hong Kong and can testify that they were able to cut and carve jade extremely rapidly. In addition to using the device for sawing, operators have at hand many kinds of carving points mounted in spindles which are exchanged for the saw blades by slacking off the leather strap and taking out the previous spindle. An illustration of this machine in use appears in Figure 160, where a skilled modern carver is shown at work.

The wooden spindle is tapered from several inches at the front where the saw blade is attached, to about 2 inches at the other. The back end is sharply tapered to fit in a greased

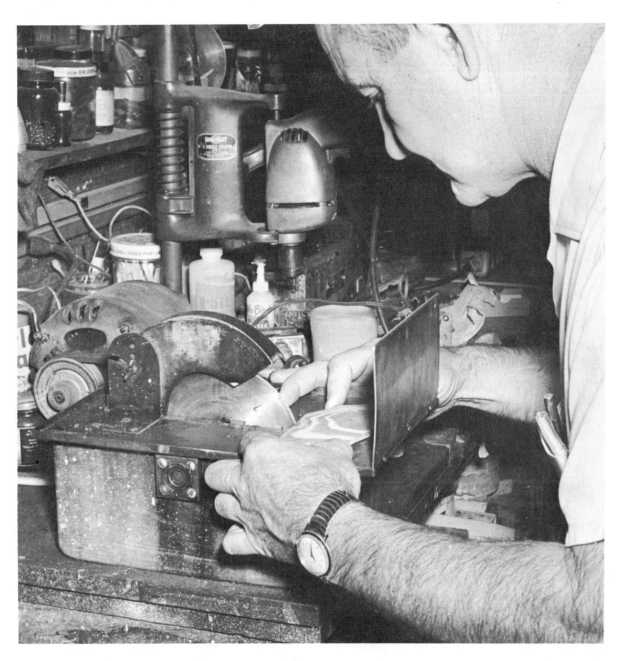

Fig. 24 Home-designed and home-made trim saw in operation. Tom Hubbard, of Whittier Gem and Mineral Society, California, is shown operating the saw, which was designed and built by Sol Stern, also a member of the Whittier society. (Courtesy Frank Hewlett Photography, El Monte, California)

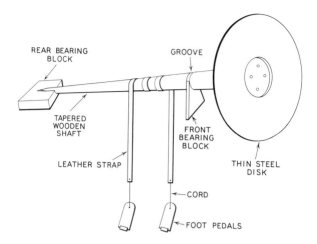

REAR BEARING BLOCK

GROOVE

TAPERED WOODEN SHAFT

FRONT BEARING BLOCK

LEATHER STRAP

THIN STEEL DISK

CORD

FOOT PEDALS

Fig. 25 The Chinese mud saw and carving machine.

socket. Bearings are of hardwood and greased for easy running. The center part of the spindle is looped over with the leather strap with the ends going down to a pair of wooden boards used as foot pedals. A thin metal hood covers the blade and keeps spray and grit from splashing about. A tub is attached to the front end beneath the spindle and serves as a place where grit can be kept and water for washing off work to check progress.

The blade is roofing tin and is fastened to the spindle by shellac dopping wax. No iron is used except in the blade itself. The inner portion of the blade is hammered into a shallow depression to stiffen the blade and make it run true. After installing, the blade is spun for an accuracy check, and adjustments are made by heating the wax to soften it and allow shifting of the blade. Several holes are drilled near the center to allow some wax to ooze through and lock the blade in place. The final step is to file the edge while spinning to true it up.

The operator sits before the machine on a wooden platform attached to the frame and pushes the pedals alternately to make the blade spin back and forth. The rough stone is held in one hand under the lower edge of the blade, the other hand being filled with loose grit which is held against the blade to keep it constantly supplied. In this way sawing proceeds with amazing speed and accuracy. The grit used is 100 or 220 silicon carbide. For smaller blades and finer work, 400 grit is used. Small slabs are supported on a wooden block resting in the palm of the hand with the object of preventing harm to the hand when the blade cuts through.

Stiffening Saw Blades. All mud saw circular blades cut faster if made as thin as possible. However, thin blades tend to wobble and dish badly unless they are stiffened by beating. The procedure is simple and can be applied not only to plain blades but also to diamond blades which have become dished during use. Lay the disk on a flat metal surface such as the top of a carpenter's table saw. Starting about an inch from the center hole, tap the blade lightly with a ball peen hammer or an ordinary hammer if a ball peen is not available, being sure that each blow lands squarely. Tap every inch or two in a spiral path about the center, turning the blade meanwhile, and gradually bring the line of blows out toward the rim. Turn the blade over and repeat. When properly done, and it may take several repetitions of the tapping, the blade will be tensioned and will resist bending. It is important that the blows start at the center each time and continue to the rim. Haphazard taps cause an uneven blade which will not run true. Practice this operation on a worn-out blade or a piece of scrap sheet metal before trying it on an expensive blade.

Power Driven Circular Mud Saws. Standard diamond saw machines can be used for mud sawing with the blade dipping into grit slurry instead of oil. However, any moving machinery parts will be destroyed by wear from the grit particles unless carefully covered. Since it is almost impossible to shield sliding carriages, the swinging arm arrangement shown in Figure 16 is useful for holding the stone against the saw. Rpms of the blade must be lower so that the edge picks up the slurry; if the blade runs too fast, it will pick up water only and leave the grit behind or sling it off before it gets to the cut.

Straight Blade Mud Saws. The straight blade or hack saw type is easier to make and less messy to use than the circular type. There is almost no limit to size and the author knows of one machine made by amateurs which runs a blade about 6 feet in length and about 6 inches in depth. Figure 26 shows one scheme for such a saw, particularly a very large one. Since the blade is likely to wobble if it is thin, it may be necessary to support it along the sides with uprights of wood. Smaller models support the blade in a frame similar to the old-fashioned buck saw, that is, the blade is stretched between posts with a rod and turnbuckle, and the entire frame supported between vertical guides as it strokes back and forth. Small saws use 18- to 20-gauge soft steel;

larger saws need thicker metal to be stiff enough.

Grit and water must be fed constantly and one arrangement is shown in Figure 26. A metal trough is rigged above the cut with a supply of grit. Water drips on the grit and washes a small but steady supply into the cut. The latter is surrounded with a miniature crater of modeling clay which funnels the grit-water mixture to the cut. Containers can be placed on each end of the cut to catch run-off, and the grit returned to the trough from time to time. The grit size used is 100 to 220.

Mud Band Saws. Converting a band saw into a stone saw is entirely practical, in fact, some museums and laboratories have done it in order to handle sections which are too large to cut with a diamond saw. The requirements are that the usual toothed blade by replaced by a plain untempered mild steel blade, and that a dolly or roller table be fitted on the normal table to allow the stone to be moved into the blade as cutting goes on. Special covers must be placed over all bearings and shafting to keep out grit; in most cases, these can be made from canvas and taped or tied over the places concerned. The most troublesome part

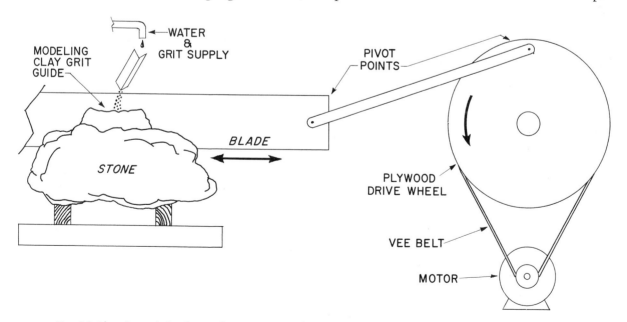

Fig. 26 Abrasive grit hack saw for stone. Very large stone sections can be cut with this type of saw.

is trying to rig up a suitable feed which will sluice just enough grit into the cut without being overgenerous. A vee-shaped trough is again used with a drip of water which can be adjusted. Modeling clay is attached to the side of the block being cut, and as the cut goes deeper, more clay is used to keep the grits funnelled where they belong.

In operation, the block of stone is propped up on the table dolly so that it cannot wobble or change position. It is moved up to the blade until almost touching. Clay is built up the side like a bird's nest, with the saw blade through the middle. The water drip is turned on and when the grit is funnelling properly, the motor is started. The stone is moved forward very slowly until it barely contacts the blade. When the initial "zinging" noise stops, it means the blade is no longer cutting. The block of stone is then moved up about $\frac{1}{16}$ to $\frac{1}{8}$ inch and cutting begun again. This process is repeated until the entire stone is cut through. Blade speed is about 900 to 1000 feet per minute; grits used are from 100 to 220.

The Wire Saw. Wire saws are still used by the Chinese to cut large blocks of jadeite into smaller and more manageable pieces. There is really no limit as to size of material since the only requirement is for the bow on which the wire is strung to be big enough to span the block. A saw can be built with the bow principle or the roller principle. In the first, the wire is strung between the ends of a wooden bow, while in the second, the wire runs be-tween two spools which alternately wind and unwind. Both saws have been made by am-ateurs and work successfully, though they are slower cutting than other kinds of mud saws.

Soft iron wire of no more than $\frac{1}{32}$ inch in diameter should be used for the cutting wire. Three strands are twisted together, although a single strand can be used. Three strands are better because the vee-shaped groove between wires grips abrasive grains and promotes faster cutting. Small saws can be made with finer wire stretched in a jewelers saw frame or in an ordinary hack saw.

The roller wire saw consists of two plywood wheels over which the ends of the wire are strung and fastened. One wheel is made to roll back and forth with a push-pull arm from a motor driven wheel. The other wheel is weighted so that it keeps the wire taut at all times. When the motor is turned on, the push-pull arm oscillates one wheel, stroking the wire back and forth across the stone.

In using a wire saw, it is necessary to chip a small groove on top of the stone to start the wire and avoid sharp kinking. A clay cup is built over the selected spot and filled with a slurry of grit. As the wire is stroked back and forth, more grit is added as necessary. As much of the wire length should be used as possible to equalize wear. When the wire has been used for some time, it should be replaced before it gets too thin because as it wears, the cut narrows, and the latter can become too small to take a new wire. This can be prevented by changing wires frequently.

4 | *Grinding*

GRINDING is the abrasive process used to give rough shape to gemstones. In lapidary work, the term refers to the use of abrasive wheels. The most common are made from silicon carbide in many sizes and shapes and employ abrasive grains of different size, depending on the purpose of the wheel. Coarse grits are used to make wheels which rapidly remove material while fine grits are used whenever the abrasive action must be slower and smoother. Amateurs use grinding wheels to shape cabochons and to preform rough for faceted gems, also for grinding bevels on flats, shaping carvings, profiling pieces for inlay work, and many other tasks.

■ ABRASIVES USED IN GRINDING

Crushed sand, garnet, emery, and other hard substances have been used for abrasive purposes in lapidary work, but silicon carbide now reigns supreme as the preferred abrasive. This extremely hard substance is formed by heating coke and sand in electric ovens. After cooling, the crude material is taken out, crushed, and carefully graded as to grain size. The loose powders are used in lapping, a process which will be described in Chapter 5, while powders cemented together are formed into whetstones and the grinding wheels of industry and gem cutting.

■ GRIT SIZES

Silicon carbide is sold in the trade under a variety of names, such as Carborundum, Crystolon, etc. As explained in Chapter 3, the finer the particles, the larger the grit number; i.e., 100 grit is coarse but 1200 grit is very fine. This grit number must always be used when ordering powders or wheels. The grits used in lapidary work, either as loose grain or in wheels, are shown in the table on the next page.

■ GRINDING WHEELS

Silicon carbide wheels for gem cutting come in a variety of sizes depending on the type of equipment used. Common sizes range from ½ to 1½ inches thick and from 6 to

TABLE OF GRIT SIZE

Grit Size	Inch Size	Micron Size	Purpose
60	.016	406	Rough lapping, grinding, tumbling
100	.0068	173	Rough lapping, grinding, tumbling
220	.0026	66	Fine grinding, lapping
400	.0009	23	Very fine grinding, lapping, tumbling
600	.00033	8	Very fine lapping
1200	—	—	Very fine lapping, prepolish

10 inches in diameter. Shaft or arbor holes are available in sizes ranging in diameter from ½ to 1 inch to accommodate various makes of equipment.

In the manufacture of grinding wheels, a small amount of clay and water is added to the loose grit and the mixture pressed into molds. After drying, the pressed forms are heated to a high temperature, which fuses the clay and cements the grit in a very strong bond. Considerable space remains between grains which permits water to penetrate and soak the wheel. This is a highly important feature in gem grinding, where water must be used to prevent gemstones from overheating or "burning" while being ground. The amount of clay used in bonding silicon carbide wheels determines how well the grains are cemented together. A larger quantity makes a "hard" grade wheel, while a smaller amount permits the grains to be broken apart readily and makes a wheel of "soft" grade. The bond varies accordingly from "hard" to "soft" and is an important feature of any grinding wheel. To understand why this is so, we must examine the action at the surface of a wheel during grinding.

A fresh wheel cuts quickly because its entire surface is covered with jagged, sharp grains of abrasive. Soon after, however, each grain becomes blunted and the rate of cutting slows down. If the wheel is hard in grade, the grains break out with difficulty and the wheel tends to "glaze" while the cutting action slows down. On the other hand, a soft grade wheel loses its surface grains quickly because they are held together with less cement. This results in constant renewal of the surface with fresh, sharp grains and fast cutting continues. Thus, hard wheels wear slowly and soft wheels rapidly, the rate of wear and cutting being proportional to the strength of the cement

bond. As a general rule, hard wheels are used for grinding soft materials like certain metals, while softer grades are used for harder materials including gemstones.

Although soft wheels cut quickly and are a joy to use in gemstone grinding, they are expensive because more of them must be used to do the same work. For this reason, very soft wheels are not favored by amateurs, who find wheels of "medium," "medium hard" and "medium soft" the best compromise between speedy cutting and economy. Although letters of the alphabet are used by makers to designate the hardness grade, several systems are employed and the results are confusing to anyone ordering wheels. It is enough to say that you want a medium hard, medium, or medium soft wheel, and that it is intended for gem grinding. Any lapidary supply house will give you the grade most suitable for the grit size you specify.

Only a few types of wheels are needed to do most grinding jobs. For rough shaping, a medium soft grade of 120 grit is most popular although 100 grit is almost as much in demand. In fine grinding, where the object is to smooth surfaces and not remove much material, a 220 grit wheel in medium hard grade is best. Sometimes very soft gemstones, such as turquois, cut too fast even on 220 wheels, and for them a medium hard wheel in 400 grit is better. The beginner will not need this wheel for most work but may find it useful as he increases skill and expands the variety of his work. To order grinding wheels from a dealer, give *thickness* of the wheel, *diameter, arbor hole size, grit,* and finally, the *grade.*

Most amateurs use wheels in two grit sizes in their grinders: a coarse wheel of 120 grit, and a fine wheel of 220 grit. These are generally placed next to each other in the same

Fig. 27 Dell Jones, of the Whittier, California, Gem and Mineral Society, demonstrating the shaping of a cabochon on a Frantom all-purpose lapidary machine. The wheel on the right is coarse grit while that on the left is fine. (Courtesy Frank Hewlett Photography, El Monte, California)

unit, as shown in Figure 27; this arrangement allows quick switching from rough to smooth grinding, and vice versa if retouching is needed. Although it is possible to use only one wheel for all grinding, the marks left by a coarse wheel are so deep that prolonged work is needed in sanding to eliminate them. A rough surface *cannot* be polished directly, and this is the reason why a series of abrasive steps is needed. In the event that only one wheel must be used, it is best to get a wheel no coarser than 120, preferably one as fine as 180. Even though the 180 wheel cuts slower at the beginning and does not leave as fine a finish as a 220 wheel, it works well for most purposes.

■ GRINDING EQUIPMENT

The simplest grinder is a steel shaft in bearings which carries one or more grinding wheels. The usual arrangement is to place the two grinding wheels, coarse and fine, on opposite ends of the shaft with bearings just inside them and the drive pulley between the bearings. This provides a balanced machine which is steady and smooth in operation. The motor is mounted to the rear and drives the shaft by means of a rubber vee-belt. Each wheel is housed in a splash hood which serves the twofold purpose of trapping water and grit, and of protecting the operator in the extremely rare event that the wheel should break while running. Water to cool the work and wash away rock dust is supplied either by a drip arrangement or a sponge in contact with the wheel. Where a great deal of grinding is to be done, it pays to equip the shop with a separate grinding arbor with two wheels. However, most amateurs buy all-purpose units, one of which is shown in Figure 27, because all essential steps in making cabochons can be completed on them for the least investment in money. These units are fully described in Chapter 8.

■ **THE GRINDING ARBOR**

Grinding wheels must spin at high rpm in order to cut well; it is therefore essential that the arbor, with its spindle and bearings, be rigid and accurate, with a minimum of vibration. Wheels that wobble or vibrate cannot grind well and they wear quickly without giving the amateur his money's worth in good work. Wheels of 6-inch diameter or less require a spindle diameter of at least ½ inch. Wheels of 8-inch diameter should be mounted on spindles of at least ⅝-inch diameter, 10-inch wheels on at least ¾-inch spindles, and 12-inch wheels on spindles of 1-inch diameter. Anything less may result in excessive and wasteful vibration. If in doubt as to what size spindle should be specified, err on the high side.

The ends of grinding wheel spindles are threaded to take nuts which tighten pairs of flanges holding wheels in place. Flanges differ from ordinary washers in that the center portion is cut away leaving only a narrow rim which grips the wheel. If ordinary flat sided washers are used to fasten a wheel in place, the greatest pressure will be placed upon a small area immediately under the tightening nut, putting a severe strain on the wheel and possibly causing it to develop cracks. Most grinding arbors are sold equipped with flanges; if they are not, the following should be obtained according to wheel diameter: wheels of 6-inch diameter use flanges of no less than 2-inch diameter; 8-inch wheels use 3-inch diameter flanges; 10-inch wheels use 3½-inch diameter flanges; 12-inch wheels use 4-inch diameter flanges. The general rule of thumb for flanges is that they should be not less than one third the diameter of the wheel.

Ball bearings are best, particularly those which are permanently sealed to keep out dust and dirt and with a lifetime supply of grease inside. Sleeve bearings and unsealed ball bearings are also satisfactory but must be protected from grit. Small metal cups called "slingers" are usually installed over unsealed bearings to sling off water and grit through centrifugal force. Most grinding arbors are equipped with slingers, but if not, you should ask for them.

■ **INSTALLING AND TESTING WHEELS**

Check a new grinding wheel carefully for cracks. Suspend the wheel from two fingers and tap it with a small stick—you will hear a clear ringing note if it is solid; a dull sound may indicate a hidden crack, in which case it should not be used. On each face of the wheel will be a circle of blotting paper bearing the manufacturer's data as well as the maximum rpm, which should not be exceeded. Since blotting paper traps water and contributes to rusting of the shaft, locking nut, and flanges, carefully remove both disks and substitute similar ones of thin rubber or cork or fiber gasket material; do not glue these in place.

Install the wheel on the arbor spindle, sliding gently to avoid scraping of the inner bearing, which is made of lead. Be certain that both flanges bear evenly on the sides and then tighten the lock nut firmly. Spin the wheel by hand to be sure the edges are free from wobbling, which is a sign of unevenness in the material used for making the cushioning disks. When the wheel is balanced, install the splash hood and start the motor, standing to one side while the wheel speeds up. Let the wheel run for at least two minutes before starting to use it. This procedure is a good one to follow every time the wheel is started.

Never allow a wheel to rest in water, either on the machine or stored in the shop. Wheels are porous and absorb enough water to make them seriously unbalanced if water-soaked on one side. *In this condition they are dangerous!* For the same reason, never turn on the water before starting the wheel.

■ SPLASH HOODS

Because water must be used during grinding, each wheel must be covered with a splash hood. In addition, this hood should be strong enough to protect the operator from harm in the event that the wheel should burst while running. This danger is not great, due to the care taken in the manufacture of wheels and the spin tests given before they are shipped. Nevertheless, it is wise to consider self-protection. The chance of breakage is greater in large-diameter wheels, and for these, heavy metal hoods are proper; hoods for wheels of 8-inch diameter and smaller can be of less substantial material. Manufacturers of grinding arbors always provide suitable hoods on request.

■ HOMEMADE GRINDERS

The one piece of equipment needed to make a grinder, or a combination grinder, sander, and polisher, is an arbor. Satisfactory arbors can be bought in hardware stores or lapidary supply houses in considerable variety. A simple type is shown in Figure 28 and consists of a ball bearing arbor with one end fitted with a grinding wheel and the other with a pulley which leads to the motor. If a double-ended arbor is selected with a drive pulley in the center, it is possible to operate

Fig. 28 Homemade equipment in the workshop of French Morgan of Morgantown, West Virginia. The grinder shown here is made from a ball-bearing arbor, one end of which supports the wheel and the other the pulley to the motor. Though simple and inexpensive to build, this arbor has helped Mr. Morgan win prizes for his cabochons.

two accessories at once, as shown in Figure 29, or, by buying another splash hood, to use this unit as a coarse and fine grinder.

All arbors must be bolted on sturdy bases of strong plywood or planking. The base also supports the motor and keeps it at the proper distance from the arbor to maintain tension on the rubber vee-belt. Select a vee-belt which will allow the motor to be placed a foot or more to the rear.

Splash hoods can be made or bought separately as shown in Figure 30. Small 6-inch diameter wheels can be housed in 1-gallon cans cut out in front and slipped into position from the rear of the wheel. Be sure all sharp edges are covered with tape to prevent cutting the hands. The top of the can traps spray while the bottom collects water and rock dust. A drain can be provided or the water in the bottom can be poured off periodically. A somewhat better hood can be made from ¾-inch plywood but all joints must be carefully sealed to prevent leakage and all surfaces heavily varnished to keep the plywood from coming apart. If you are able to solder, good pans can be made from

Fig. 29 A first class combination grinding and sanding arbor which can be bought in parts, as shown. A polishing buff can be substituted for the drum sander on the right to allow a full range of operations in cabochon cutting. The disk on the lower right is cemented to the end of the sanding drum with contact cement which enables it to be removed when necessary. (Courtesy The Ducketts, Medford, Oregon)

galvanized sheet to suit any size grinder you may use.

■ ELECTRICAL HAZARDS

Because many lapidary operations involve the use of water near electrical equipment such as motors, lights, and switch boxes, it is a good idea to say now that carelessness in handling electrical wiring can result in very severe shocks and perhaps even death. Newspapers often carry accounts of persons killed by ordinary household current because appliances such as radios, toasters, etc., were used with wet hands while another part of the body was touching a "ground" such as a sink, bath tub, or water pipe. This can happen in the lapidary workshop and it is absolutely essential that proper preventive steps be taken ahead of time. This is one of the reasons why arbors are used with the motor placed behind where it will not be sprayed by water from the wheels. Bench grinders, so commonly used in home workshops, can be converted to gemstone grinders, but since their motors would be

Fig. 30 Splash hood for grinding wheel. This item can be purchased separately for use in homemade units. This hood is fitted with water connection and valve, and adjustable spray shield at the forward upper lip. (Courtesy Rock's Lapidary Equipment & Supplies, San Antonio, Texas)

subject to constant wetting by wheel spray, they are likely to cause electrical shock. However, any electrical motor labeled "explosion proof" is specially sealed to prevent dust, moisture, or grease from reaching the parts inside carrying a live current and is suitable for gemstone grinding even when wetted repeatedly. Switches should be placed away from the motor since they too carry current which can leak to wet hands. A most convenient, simple, and foolproof arrangement is to plug any motor into an overhead lamp socket with a pull-chain on the socket. Attach a piece of plastic cord to the chain and turn the motor on and off by pulling the cord. In this way, you will not touch any metallic part which could be carrying current.

■ WATER SUPPLY

There are several ways to supply water to grinding wheels. The best is to use a drip or spray on the face of the wheel. A spray which covers the entire cutting face is better than a drip since the latter tends to drop the water only in the center of the wheel. Unfortunately a spray head is almost impossible to buy and one must make one's own. This can be done by using a piece of metal tubing bent at right angles. The bent portion is placed parallel to the cutting face of the wheel and adjusted so that it is only a fraction of an inch away. This portion of the tube is drilled with four to six very small holes after the open end has been pinched off and folded over to prevent leakage. The other end is connected by tubing to the household water supply.

Another method uses a sponge placed under the grinding wheel and resting in water. The idea is that enough water will be wiped from the sponge to keep the face of the wheel wet. This works well if wheels do not spin too fast. Still another method uses a piece of thick porous cloth or a piece of carpeting resting on the upper face of the wheel as shown in Figure 31. The water is supplied to the cloth and the latter spreads it over the face. Since the cloth wears to the same shape as the wheel

Fig. 31 Roughing out a gemstone using a large silicon carbide wheel. Note the position of the hands. Several folds of cloth above the wheel are used to spread water evenly over the face of the wheel; the water is supplied from a can above the wheel hood. Scene taken in a professional lapidary establishment in the famous German gem cutting center of Idar-Oberstein. (Courtesy W. Fischer; Rassmann Photo, Idar-Oberstein)

face, it does a good job in spreading the water evenly.

Some grinding units come with water nozzles which need only to be connected, as in the unit shown in Figure 27, but other units meant for sponges have no provisions for drip water; the top of their hoods must therefore be drilled to convert them. This is not difficult, and many amateurs who find the sponge method less than satisfactory convert their grinders to the drip type.

A good water supply is all-important in grinding. If a wheel appears whitish during grinding, it shows that rock dust is accumulating on the surface and clogging the wheel. This not only makes the wheel less efficient but could overheat the gemstone causing it to crack. The cure is to increase the supply of water. In workshops where city water is un-available, or where drain water cannot be dis-posed of easily, a good water supply can be had by buying a small water pump fitted to a five-gallon can and delivering water to the wheels from the can itself. The water drains back into the can, where the grit settles in the bottom. One advantage of this arrangement is that the water can be kept warmer and is therefore more comfortable than if a fresh sup-ply of cold water were being used. When con-siderable sludge has accumulated, empty the can and refill with clean water. Since rock dust and silicon carbide grit are heavy, they settle quickly and clog standard plumbing. Do not drain grinding wheel pans into household plumbing or an expensive cleaning bill is sure to result.

■ GRINDING WHEEL SPEEDS

Silicon carbide wheels are most efficient when run at surface speeds of 4,000 to 6,000 feet per minute. Surface speeds vary with the diameter of the wheel, a small wheel hav-ing to turn faster than a larger wheel in order to get the same surface speed at the rim. The rpm required to obtain a selected surface or "rim" speed can be determined from the Table of Rim Speeds for Saws and Wheels in Appen-dix 1. This table shows, for example, that if a rim speed of 4,000 feet per minute is wanted, it can be obtained by spinning a 10-inch wheel at 1,530 rpm, an 8-inch wheel at 1,910 rpm and a 6-inch wheel at 2,550 rpm. Notice that as the wheel becomes smaller the rpm must increase in order to get the same rim speed. This point is important because grinding wheels decrease in diameter as they wear and require a higher rpm if the same surface speed is to be main-tained. This problem is solved by running the newly installed wheel at about 6,000 feet per minute rim speed through a proper motor and arbor-pulley combination and suffering the loss in efficiency as the wheel decreases several inches in diameter. Below this, the pulley com-bination should be changed to give a higher rpm to restore rim speed.

Before settling on a rim speed for whatever size grinding wheel you install, you must con-sider the fact that every grinding wheel is limited to an rpm beyond which it cannot go without bursting. This limiting rpm is printed on the label of each wheel and *must not be exceeded*. Although each wheel is tested at the factory beyond this speed, it is foolhardy to exceed it even slightly; it is safer to keep be-low the limit. With this in mind, be sure that the wheel you are planning to use can be run at 6,000 feet per minute without exceeding the safe rpm; if it cannot, then it must be run at some lower speed which will be safe. Most manufacturers of lapidary equipment are well aware of these considerations and are careful to furnish complete instructions as to what rpm should be used.

A peculiarity of grinding wheels is that they seem to get softer as they wear or seem to get harder if the rpm is increased. The practical effects are that wheels wear slowly at first and with increasing rapidity as their diameter de-creases. Also, if the rpm should be increased, the wheel wears less and appears harder; whereas if the rpm is decreased, the wheel wears quickly and appears soft. This behavior of grinding wheels can be put to good use by the amateur who cannot always run his equip-ment at the best speed. If only a low rpm can be obtained, then a harder wheel should be installed and vice versa; whereas if a wheel wears too quickly and it is possible to increase the rpm, then it can be made to wear normally by speeding it up.

The author's experience points toward a combination of high rim speeds with medium to medium-soft wheels as being most efficient.

■ KEEPING WHEELS SMOOTH

Because grinding is mostly free-hand, it is impossible to prevent development of pits and bumps on the face of the wheel. Bumpiness is less likely to develop if large wheels are used and the work supported as steadily as possible. If the work is held free-hand, then it helps to use an even larger wheel since this delays the development of bumpiness for a longer time. This principle is well understood in the professional cutting shops of Idar/Oberstein in Germany, where the picture shown in Figure 31 was taken. The lapidary is grinding a rough gemstone to shape on a silicon carbide wheel which is far larger than most amateurs ever use. Such large wheels are very steady running and resist development of bumpiness almost indefinitely. Unfortunately, few amateurs have such large wheels and for them, the problem of bumpiness is severe and annoying.

Slight bumpiness is tolerable but when it becomes severe, it is necessary to dress the wheel face to return it to smoothness. Several methods are used to do this: (1) smoothing with a star wheel dresser, (2) smoothing with a diamond point, and (3) smoothing with a block of abrasive.

The star wheel dresser consists of a series of star-shaped hard steel wheels which fit loosely on a small shaft, which in turn is attached to a long, stout handle of steel. As the star wheels revolve, they vibrate from side to side and scrape off the outer layers of the grinding wheel. This tool is commonly used in machine shops in the manner shown in Figure 32.

Diamond points are small crystals of industrial diamond imbedded in the ends of steel rods. Several types are shown in Figure 33, while Figure 34 shows one held in a special jig. This type of dresser is easy to use, removes material quickly, and is not expensive considering how long one lasts.

The third method of dressing involves rubbing down the face of the grinding wheel with a block of abrasive, usually silicon carbide specially pressed into "brick" form. It is much slower than either of the other two, but where a very smooth surface is wanted it is probably somewhat better. Its use is shown in Figure 35.

■ MAKING A DIAMOND POINT DRESSER

Certain lapidary equipment dealers supply loose industrial diamond, and if

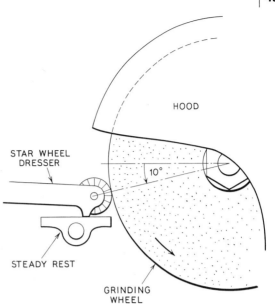

Fig. 32 Star wheel dresser in use, showing how wheels run in contact with grinding face and somewhat below the horizontal.

one can get a ¼ to ½ carat crystal at reasonable cost, it is easy to make a single-point dresser, as illustrated in Figure 36. Begin with the rod. Saw off a piece of ½-inch mild steel rod to a length of 6 inches; square off one end and drill a hole in it slightly larger than the diamond crystal. Slip the crystal into the hole, being

Fig. 33 Two types of diamond grinding wheel dressers. *Left.* A single point tool with a small industrial diamond protruding from the end. *Right.* A multiple-point tool containing seven separate diamond crystals. This tool dresses wheels faster and more smoothly but is also more expensive. (Courtesy Highland Park Mfg. Co., South Pasadena, California)

Fig. 34 The Highland Park wheel-dressing jig. A seven diamond dressing tool is inserted in the jig block and the latter is passed on a stout metal platform in front of the spinning wheel to dress the cutting face. (Courtesy Highland Park Mfg. Co., South Pasadena, California)

types, the tool is readied for use by grinding away the top of the rod until the point of diamond crystal appears.

■ USING WHEEL DRESSERS

Star wheel dressers must be rested on a firm support before they can be used. Some grinding units are equipped with work rests but often you must provide your own support. A heavy block of steel or iron is excellent; a block of stone or brick will do. The support must be high enough so that the star wheels will contact the grinding wheel face at a point about ½-inch below the center. This is shown clearly in Figure 32. The star wheel dresser is applied lightly to the moving wheel until the disks begin to rotate and chatter. Always use light pressure, since jamming will do nothing but wear away the star wheels rapidly. Slowly move the dresser across the face of the wheel until no low spots are present and the face is square and true. Dressing may be done with the water supply cut off if desired, but considerable dust will be raised. Since wheels soften slightly when wet, a faster job can be done by leaving the water supply on, but the dresser should be dried afterward to prevent rusting. Figure 37 shows common mistakes in wheel dressing as well as a correctly shaped wheel face.

A diamond dressing tool is best used on a support if available but can be used freehand with practice. Only the lightest of cuts should be taken, to avoid cracking or splitting the diamond. Grip the tool in one hand and support this hand with the other. Bring the diamond point into contact with the wheel about ½ inch below the center of the face and sweep the point across from side to side. Do not press the point *into* the wheel but let it "tick" on the high spots until these are worn down. Stop the wheel from time to time to check progress. If the tool is allowed to "ride" on the surface, it will dip into each hollow and only make the bumpiness worse. The wheel is most quickly trued wet but may be trued dry if the resulting dust is not objectionable.

sure it reaches the bottom. Place upright in a vise, and with a hardened steel punch or drift, peen the steel over the diamond with light taps, being very careful not to strike the diamond itself. The diamond should now be locked in and you may either continue peening until it is completely and snugly gripped by the steel, or you may fill the crevices around the diamond with silver solder or spelter. In the soldering method, the only safeguard required is to be sure that both the diamond and the rod are absolutely free of grease or oil; the slightest trace of either will prevent good adhesion of the solder. Heat the rod with a blow torch or in a gas flame until it is hot enough to melt the solder (do not fear for the diamond, which is capable of being heated white-hot without damage). As soon as the rod is hot enough, the solder will flow completely around the diamond and, after cooling, will grip it firmly. Sometimes not enough space exists between the diamond and the walls of the cavity and it may be necessary to fill the latter with molten solder and with a pair of tweezers to push the diamond below the surface until the solder freezes. In both peened and soldered

Fig. 35 Method of truing sandstone grinding wheels in Idar-Oberstein, Germany. Springy sticks are used to push a small piece of sandstone into the grinding wheel face. In time, the face is flattened to the point where it can be used again. (Courtesy W. Fischer; Rassmann Photo, Idar-Oberstein)

With the dressing jig shown in Figure 34, it is far easier to smooth a wheel, because the entire tool is supported on a steady-rest and can be swept from side to side without chattering or bumping. However, this tool, like the others, cannot be jammed into the face; it must be moved forward in the block just enough to contact the high spots and then locked into position. After the first pass, it is unlocked and

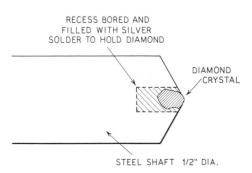

RECESS BORED AND
FILLED WITH SILVER
SOLDER TO HOLD DIAMOND

DIAMOND
CRYSTAL

STEEL SHAFT 1/2" DIA.

Fig. 36 Detail of diamond dressing point, showing method of mounting.

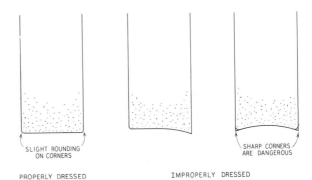

SLIGHT ROUNDING
ON CORNERS

PROPERLY DRESSED

SHARP CORNERS
ARE DANGEROUS

IMPROPERLY DRESSED

Fig. 37 Properly and improperly dressed grinding wheel faces.

moved slightly forward, relocked, and repassed over the face. This process is continued until dressing is finished.

■ HOW TO USE GRINDING WHEELS

The position of the stone while being ground is highly important, since it must be held in a "trailing" position like a knife used to spread butter on a piece of bread. If a jagged edge of stone is forced into the wrong direction on a grinding wheel it will result in "catching." This in turn will cause a bad nick on the face of the wheel and, quite likely, the stone will be twitched out of the fingers or broken by the force of the impact. This is our first rule for the use of a grinding wheel: always grind with the rotation of the wheel and not against it. This principle is being used by the operator shown in Figures 27 and 38.

Another important rule is to give the work adequate support. In machine shops where grinders are used extensively, small platforms directly in front of the wheels are used to brace the work and thus keep it from vibrating or "chattering." Unfortunately steady-rests can seldom be used in gemstone grinding because the sweeping curves of cabochon stones require that the position of the hands be changed constantly to create the desired shape. Without support, however, it is an easy matter to set up chattering or bumping, especially if the wheel is the least bit out-of-round. Some cutters rest their wrists or forearms on the edge of the splash pan. This provides additional support and proves less tiring. However, perfectly good work can be done by holding the work as close to the point of contact as possible with one hand and placing the other hand underneath as an additional brace. This is clearly illustrated in Figure 27 where the operator is holding the mounted stone by the shaft of the dop stick and supporting that hand with the fingertips of the other. In this position, he is able to control accurately the movements of his hands.

Another rule that must be followed governs the size of the stones which may be ground on a wheel of given diameter. In general, very

large pieces cannot be worked on small wheels without setting up severe bumping. When a wheel is first used, the surface is even and smooth. If a heavy stone is brought against the rapidly moving surface it will be almost impossible to feed it steadily enough to prevent bumping. Only one bump is needed to start the cycle, because as the wheel turns, the edge of the pit caused by the bump will catch it and bounce it a fraction of an inch. Then when it is brought back by the pressure of the hands, another pit will be made and another, until in a matter of seconds the wheel has lost its accuracy. In a very short time the bumping becomes uncontrollable and, if allowed to continue, will surely crack the stone if not the wheel. Experience shows that 6-inch wheels should not be used to grind stones larger than about 2 inches in diameter, first-size stones may be ground with care on 8-inch wheels, while larger specimens may be done safely on 10-inch and 12-inch wheels. Fortunately our grinding chores seldom call for whittling away at stones larger than our thumbnails but even then it is wise to remember that bumping will occur sooner or later, and when it does, the wheel should be resmoothed immediately with a dressing tool.

The avoidance of bumping is a difficult problem and will never be solved completely so long as work has to be held freehand. However, certain things will delay the appearance of bumping—or at least keep it in check. First, one must acquire steadiness, training the hands and wrists to hold the work so that it is fed to the wheel gently yet firmly. Second, one should avoid jamming sharp corners of the rough into the face of the wheel because this will cause pitting, followed immediately by bumping. Third, avoid grinding away material too fast, for this will cause bumping as well as wasteful use of the wheel itself. And finally, bumping should never proceed to the point where deep pits develop; the deeper the pits, the more unused wheel material must be removed to even up the surface. Because bumping is far more likely to begin on small wheels, the professional cutters of Idar/Oberstein sel-

Fig. 38 Extremely large sandstone grinding wheels as used in some professional gem cutting shops in the cutting center of Idar-Oberstein in Germany. Such large wheels resist bumping and stay in round for a long time. (Courtesy W. Fischer; Rassmann Photo, Idar-Oberstein)

dom use grinding wheels smaller than 12 inches diameter and at least 2 inches thick. In some cases, as shown in Figure 38, very large sandstone wheels are used which, though they may not cut as fast as silicon carbide wheels, are satisfactory for rough or heavy work. It isn't practical for amateurs to use such large wheels but the lesson is plain: if you can, buy large wheels mounted on heavy arbors; the larger, the better.

■ SIMPLE GRINDING PRACTICE

Set up your grinding wheel as instructed by the manufacturer and review the hints given at the beginning of this chapter. Be sure to carry out the tests and safety precautions. Select a piece of rough material, preferably a sawed slab about 2 inches square. Start the wheel and adjust the water supply until all of the wheel surface is wet. Hold the slab with the thumb and forefinger of each hand, doubling the forefingers under so that the slab rests on the knuckles. This is a very strong, steady, and useful grip. Now advance the edge gently toward the wheel face and grind off a tiny bevel, being sure that the slab is pointed downward in the same direction that the wheel is spinning. This will prevent the sharp edges from gouging the wheel. Run the slab back and forth a few times just to get the "feel." Examine frequently to see what the effects are. Try grinding off projecting points and perhaps even shaping the piece of rough into some sort of geometrical pattern. Note at the same time how close your fingers are to the wheel; remember—the wheel cuts! Care must always be exercised that you do not absent mindedly let some part of your hand contact the wheel.

After satisfying yourself with the action of the wheel on the slab, break the slab in half and try more grinding. You will note now that the piece is more difficult to hold because there is less of it. However, practice anyway because many stones you grind later will be even smaller, and much skill is needed to handle those as small as a dime. Now take a bit of slab again and draw a portion of a circle on it with a pencil made from a piece of aluminum wire or sheet. Deliberately grind to this outline, being as accurate as you can; examine your effort frequently. Next, try to square the edges so that the corners will be right angles. To do this you will need to hold the slab nearly at right angles to the face of the wheel. All of this is practice, but it accomplishes the two things you need to know at this stage of the game—what your grinding wheel will do, and how to control your hands to obtain the shape you want.

In addition to the simple exercises above, try grinding bits of unsawed rough, roundish pebbles, and a variety of gemstones both soft and hard.

If your grinding unit has both a coarse and fine wheel, do your practicing on the first for that is the one which will remove most of the material. Try the fine wheel afterward to see how smoothly it cuts in comparison to the coarse wheel.

■ GRINDING HINTS

Experiment with gripping the stone in various positions—this gives experience which will be helpful later on and will also strengthen your fingers.

Try a bit of every material on hand to see how it reacts to the wheel; try especially softer gemstones like turquois, opal, and serpentine. Note that these stones may grind away too fast if you are not careful. This is an important point to remember in grinding cabochons, where overshooting the mark may mean you have to start all over again.

Try grinding bits of slab from 2 inches in size to a mere ½ inch; note the difficulty in holding the smaller pieces with any sure control. Do not be discouraged if you lack sureness; few beginners can grind such small stones with accuracy.

When grinding slabs, avoid chipping by grinding a very small bevel on the sharp edges first. As the bevel disappears, renew it. This principle is the same as the one used in woodworking by the carpenter who planes a small bevel on the end-grain of a board to keep the edge from splitting. Gemstones won't usually split but they will chip badly.

Small surfaces may be flattened by using the side of the wheel instead of the face. Don't allow the stone to get hot, which can happen if the side of the wheel is not wet enough. Test for overheating by feeling the ground surface with your fingertip or pressing it against your cheek.

If the grinding wheel shows whitish patches, the rock dust is not being washed off and more water is needed. If the gemstone is warm to the touch, this also indicates lack of sufficient water. In severe cases an overheated stone will crack or check.

Remember practice makes perfect—and nowhere is it so true as in grinding. It is here that the form of the gem is established and it is in this stage that most gems are ruined, no matter how well subsequent steps are done. Get as much practice as you can on cheap material before you attempt work on a fine piece of rough; you may be impatient to get results immediately but the delay is worth it.

For a more detailed description of the grinding methods used in cabochon work, refer to Chapter 11, "How To Cut Cabochons." The material given there, combined with the material in this chapter, will give you all the information you will need to do any gemstone grinding job.

5 | *Lapping*

THE process of lapping is simple and consists merely of rubbing a stone on a flat plate charged with loose abrasive grit. It is used wherever a flat surface is wanted as in specimen "flats" or "transparencies" where the object is to show the beautiful colors or patterns of agate, petrified wood, etc., or in book ends, table tops, inlay, mosaic work, etc., where flat surfaces are also required. As in grinding, it is usual to begin with coarse grits in order to level surfaces as quickly as possible, and then to finish with grit fine enough to permit polishing afterward.

The principle of lapping is shown in Figure 39. As the stone and lap move in opposite directions in relation to each other, grains of grit roll between the surfaces. The metal of the lap is soft and yields slightly but the stone is unyielding and therefore chips as shown. Multiplied many times by the number of grains, the surface of the stone is soon covered with numerous minute pits. When cleaned off it looks frosted. The frosting is perfectly uniform when the entire surface of the stone has been lapped properly but streaks or areas of slightly differ-

ent luster mean places where lapping has not removed the old surface. As smaller size grit is substituted, the frosting becomes finer and finer until it actually becomes semi-transparent. It is usually at this stage that the stone is ready for polishing.

The parts of a lapping rig are shown in Figure 40. Although these are sold as a kit so that amateurs can make their own rigs at less

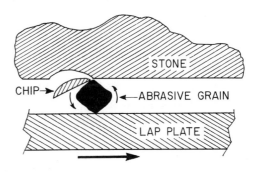

Fig. 39 The principle of lapping. As the lap plate moves, it rolls the sharp-cornered grains of abrasive between the lap and the stone. Each grain corner causes the stone to chip, as shown, and it is this effect multiplied many times over which gradually wears away the stone.

Fig. 40 Parts for a homemade lapping rig. *At left.* Vertical shaft with thrust and side bearings. The large pulley provides slow lapping speed. *Lower right.* Steel lap which screws on top of shaft. *Background.* Splash pan. (Courtesy The Ducketts, Medford, Oregon)

expense, the parts are basically the same as in any other simple lapping unit. A vertical shaft which supports the lap is the heart of the unit. At the top is a threaded portion upon which the lap plate screws but only far enough so that the top of the plate and the shaft are flush. This permits the entire surface of the plate to be used, an important point as will be explained later. The shaft also supports a large-diameter pulley designed to turn the lap at slow speed so that grits will not be slung off. The bottom of the shaft is fitted with a thrust bearing to take the considerable weight of the shaft, the pulley and the lap plate. The splash pan is removable so that it can be cleaned out.

Lap plates can be made of almost any metal but the most satisfactory is mild steel or cast iron. Lead laps are also used but abrasive imbeds in the surface and the cutting action is slower.

■ GRITS USED IN LAPPING

Silicon carbide grit, bought in pound lots, is the favorite abrasive for lapping. Where very large surfaces are to be lapped the grit may be as coarse as 50 or 60 in order to speed up the initial flattening of the surface. Surfaces of about 8 inches or so in diameter may be quickly lapped at the beginning with

100 or 120 grit, but most amateurs seldom tackle anything that large, and therefore use 220 grit which is coarse enough for almost all jobs. If you buy a lap plate of 14 inches or less, plan to stock a pound or two of 220 silicon carbide grit for the first grind. The next grind uses 400 grit, and the very last uses 1200, a very fine whitish powder which imparts a very high gloss just prior to polishing. One pound of 1200 will last a long time since only a little is used; in fact, if it is used too thickly on the lap plate it will not cut properly. Both 400 and 220 are used in about the same proportions and should be bought accordingly.

The cost of grit rises with decrease in size, the 1200 costing considerably more per pound than the 220 grit. Many amateurs make a practice of saving the grit sediment from the bottom of their grinding wheel splash pans for first lapping. Since this residue is mainly grit torn off the grinding wheels, there is little reason not to use it for this purpose. It is not as accurately sieved as new grit, but since the surface left by its use is going to be smoothed out by later operations, it makes little difference how irregular it is.

■ **ACCESSORY EQUIPMENT FOR LAPPING**

With the lapping rig set up and a stock of 220, 400, and 1200 grit on hand, one needs only some wide-mouthed jars, glasses, or discarded cups to hold each grit size. Also needed are small brushes of about 1 inch in width, one for each grit, to use in applying the mixture to the lap, as shown in Figure 41. Each container should be labeled to prevent mix-ups. Some amateurs have found it cleaner and more efficient to store grits in "squeeze bottle" containers, such as the catsup and mustard dispensers which are for sale in shops, and to apply grits by shaking the bottle and squeezing. However, a brush does provide somewhat better distributing action while the lap is running.

An important item during lapping is a deep bucket filled with water to which detergent has been added, for use in washing off the hands

Fig. 41 The lapping process. The essentials are shown: a horizontal steel lap (stopped for clarity), glass jar with grit-water mix, and a brush for applying the mixture to the lap. The tub is lined with newspapers which will be discarded as soon as this stage of lapping is completed.

as well as the specimen. A small fingernail scrub brush or toothbrush is used to clean off every particle of grit. Keep the bucket next to the machine so that you can lean over and wash off specimens at any time you wish to inspect them. Because grits are heavy, they will promptly sink to the bottom and will not contaminate the next grit; discoloration of the water is due only to extremely fine particles of abrasive and stone which are too fine to cause scratching.

■ **USING THE LAP**

Before starting, line the lap pan or trough with several layers of newspaper, tucked under the lap and neatly folded over the edges of the pan. Secure in place with clothespins. When the first lapping operation is over, peel off the paper on top and discard. Thus whenever a specimen happens to fall into the tub, it will not be contaminated with a coarser grit. This scheme also prevents unnecessary dirt accumulating in the tub and stops corrosion of the metal. In this connection, it must be remarked that aluminum corrodes badly with ordinary detergents, which seem to react chemically with this metal. To prevent such corrosion, coat the inside with good paint or with melted wax.

The objective in lapping is to flatten the surface to remove saw marks, pits, and other irregularities by using successively finer grades of grit until the surface is smooth enough to take a polish. There are no shortcuts; the temptation is to skip or skimp stages but the penalty quickly shows up in polishing when it is discovered that no amount of pressure or application of powder will cause deep pits or scratches to disappear.

Examine the specimen to be lapped; note if any snags or projections mar the surface. Either snip these off with pliers or grind them off. Pour about an inch of 220 grit (or coarser if the specimen is large) into the jar or cup; add an equal amount of water and a pinch of detergent; stir well and apply a brushful to the rotating lap near its center. Put the specimen on the center of the lap and, with a circular motion, spread the grit until the whole surface of the lap is covered. Listen to the noise made as the grit begins to work. At first it will crackle, then, as the grit pulverizes, it changes to a swishing noise. This indicates the slowing of cutting action and another brushful of abrasive should be added. Don't get too much water in the brush—just enough to make the mixture on the lap like a thin mud. If too much water is put on the lap, the grit is flung off and lost in the splash pan. Too little water will result in the lap running dry and this is also to be avoided.

As lapping proceeds, it is necessary to clean the specimen to see how flat the surface has become. This is important because any small rough spots remaining will call for long periods of lapping with the next finer grit before they are removed. One of the best ways to inspect flat surfaces is to hold the specimen at a low angle under a good light and let the rays reflect toward the eyes. Any slight "frosted" spots indicate unfinished places and will show clearly because their surface texture is different from the rest. Lap until you are *certain*

that the surface is uniform—then lap two more minutes for good measure. Another way to be sure that all previous lapping marks are removed is to cross-hatch the surface with an aluminum pencil. Cover every portion. When the next lapping is finished, all marks will be gone.

When the specimen is ready for the 400 grit, stop the motor, clean the lap plate and the specimen by brisk scrubbing in slightly soapy water, then scrub your hands and wrists, paying particular attention to the fingernails. Put the old grit and brush away and line the splash pan with clean newspaper so that in case a specimen should fall into the tub, it will not accidentally pick up particles of coarser grit. It takes only *one* large particle to put a deep scratch across the face of what would otherwise be a perfect job.

Although coarse grits permit the specimen to ride rather easily on the revolving lap, finer grits have a tendency to "grab" the specimen from the hands, sometimes with considerable violence. This usually happens when the grit mixture on the lap gets too dry. Guard against this, particularly when using 400 and 1200 grit.

As finer grits are used, cutting becomes slower and a longer time is needed to remove all previous marks. Inspect closely to be certain that the specimen is really ready for the next step. After completing the 400 grit stage, which is the same as the 220 grit as far as technique and precautions are concerned, go on to the 1200.

In using 1200 grit, charge the brush with a minimum amount of grit. Stir the mixture briskly until the water appears cloudy; a brushful of this water will be about right. Applying a paste of 1200 grit merely wastes it. When you complete the 1200 grit stage, the surface of the specimen should be finely frosted, almost glossy. Check for any spots that may have been overlooked—this is the last chance before polishing! When the specimen appears uniform in texture with no scratches, it is ready for polishing—a technique which will be described in the next chapter.

■ LAPPING VERY THIN FLATS

Sometimes it is desirable to lap and polish very thin slabs of gem materials, for example, iris agate or moss agate. Iris agate displays wonderful colors when held before a strong pin-point light but the effect is at its best when the slabs are as thin as possible. Much moss agate and other types of agate show beautiful markings or coloration and must be treated the same way. However, it is almost impossible to hold very thin slabs, much less do any lapping and polishing on them, and there is a strong likelihood that they will break somewhere along the line. To avoid these troubles, cement the slab to a backing of some kind, preferably another stone slab or a piece of plywood. The backing should extend to the edges, and for this reason plywood is more practical, since it can be easily trimmed to shape. The slab is cemented with a mixture of beeswax and paraffin, or beeswax alone. Warm the plywood, coat with wax, warm the slab and apply to the melted wax surface. Now all lapping can be done safely since not enough heat is generated to melt the wax and cause slippage. However, if polishing is to take place on a felt buff where considerable heat is generated, a different cement must be used. Ordinary cabochon dopping wax or stick shellac are both useful in such a case and may be applied or removed with heat. If not much wetting is to take place, white polyethylene glue is satisfactory, but one must then wait for the cement to set and wait even longer for the cement to soften in warm water when separating the slab from its backing. Epoxy resins are excellent but removing the stone from the backing must be done by soaking in solvent and this takes considerable time.

■ KEEPING A LAP PLATE TRUE

The tendency for most beginners is to lap specimens at a place about halfway between the center and the rim of the lap plate. In a short time the metal is ground away in a circular belt and a pronounced "saddle" occurs. Naturally the exact curvature of this saddle will not fit all size specimens and it will be just that much harder to lap the next specimen. The secret of keeping the lap plate flat is very simple: *use all of the lap at all times*. This is done by sweeping the stone constantly from one edge of the plate to the other, crossing the center and overlapping the edge a little each time. Slow up the sweep as you near the center of the lap because this part is revolving more slowly and a longer period of abrasion is required. If you observe this simple rule, your lap will remain remarkably flat and the amount of time you must spend on each succeeding operation will be less.

■ LAPPING HINTS

Some authorities recommend adding a spoonful of clay powder to loose grit to cause the water-grit mixture to adhere better to the lap plate. The author has found this to be unnecessary, the fine particles of rock abraded from the specimen serving the same purpose.

Scratches are most often caused by failure to clean up carefully, but some specimens have holes and pockets which are almost impossible to clean out. When this is the case, seal the pockets with paraffin, which can be removed later by soaking in gasoline or warm water. Gasoline is safer, as warm water may crack the gem material. Another excellent and permanent sealer is clear epoxy resin, which can be forced into cracks or openings and allowed to cure. Being transparent, it scarcely alters the appearance or color and need not be removed afterward, even for polishing.

Scratches may sometimes be avoided by grinding a tiny bevel around the edge of the surface to be lapped. The bevel should be only enough to remove sharp edges.

A "fake" polish can be given to lapped surfaces by drying thoroughly and coating with transparent colorless lacquer, the new plastic spray types being very good. Such specimens can always be relapped and polished if desired.

There is quite a difference in handling large

and small specimens on a lap; the larger ones being easier to grip. Practice helps here. Also, in small specimens there is a tendency to "tilt" the work and actually cut two flat areas on the bottom instead of one. This can be avoided by gripping the specimen as close to the lap plate as possible, using fairly light pressure.

It is possible to grind shallow curves on a lap by placing more pressure on one side of the specimen to develop a flat bevel, then doing the same on the other side. With a gentle rocking motion, a smooth curve can be ground. This can be finished with successively finer grits until ready for polish. This treatment is popular in Germany for agate nodules.

■ AUTOMATIC VIBRATING LAPS

Several excellent automatic lapping machines are available which greatly reduce the amount of personal attention the cutter needs to pay to lapping. The principle is simple: an electric motor drives an eccentric shaft connected to the lap plate, causing it to vibrate or oscillate so rapidly that stones placed on the surface remain almost still while the lap moves beneath them. Because there is some movement of the stones however, the edges are protected from chipping by encircling with rubber tubes or bands. The laps used are of metal with grooves in various patterns designed to allow the water-grit mixture to circulate beneath the specimens. One model is illustrated in Figure 42, another in Figure 43.

The lapping procedure generally follows that described for hand lapping but there are some differences. One manufacturer recommends that the first grind use 80 grit, which, though very coarse, crushes after several hours of operation into finer and finer grit. The surface left is smooth enough to go to the next stage using 400 or 600 grit. As in regular lapping, all specimens and machine parts must be thoroughly scrubbed between stages. The time required for coarse lapping is from six to seven hours, and from five to six for fine lapping, depending on the weight of the specimens. Large

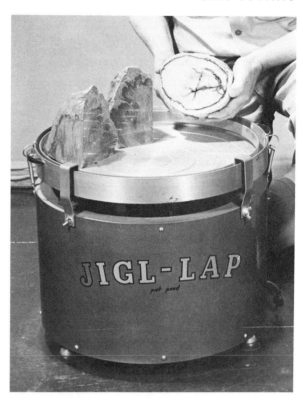

Fig. 42 The Jigl-Lap automatic lapping machine. The top plate is thinly covered with a grit-water mixture; the spiral groove helping to distribute the grit. When the machine is turned on, the top oscillates and grinds the bases of the specimens. (Courtesy Wesley Banta, North Bend, Washington)

heavy blocks take less time than thinner and lighter specimens. For thin slabs, additional weight is added to speed lapping. Polishing is done on the same machine with a soft polishing pad installed and charged with polishing powder and water. Polishing takes seven to eight hours, depending on weight and type of material.

Although many hours are consumed in completing specimens from lapping to polishing, very little is hand labor, and the large area available permits treating a number of specimens at the same time. Automatic machines also make it possible to get very accurately lapped surfaces and polishes superior to those obtainable with ordinary methods. Manufacturers of these machines supply detailed instructions which should be followed for best results.

Fig. 43 The Vi-Bro-Lap automatic lapping machine. *Left.* Details of machine showing scored lap plate on top, drive shaft, supports, and motor. *Center.* Lap plate tilted up to show ease of removal and details of scored plate. *Right.* Lap plate loaded with stone sections being polished. Best results are obtained by trying to cover most of the area during lapping and polishing operations, thus keeping the surface flat for the longest period of time. (Courtesy Vi-Bro-Lap, Yakima, Washington)

■ OVER-ARM LAPPING MACHINES

Adapted from standard stone polishing machines used for many years by stonecutting and monument works, smaller over-arm lapping machines, such as shown in Figures 44 and 45 are meeting with the enthusiastic approval of many amateurs. The principle of operation is simple: a motor driven flexible linkage rotates a lap plate *over* the work, which rests on a table in fixed position. Various accessory plates are provided which are interchanged to allow all operations from lapping to polishing. In operation, slabs or blocks of material are imbedded in plaster of Paris in a tray which is fixed to the table, as shown in Figure 45. A water mixture of grit is placed on the slabs and rubbed with the steel lapping plate until all specimens are flat. Grits are changed as in regular lapping until surfaces are smooth enough to be polished. At this time a polishing buff is substituted and the work is polished to smoothness. Because considerable pressure can be brought to bear, all steps are completed rapidly and very large sections of material can be handled. Complete instructions for each machine are furnished and should be followed.

■ HOMEMADE OVER-ARM LAPPING MACHINE

Figure 46 shows an over-arm lapping machine which can be made from wood parts plus a standard lapping arbor. A stronger rig can be made from metal. This machine is standard in the optical industry but only lately has been used by amateurs for making flats. The principles are simple and sound. The stone slab is cemented to a flat piece of iron about ½ inch thick, known as a "runner." In the center of the runner is bored a shallow vee-shaped hole, as shown in Figure 46. The point of the pivot attached to the over-arm rests in this hole and, when the machine is in operation, allows the stone slab to rotate and to adjust itself to the lap surface, in case the latter is not parallel to the surface of the mounting plate. This is important during pitch polishing because when pitch laps are made it is difficult to get the surface parallel to the top of the lap plate upon which the pitch is poured. Consequently it often happens that when the pitch lap is installed, the top surface wobbles slightly as it turns. Were it not for the shallow hole on the runner which allows the flat section of stone to follow the lap as it wobbles, it would be impossible to do a good job.

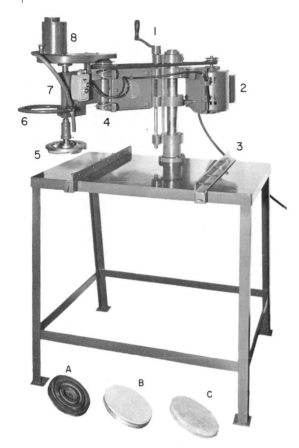

Fig. 44 Highland Park over-arm lapping machine. The table measures 2 by 3 feet, and vertical adjustment permits polishing a slab 12 inches thick. 1. Head raising and lowering handle. 2. Motor. 3. Adjustable slab clamps. 4. Arm pivot. 5. Spiral iron lap installed. 6. Hand-held guide ring. 7. Motor switch box. 8. Water reservoir. A. Cast iron lap. B. Felt polisher. C. Leather polisher. (Courtesy Highland Park Mfg. Co., South Pasadena, California)

In making this machine, provide a good stout piece of plywood or metal for the mounting plate. The arbor unit is bolted on at one end, while a wooden post at the other supports the over-arm assembly. A large lag screw serves as the horizontal pivot and, by means of adding or taking away washers underneath its head, the over-arm can be raised or lowered to suit different slab thicknesses. The yoke can be made of metal, although good hard wood will do. The wooden arm fits into a slot in the yoke and pivots on a through-bolt. A large bolt with one end ground to a point, is used for the pivot which fits into the runner hole. If a large bolt

is not available, a section of threaded steel rod will do as well. A hole is bored through the arm to take the bolt and its position up or down is set by a nut underneath.

The rough slab is heated and cemented to the runner by dopping wax, or by a half-and-half mixture of rosin and beeswax. Warming must be gentle to prevent the stone from cracking. It is safer to cement the stone using epoxy resin but difficult to remove it afterward unless stone and runner are soaked in special epoxy solvent. Cabinet makers glue will also cement slabs to runners and can be removed by soaking in warm water. Once cemented, the stone is left attached to the runner until polishing is completed.

The stone slab is lapped with grits as described previously until it is smooth enough to polish. At this time, the grit lapping plate is taken off and another put on for polishing. For good work, the polishing surface can be Pellon, cemented to a metal lap with contact cement. For undercutting material, use a pitch lap with rouge or cerium oxide as the polishing agent. Making a pitch lap is described in the following section.

The advantages of the over-arm machine are that considerable pressure can be applied during lapping and polishing, and it is easier to keep the stone from "grabbing" since it is not held in the fingers, as in ordinary work. Furthermore, much larger sections of stone can be handled, since the entire area is swept back and forth across the lap as work progresses. Also, the lap is kept flat since all of its area is used; this means a flatter surface on the stone and a much better polish.

■ MAKING A PITCH LAP

Prop up a metal lap so that the top is level. Rim the edge to about ¾ inch with masking tape to provide a dam. Melt optician's pitch until it is smoking hot. Be careful that it does not catch on fire! Pour the hot pitch on the lap to ½-inch depth and let cool. Score the pitch by drawing straight lines across it with a ⅛-inch thick piece of metal strip, heated very

Fig. 45 Victor over-arm lapping machine. Note how large slabs and terrazzo-like work pieces can be ground and polished with this machine. (Courtesy Victor Valley Gem Shop, Fallbrook, California)

hot. The grooves should be about as deep as they are wide. Criss-cross them so that they are about 1 inch apart and divide the surface of the lap into 1-inch squares. Let the pitch cool again, then remove the ridges left by scoring; use a thin scraper or razor blade, being careful not to mar the surface of the squares.

Although the lap is now quite flat, it must

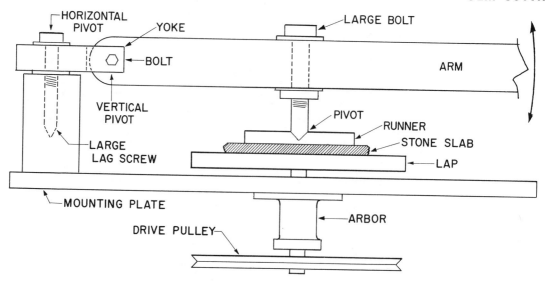

Fig. 46 Schematic drawing of over-arm lapping machine. The vertical post on the left, the yoke, and the arm, can be made from hard wood. The horizontal pivot allows the stone slab to be swung from side to side, while the vertical pivot allows the arm to be raised.

be smoothed before use. This is done as follows. Select a piece of scrap plate glass larger than the lap; place upon a firm flat surface. Clean the top and smear with a watery mixture of cerium oxide. Heat the pitch lap in warm water until the pitch is easily dented by the fingernail. Wipe off excess water and press down upon the plate glass. Add weights and let cool. The warmth of the pitch should have allowed it to flow and flatten while pressed against the glass. If the entire surface is not flat, repeat the process. When the surface is perfect, the lap is ready to install and use. Although a pitch lap is meant for polishing large surfaces, it can also be used for polishing faceted gems, but very light pressure must be used and the scores made narrower and shallower.

Opticians pitch is made by melting together 5 pounds of rosin, 1 pound of roofer's pitch or burgundy pitch, and ¼ pound beeswax. This mixture burns quickly and is a dangerous fire hazard. Do the melting outdoors, away from any building. Use low heat, preferably an electric hot plate. Stir during melting. When thoroughly mixed, pour into several small clean cans so that small batches can be had without having to heat the entire mixture again.

6 | *Sanding*

Tʜᴇ last step in preparing many types of gemstones for final polish is to sand their surfaces. Although this process is mostly used for cabochons, many use it for flats in lieu of last fine grit lapping stages described in Chapter 5.

■ PRINCIPLES OF SANDING

The term "sanding," like many other terms in gem cutting, has a broad meaning. For most amateurs, sanding means the use of a flexible sanding cloth, either covering a rotating wheel or as a continuous belt moving over two pulleys. Actually the term sanding also covers the use of wooden disks, suitably grooved to accommodate various shapes of cabochons and charged with loose grit. In any case, the primary feature of all sanders is a yielding surface. The need for flexibility is made clear when one considers the condition of the surface of a cabochon gem as it leaves the fine grinding wheel. No matter how skillful

the cutter, the surface will be covered with flat spots left by the grinding wheel. The flexible sander removes these and associated scratches and smoothly curves the surface in preparation for polishing.

■ SANDING CLOTH

The best material for sanding is stout cloth covered with a layer of silicon carbide grit. The grit varies from very coarse to very fine but only two or three sizes are usually needed. For coarse sanding, 220 grit is popular, followed by 400 or 600 grit for finer sanding.

The type of glue used to cement the abrasive to the cloth is important since it determines whether or not the cloth can be cooled with water during sanding. Ordinary sanding cloth is made with a water-soluble animal glue similar to cabinet maker's glue and soon disintegrates if wetted. Another type is impregnated with plastic resin glue and is impervious to the effects of water. This kind is known as "wet-or-dry" from the term used by the Behr-Manning Company in advertising this material. Of the two kinds, the latter is far more expensive.

Sanding cloth is available in disk, strip, and belt form, depending on the type of equipment used.

■ WET SANDING VERSUS DRY SANDING

Prior to the making of wet-or-dry cloth, all sanding had to be done dry. Due to its peculiar advantages wet sanding is now favored despite the higher cost of wet-or-dry cloth. The most common hazard of dry sanding —frictional heat—is completely eliminated by the use of water on wet-or-dry cloth. Heat is dangerous because it melts the dopping wax and may cause the stone to shift position or drop off the dopstick. Also, some gemstones are very sensitive to heat and will crack unless they are kept cool during all stages of cutting. Among these is opal, an expensive gemstone whose loss through accident can be ill-afforded by most amateurs.

Another excellent reason for using wet-or-dry cloth is that the constant washing with water eliminates clogging of the surface with debris. In using dry cloth, the surface is soon loaded with gemstone dust and the cutting action is slowed.

A final reason for using the wet sanding technique is that a superior finish is given to the gemstone because the amount of water falling on the sander can be regulated to give a deep or shallow cut, depending on the quantity used. If a large amount is used, it acts like a lubricant and keeps the gem from receiving more than a gentle abrasion, whereas if the water is reduced, the stone touches the surface more directly and is cut away more rapidly. The ability to regulate the depth of cut is most useful in the treatment of soft stones but is also valuable for any gemstone, regardless of hardness, for putting on the last fine gloss prior to polish.

■ SUBSTITUTES FOR SANDING CLOTH

Because it is less expensive, some experimenters use sandpaper in place of cloth but paper is not very flexible and, with the pressure of sanding, it tears quickly. If very small stones are being treated, sandpaper cemented to a stiff backing will do quite well.

Although seldom as good as commercial cloth, homemade cloth can be prepared. The materials needed are heavy denim or twill of close weave, silicon carbide grits and cabinetmaker's glue. The most important part of the process is to make the glue so that it will spread thinly and evenly.

Cabinetmakers glue can be bought by the pound and is sold as dry brown flakes. Place a quantity of the flakes in the top of a double boiler or in a can. Enough water is added to cover the flakes. Set the pot aside and allow the glue to soak for twenty-four hours. At the end of this time, place the container in simmering hot water and stir the glue until dissolved into a uniformly thin mixture; it is now ready to use.

Stretch the backing cloth over a flat smooth piece of board. Tuck the edges under and tack in place to avoid all wrinkles. Using a small, stiff, bristle brush, apply a thin film of glue to the cloth, working it in well to assure a good bond with the fabric. Do this quickly, as the glue sets rapidly and will then refuse to grip. Cover an area of cloth corresponding to the size circle you need. As soon as the cloth is covered with glue, dust on a uniform layer of abrasive, using a flour sifter or similar utensil for the purpose. Shake off excess abrasive and allow to dry thoroughly. Some time can be saved by making a number of disks at once. When dry, the cloth is removed from the board and cut into desired sizes and shapes. It is applied and used like regular sanding cloth. Note that this process is only for "dry" cloth because the glue used is water-soluble. It is possible to make a similar cloth using waterproof glue.

■ DISK SANDERS

As the name implies, disk sanders are circular plates or frames covered with sanding cloth. The simplest type, shown in Figure 47, is a steel disk with a tapped and threaded stock which permits it to be screwed to the shaft of an arbor. The disk is covered

Fig. 47 Allen combination disk-drum sander. The aluminum casting is covered on the outside with sponge rubber to provide a resilient surface for the sanding cloth. The drum portion is used for coarse sanding of cabochons and flats. The disk portion, fitted with fine sanding cloth, is useful for cabochons or other rounded shapes. (Courtesy Belmont Lapidary Supply, Belmont, California)

with sponge rubber sheet to provide resilience and the sanding cloth is attached to the rubber with pressure sensitive cements. A popular brand is known as Peel-'em Off. Cements of this kind permit disks to be attached firmly yet allow them to be removed later, either to change grit size or to discard worn out cloths.

A different type of disk sander is depressed in the center to allow curved gem surfaces to be sanded easily while the outer portions are used for shallow curves or for flat places. In sanders of this kind it is necessary to attach the cloth by means of a snap-rim or a heavy spring which encircles the cloth and presses into a groove around the rim of the disk. To make sanding cloths fit snugly, it is necessary to cut out vee-shaped notches along the edge. Draw a line, about 1 inch from the edge, completely around the margin of the cloth disk. Cut notches about an inch apart from between the edge and the pencil mark. The spaces provided allow the sanding cloth to wrap snugly and smoothly over the rim of the sander and leave

the working face wrinkle-free. A bulge or wrinkle will wear away and tear before the rest of the cloth is used up.

The working surface of disk sanders can vary from flat to concave or convex, or a combination of these. Others types merely support the cloth at the rim allowing the surface to sag under pressure and therefore conform automatically to the cabochon shape. Each type has its merits and all turn out satisfactory work. The author's preference is a disk sander with a shallow convex curvature.

■ DRUM SANDERS

Figure 48 describes better than words, the piece of equipment known as a "drum sander." It is fitted with a piece of

Fig. 48 Drum sander fitted with sponge rubber backing over which strip abrasive cloth is stretched. The ends of the cloth are placed in the slot at the lower right and tightened by the locking lever. (Courtesy Rock's Lapidary Equipment & Supplies, San Antonio, Texas)

sponge-rubber cushion and slots are provided for inserting the ends of the cloth strip and locking them firmly in place. It is usually operated vertically, although it can be run in other positions. Simple and rugged in construction, it is suitable for sanding both curved surfaces and flats. Cloth stripping in rolls is used, a piece of the correct length being cut off whenever replacement is needed. There is some hazard to the hands from the sharp edges but ordinary care will prevent accidents. Width of the cloth varies from 2 inches upward, with 3 inches being most useful. One advantage of the drum sander is the relative cheapness of the cloth in strip form as compared with disks. If wet-or-dry cloth is available, this type may also be used for wet sanding.

A new type of drum sander is shown in Figure 49. It uses an endless cloth belt slipped over a deflated rubber tire which is then inflated to tighten the belt. The surface is very resilient if the air pressure is low or can be made firmer by increasing the pressure. Because of the thinness of the rubber tire and the fact that there is air space beneath, this sander is somewhat cooler in operation and is able to conform to many degrees of curvature in gemstones and other lapidary objects.

■ **BELT SANDERS**

The belt sander consists of an endless belt of abrasive cloth passed over two rubber-faced pulleys at some distance apart, one of the pulleys being run by a vee-belt from the motor. A stout frame supports the pulleys and a special release on the "idler"

Fig. 49 A unique sanding drum inflated by air to any desired pressure. The endless cloth belt in the background is slipped on the deflated drum and held in place firmly when the latter is inflated. The surface provided is very resilient and conforms to the shape of rounded gemstones. (Courtesy R. H. Dollar Co., Cleveland, Ohio)

pulley permits it to be lowered to allow belts to be slipped on and off quickly. These features are shown in Figure 50, while Figure 51 shows a belt sander in operation. An advantage of the

Fig. 50 Alta belt sander with back-plate and steady-rest installed. The back-plate provides a firm area for sanding flats while the area between the back-plate and the upper pulley is yielding and therefore suitable for sanding rounded forms. (Courtesy Alta Industries, Fresno, California)

belt sander over other types is that slabs and flats may be sanded as well as any rounded surface. Where the belt passes over a pulley or over a flat back-plate, as shown in Figure 50, the surface is very firm and excellent sanding of flats is possible at this point. The cloth area between pulleys is unsupported and yields under the pressure of a rounded gem thus conforming to its shape. All belt sanders are expensive as compared to other types.

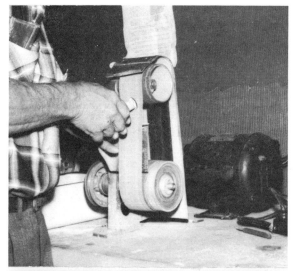

Fig. 51 Using the belt sander. Note how dopped cabochon gems are held against the flexible portion of the sanding cloth belt, and how the belt conforms to the rounded surface of the gems. Because of this it is possible to round such gems smoothly and make them almost geometrically perfect. Belt stopped for clarity. (Courtesy Alta Industries, Fresno, California)

■ **RUBBER SANDING WHEELS**

Small to large abrasive-impregnated rubber wheels have been used for many years for cutting and polishing metal, especially in the jewelry trade. In the last decade they have become standard items of equipment in the lapidary shop. Because they are less yielding than cloth-surfaced sanders, they find special application in smoothing the surfaces of very hard gemstones such as catseye chrysoberyl, star sapphire and ruby. Amateur carvers are also using smaller sizes for sanding since the edges of the wheels can be shaped to fit into narrow grooves or depressions.

Rubber sanding wheels are made by mixing abrasive grains with rubber and curing in molds to achieve the proper shapes. Fast or slow cutting action is achieved by varying the proportion of abrasive grain to rubber, while surface finishes are varied according to the size grit used. Water must be fed to these wheels to prevent surface burning due to friction, although if one does not mind the smell of burning rubber they can be used dry, providing care is taken not to overheat the gemstone. They can be used for all materials but are really better for hard gemstones, for the firmness of surface makes them likely to put flat spots on soft gem material unless great care is used to keep the gem moving during sanding. These wheels are expensive but last a long time and do not require the frequent changing that is necessary with sanders using cloth.

■ WOOD SANDERS

A soft wooden disk several inches thick can be used for sanding very hard gems. The wood should be "diffuse porous," that is, all of the pores are distributed evenly over the surface with no pronounced change in structure between summer and winter wood. Poplar, birch, boxwood, holly, teak, and mahogany are several that show this structure and are therefore suited for sanding wheels. Such wheels are turned out on a woodworking lathe; both sides are made parallel and grooves of varying curvature are turned into the rim or the face, depending on whether the wheel is to be used horizontally or vertically. The wheel is run at about 500 rpm and the groove most nearly corresponding to the shape of the gem charged with a water-grit mixture. Firm pressure is used to start the cutting action and to imbed the abrasive into the wood. Water must be supplied often to keep frictional heat

from becoming dangerous. Sanding wheels of this type are particularly advantageous with very hard gemstones such as chrysoberyl and sapphire, where ordinary methods take too long. Wooden sanding wheels charged with various sizes of diamond powder are effective for hard gemstones not only for sanding but also for polishing, if the diamond powder is fine enough. The use of wood for sanding and polishing is a very old technique which does not receive the attention it should from present-day lapidaries.

■ LEATHER SANDERS

Disk or drum sanders fitted with leather are excellent for fine sanding of many gemstones which would sand poorly on ordinary abrasive cloth. Thin leather is used, either backed with felt or sponge to provide a yielding surface, or stretched over a disk sander and allowed to sag in the middle. Although grits as coarse as 400 can be used, the author has had greatest success using a thin slurry of 1200 silicon carbide. This combination is startlingly successful on notorious undercutters such as jade, rhodonite, dumortierite, and others. It is equally good for sanding tourmaline and garnet, also the metallic gemstones such as pyrite, niccolite, smaltite, etc. The latter are almost impossible to sand with ordinary cloth because numerous minute pits develop but with 1200 on leather such pits are quickly and entirely eliminated.

Leather is also used successfully with diamond powder, applied as a mixture with oil, vaseline, grease, or plastic cement. The extremely fast cutting action of diamond allows sanding of cabochons which otherwise develop low spots due to varying hardnesses in the gem. This method is expensive due to the cost of diamond powder, but where fine finishes are necessary on undercutting stones, it is hard to find a better way. Very stiff sole leather is also useful with diamond and leaves superfine finishes on hard gemstones such as chrysoberyl and corundum.

■ MISCELLANEOUS SANDERS

Close-woven cloths such as canvas have been used for sanding effectively. In German cutting centers, wooden drums have been covered with canvas for this purpose. Loose grit applied with a brush is used. Firm rubber sheet, linoleum, masonite, and even hard felt have all been used but offer few advantages over standard methods.

■ SANDING SPEEDS

Since sanding is really the same process as grinding (with the factor of surface flexibility added), it is only reasonable that sending speeds should approach those found for grinding. Unfortunately, certain types of sanders cannot be run at high speeds without paying a penalty. Wooden disk sanders, for example, if run at high speeds, throw off loose grit as rapidly as it is put on, while impregnated rubber wheels lack the strength of vitrified silicon carbide wheels and cannot be run as fast. Many disk sanders with snap-rims have enough play in the rim to become severely unbalanced at high speeds. Of all types used, the belt sander, the disk sander using a cemented cloth disk, and the drum sander (properly balanced) seem to be the only kinds that can be brought to high speeds without disadvantage. High speed in a sander is desirable for several reasons: heat dissipates more quickly in the dry-cloth types, abrasive action is faster and therefore less tedious, lighter pressures can be used because cutting action is faster, and the tendency of some gemstones to undercut is markedly reduced. A word of explanation on the term "undercutting" is in order since you will encounter it frequently from now on.

■ UNDERCUTTING

Many gemstones are uniform in "grain" or inner structure and may be sawed, ground, sanded, and polished, with the same ease in all directions. Others have pronounced differences in structure which cause them to be weaker in certain directions, somewhat resembling wood in this respect. For this reason, some gemstones show hard and soft spots and a difference in their ability to wear away. Sometimes a gemstone consists of two or more minerals with varying properties. In all cases, the differences in structure show in sanding and polishing because the weaker portions wear away at a faster rate and leave the surface of the gem mottled and pitted. This is called "undercutting" or "lemon-peel," the latter term taken from the resemblance to the pitted surface of lemon rind.

Undercutting is seldom troublesome in grinding, but is likely to occur during sanding. Its effects are greatly reduced if the sanding is done at high speed.

■ RECOMMENDED SPEEDS

As said before, grinding wheels are run at surface speeds of from 4,000 rpm to 6,000 rmp and sanders should approach these speeds if possible. Because of mechanical limitations and vibration, it is doubtful if most sanders can be run at surface speeds in excess of 4,000 feet per minute. Speeds from 4,000 rpm to 3,000 rpm must be considered as acceptable. Speeds below 3,000 rpm are to be avoided if equipment can run faster without harm.

Recommended Sanding Speeds

Type	Diameter	Surface Speed (feet per minute)	Required Rpm
Snap-rim disk	6-inch	3,000	1,910
" " "	8 "	"	1,430
" " "	10 "	"	1,145
Cemented disk	6 "	4,000	2,550
" "	8 "	"	1,910
" "	10 "	"	1,530
Drum	6 "	"	2,550
"	8 "	"	1,910
"	10 "	"	1,530
Belt	4 "	"	3,820
"	4 "	3,000	2,865

Note: On disk sanders, only the extreme outer portion will deliver the surface speed given in the table above; the surface speed will diminish quickly toward the center as the diameter decreases. For rubber bonded sanding wheels, use the rpm recommended by the manufacturer.

■ WATER SUPPLY TO WET SANDERS

The problem of supplying water to sanders may be solved by means similar to those used on grinding wheels; however, not so much water is needed and sometimes only a steady drip will do.

Disk sanders spinning in a horizontal plane are easy to keep wet since a small-diameter hose or tube can be led from overhead to cause the drip to fall in the middle of the sander; centrifugal force will spread the water over the cloth. Disk sanders spinning in a vertical plane can be watered in the same way, but the water must be under pressure to be sure that it strikes the surface. On drum and belt sanders, it is best to have several drips of water falling on the cloth to be certain that the entire width is kept moist. In all cases where water is used, a splash hood should be installed to trap spray and grit.

Another solution to the problem of supplying water is to use a squirt bottle or plastic squeeze bottle to direct a spray on the working face. An ordinary window cleaning squirt bottle is good but a squeeze bottle can apply more water at one time.

■ SANDING SLABS AND FLATS

Sanding of any flat surface is done best on belt or drum sanders. It is difficult to sand flats on disk or wheel sanders, although the latter can be used if the surface is absolutely flat. To work on flat surfaces, the sander must be curved enough to apply considerable pressure at any point. A flat disk, for example, yields under the pressure of sanding, and the only parts of the specimen to receive effective smoothing will be the edges. In a belt or drum sander, on the other hand, the area of contact is reduced to a narrow zone across the specimen and as much pressure can be used as necessary to do the job.

During sanding the slab should be grasped with both hands for maximum firmness, as shown in Figure 52. The grip is simple: make a fist of each hand with the thumbs up, touch

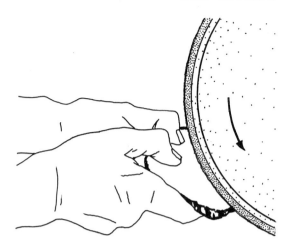

Fig. 52 Holding a flat slab against the sander, in this case, a drum sander. After the lower area of the slab is sanded, it is turned and another area sanded until the entire slab is done. Note that the slab trails.

the fists together, knuckles-to-knuckles; the slab will rest on the upper side of the index finger knuckles while the thumbs will press it down firmly in a very secure grip. The upper side of the slab is now placed against the bottom of the drum sander in a trailing position, and the lower portion of the slab is exposed to sanding. The same sort of grip is used with the belt sander except that the slab must be pressed against those portions of the cloth that are supported firmly from beneath by the rollers or by back-plates. Note that in each case the slab *trails,* that is, the sharp edge cannot dig into the sanding cloth and tear it. This is a very important point to remember in all types of sanding, since it is possible to injure the hands by carelessly allowing the slab to "stub its toe."

After one part of the slab is sanded, the specimen is turned around and a new area exposed, using the same grip. In this way all outer portions will be sanded except a portion near the center. In this case, carefully extend the first two fingers of one hand underneath the slab to apply the necessary pressure at exactly the point where it is needed.

Special Tips on Sanding Flats. Be careful not to stay too long on one spot—a deep ridge or groove may develop, or a rippled appearance on the surface. Keep the slab moving constantly. This is particularly important when using rubber-bonded wheels.

If saw marks are very deep, it will pay either to lap the surface flat with 220 grit, followed by sanding with 220 cloth, or to sand first with fresh 100 or even 80 grit cloth, and then with 220 grit cloth.

A fair surface is left using fresh 220 cloth followed by well-worn cloth of the same grit, but a better polish will result if the last sanding is given with 400.

Try to have several slabs or specimens ready for sanding at one time; as one slab becomes hot it can be set aside to cool while another is substituted.

The sanding of large specimens, such as sawed nodules, book ends, blocks, etc., follows the same technique used for slabs, but naturally the grip must be changed to accommodate the shape of the specimen. In most cases, it will suffice to rest the piece in the curved palm of one hand, grip it along the edges with the fingers, and apply it to the sander face up.

In dry sanding, heat is quickly generated but must never be allowed to reach the point where the specimen will crack. Being thin and in direct contact with the fingers, slabs rapidly transmit heat to the fingers and give automatic warning of danger. In larger specimens, this warning is lacking and one must touch the surface frequently to test for heat. In wet sanding, of course, these precautions are unnecessary.

■ SANDING CURVED SURFACES

Most of your sanding will be done on curved surfaces such as tops of cabochons. In many ways rounded stones are easier to sand because the shape allows much pressure to bear on any given point. Because of this curvature, even a perfectly flat disk sander can be used successfully for almost all cabochon sanding jobs. In larger cabochons, however, where the top is shallowly curved, the flat sander is not so effective; for this reason, the author prefers disk sanders with a pronounced dome shape to the top.

The methods of sanding curved surfaces follow almost exactly those given for slabs and flats. The special technique of sanding cabochons is discussed in Chapter 11—How to Cut Cabochons.

■ IS IT SANDED ENOUGH?

The question: "Is it sanded enough?" is best answered by comparing sanded parts against those that are still unfinished. All saw marks or lapping marks should be gone and the finish should be glossy and uniform. A useful trick to be sure your work is done is as follows. Sand the cabochon or flat in one direction only. Now turn it to right angles and sand again. If any traces of the first set of marks remain, you have not sanded enough. Do this during coarse sanding and finish by leaving the final parallel marks all in one direction. Note this direction. Now go to fine sanding and sand at right angles to the coarse sanding marks. If any coarse sanding marks remain, you have not sanded enough. Old marks left behind represent deep scores and will cause trouble in polishing if they are not removed now.

■ SANDING VERY HARD GEMSTONES

There are two gemstones which are classed as very hard, requiring special sanding techniques not ordinarily needed for softer stones: corundum, better known as sapphire or ruby, and chrysoberyl. For both sapphire and chrysoberyl, preliminary sanding is done using coarse and fine sanding cloth, but these steps only partly smooth the surface and do little to prepare for polishing. The surface must be further smoothed either by sanding on wood with various grades of diamond powder or by sanding on rubber-bonded wheels. The first method is far better but is more expensive due to the cost of diamond powder.

Sanding with Diamond Powder. Wooden disks of close-grained stock are turned on a lathe to about 8 inches in diameter and about

1 to 2 inches in thickness. While they are in the lathe, concentric rounded grooves are cut in their working face to various depths and curvatures to accommodate a variety of stone shapes. Either the edge of the disk or one side may be grooved, depending on which position the disk will be run.

For first sanding, mix 400 grit diamond powder with vaseline. Be sparing with the expensive powder, using an amount about the size of a large match head to begin with. Mix this with several times that amount of vaseline, using a toothpick to stir, and apply the mixture to the desired groove. Because several grit sizes of diamond powder will be used, each grit should be applied to its own groove in order to prevent contamination. If the side of the disk is being used for sanding, apply the coarse powder in a groove nearest the edge and fine grit toward the inside. This will also prevent contamination in the event any of the powder is slung outward by centrifugal force. Spot the vaseline-diamond mixture evenly around the selected groove and smooth out with a finger tip until the whole groove is covered with fine film. The disk is now ready for sanding.

In operating wooden wheels, use 200 to 500 rpm. Heavy pressure is necessary to get good cutting action, but beware of overheating the stone. For sapphire or chrysoberyl, the heat developed is not harmful, but it may soften the dop wax and cause shifting of the stone or smearing of the groove with wax. If the stone becomes hot, dip in cool water until the wax hardens again. In a very short time, necessarily interrupted by frequent cooling-off periods, the gemstone will become glossy, as pits left by previous operations disappear. Continue sanding until *all* have disappeared; to stop now will require a very long period of fine sanding later.

When satisfied that further work will not improve the stone, switch to fine sanding after

carefully cleaning off the surface of the gem with lighter fluid. Charge a clean groove with 1200 diamond grit in the same way as before and continue sanding until the scratches of the 400 operation have been eliminated. For final polishing repeat the process using 3200 or 6400 diamond powder.

Some cutters use ordinary leather in lieu of wood. The leather may be flexible and backed with sponge rubber, or it may be stiff sole leather glued to a wooden disk and suitably grooved. Needless to say, diamond powder is very useful for cutting all sorts of gemstones, but its expense militates against its lavish use.

■ **SANDING WITH RUBBER WHEELS**

Rubber-bonded sanding wheels are used successfully in preparing sapphires and chrysoberyls for final polishing. It is still advisable, however, first to use a coarse cloth for a preliminary sanding before going to the rubber wheels. Wheels of two grit sizes are needed to do a good job, 120 (coarse) grit followed by 220 (fine) grit. Water is necessary at all times, but judgment must be used as to the quantity applied. Too much will cause the gemstone to slip over the surface without being cut rapidly, too little may wear the wheel excessively. If possible, rubber wheels should be run at highest safe speeds to improve cutting action.

■ **MISCELLANEOUS SANDING HINTS**

Worn out dry-type cloth can be rejuvenated by wetting and brushing with a sponge or rag. Dip in water and apply near the center; rub loosened grit outward with brushing strokes. This turns over dull grains near the outside and brings unused one from the center, where less sanding is done. Allow the standing cloth to dry before reusing.

7 | *Polishing*

T HE final step in the preparation of lapidary projects is polishing. The brilliant and fantastically smooth surfaces typical of polished gems are produced by pressing the work with considerable force against soft materials such as felt, leather, cloth, or wood which have been charged with a watery mixture of polishing agent. Why a polish forms at all under such conditions has puzzled investigators and even now is not fully understood. Some authorities believe that polish is only a form of abrasion carried to the point where scratches are so small that they cannot be seen. Others disagree and believe that a polish is a very thin layer of material which has melted and smeared like butter under a hot knife. In any case, the polish forms, miraculously it is true, but only if the surface has been properly treated beforehand. This is why in previous chapters emphasis has been placed on thoroughness in grinding and sanding, for without careful preparation, polishing efforts will be wasted.

■ **POLISHING AGENTS**

Most polishing agents are oxides of metals, for example, jeweler's rouge, an oxide of iron, green rouge or chromium oxide, and others such as tin oxide, cerium oxide, etc. Oxides are generally very hard and melt only at high temperatures. Recent investigations in the cause of polish point to the high melting temperatures as having a bearing on their ability to polish but to say that hardness or high melting points explain their action is to oversimplify the problem. For example, sapphire, a tremendously hard gemstone, is polished with tripoli, a much softer material which melts at a lower temperature. Probably hardness of polishing agents has something to do with their ability to smooth gemstones but other unexplained factors must have an influence too.

■ **POLISHING AGENT CHARACTERISTICS**

The characteristics of the principal agents used for polishing gemstones are given below. The chemical name is followed by common or trade name, color, solubility, and uses in lapidary work. The preferred powder-polishing lap combination for every gemstone is given in Chapter 19—The Description and Treatment of Individual Gemstones.

Aluminum Oxide. Alumina, levigated alumina, diamontine, sapphire powder, ruby dust, ruby powder, Ruby Dix, Linde A, etc. All are chemically identical but vary in purity according to method of manufacture. Several, such as those with "ruby" in the common name, are made from crushed synthetic corundum. Linde A is the most carefully graded, showing remarkable consistancy in particle size. All are white except those made from synthetic corundum, which are pink. For practical purposes, aluminum oxide is insoluble. All are used extensively in polishing metals and gemstones. For tumbling or cabochon work in quantity, levigated alumina is popular because of its cheapness but does not polish as quickly or as well as Linde A, tin oxide, or cerium oxide. For soft or undercutting stones, Linde A has no peer when used on leather or wood.

Carbon. Diamond, bort, boart, carbonado. Colorless, yellowish, or grayish. Insoluble. Prepared by crushing diamonds unsuitable for gem purposes and grading the powder to size. Polishing powders range from 3200 grit to 6400 grit.

Ceric Oxide. Cerium oxide, cerium. Yellowish-pink. Soluble in concentrated sulphuric acid or concentrated nitric acid. Insoluble in dilute acids. A similar agent composed of rare earth oxides is known as barnesite and is equal to cerium oxide as a polishing agent. Ceric oxide is the preferred polishing agent for all members of the quartz family except certain kinds which tend to undercut, such as tigereye, which are better handled with Linde A. Excellent for all beryls.

Chromic Oxide (Chromium Sesquioxide). Chrome, green chrome, green oxide of chrome, etc. Dark intense green. Stains badly and is messy to use, difficult to remove from hands, clothing, etc. Tends to be non-uniform in size and may scratch. Much used for polishing cabochons, especially undercutting material. A favorite for jade. Out-performed in every respect by Linde A. Because of staining, should not be used on any light colored stone containing cracks, fissures, or pockets.

Ferric Oxide. Red oxide of iron, rouge, jeweler's rouge, London red rouge. Chemically identical to hematite. Dark brownish-red. Stains badly. Soluble in hydrochloric acid. Seldom used for lapidary work because of availability of cleaner compounds which are equally effective; however, it can be used for polishing many gemstones.

Silicon Dioxide. Tripoli. Chemically identical to quartz. Derived from pulverulent rocks containing siliceous remains of diatoms. Properly purified, this agent is quite uniform. White to pale brownish-yellow. Slightly soluble in strong, hot, alkaline solutions; soluble in hydrofluoric acid and hot-water solutions of ammonium bifluoride. Used extensively for polishing agate and many other gemstones. Sometimes recommended for polishing sapphires on tin or typemetal laps but not as satisfactory as diamond.

Stannic Oxide. Tin oxide, tin. "Putty powder" is a compound of indefinite composition supposedly containing tin oxide, calcium or magnesium carbonate, and a small quantity of oxalic acid; it can have little significance in lapidary work because of its varying characteristics and the availability of better agents. Pure tin oxide is creamy white. Fresh powder looks lumpy but breaks down with the addition of water. Decomposed and then dissolved by strong solutions of potassium or sodium hydroxide.

Zirconium Dioxide. Zirconia. Rich reddish-brown. Soluble in sulfuric acid or hydrofluoric acid. Reacts in the same way as cerium oxide as a polishing agent.

■ STORAGE OF POWDERS

Keep all polishing agents in separate containers, clearly marked to prevent confusion. Containers must be dust-tight and stored away from sanding or grinding equipment. They may be stored with polishing buffs on shelves with a cloth curtain to keep out dust and dirt.

A handy way of applying agents is to mix some of the powder with water in polyethylene "squeeze bottle" plastic dispensers. Shake the bottle to mix the powder and water, then squirt as much as is wanted on the buff. Do not mix too much at one time as some, notably cerium oxide, cake when dry. This can be prevented by tightly capping bottles to prevent water evaporation.

■ POLISHING AGENTS IN BAR FORM

Recently, polishing agents have been mixed with water-soluble, semi-solid material and cast into bars or blocks which are applied to damp buffs by holding them against the spinning surface. By varying the dampness of the buffs, it is possible to build up as much powder concentration as is necessary. One of these bars is shown in use in Figure 53. The same firm sells abrasive grits in similar containers as well as standard polishing agents.

■ POLISHERS

There are two general types of polishers—those for polishing of cabochons, flats, spheres, and other work demanding little accuracy, and those for polishing geometrically flat surfaces such as on faceted gems. The first type embraces buffs constructed from yielding materials, such as fabric and wood, the second includes flat plates of metal, plastic, or wood, less yielding under pressure and more capable of providing the accurate surfaces desired.

Fig. 53 Polishing agent in bar form. Cerium oxide is shown here being applied to a spinning polishing lap. The binder is water-soluble and allows the mixture to be washed off readily when necessary. (Courtesy Bruce Bars, Bruce Products Corp., Howell, Michigan)

The latter will be dealt with in detail in Chapter 14—How to Cut Faceted Gems, while the following sections of this chapter will deal with the polishers useful for cabochon work and other common lapidary projects. The polishers used in facet work are customarily called "laps" and those used in cabochon work are called "buffs."

■ POLISHING BUFFS

The construction of a buff is of far less importance than is true for many other items of lapidary equipment because no great accuracy is needed and the running speeds are low. From the mechanical standpoint, however, some designs are better than others. As in sanding, polishers can be disks, drums, wheels, and belts; the simplest are wheels and disks.

■ SOLID FELT WHEELS

The most popular polisher is a solid felt wheel made of top-quality compressed wool. The best is called "rock-hard" and it is essential that this quality be specified because other kinds are soft and wear too quickly. Felt wheels are available from midget sizes for jewelry work to wheels of 12 inches in diameter and 2 inches or more in thickness for lapidary work. Because felt is not as strong as other materials, it is necessary that felt wheels be at least 1 inch thick, with 1½ or 2 inches preferred. Supporting flanges should be about one third of the diameter of the wheel to add stiffness and to prevent slipping on the arbor shaft. Felt polishes best at slow rpms, and speeds of 1000 to 2000 surface feet per minute are recommended. Excessive speed makes the surface appear harder, but much polishing agent is slung off by centrifugal force and wasted. Wear is rapid if only the center portion is used and a groove allowed to develop; *all* of the surface must be used to keep the working face reasonably square. This becomes important whenever a flat surface is polished, since a badly worn buff can only present a fraction of its useful surface.

Felt of all kinds contaminates easily, and care must be taken to keep dirt and dust away. The buff should be covered when not in use, or, if removed from the machine, wrapped in clean newspaper before storing. Do not mix powders on a felt buff if you can avoid it; if you settle upon cerium oxide as your favorite polishing agent with a felt buff, try to use only that agent on that buff. Contaminating particles can be removed by touching the surface of the spinning buff with a block of pumice. This is also a good way to true the surface.

■ BUFFS USING SHEET FELT

Sheet felt is used on disk polishers from 6 inches in diameter to as large as 16 inches in diameter. Sheets less than ¼ inch thick are seldom practical unless they are glued down carefully; otherwise they tend to wrinkle and tear. Horizontal disks often have the felt secured only in the center and depend upon friction between the felt and the disk to keep the sheet from twisting; it is better, however, to fasten it all the way around the edge if the construction of the disk permits.

The curved buff shown in Figure 54 was designed by the author to provide greater choice of surfaces for polishing. With this buff it is possible to easily polish flats as well as cabochons. The curvature allows considerable pressure to be exerted at any point upon a slab or cabochon. The wood body is constructed by cutting out three circular disks of mahogany or other fine-grained wood, crossing the grains, and then cementing with waterproof cement. The resulting cylinder is then turned on a lathe to the cross-section shown; afterwards it is sanded and heavily varnished. The recess on top is for a hold-down nut, but if the arbor hole is bored undersize and then threaded, the entire top surface can be left unbroken. Sheet felt is soaked for about five to ten minutes in hot water to make it pliable; it is stretched over the buff and smoothed along the bottom edge to remove wrinkles. Wrap the bottom with stout twine. Cut a hole in the top and tack

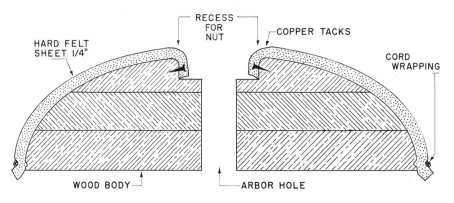

Fig. 54 Cross-section of felt-covered wood buff. The wooden sections are crossed and glued to prevent warping, and varnished heavily afterwards. This buff may be any size.

the edges of the felt around the bottom and the buff is ready for use.

Sheet felt has been used for drum-type polishers, but since it is difficult to fasten down the ends of the strip and since solid felt wheels are available, its use does not seem worthwhile.

■ LEATHER BUFFS

Solid leather wheels have been used for many years for polishing jewelry as well as for polishing gemstones, including carvings. Because of the availability of hide leathers, solid wheels are not really necessary, and suitable substitutes can be made easily. Any kind of leather is useful for polishing, but it should be simple tanned leather without artificial coloring or finish. Leather may be glued to disks, stretched over forms, similar to the wooden buff shown in Figure 54, or employed in any number of arrangements to make successful polishers. Figure 55 shows a useful polisher using thin leather stretched over a hollow-back wheel.

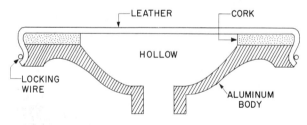

Fig. 55 Construction of the Rock leather polisher for cabochons. The center portion presses down and conforms to the curvature of the gem while the outer ring is backed with firm cork. The stem can be obtained with a set screw or with threads.

Leather is satisfactory for almost any gemstone, but it finds its greatest use in polishing undercutting materials such as jade, lapis, rhodonite, serpentine, etc. Furthermore, almost any agent may be used on leather, with chrome oxide and Linde A being the favorite, the latter preferred. Stones which merely achieve a dull gloss on felt, even after prolonged polishing, are almost always brought to a brilliant finish on leather. If only one buff is to be employed by the amateur lapidary, it should be leather because it will polish almost everything; whereas felt, although much faster for certain gemstones, will not polish undercutters.

Leather is extremely economical to use, a single skin stretched over a polisher lasts for months without visible wear. The greatest drawback to leather for polishing is its slowness and the fact that it seems to polish best when almost dry. The latter characteristic sometimes causes considerable heat to be developed in the gemstone with some danger of the dopping wax melting and the stone coming off the stick.

Thick sole leather is used with diamond dust for polishing very hard stones in the manner described for sanding. It may also be used effectively with standard powders but generally the stiffness of sole leather prevents it from conforming to the shape of cabochons resulting in only a small area being polished at a time. For this reason, most leather polishers use skins of ⅛-inch thickness, or slightly less, the greater flexibility permitting far more contact area on the gem.

Leather is obtained from lapidary supply houses, hobby shops or cobblers' supply houses. Whenever flexible leather is required, ask for "elkskin" since this has the desired thinness and flexibility. There are two sides to a skin, the smooth, hair side and the rough, fibrous, flesh side. The author has not been able to see much difference in either side as far as polishing efficiency is concerned but prefers the smooth side because it is less likely to catch foreign particles which cause scratching.

■ CLOTH BUFFS

Cloth buffs made from many circular disks of unbleached muslin sewed together are used with considerable success for polishing but have to be run at high speeds to make the working face stiff enough to resist the pressure of the gemstone. As a result of this high speed, much polishing powder is thrown off the wheel and if the edge of a gem is caught during polishing, it too will be thrown off violently.

Cloth can be used on disk or drum buffs but only the thick or closely woven types can stand much use without fraying and tearing. Canvas is used, as are certain twills and special napped cloths designed for polishing flat mineral specimens. Excellent results have been had with polishers made of clean wool carpeting. A stout cloth has been developed for belt sanders and offers advantages similar to those stated for sanding on this type machine. Heavy cloth may also be stretched and tacked over wooden forms for polishing, the only precaution being to tack below the edge so that no tacks extend into the area used for polishing.

Cloth buffs should run at speeds not exceeding 500 rpm except those of stitched muslin which may have to be run as high as 2,500 to 3,000 rpm in order to be stiff enough to be effective.

■ POLISHING WITH PELLON

Pellon is a cloth-like plastic material used extensively for linings and stiffeners in clothing. It is also singularly efficient for polishing gemstone and mineral flats. For this purpose, Pellon disks are cemented to metal laps with contact cement and charged with watery mixtures of polishing agent. It is possible to use Pellon on curved surfaces and soft backings but it tears easily if hooked with a sharp corner. Pellon disks, already coated with cement and ready to apply to laps, are sold by lapidary supply houses. Pellon by the yard, in various weights, is also available in yard goods stores but is not as easy to use as the prepared disks. Standard contact cements can be used to cement unprepared Pellon to suitable laps.

A Pellon-coated lap is simple to use: merely brush with a thin, watery mixture of polishing agent, start the motor, and hold the flat specimen to the lap. Due to the porous nature of the Pellon, there is very little jerking or tugging, however, when friction increases appreciably, the lap is drying and needs to be wet again. Since Pellon cannot stand much heat, check the specimen frequently to see that it is not getting too hot.

Since Pellon laps are most efficient when perfectly flat, insure smoothness by applying contact cement in a thick uniform layer. Iron disks to remove wrinkles before applying and, after application, rub gently to eliminate trapped air bubbles.

Although Pellon has been claimed to be effective for many kinds of gemstones, the author has found it no more efficient than standard polishers for undercutting gems. However, it is *by far* the best polishing material he has ever used for quartz family gemstones and others which consist of single minerals or are uniform in composition. It polishes rock crystal and chalcedony flats with a speed and perfection of surface which would be hard to duplicate by any of the standard methods. Cerium oxide has been found extremely effective as a polishing agent; also Linde A.

■ WOODEN BUFFS

Ordinary wood has been used for many years for polishing gems, the famous gem-cutting centers of Germany and France using beechwood for this purpose. Any "diffuse-porous" wood is suitable for polishing. Teak, mahogany, beech, birch, cherry and other fruit woods, holly, poplar, and gum are all useful. Wood can be made into disks, drums, or wheels, the surfaces left flat or cut into a variety of grooves to give greater contact area with the gem. Since the wheels will be used wet, warping may occur but can be partially prevented by impregnating with melted beeswax. Similar in action to leather, wood buffs will do wonders with undercutting materials and with many of the harder gemstones that polish either slowly or with difficulty on other buffs.

Grooved hard wood buffs are commonly used for polishing cabochon sapphire, ruby, and chrysoberyl. After preliminary smoothing, as described under sanding, final polishing is done with 6400 to 8000 diamond powder. The diamond is mixed with grease or oil; one authority recommends lipstick, which is of the proper consistency and whose color tells whether too little or too much is being applied to any place on the lap. Professionals use lignum vitae wood for diamond powder polishing of corundum gems, but almost any hard wood is satisfactory. Diamond tends to sink into softer woods and these should be avoided.

■ CORK LAPS

A good polisher for cabochons and small flats is made from ³⁄₁₆-inch or ¼-inch sheet cork cemented to a metal lap. Suitable sheet cork is available from automotive parts suppliers, or if they do not have thick sheets in stock, they can tell you where to get it. Cut the sheet to fit the lap and cement on with contact cement or pitch-rosin mixture. If the latter is used, the lap must be heated until the mixture melts upon it readily. Press with weights but be sure the cork lies flat. The firm surface of this lap makes it particularly useful for the polishing of undercutting materials.

■ NON-WARPING WOODEN LAPS

The warping of wooden buffs is not a serious handicap to polishing of cabochons where only curved surfaces are involved but a warped wooden disk is completely ineffective for polishing large flat areas. To solve the problem of how to use the splendid polishing action of wood without suffering the penalties of warping, the author hit upon the idea of cementing wooden blocks to a metal lap. Although each wooden block swelled as it absorbed water, the level of the lap surface was not affected and retained its flatness. This lap is especially useful for polishing large flat areas of jade with chrome oxide. It is shown in Figure 146 and is made as follows.

Select an aluminum or steel lap at least ¼-inch thick. Clean all oil, grease, dirt, and corrosion from the surface and score heavily with very coarse garnet paper. Do not touch the surface again with bare hands. Cut strips of diffuse-porous wood to about ½-inch square in cross-section. Cross cut into blocks from ¼-inch to ³⁄₈-inch thick. Coat the prepared lap liberally with epoxy resin, preferably the type that does not require heat curing. Starting at the middle of the lap, and at least 1 inch away from the bolt hole if there is one, attach the wooden blocks, making sure that the end grain is up. Overlap them like bricks in a wall but leave ¹⁄₁₆-inch space between them. Work outwards until the entire surface is covered. Near the edges and near the inside, split some of the blocks to fill all spaces. Set aside on a level place to prevent the blocks from drifting and let cure thoroughly.

When the epoxy resin has set hard, place the lap in a lathe or on a rapidly spinning arbor and file the surface until it is flat. File the edges of the blocks along the rim to avoid sharp corners which may snag flats being polished. To use this lap, brush with a watery mixture of polishing agent and apply flat specimens by hand. For jade, strong tugging means that the lap is on the verge of drying out and that polishing is taking place. However, since wood laps dry quickly and overheat, cracking of gemstones more fragile than jade is a real danger. Guard against this by frequent checking for warmth in the slab itself.

It is absolutely necessary when using epoxy cement that the metal lap surface be completely clean and heavily scored or scratched. Without these precautions, the wood blocks will not stick.

■ PREPARATIONS FOR POLISHING

Install and test the polishing buff for proper operation before charging with a polishing agent. Mix about a teaspoonful of agent in a glass jar or dish with several times that amount of water. Add several drops of household detergent or a pinch of the dry type, to the powder-water mixture. Detergents contain a "wetting agent" which causes water to soak more quickly and aids the polishing powder to distribute itself more evenly. Household detergents are not harmful to buffs.

Each polishing agent should have its own container and its own brush. The powder-water mixture is applied by dipping up the thin solution. Do not apply the thick portion which settles on the bottom, but stir this up each time to get it well mixed with the water. Applying an excessively thick paste of powder merely glazes the buff and slows the polishing action and wastes the agent. For felt buffs, apply only enough mixture to color the felt strongly; add more every few minutes, but be sure that the surface does not become thickly coated or sticky. When using leather, be far more sparing; use only enough Linde A or chrome oxide to change the color. Too much powder on leather causes glazing and slows polishing action. In all cases, supply enough mixture to keep the buff damp but not wet and just enough powder in the mixture for good polishing action.

■ POLISHING TECHNIQUES

In general, the handling of specimens during polishing follows the same methods used in sanding. The principle of cabochon polishing is best shown in Figure 56, in which a large cabochon on a dop stick is

Fig. 56 Proper position for holding dopped cabochon when polishing on horizontal felt buff. Note how fingers surround dop wax (in black) and rest on back of cabochon. The arm is in "trailing" position and the edge of the stone (to the right) is raised slightly to avoid catching the edge.

being held against a buff. The operation appears simple—and it is simple—but several points are worth mentioning to prevent difficulties. Note first that the fingers of the hand are gripping the dopstick at a very low point, directly behind the stone. In this way the stick is held firmly under perfect control and at the same time, the stone is supported by the fingertips. Note also, that the edge of the stone is raised from the buff to prevent catching. Although buffs generally turn slowly, catching an edge is still a serious matter because it may tear the buff or break the stone off the dopstick. As in sanding, it is essential that the stone *trail* on the buff. As polishing progresses, the stone is turned to expose a new area until the entire surface is completed.

Much pressure must be used in polishing regardless of the type of buff. However, the better the sanding job, the easier it is to bring up a polish with less pressure. Pressures vary from several ounces to many pounds, depending on the size and kind of gemstone. For a cabochon 2 inches wide, 10 pounds pressure may not be enough, while a small gem of ½ inch in size may polish quickly with only the pressure needed to push a doorbell button. Experience will show what works best with various materials in various sizes. Remember that heavy pressures create heat which could crack the gem or soften the wax holding the gem on the dop stick and cause it to shift position or fall off.

It is wise to adopt a system in polishing to be sure that every portion is gone over throughly. The author uses the following method. Whether the piece is a slab, block, or curved surface, polish the edges first until a lustrous finish completely encircles the untouched area in the center. Keep a box or roll of disposable tissue to wipe off the work frequently and permit careful inspection.

Clean the surface thoroughly, since only a trace of polishing powder can hide small defects such as scratches and unfinished patches. Tilt the work slightly to polish the center portion and again inspect results. When the entire surface appears complete, clean carefully and examine with a critical eye, holding the stone under a strong light. This is the time to find and correct defects. Remember, wipe the surface carefully and use a strong light for examination. A severe test for polish perfection is to try to see the cleaned surface with a 5–10X magnifying glass. A perfectly polished surface is almost impossible to see even when magnified.

Almost any properly sanded gemstone begins to show a polish within seconds; if it does not the surface has not been properly sanded or the wrong powder-buff combination is being used. Check the combination recommended in Chapter 19 for the particular mineral being polished to be certain it is correct. Not all minerals polish on the same combinations and it is important that the proper one be used. If the work has not been correctly sanded, there is little to be gained by trying to polish. Take the gem back to fine sanding or even coarse sanding and re-do the surface until smooth.

■ POLISHING UNDERCUTTING GEMSTONES

Felt buffs polish most common gemstones but there are some that undercut and require wood or leather buffs. Polishing an undercutting material on felt results in pits and depressions which deepen with prolonged effort. If a material thought to be non-undercutting begins to develop pitting on felt, stop immediately and switch to wood or leather. Further polishing on felt may ruin the surface to the point where resanding is necessary.

To prepare a leather buff for polishing, wet the surface with water to which a bit of detergent has been added. Upon soaking, the leather becomes dark in color, softens and is more flexible. Run for a few minutes to drive off excess moisture. Now apply chrome oxide or Linde A in small amounts, remembering that an excess is merely wasteful. Apply the work with firm pressure, starting at the center of the buff and working outward. There will be an excess of water, making the gemstone slide on the slippery surface of the leather. It is not until the leather is barely damp that a friction or "tug-

ging" occurs which is quite strong and, if the work is not held firmly, may cause it to be plucked from the operator's hands. Strong friction means the leather has reached the proper condition for polishing, as a quick check of the gemstone surface will show.

Since the proper condition of leather is a state approaching dryness, it is essential that it be kept this way by occasional drops of water near the center. When the water is applied, a momentary slipping occurs, but friction again asserts itself and polishing continues. Much heat develops during this semi-dry stage and frequent cooling of the gemstone is necessary to prevent softening of the dopping wax.

Harder gemstones, such as jadeite, nephrite, and rhodonite, need more pressure and a buff which is barely damp. Softer species, such as tigereye, moonstone, and opal, can be polished easily with more moisture and less danger of overheating.

The use of wood follows the same practice specified for leather but its firmer nature permits use of more moisture to achieve the same results. In most cases, tin oxide on wood will polish everything and is recommended over Linde A because it is cheaper.

Wood and leather buffs should be run at very slow rpms, not over 500 and preferably about 200. Slower speeds produce better polishes but equipment limitations sometimes prevent getting an rpm as low as one would like.

■ DISCOLORATION BY POLISHING AGENTS

Polishing agents creep into pores and openings in gemstones and may discolor them. It is better to prevent this from happening than to try to disguise or remove discoloration later. Several methods of sealing pores have already been discussed under lapping in Chapter 5, but there are other methods which should be mentioned here. Since the final shape of the cabochon is not obtained until after fine sanding, it is at this point that the sealing of pores must be done. As a temporary measure, pores may be packed with a water soluble substance such as hard soap which serves to keep polishing agents from penetrating deeply. If polishing is brief, soap will last, but if prolonged, it may be washed out. Paraffin is useful but requires that the gem be warmed and then dipped in melted paraffin. As it cools, the paraffin will be drawn inside crevices and pores. Scrape off excess paraffin to keep it from contaminating the buff. Another method is to soak the gem overnight in a solution of water glass. Later this is allowed to harden and stays hard long enough to finish the polishing job. What is left is removed by soaking the gem in warm water. This method is useful for very fine pores such as are found in some catseye gems. Perhaps the best method of all is to soak the gem in a colorless epoxy resin, but in order to obtain penetration, it will be necessary to remove the gem from the dop stick and heat it on the dopping stove until it is quite warm and all water in the pores is driven off. It is then brushed with a film of warm epoxy which is forced into the pores by atmospheric pressure as the gem cools.

8 | *All-Purpose Units*

THE ideal shop has separate pieces of equipment ready at a moment's notice to do the several tasks called for even by a simple project. If commercial work is being done, a complete shop is vital to efficiency and saving of time, however, for most beginners, it is neither necessary nor wise to spend the money required. Later, when it is decided to do a greater variety of work, is time enough to think about separate machines. Usually beginners start by buying an *all-purpose* unit, which, as the name implies, means that many lapidary operations can be done on the same machine. Most all-purpose units are designed for cabochon cutting, but some permit lapping, slab sawing, sphere making, and even faceting, if the necessary accessories are obtained. All-purpose units range from small inexpensive models, to some which are large and sturdy and fitted with many accessories for a large variety of work.

There are many advantages to all-purpose units—and also disadvantages. Small size is attractive if workshop space is limited or unavailable. There is no doubt that separate machines for sawing, grinding, sanding, and polishing take much more bench space and require several motors with separate wiring, plumbing, lighting, etc. Much of this space and cost can be saved with an all-purpose unit. However, separate machines are designed to provide the best performance possible, while in the all-purpose unit, many compromises must be made to combine operations. For example, if a saw is attached, it is not always as versatile as one wants, and if it runs continuously because it cannot be disconnected from the drive shaft, it will keep throwing small quantities of coolant spray at all times unless the tank is drained. In some units, particularly those with a vertical shaft, only one accessory can be installed and operated at once. This means time wasted in switching from one accessory to another. In the case of exchanging grinding wheels, imbalances can occur because the wheels seldom fit exactly as they were before. With a horizontal shaft, once the wheels are put on and correctly trued, they need not be disturbed again until they wear out.

■ HORIZONTAL SHAFT UNITS

The most common all-purpose units use horizontal shafting upon which are strung various accessories. Among them are usually one or two grinding wheels, a drum sander, sometimes a disk type sander at the end of the shaft, an interchangeable polisher, and perhaps a trim saw. The motor is usually placed in the rear out of the way, while power is delivered by a vee-belt from the motor to a pulley near the center of the shaft. When grinding wheels wear out, it is necessary to unbolt various parts of the machine in order to remove the old wheels and install new ones, however, the operation takes only about thirty minutes.

A small beginner's unit, and a great favorite, is the Allen Junior, shown in Figure 57. It measures 16 inches in length and 8 inches in width. Coarse and fine grinding wheels of 4 inches in diameter are provided, along with a 4-inch diamond trim saw, sander and polisher.

Another very small unit designed for a complete range of operations is the Covington "Little Gem Shop," shown in Figure 58. It also uses a 4-inch diamond blade with interchangeable grinding, sanding and polishing accessories to fit the shaft shown at the right. A larger unit made by the same firm is shown in Figure 59 where two operations are being performed at once. This unit features 8-inch diameter grinding wheels, sanding drum and polisher as well as a trim saw shown at the extreme left. The M.D.R. unit shown in Figure 60 employs similar horizontal shaft construction and has proven to be a very sound unit of high reputation. Grinding operations are performed in the center and sanding and polishing on the right hand shaft extension. The trim saw is shown on the left. Figure 61 illustrates the Highland Park Junior unit.

All units illustrated may either be placed upon table tops or installed in stands designed for them specially, as shown in Figure 59. Stands are advantageous because they can be used to store all accessories as well as powders, cloths, and other supplies which are used.

Fig. 57 Three views of the Allen miniature all-purpose unit in operation. *Top.* Using the trim saw feature. *Center.* Shaping a cabochon on the coarse grinding wheel. *Bottom.* Polishing a cabochon. On the left is the sanding disk which has been removed to install the polisher. (Courtesy Belmont Lapidary Supply, Belmont, California)

■ VERTICAL SHAFT UNITS

Almost as popular as horizontal shaft units are those in which a single vertical shaft passes upward through an enclosing

Fig. 58 Covington "Little Gem Shop" all-purpose unit. The trim saw shown on the left is fitted with a 4-inch blade, while grinding, sanding and polishing are done on the right hand shaft extension by using interchangeable accessories. (Courtesy Covington Engineering Corporation, Redlands, California)

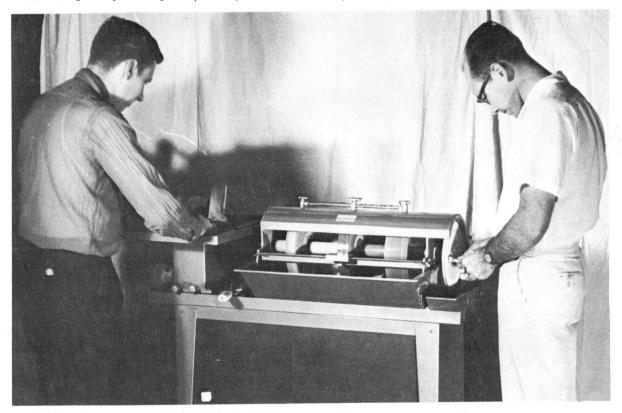

Fig. 59 Covington No. 423 all-purpose unit in operation. This larger unit accommodates several operations at once as shown here. The operator at the left is using the trim saw while the other person is sanding a cabochon. (Courtesy Covington Engineering Corporation, Redlands, California)

Fig. 60 The M.D.R. No. 53 cabochon unit. This all-purpose machine permits sawing, coarse and fine grinding, sanding and polishing of cabochons. Other types of work can also be done. (Courtesy M.D.R. Manufacturing Co., Inc., Los Angeles, California)

Fig. 61 Highland Park "Junior" all-purpose unit which features 6" accessories including grinding wheel, trim saw, sander and polisher. (Courtesy Highland Park Manufacturing Co., South Pasadena, California)

splash pan, as shown in Figure 62. The top of the shaft is fitted with a flange and threaded to take accessories which are tapped to fit the threaded portion, or slip over the shaft and rest on the collar where they are locked in place with a nut. Other units of similar type are shown in Figures 63 and 64.

Normally, accessories consist of grinding wheels, disk sanders, polishers, and a saw blade. The latter is used with a clamp arm which holds the stone and swings into the blade, as shown in the left hand picture of Figure 62 and in Figure 63. In addition, plain steel laps can be obtained for lapping, also tubes for making spheres and accessories for

faceting. Some accessories for the author's machine are shown in Figure 65.

Vertical shaft units sometimes suffer from inaccuracies in their bearings which cause the vertical shafts to lean slightly to one side. In sawing and faceting this leads to inaccurate alignment and poor results. Most units would be greatly improved by fitting them with a heel bearing as well as the one normally provided, since this would suspend the shaft between two bearings and counteract the tendency of the vee-belt to pull the shaft out of line. Misalignment can be prevented or postponed by tightening the vee-belt only enough to obtain the necessary friction to

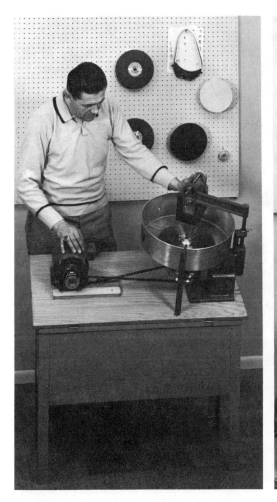

Fig. 62 Hillquist 3V compact lapidary unit. *Left.* Unit shown being used as a saw. The rock is clamped in the swinging arm and brought against the saw by means of a cord and weight (not shown). *Right.* A grinding wheel has been installed. This unit features the use of many accessories including sphere cutters, faceter, and others. (Courtesy Lapidary Equipment Company, Seattle, Washington)

drive the pulley on the vertical shaft. In comparison, it will be noted that all horizontal shaft units are suspended by at least two bearings, in some cases, more. They are therefore inherently more accurate.

Despite the inherent deficiencies of vertical shaft units, they present strong advantages which are much in their favor. They are very effective in lapping and avoid the necessity of buying a separate unit for this important lapidary operation since only a lapping plate is needed to convert the unit. By buying a set of sphere cutters, they can also be used efficiently for this purpose. However, the greatest advantage that the author has found for the

larger units of this class is that it is possible to grind cabochons and facet preforms more accurately because the point of contact of the gem with the grinding wheel is always in plain view. This operation is shown in Figure 66. Unfortunately, few units are large enough to permit this kind of work and the smaller vertical shaft units have no room in the tubs to work on the edge of the wheel and grinding must be done on top or actually on the side of the grinding wheel. Since the point of contact is less sharp than if the gem were being ground on the edge of the wheel, cutting is slower, and the wheel is almost impossible to true once it begins bumping. It is unfortunate

Fig. 63 Covington No. 301 horizontal all-purpose unit. The cord for pulling the rock into the saw blade is shown with a rock already placed in the clamp. As in the unit shown in Figure 62, the saw accessory is removable. (Courtesy Covington Engineering Corporation, Redlands, California)

Fig. 64 Gemlap all-purpose unit being used to grind a cabochon. A special hollow-center grinding wheel is mounted upon the spindle. Note water supply. (Courtesy Brad's Rock Shop, Ferndale, Michigan)

that much more design talent has been placed in horizontal shaft units than in vertical shaft units because, in the author's opinion, the latter could be greatly improved.

■ HOMEMADE ALL-PURPOSE UNITS

As in other pieces of equipment for lapidary work, the amateur can also buy the components needed to make his own all-purpose unit. At present, only components for horizontal shaft units are available. A large variety of combinations is possible depending on the size of the shaft, spacing of bearings, and other factors. Figure 67 shows the Rock arbor unit and how its usefulness can be expanded by adding accessories. Figure 68 shows a Highland Park arbor with several accessories attached. With such basic arbors, the amateur can save considerable money at first. However, as other accessories are added, the costs will be about the same in the long run as if a complete all-purpose unit were bought in ready-to-run condition.

Fig. 65 Accessories for a vertical shaft all-purpose lapidary unit. *Top left.* Felt-covered polishing buff (see Figure 55). *Top right.* Poplar wood blank ready to be turned into a polisher for undercutting gems or for very hard gems. *Bottom right.* Leather disk polisher. *Bottom left.* View of bottom of disk sander showing attachment hole and snap rim used to hold sanding cloth in place.

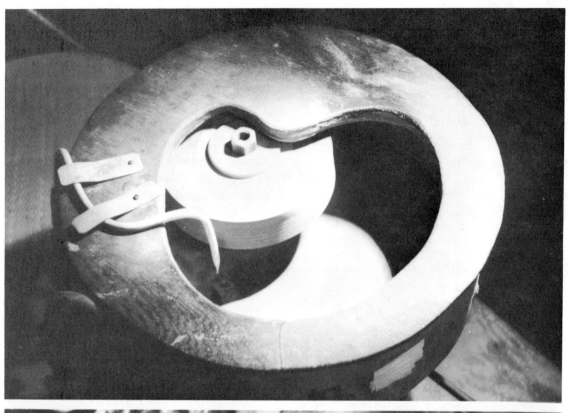

Fig. 66 The author's method of grinding cabochons on a vertical shaft unit. The tub is fitted with a waterproof plywood splash shield, and a bent metal tube delivers a spray of water to the side of the grinding wheel. As the lower photo shows, it is possible to see exactly what is being done during grinding.

Fig. 67 A basic outfit for making homemade all-pur-pose lapidary units. By adding accessories as shown, it is possible to make grinders, sanders and polishers.

(Courtesy Rock's Lapidary Equipment & Supplies, San Antonio, Texas)

Fig. 68 Highland Park Model B-1 arbor with some accessories installed. The basic shaft is supported by ball bearings at the center on each side of the pulley. The left end of the shaft is fitted with a grinding wheel while the right end is fitted with sanding drum and disk polisher. (Courtesy Highland Park Manufacturing Co., South Pasadena, California)

9 | *Drilling*

Drilling is used for many purposes in lapidary work, as in piercing beads for stringing, boring attachment holes, and hollowing out cavities in large blocks of material. String holes and attachment holes are usually very small in diameter but holes drilled for hollowing out cavities may be several inches or more in diameter. Various types of gemstone drill bits are shown in Figure 69.

■ NEEDLE DRILLS

The finest holes of all are drilled with steel needles, using crushed diamond for abrasive. Such drills have been used for centuries, and all work in the same way. The needle is mounted accurately at the end of a small, light shaft which is then spun rapidly while diamond powder is supplied to the point. For motive power and still in use is the "bow drill," in which a light wood spindle bearing the needle is stroked back and forth by several turns of twine fastened to a bow. Generally the spindle is hung from a bracket, leaving the

lower end free. The operator lifts the bracket, places the gem to be drilled under the needle, and strokes the bow. Because extreme delicacy of touch must be used to prevent bending or breaking the delicate needle, this kind of work can only be done well after years of practice. Most amateurs do not have the skill nor the patience to drill in this way and other methods are commonly used.

■ TUBE OR CORE DRILLS

An easier and more certain method of boring holes is to use a length of rotating tubing whose point is supplied with abrasive grit or coated with sintered metal containing diamond. It is impossible to drill as fine a hole with tubing as is possible with a needle, but for most purposes the holes are small enough. The principle of the tube drill is illustrated in Figure 69 where a small tube and a large tube are shown with corresponding holes in pieces of rough gem material. The tube cuts a circular channel as it spins and

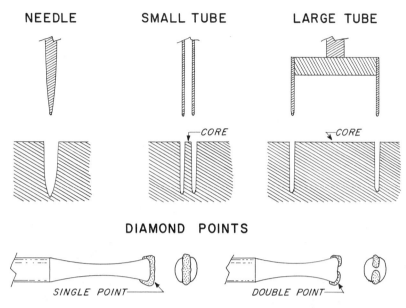

NEEDLE   SMALL TUBE   LARGE TUBE

CORE   CORE

DIAMOND POINTS

SINGLE POINT   DOUBLE POINT

Fig. 69 Various types of gemstone drill bits.

therefore leaves behind a slender or stout core, depending on the tube diameter. When the drill is large and purposely used to obtain a cylindrical section of stone, as shown to the right of Figure 69, it is known as a core drill. Small-diameter bits are used with loose abrasive but large-diameter bits may be coated with sintered metal containing diamond.

Tubes used for boring very small holes are made from bronze, brass, stainless steel, or ordinary steel. The material is not too important providing it is not too soft. The effective limit to size is about $1/16$ inch—anything smaller is apt to jam. Small-diameter bits require accurate drills to run them, since the slightest wobbling soon causes wear on the sides and gradual closing of the tube opening. The slender core, shown in the center illustration of Figure 69, tends to break into small sections which work their way up into the tube. If these should jam, the face of the tube becomes plugged with stone and drilling stops. One drill takes care of this by providing a needle which automatically dips through the tube and pushes out the small bits of stone as fast as they enter. In large tubes, this is not a problem.

Small-diameter tubing such as shown at 1. in Figure 70, is available from makers of automatic drills. Many amateurs use the tubing that comes in ball-point pens and find it satisfactory. The outer tubing in the ink container is usually about $1/8$ inch in diameter while the tip tubing is about $1/16$ inch. Sections are cut as needed, avoiding the crimped part. Before use, the working edge of all tubing should be carefully squared to perfect flatness.

Large-diameter tubing is available in steel, particularly in a thin-walled type known as "Shelby" tubing. This is the kind used in the Koning core drills shown in Figure 71. However, copper, brass, and steel tubing of many types can be used but should be thin-walled to reduce as much as possible the actual area of the stone that must be cut away. Similar bits can be made at home if one has a metal-working lathe or if one can buy a mechanics hole saw, which consists of a metal disk, with stem, fitted with circular grooves to take various sizes of tubing. One type available in hardware stores takes tubes from 1 to $2\frac{1}{2}$ inches in diameter. A twist drill is provided in the center but this must be cut off, since it cannot drill stone. The tubes provided with such hole saws are designed to cut wood and metal. However, suitable thin-walled tubing can be bought in short lengths from junk dealers at nominal prices.

Fig. 70 Koning Vibra-Drill. The principle behind this drill is simple and sound; as the motor turns the drill tube, the stone slab, held in a clamp, is rapidly vibrated up and down to allow fresh grit to enter the hole and spent grit and powdered stone to leave. 1. Drill tube, extending down hollow shaft to 8. 2. Friction drive. 3. Motor switch. 4. Power receptacle and vibrator switch. 5. Vibrator. 6. Vibrator arm. 7. Stone clamp. 8. Slab in process of being drilled. The small cone of clay containing brasive and water has been omitted for clarity. This machine drills through ¼ inch of hard gem material in six minutes. (Courtesy Frances Paul Crafts, El Monte, California)

Fig. 71 Koning Vibra-Drill accessories used for core drilling. The upper row shows various sizes of core drills with which the rings of stone shown on the lower right may be cut. The tubes can be separated if desired. Note that the tubes are notched along the working edges to permit better distribution of grit. (Courtesy Frances Paul Crafts, El Monte, California)

■ LARGE DIAMETER CORE DRILLS

For large projects in which it is desired to hollow out deep cavities or to obtain large rings or cores of stone, it is necessary to use the same type of bits that the Chinese carvers use, namely sheets of tin plate wrapped around suitable steel or wood cylinders. These are fitted with accurately-centered stems which are gripped by the jaws of the chuck in a drill press. One method uses a piece of hardwood bored in the center for a section of threaded rod or bolt. The rod is attached by two nuts, one at the top of the wood block and one at the bottom. This is chucked in a lathe and the wood turned to the diameter wanted. Since the metal rod is used as the center, the wood will be perfectly concentric and an accurately running core bit will result. Better devices can be made by turning steel bar stock into bits

of various sizes. The cutters are made by rolling galvanized sheet or roofing tin into cylindrical forms, leaving a gap of about $\frac{1}{16}$ to $\frac{1}{8}$ inch when the sections are tightly fitted to the tool. The metal sheet is fastened to the disk with tube clamps or by small screws. Where wood cylinders are used, the metal sheet is attached by wrapping tightly with many turns of strong twine, which are then varnished to make them waterproof. Tin cans can be used but it is difficult to cut them without deforming them. Suitable sheet metal and facilities for rolling strips into uniform rolls may be found at roofers or tinsmiths shops. Small-diameter tubes can be made by cutting rectangular strips of metal and passing them through jewelers' drawplates. If closed tubing is used, the edges should be notched, as shown in Figure 71; if rolled sheet is used, a gap should be left between the ends. The notches or gaps provide channels for fresh grit to reach the working edges.

■ DIAMOND POINT BITS

Very efficient drills are made by imbedding small bits of diamond in slots cut in the end of thin drill rod, as shown in Figure 69. The single point bit is not as efficient as the double point bit, but is easier to make and less likely to be damaged in use. To make one, obtain some lengths of thin drill rod in various diameters to about ⅛ inch and an assortment of diamond chips or small single stones of the kind known as bort. Diamond chips are less desirable because they split during use but are easier to get than properly shaped bort crystals. The end of the drill rod is annealed by heating to cherry red and allowing to cool. The end is then squared and slotted with a jeweler's saw; the slot can be enlarged slightly by using a thin riffling file. Select a piece of diamond of rectangular shape and somewhat wider than the diameter of the drill rod; insert into the slot and gently pinch the ends over with a pair of pliers. Use as little force as possible, to prevent splitting the diamond. Examine with a magnifying glass to see that the steel is pinched over properly. Dip the end in silver solder flux and heat. Now heat once more and apply silver solder. Properly done, the chip will be completely enclosed in steel with spaces filled with solder. The bit is now taken to a grinding wheel and the excess metal cautiously cut away until the diamond chip appears on front and sides. The neck is made slender as shown in Figure 69 by placing the bit in the drill chuck and filing while it spins. Double point bits are more difficult to make, especially in small sizes. Professional bits are made with two matched bort crystals of minute size and with great care to insure proper anchoring.

Because of the delicacy of diamond point bits, they must be used with extreme caution and very little pressure. As a matter of fact, they drill better and last longer when used with as little pressure as possible.

■ PLATED DIAMOND BITS

Several manufacturers now market small, solid steel bits charged with diamond powder and which require no recharging for the life of the bit. These are made by coating the steel rod with diamond powder and covering the particles with heavy chrome plate electrolytically deposited. Bits of this type, plus small grinders and disks in various sizes and shapes, are used by dentists and are available from dental supply houses. Some are also stocked by lapidary equipment suppliers. A typical bit was tested by the author. It measured ³⁄₃₂-inch diameter at the shank, with about ¼ inch of the point recessed to provide side clearance. The tip was a ball point plated around the tapering shank and studded with minute diamond particles. The diameter of the ball was somewhat over ⅙ inch. This bit was used with a hand electric tool and drilled holes in ¼-inch agate and chert in from six to eight minutes. The resulting holes were somewhat less than ³⁄₃₂ inch since the shank of this diameter would not fit in the holes. Because of this, and the limited length of the recess on the shank, this bit could not drill holes deeper than ¼ inch. The results were good and the quality of the hole excellent. Other bits of this type useful for carving will be described in Chapter 17. A variation of this bit is fitted with a cone at the tip and is used to ream the edges of holes to make them smooth as for stones which are to be strung on cords.

■ ABRASIVES FOR DRILLING

The standard abrasives are silicon carbide, boron carbide, and diamond. Of the three, silicon carbide is used most because it is readily available in all sizes and is far cheaper than the other two. Boron carbide is harder but the grains are not as sharp-cornered as either silicon carbide or diamond; it is consequently slower in action. However, it is tough and therefore does not crush easily.

Diamond powder, though expensive, is best for drilling because it cuts fast and imbeds itself in the metal bit, thus promoting the rubbing action necessary for best cutting. Both silicon carbide and boron carbide tend to roll rather than to imbed, and consequently their cutting action is more in the nature of lapping. Some amateurs use a mixture of diamond powder and boron carbide and claim that this is cheaper than pure diamond but faster than silicon carbide or boron carbide alone. Diamond powder of 100 to 200 grit is useful for most purposes, but 400 should be used for very small holes. Similar sizes are required for silicon carbide and boron carbide.

■ **DRILLING PROCEDURE—SMALL HOLES**

Place at hand, in addition to bits and drilling machine, some modeling clay, paraffin or beeswax, some flat pieces of wood, and some thick washers or nuts to function as dams to hold the grit around the hole being drilled.

The piece to be drilled, generally a slab or other flat object, is heated gently and cemented with wax or paraffin to a flat piece of wood. The wood provides a steady platform for holding the stone and for clamping the work to the drill table so that it cannot move about while being drilled. The wax holds the stone to the wood and provides support underneath to prevent the edges of the gem from crumbling as the drill pierces through. If possible, start drilling on a flat surface; center the work directly under the bit and lower to mark the spot. Clamp the wood block to the drill table. Heat a washer or nut until hot enough to melt wax and place over the spot to be drilled. This will act as a small container for the grit mixture. Place a dab of grit and water at the point of drilling; lower the bit and start the motor. Stop after a few seconds to check accuracy and re-adjust as necessary.

It is very important to lower the bit as gently as possible, especially if a polished surface is being drilled or if the surface is curved. The idea is to let the point cut a small channel without wandering off, and this can only be done by the lightest contact. When a minute circular groove has been cut and the bit is seated firmly, turn on the machine for steady

drilling. Fill the space around the bit with grit and water; check frequently to see that this mixture is not used up.

Automatic machines, such as that shown in Figure 70, provide an up-and-down motion of the bit which allows fresh grit to fall under the tube and helps wash out crushed stone and spent grit. Without such a machine the drill point will have to be raised and lowered every few seconds by hand.

Once the work starts, do not square off the end of the tube or needle, for it will then jam when it is reinserted in the hole. It is best to wait until breakthrough and then turn the stone over and drill from the opposite side to equalize the size of the bore. If a tube drill is being used, be sure that the end is square and slightly flared before starting. Test the bit while running to be sure that it is spinning accurately. If it is whipping or wobbling, bend the tube gently until it is straight.

When the hole is nearing completion, proceed slowly in order to make the breakthrough as gentle as possible. As soon as the point has passed through, stop drilling, reverse the piece, and drill from the other side.

Drilling is a delicate task and requires patience. Success lies mainly in gentle pressure at all times, as well as frequent up-and-down movement of the drill to clear debris and permit new abrasive to enter the hole. For these reasons, automatic drills for boring small holes are a good investment. However, many amateurs drill so infrequently that they prefer to send their drilling jobs to lapidary shops which specialize in this work. These shops charge about $.50 per hole of about ¼-inch depth.

If a large amount of drilling must be done, it may even be advantageous to send the work to Germany, where the charges are much less and the quality of the work very high. Inquiries should be directed to: Handelskammer, Idar-Oberstein, Germany. Correspondence to this address will reach the chamber of commerce in the famous twin gem-cutting cities of Idar-Oberstein and will be forwarded to a commercial concern prepared to do the work.

Certain gem materials are easier to drill

than others; mainly the softer stones and those with crystalline structure, such as rock crystal, amethyst, citrine, beryl, feldspar, etc. The most difficult are those which have a compact fibrous structure or which contain several minerals of varying hardness. Jadeite and nephrite are especially difficult to drill, as well as the relatively soft gemstone williamsite, which contains specks of chromite, a much harder mineral. Agate is also difficult to drill because of its finely granular structure, which causes it to react in a manner similar to jadeite and nephrite. In any fibrous or granular mineral, drilling will be slow and tedious.

■ **DRILLING PROCEDURE—LARGE HOLES**

In general, the same arrangements are used as for drilling small holes. However, it is often convenient to clamp or cement the work to the bottom of a pan which is then filled with grit and water to provide the necessary abrasive bath. Slabs should first be cemented to flat pieces of wood. If large blocks of stone are drilled, it may be wasteful to place them in pans, and it is better to use modeling clay to build a dam around the work point. At least ¼ to ½ inch of abrasive mixture should surround the bit to insure that the cut will be properly supplied. If the surface of the stone is rough and uneven, lower the spinning bit as gently as possible, since the first contact will be on a very small area and the metal may scrape off and ruin the edge. Once the circular channel is begun, the only attention needed is to raise and lower the bit from time to time, and to be sure that the abrasive slurry covers the work.

■ **COOLANTS**

Some authorities recommend kerosene, turpentine, or light oils to suspend the grits and cool the work. However, the Chinese, who are as expert as any, use only water with silicon carbide for drilling and mud

sawing. Oils may be used with diamond, for which they have great affinity, and possibly may be better. Oils are also thicker than water and do not splash as much, and for this reason, may be preferred if drill bits turn at high speed.

■ **DRILLING SPEEDS**

Small diamond bits should turn from about 4,500 to 5,500 rpm; small tubes from 2,000 to 3,000 rpm; and large tubes from 2,000 rpm downward, depending on diameter; larger diameters require slower speeds. Faster speeds can be used for any of the type bits mentioned, but splashing occurs and the ability of the grits to seize and attack the stone is reduced. Slow drilling speeds are used by the Chinese carvers and also by the German lapidaries, who are very skillful in drilling extremely small holes with bow drills.

■ **HOMEMADE DRILLING RIGS**

Small holes have been bored successfully using an ordinary electric hand drill. The drill is fitted into a wooden trough and strapped in place so it cannot move. A piece of wood which fits snugly into the trough is squared at one end and the piece of stone to be drilled, dopped to this end. The block is slid along the trough to contact the spinning bit held in the jaws of the drill chuck. This rig can be run in horizontal position or can be converted into a workable vertical stand. Some small electric drill kits are equipped with vertical stands and with a little ingenuity these can be made into satisfactory drilling rigs.

Some amateurs have made their own automatic drilling rigs, like the model shown in Figure 72. However, though seemingly simple in construction, these rigs have required the greatest care and skill to make a true-running spindle and to provide a means for raising and lowering the drill to allow fresh grit to enter the hole.

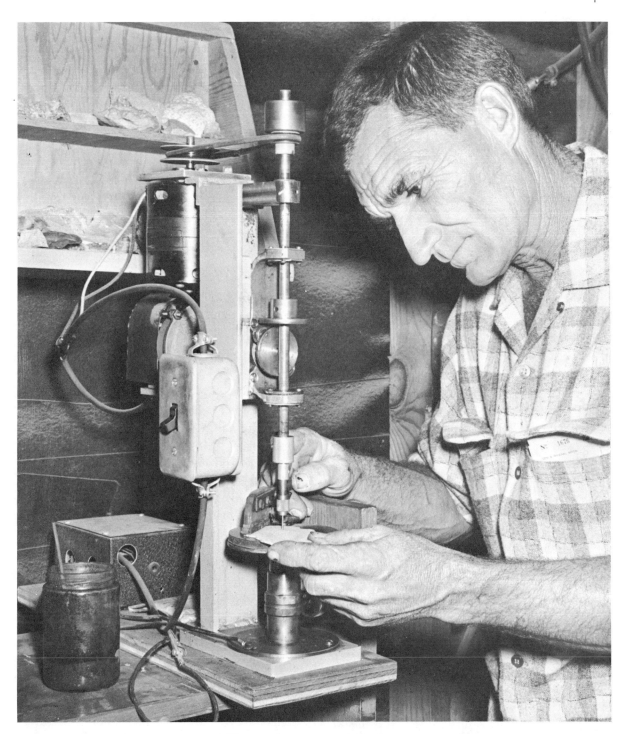

Fig. 72 Bill St. John of the Whittier, California, Gem and Mineral Society operating a drilling machine designed by Sol Stern, a fellow member. The drill features an automatic electric cut-off to avoid breaking through the bottom of the slab. (Courtesy Frank Hewlett Photography, El Monte, California)

10 | *Cabochon Gems*

Before proceeding with the actual cutting of a cabochon, we must know what the finished stone will be used for. Will it be used in jewelry; if so, what kind? Or, if intended as part of a collection, are shape and size important? The answers to these questions give purpose to your cutting and lead to more worthwhile results.

■ SELECTING A STYLE OF CUT

The shapes of cabochons are many but only a few are standard. These are: the oval (really an ellipse), circle, angular or polygonal, heart, pendant, and cross. Hearts and crosses are attractive but difficult to do. A variety of shapes is shown in Figure 73.

The selection of a shape must be governed by practical considerations. The long, narrow navette, for example, is intriguing, but if meant as a ring stone, it presents serious problems. Not only is it more difficult to set, but its sharply pointed ends may catch on clothing and result in bending or breaking the ring. Cabochons are seldom practical for brooches

unless cut thin in cross section to reduce weight. If too heavy, they hang improperly from the clothing. Commercial cutters cut such stones thin, sometimes even hollowed on the back, and always with the idea that gem material is more economically used in thin slices. Earrings of the screw type are easily lost if too heavy; they must be cut thin to be practical. Bracelet stones cannot be too large. If meant to be set in a series of links, they should be small enough to allow the assembled bracelet to curve smoothly and gracefully around the wrist.

Cabochons are sometimes cut thick deliberately, as in the case of moonstones, catseyes, and star stones, or gemstones which are too fragile to be cut thin. Amazonite, the lovely green feldspar, for example, possesses several easy cleavages, and unless it is cut thick it breaks apart during cutting. Some transparent and translucent gems, such as amethyst and rose quartz, may, in thin sections, look washed out. Obviously, color intensity determines how thick such gems should be cut.

Cabochon shapes are classified not only as

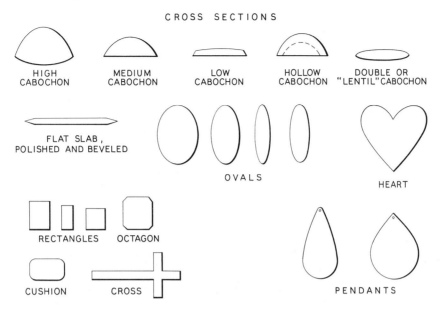

Fig. 73 Various cabochon shapes.

to outline but to cross section as well. The most common is flat on the bottom with a curved top. Starting from sawed slabs, this kind is easiest to make and also easiest to set in jewelry. If both top and bottom are rounded—the top usually more so—it is known as a "double-cabochon." If thin, it is called a "lentil" in allusion to its bean-shaped cross section. The hollow cabochon is used to lighten color. The back of the stone is ground away with sphere-shaped cutters and polished. It is almost exclusively used for dark red almandine garnet or "carbuncles," which would appear black without such hollowing. Simple yet highly satisfactory large stones are made from thin, flat slabs polished on both sides and the edges finished in single or double bevels. This cut is well suited to pendants and brooches.

The upper curvature of cabochons is further classified as to steepness of curve. A shallow curve makes a "low" cab, and as the curve steepens, "medium" and "high" cabs. All of the forms and cross sections mentioned are shown in Figure 73.

■ ORIENTATION

Many minerals show special effects due to certain optical properties or in-clusions. The silvery or bluish sheen of moonstone is due to an optical property, while the bright streaks of light which cross the apex of star stones are a visual effect due to many fine hair-like inclusions. In order to show these effects to their best advantage, it is necessary to cut the gem in a certain direction. The determination of this direction is called *orientation*. Each effect will be described, as well as how to take advantage of its presence in rough gemstones.

Play of Color. Only opals display shifting hues as stones are tilted back and forth. This effect is called *play of color*. Light rays are broken into exceptionally pure prismatic colors as they traverse the stone but the colors are stronger in certain directions than in others. Much Australian white opal occurs in seams and in these, the best color is seen edge on, as shown in Figure 74. If the seams are thick enough, stones should be cut across them. Black Australian opal is seldom found in more than wafer-thin seams and special care must be used to get worthwhile gems. A thin seam of good color is flattened on one side until the color begins to show, then a flat piece of waste opal is cemented to this side to add thickness. The stone is turned and the opposite side

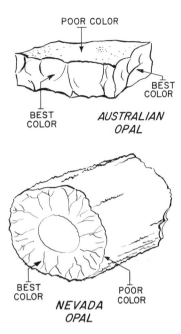

Fig. 74 Orientation of opal to obtain strongest play of color in finished gems. The best color in Australian opal often occurs on edges of seams. Similar differences are noted in Virgin Valley, Nevada, opal. The latter commonly occurs as precious opal replacement of wood limbs, as shown here.

cut into a very low cabochon which when completed is called a "doublet." This construction is made necessary solely by the thinness of the gorgeously colored seams; of course, better gems result from thicker rough.

Catseye Gems. If a transparent or translucent mineral contains numerous thin, hairlike fibers of another mineral, light reflected from a polished surface displays a fibrous sheen like satin or silk. This effect is called *chatoyancy* and is responsible for the streaks of light in catseye gems and star stones. Almost any fibrous gem makes catseyes but the best are cut from minerals which would be transparent were it not for inclusions. Orientation for cutting is simple—the fibers must lie flat on the bottom of the cabochon. If the stone is oval in outline, the fibers must also lie across the long axis of the gem. The making of a catseye from a piece of tourmaline is shown in Figure 75. The only real trick is to be sure that the base of the cabochon is parallel to the fibers.

Star Stones. Two or three sets of needles in a gemstone provide stars, or the effect known as *asterism*. Each set of needles gives off its own line of light and if the stone is properly oriented, cross on top to produce the star. If two sets of inclusions are present, a four-legged star will be produced; if three, a six-legged star. Unfortunately, most star stones contain very minute needles which are less easily detected than are the single sets in catseyes, so some care and extra trouble are required in locating the apex of the star. The simplest way is to round off and polish about one third to one half the surface of the rough and inspect this area directly under a point of light, such as a single overhead bulb or a pencil flashlight. Tilt the stone slowly back and forth and note where the legs cross; mark this spot with an aluminum pencil. Recut the stone to place this spot on top of the finished gem. Even if the apex of the star is not seen, any two legs converge toward the cross-over point and the latter can be located with reasonable accuracy. Examination must be under a single-point source, *not* diffused light such as that from fluorescent fixtures and bulbs covered with milk-glass bowls. Have the light directly overhead during examination. Figure 76 shows how star stones are produced from either well-formed crystals or from irregular bits of rough. Figure 77 shows

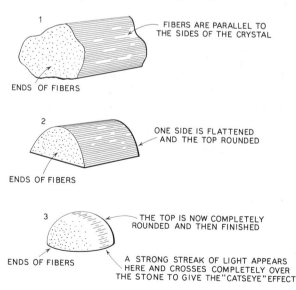

Fig. 75 Producing a catseye from a tourmaline crystal.

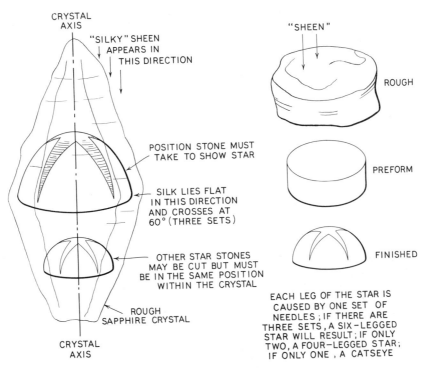

Fig. 76 Producing a star gem from a sapphire crystal.

both a splendid catseye and star ruby, each with strong, well-defined streaks of light.

Chatoyant Gems. Not all gems showing chatoyancy produce catseyes and stars; fibers must be straight for either to be possible. Much material is found with crumpled and twisted fibers thereby eliminating catseyes and stars but permitting others almost as attractive. In these, the reflections of light will be twisted and bent in graceful, silky highlights, making shifting patterns of light and dark as the stone is moved back and forth. The most popular material in this class is tigereye, a form of quartz enclosing thousands of fibers of golden and blue color. Best effects are obtained by slabbing the rough as nearly parallel to the fibers as possible. Since an eye effect is impossible, the gem can be made with the fibers running across the outline at any angle as long as they are roughly parallel to the base of the cabochon.

Aventurescence. When a clear gemstone contains many small, flat inclusions which strongly reflect light, the effect is called *aventurescence*. Quartz and feldspar commonly show this effect and are used to make attractive gems. In most cases, the platelets are arranged in a certain plane and the base of the cabochon must be cut parallel to it. Aventurine gems are not effective unless the top is cut very low. The most prized variety is a feldspar from Norway with numerous reddish-orange scales that shine all at once when caught

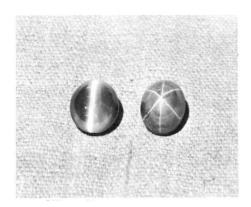

Fig. 77 Catseye and star cabochons. *Left.* Forty carat chrysoberyl. *Right.* Star ruby weighing 33¾ carats. (Courtesy Smithsonian Institution)

under a light, and on this account, is called *"sunstone."*

Schiller. Similar in effect to aventurescence, *schiller* is the technical name given to stones which, by virtue of many flat separations or partings, usually along cleavage planes, show a strong reflection in certain positions. Amazonite often displays schiller, as do other feldspars. Orientation is the same as for aventurine.

Adularescence. Named from the adularia variety of feldspar which displays this effect, *adularescence* is the name applied to the soft bluish or silvery gleams shown by moonstone. In rough material, the effect can be detected easily if the stone is dipped in water and then examined. The stone is turned about under a pinpoint light and the direction of sheen noted. Cabochons must be cut parallel to the side showing the sheen.

Labradorescence. The beautiful display of colors in labradorite feldspar is called *labradorescence.* Normally black to gray, labradorite is unimpressive unless it shows this effect. Then, as the specimen is turned under the light, a startling transformation takes place. Intense hues sweep across the stone, a rich blue predominating, but greens, reds, oranges, and yellows also appearing in some pieces.

The correct orientation procedure for gemstones showing *aventurescence, schiller, adularescence,* or *labradorescence,* is pictured in Figure 78. The stone is held under a strong light so that the rays pass as close to the eyes of the observer as possible. The stone is then twisted and turned until the effect appears on some side of the specimen. It is then taken to the saw and a cut made parallel to this side. Several trial cuts may be necessary at slightly different angles before the effect appears on the sawed surface when held squarely under the light. If it is necessary to tilt the sawed surface to make the effect appear, it indicates that the saw cut is not parallel and another cut should be made to correct the error. During

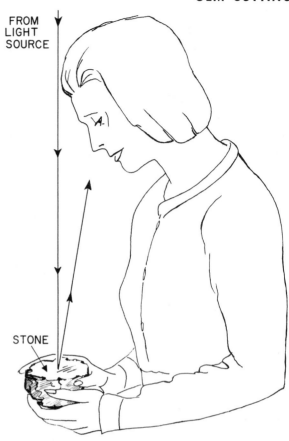

Fig. 78 Orienting feldspar under a light source. The light bulb should be directly overhead and the rays should pass as close to the forehead as possible. The stone is then turned about until the effect appears on top.

examination, the rough material should be dipped in coolant oil, kerosene, or even water to make the effect stand out and orientation easier.

Iridescence. In some chalcedony nodules, deeper layers are coated with thin films of iron oxide. Light reflected from these films is broken up into many colors similar to those seen in an oil film on water. If outer layers are carefully ground down to a little short of the oxide layer, and then polished, the stone appears iridescent. Although grinding as close to the film as possible produces more vivid color, going below destroys the color-producing layer of iron oxide and the effect is lost. Chalcedonies of this type are popularly called "fire" agate.

Iris Agate. Agate is composed of extremely fine crystals of quartz built up in successive layers during growth. If these layers are numerous enough, a thin section sliced through them may show a rainbow display of colors when held at arm's length before a strong point of light. Iris agate, as it is called, is quite rare; however, any agate deposit yielding highly translucent material may also produce iris. The presence of iris cannot be told by appearance alone; a thin slice must be taken off, wetted with oil, and tested in front of the light. In cutting iris agate, slices should be as thin as possible for best color and taken from the center of nodules. Orientation is important, otherwise the effect will not appear unless slabs are tilted. Figure 79 shows how an iris agate nodule must be cut for best results. The saw must cut through the bands in the agate at right angles.

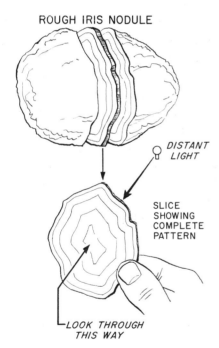

ROUGH IRIS NODULE

DISTANT LIGHT

SLICE SHOWING COMPLETE PATTERN

LOOK THROUGH THIS WAY

Fig. 79 Orientation of iris agate to show best iris effect. The most colorful slices are taken out of the center of the nodules.

Pattern Effects. Many gemstones are cut to produce thin translucent slabs which display beautiful colors or patterns when held to a light. Such *transparencies,* as they are called, are then polished and cemented to glass or plastic and illuminated by a light from behind. Agate displaying complete loops or rings is specially prized since it often combines perfect pattern with vivid coloration. Other patterns are found in many gemstones and the alert amateur watches for them and may prefer not to cut the rough into cabochons but to take slices which can be lapped and polished whole. However, for cabochons, pattern is frequently the most interesting feature, and whenever possible, should be shown to best advantage. Montana, Texas, and Oregon agate frequently contain small areas where other minerals have grown in the form of miniature trees, bushes, etc., or have combined with banding to create landscapes. If such areas are carefully sliced from the specimen and the design is framed by the outline of the cabochon, beautiful gems will result.

■ **CHOOSING CABOCHON MATERIAL**

The beginner is often puzzled and confused by the great variety of cabochon material offered for sale, and sometimes makes poor choices because he does not know what to look for. In the Quartz family alone, there are dozens of kinds of agate and jasper from which to choose, not to mention the many varieties of petrified wood. Whatever material is finally selected should be on the basis of quality, and this can only be told by careful inspection. Good rough must be solid, free of cracks and holes, and uniform in texture. Material with many cracks falls apart when slabs are sawn from it, but even so, if the smaller pieces are colorful and solid, and large enough for cabochons, they may be useful. Natural cracks often show iron stains, and the cracks appear as dark brown to black films. Material which has been broken by hammers is often penetrated by numerous small cracks beneath the places where hammer blows have been applied, and the cracks appear white because they are filled with air. Rough of this sort should be avoided because numerous unseen cracks may be present inside and limit the amount of usable material.

Many kinds of jasper contain soft spots where silica-bearing solutions which permeated the original formation did not completely fill all the minute pores. As a result, such spots seldom take a polish and in many cases, undercut badly. A time honored test for material of this kind is to wet the surface and see if the water remains on top or is soaked up. If it disappears in a few seconds, the material beneath is porous and will not polish. No matter how attractive, it is a poor risk, because no amount of skill will create a good finish. Slabs of cabochon rough are often displayed for sale in flat water-filled pans and of course, look much better than they would if dry. If allowed to soak for awhile, even porous spots will absorb enough water to look sound. Before buying doubtful material, remove the slab and allow the surface to dry thoroughly. By holding the slab to a strong light at a glancing angle so that the light is reflected from the surface, the lack of uniformity in texture, if any, will become apparent.

Soft inclusions which "pull out" during polishing are common in moss and plume agate and in most cases, are unavoidable evils. However, some types are more solid than others and perfect polishes can be obtained. Other gems which contain inclusions and are difficult to polish perfectly are aventurine quartz, poor grades of chrysocolla chalcedony, petrified wood which often contains small crystals of quartz, rhodonite, etc.

What kind of cabochon material should the beginner choose for his first gem cutting attempts? Without doubt, it should be uniform material, hard and tough enough to withstand some abuse, and to allow some mistakes in shaping which can be corrected. In this class is much agate and chalcedony and it is recommended that the first attempt be made upon Montana or Mexican agate, or Brazilian agate. The first cabochon should not be over about ½ inch in size so that progress is rapid and one avoids frustrations. As experience is gained, larger cabs can be attempted in common materials and ordinary sized cabs in some of the softer or undercutting materials. Soft gemstones such as opal should be avoided at first, since some skill is needed to shape them properly.

As a final word, avoid buying large blocks of material unless you own a slabbing saw. The temptation is to break up such blocks and in the process, much good material is usually ruined. On the other hand, if you have a friend who owns a slabbing saw, the block can be sawed on a "shares" basis, the saw owner receiving one third to one half of the yield in slabs for the time and cost involved in sawing. Large blocks may also be sent to various individuals or firms who charge from five to ten cents per square inch for sawing rough.

11 | *How to Cut Cabochons*

C ABOCHONS are ordinarily begun from sections of sawed slabs but they may also be cut from single pieces of rough of considerable thickness, as is usually the case with precious opal, star sapphire, ruby, garnet, and other pieces which do not occur in large masses. When buying slabs or sawing your own, remember that larger stones need thicker slabs. Thin slabs can be used for large cabs but the extremely shallow curvature required for the top is difficult to grind and difficult to sand. On the other hand, an overly thick slab requires much grinding to bring the crown to ideal proportions. The useful range of slab thicknesses runs from ⅛ to ¼ inch but exceptionally large cabochons may need slabs up to ⅜ inch or more. It is best, when sawing, to cut some thin and some thick to cover all possibilities.

Remember to clean the oil from slabs immediately after sawing. A greasy surface hinders marking of outlines and causes other difficulties later. Most slabs have sharp projections left from sawing. Snap these off with a pair of pliers to permit the marking template

to lie flat on the slab. At this stage, some amateurs lap one side of the slab, prior to marking, to remove saw marks and leave the surface sufficiently smooth so that no further finishing is necessary. This step has much in its favor, but unless the saw marks are extremely deep, it is preferable to wait until later.

The choice of the best place on the slab to cut a cabochon must be practical as well as artistic. It does little good to mark the most beautiful pattern or spot of color if a large flaw or crack passes through it. Before outlining, examine the area to see that it is the best available, then turn the slab over to see that the other side is the same quality. The most common fault is trying to make a larger cab than can be reasonably expected. Some gem material is deceptive as far as flaws are concerned and only very careful examination shows the fine, hairline cracks that must be avoided. Massive granular material is most troublesome, while smooth-grained types such as agate and jasper show flaws plainly. When found, flaws should be marked to be sure that they are not included in the cabochon outline. A selection of possible outlines is shown in Figure 80 and illustrates how a large variety of

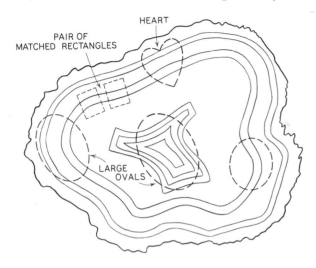

Fig. 80 Various pattern selections on a slab of agate.

shapes can be cut from a single slab of agate. To visualize the best patterns, use the template in the manner shown in Figure 81. As the template opening is passed over the slab, the best pattern will soon be seen and this can be marked as described below.

■ MARKING TEMPLATES

The sweeping graceful curves of a well-cut cabochon are obtained by using templates with openings of many shapes and sizes. When a shape has been chosen, it is marked on the slab and serves as a guide for further work. Draftsmen's templates can be used and are purchased at any store selling drawing supplies. For gem work, several excellent plastic templates are available with openings of "standard" size; in other words, stones cut accurately to fit the openings will also fit ready-made jewelry mountings calling for these sizes. Many beginners make their own jewelry by cutting cabs to standard sizes and then buying the mountings at low cost. All that is necessary to complete the jewelry is to bend some prongs over the stone. If mountings are handmade, standard sizes are not im-

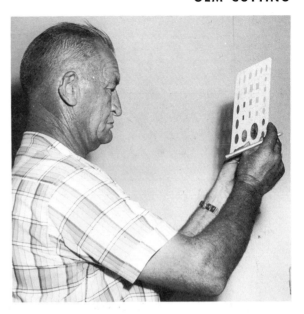

Fig. 81 Nick Potskoff of the Walt Disney Gem & Mineral Society shows how a template and a slab of gem material are held to select the best pattern for marking a cabochon. View in the society's shop on the studio lot. (Courtesy Circle C Walt Disney Productions)

portant, since the mounting is made to fit the gem and not the other way around. In the jewelry trade, stone sizes are given in millimeters, of which there are about 25 to the inch. Thus a gem of 12 by 10 millimeters measures about ½ inch in length and about ⅖ inch in width. Illustrations of marking templates appear later in this chapter.

■ MARKING PENCILS

Lead pencils are not much good for marking gem material because the graphite washes off too easily. Bronze and aluminum wires or rods are much better and should be used instead. Grind a narrow point on the end to be used.

■ OUTLINING

When ready to mark the slab, lay the template flat, insert the sharp point of the metal pencil into the opening, and run it along the inner edge, as shown in Figure 82.

Fig. 82 Marking an oval stone using a plastic template and pointed piece of aluminum wire.

Get as close to the edge as possible, tilting the pencil as shown in Figure 83. The mark must be easy to see at all times, so retrace if necessary without thickening the line. Although this is a simple operation it must be

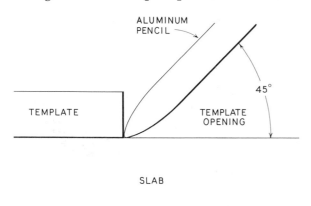

Fig. 83 The proper way to mark a cabochon outline.

remembered that the pencil outline is your only guide to accuracy and therefore it must be marked with care. Since the metal point wears quickly, have a file or piece of sandpaper handy and resharpen for every outline.

Remembering that the marked side of the slab will be the *bottom* of the cabochon, be sure to place the mark on the *poorest* side of the slab so that the best side will be the top of the finished stone. Be sure to line up the outline correctly with the pattern on top of the slab. Some amateurs do this by making an outline on the best side of the slab first, then re-marking the bottom after the slab section has been sawed from the rest of the slab. A recent innovation in cabochon templates makes this job far easier than it used to be. The new template is made with two identical sides separated by a space of about ¼ inch. The slab is slipped in between and when the best outline is found, the template and slab together are turned over and the same outline inscribed on the other side. In this way there is no chance that one will make mistakes and find out, too late, that the best pattern is being cut away during shaping because the outline was marked in the wrong place.

■ TRIM SAWING

Marked slabs are trim sawed to cut away the cabochon blanks. Before using the saw, clean off the table to prevent chips of stone getting under the slab. A tippy slab is hard on the blade and can cause it to jam, usually resulting in breaking the slab. Do not saw too close to the outline—for safety's sake leave ⅛-inch clearance. Even tough gem material chips, and sawing too close causes chipped places to run over the template mark. Slow straight feeding eliminates serious chipping.

Blanks are further sawed to remove large projections, leaving the inscribed outline surrounded by a series of flat cuts.

■ NIBBLING

Since the trim saw makes only straight cuts, the blank is surrounded by triangular projections of waste material. Instead of grinding these away, which is a tedious job, a pair of pliers is used to break off or "nibble" the useless points. An ordinary pair of slip-joint pliers—the cheaper the better—can be used and if the jaws are reground, will last for a long time. Figure 84 shows nibbling of a cabochon blank.

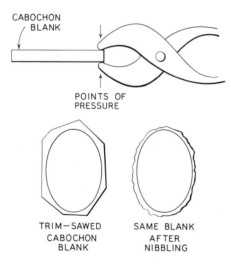

Fig. 84 Nibbling a cabochon blank.

To work the pliers successfully, strong pressure must be used and at the same time, the blank must be twisted to break off a chip of stone. A little practice is needed to get just the right balance between pressure and twist-

ing. Twisting alone is usually fruitless because most of us do not have enough strength in our hands to break a tough piece of gem material, while pressure alone generally results in crushing the edges of the blank without, however, removing more than a few scraps of material.

Not all gemstones can be nibbled. Some, such as jade and rhodonite, resist all efforts to do a good nibbling job, but others, such as agate, nibble easily. It pays to practice on scrap material from the same slabs which will be used for gems. Test them and see how they behave. Materials which cannot be nibbled must be ground to shape.

■ GRINDING THE OUTLINE

After nibbling, the blank is ready for grinding. In this step, the stone is held lightly against the coarse grinding wheel and projecting points removed. The stone is held with the aluminum mark uppermost, where it can be seen at all times. Grinding continues until an even $\frac{1}{16}$ inch border encircles the mark. Do not grind closer because some material must be left to take care of losses in later steps. It is also true that no matter how carefully marks are made, they actually fall short of the true size because the pencil point can never go entirely into the corner of the template opening. The border compensates for this and for the reduction in size due to later work. In grinding the profile, sweep the blank from side to side to make smooth curves. *Be as accurate as you can!* This is *most* important.

A useful stunt for accurate outlining, which gives a bevel around the stone at the same time is illustrated in Figure 85. A steady-rest is used in front of a vertical grinding wheel, but the secret of success lies in the leather strip which, becoming water soaked, allows the stone to slide about under excellent control. Bare metal or even wood has a tendency to catch the edges of the blank and thus gives jerky movements, which result in irregular outlines. Note how the raising of the steady-rest above the horizontal permits a bevel to be

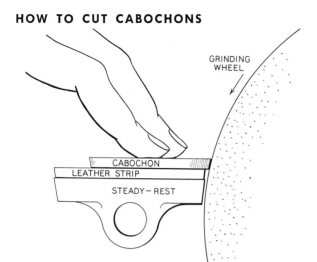

Fig. 85 Profiling a cabochon using a steady-rest.

thick to take care of the double curvature, the profiling operation is followed by marking of the girdle. Inscribe a mark around the edge of the blank and at a suitable distance between top and bottom. This mark serves as a guide for grinding both top and bottom.

■ BEVELING

Refer at this time to Figure 86 which shows the basic steps in shaping a cabochon. Notice that all ordinary cabochons have a tiny bevel ground on the lower edge of the base. This bevel strengthens the corner, which would otherwise chip. Grind the bevel in as you go along, always keeping it a bit ahead of the grinding being done on the sides of the blank. As the blank is reduced to its $\frac{1}{16}$ inch border around the aluminum mark, the bevel should just touch the mark. The blank then looks like No. 1 in the diagram. When this stage is reached, the stone is ground further by hand or can be mounted on a stick to make handling easier and more accurate. Beginners should take the latter step since considerable skill, only acquired after long experience, is needed to grind cabochons without

ground on the edge of the blank. This bevel is necessary on most cabochons to permit them to be fastened securely into settings.

If, by chance, the pencil mark is ground away, it is almost impossible to estimate the proper curvature of the outline, with the result that the shape of the stone will be lost. It is best to remake the outline using a smaller template opening of the same shape.

For double-cabochon blanks, which are cut

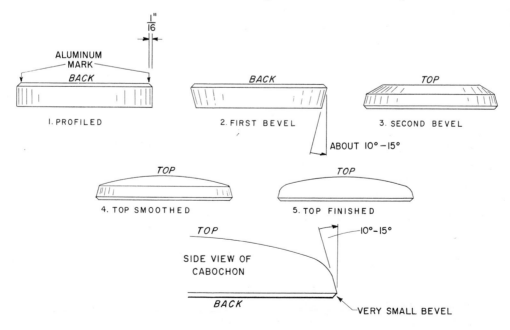

Fig. 86 Shaping the cabochon.

this aid. The stick upon which the gem is mounted is called a *dop* or *dop stick;* the process is called *dopping*.

■ DOP STICKS

Satisfactory dop sticks are cut from hardwood doweling purchased in any lumber yard. The best is maple or birch; doweling made from softer woods, or woods with coarse grain, is not nearly so good. Cut the doweling into 4- to 5-inch lengths, with good square cuts across the ends. Shorter lengths are difficult to grip and longer lengths are awkward. One end of the dop stick is rounded slightly to fit into the palm of the hand without cutting or scraping the skin; the other end is left square.

Because of the many sizes and shapes of cabochons, it is wise to stock dop sticks in diameters of ⅛ to ¾ inch. The most useful sizes are ¼, ⅜ and ½ inch. After some experience is gained, it is more efficient to cut a number of stones at once, going through all stages with each batch and thus saving time. For this reason, a dozen dop sticks of each size are not too much to have on hand.

Metal dop sticks are also available and have the advantage of not absorbing water and swelling. Wooden dowels sometimes swell enough to crack the dop wax.

■ DOPPING WAX

Sealing wax and stick shellac are used to make dopping wax. Most mixes consist of sealing wax, stick shellac, powdered clay, and a small quantity of beeswax. The sealing wax and clay give "body" to the mixture, the shellac adds "stickiness," and the beeswax helps to make the mixture more uniform and lowers the melting point. Under ordinary conditions of temperature, dopping wax shrinks little and is not likely to separate from the gemstone—a very important property. Because commercial wax is cheap and scientifically blended and a little can be used over and over, it does not pay to make your own. After re-

peated meltings, however, all waxes become brittle and when this happens, discard your stock and buy more.

To apply wax, melt broken-up sticks in a small can over a very low flame. Do not allow the wax to pop or fume; wax is weakened by excess heat. When it is thoroughly fluid, dip each dop stick into the wax about ½ inch deep and hold a moment for the wax to make a good bond to the wood. Remove and set upright, wax end down, on a smooth metal plate. When the wax cools, a small cone at the business end of the stick results. This platform supports the gemstone. If more wax is needed to make a larger cone, re-dip after the first layer congeals. Figure 87 shows a series of dop sticks ready to be used.

After dops have been used several times, some of the wax is lost and it is necessary to add more. It is convenient to supply this wax in the form of grains, which can be dipped up by the heated dop and shaped with a cold knife blade, rather than by melting the whole can of original wax. A can of granular wax can be seen in Figure 87 where it is available during dopping. The wax is made granular by melting and dribbling on to a polished metal plate or piece of glass. The cooled driblets are then broken into small bits.

■ DOPPING STEPS

A good bond between gemstone and wax requires that both be hot; a cool joint will break during grinding. The arrangements for dopping are shown in Figure 87. The oven for heating the stones is a fruit juice can with side openings for an alcohol lamp. The lamp should have a wick-trimming wheel to regulate the height of the flame. Granular wax is contained in the low can in the foreground and is dipped up as needed, while to the right is a bottle containing liquid shellac. To the left is a sheet of metal for cooling stones once they have been stuck to the dops. To avoid cracking the stone by overheating, the lamp wick is trimmed until the flame is about ½ inch high. As

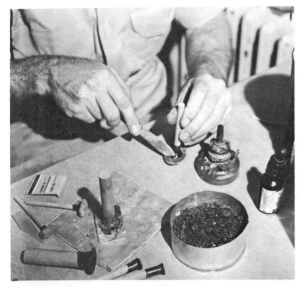

Fig. 87 *Top.* Shaping warm dopping wax about the base of a cabochon. *Bottom.* Making last-minute adjustments to be sure that the gem is square on the dopstick. Note dopping equipment, including warming oven at upper right, alcohol lamp, supply of dopping wax in foreground, and dopsticks waxed for attaching cabochons at lower left.

the stones heat, the flame is raised slightly. Naturally, if the entire top of the can is covered with stones, more flame will be needed to heat them all to correct temperature. To judge the temperature, place a drop of liquid shellac on the back of each stone after it has heated for a few minutes. When it bubbles violently, the gemstone is ready. The shellac also adds

strength to the bond between stone and wax. Stones dopped in this manner seldom come off.

When the stone reaches the proper temperature, a dop of suitable size is held in the lamp flame to soften the wax and immediately stuck to the back of the gem blank. The stone is lifted off the can by the dop stick in one quick motion and set on the table. Mould the wax around the stone and the wooden shaft to form a good support for the back. The dopping process is shown in Figure 87, while the appearance of a properly dopped stone is shown in the diagram in Figure 88. While the wax is still tacky, the stone is carefully centered on the dop, reheating as necessary to keep the wax pliable. This is also shown in Figure 87.

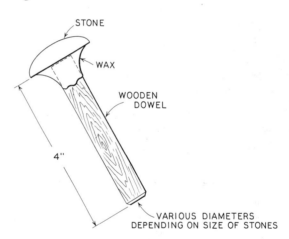

Fig. 88 A cabochon properly dopped.

■ DOPPING SENSITIVE STONES

Most gemstones can be heated to a degree which makes them too hot to hold, but some will crack at high temperatures while others can stand considerable heat if it is applied gradually. Opal and obsidian are heat sensitive and require gentle treatment to prevent cracking. To be safe, consult the remarks about heat sensitivity given for each gemstone in Chapter 19.

To avoid shock, or to raise temperature gradually, place a piece of thin cardboard on top of the dopping can and rest the stones on the cardboard. For one or two stones, a piece of book-match cover is just right. Instead of using liquid shellac to test for temperature, place a tiny chip of stick shellac on the stone. When the chip melts, the stone is warm enough to dop. Stick shellac can be bought at paint supply stores. The use of a chip of shellac is safe and accurate. Without some sort of indicator, it is easy to overheat and crack stones before any sign of danger is noticed.

Sensitive gemstones must not be placed on cold surfaces after dopping; sudden cooling will crack them as easily as sudden heating. They should be placed on paper or cardboard until cold.

■ ROUGH GRINDING THE TOP

After stones have been dopped and readjusted to sit squarely on the dopsticks, set them aside to cool.

Install and prepare the rough grinding wheel for use. If it requires truing, do this after the water has been turned on. Remember that the water is turned on *after* the wheel has started and turned off *before* it stops.

The first step in grinding the top is to put a broad bevel around the edge, sloping from the bottom toward the top at an angle of about 10° to 15°. Study the steps shown in Figure 86; note the sequence and the appearance of the gem after each step. Beveling leaves the cabochon wider at the base, permitting it to be set securely in jewelry. If a vertical wheel is used, proceed as follows. Hold the dop in the fingers of the left hand close to the base of the cab, as shown in Figure 89. Use the right hand to twirl the dop and thus grind an even bevel around the stone. The left hand is the steadying hand and, if the stone is oval in outline, also brings the stone closer and further from the wheel to accommodate the varying width. The right hand also steadies the stone but is used primarily to turn the dop.

Do not try to make the first beveling cut to full depth; take off a narrow cut in one continuous twirl of the dop. Repeat frequently, taking off a little each time until the bevel reaches the base of the cabochon. Be sure that

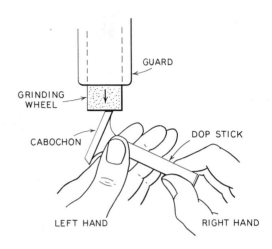

Fig. 89 Grinding a bevel (as seen from above).

this beveling cut does not go *beyond* the base or you will cut into the outline and destroy its proportions.

After the bevel is cut, another cut is made along the top, as shown in Figure 86. If the cabochon is thick, it may be necessary to cut as many as three or four steps to shape the stone. Do not work on a small section of the stone at the expense of other areas. The aim of grinding at this stage is to preserve the form of the cabochon outline and project it upward until the top is smoothly and pleasingly curved at all points.

If a horizontal grinding wheel is used, such as shown in Figure 66, the same grip is used but the stone is *trailed* on the edge of the wheel; in other words, the tendency of the wheel is to pull the stone out of the hands rather than to push it into the hands.

At this stage of grinding, trouble is sometimes caused by soft spots in the stone. Such places tend to grind away faster and therefore require less pressure. Grind once completely around the stone, then check the width of the ground off portion. If the width varies considerably it shows that soft spots are present and these must be ground with less pressure.

Once the top is covered with concentric bevels and the basic form established, smooth out the sharp edges, using the same hand hold as before but with wrists loose and flexible. Sweep the stone back and forth rapidly while rotating the dop with the fingers of the right hand to assure covering all spots.

A few words of caution: the basic shape of the stone is established in rough grinding, do not cheat yourself out of a fine gem by taking short cuts; be sure the top is smoothly curved, avoid that very common fault of leaving a flat spot directly on top of the cabochon; check progress by holding the stone edgewise to see the cross-section; avoid lingering in one spot, the overgrinding which results is as disastrous as cutting one leg of a chair to make it sit squarely, the more you cut, the more correction is needed elsewhere. The scheme of shaping given here produces the final form all at once, not in fits and starts. Common grinding defects are shown in Figure 90.

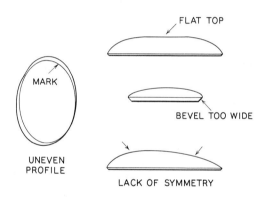

FLAT TOP

BEVEL TOO WIDE

MARK

UNEVEN PROFILE

LACK OF SYMMETRY

Fig. 90 Common cabochon grinding errors.

■ FINE GRINDING

When you are satisfied that the outline is preserved, the bevel evenly cut and the top smoothly curved with no flat spot, the stone is ready for fine grinding. In the last step, the basic form was given to the gem; now the surface is smoothed to prepare it for sanding.

In fine grinding, texture of surface is important and every deep scratch left by rough grinding must be removed. For this reason, the wheel must be dressed as smoothly as possible. The wheel is further smoothed by using a piece of grinding wheel or hard brick held to the face to remove the last few small but sharp projections.

Using light but firm pressure, go over the entire surface of the gem, starting with the bevel. Fine grinding leaves a much smoother surface than rough grinding and untouched spots will be apparent. To be sure that all deep scratches are removed, dry the gem and inspect under a strong light. Mark with pencil all areas that need retouching.

In fine grinding there is a tendency to "burn" the stone because of friction. Burned spots cannot be seen when the stone is wet but can when dry. Burning indicates too much pressure or too little water. Burned spots must be removed before continuing.

■ COARSE SANDING

New sanding cloth is very sharp—used on a small cab it can easily remove enough material in a few seconds to destroy the shape. The purpose of sanding is to smooth and not to shape, and for this reason a new cloth needs to be "broken in" so it cuts well but not too fast. Break in cloth by sanding upper parts of large cabs or a piece of agate pebble. After the cloth is worn a bit, small stones can be handled safely.

In dry sanding, cloth loads up with stone powder and becomes smoother and less abrasive. In time, it develops a glaze and stones sanded on it become almost polished. In wet sanding, the cloth is washed constantly by water, and powder is removed as fast as it forms. A wet sander therefore cuts better for a longer time, but the surface is less smooth. As a second sanding with fine cloth is required anyway, this is not serious and can even be an advantage. The better cutting action of wet sanding cloth is more likely to remove deep scratches, which may be covered over by the superficial gloss of dry sanding. The advantages of keeping stones cool in wet sanding is also of enormous benefit. For the reasons given, it is generally better to use wettable sanding cloth.

Begin sanding on the sides of the gem, then go to the top. As in grinding, keep the stone moving back and forth, using sweeping and rocking motions to round the top. Pay special attention to the center of the top, since this tends to be neglected in sanding as in grinding. Next, give attention to the places where the curve of the top breaks over the edge into the beveled sides. Inspect the stone after every two or three swipes across the sander.

In disk-type sanders, the slowly-moving center gives gentle action when needed while the outside, moving at a fast clip, is quick in action. Disk sanders with raised crowns are useful for removing stubborn scratches because greater pressure can be applied wherever the curve is steep.

In dry sanding, be careful not to overheat the stone, sand a little, then check for heat by touching the stone to your wrist or cheek. It should never become so hot that the dopping wax softens and the stone shifts positions. Carelessness results in the stone coming loose and possibly shattering, while the dop stick rubs against the cloth and smears it with wax.

Drum sanders have a uniform, constant-speed surface, so one place is as good as any other for sanding. Belt sanders provide a slack area between rollers where the cloth curves around the stone and promotes rounding. Areas directly over the roller, or close by, provide firmer and less curved surfaces. By selecting the proper spot, every degree of curvature and stiffness of surface can be had.

Undercutting materials first cause trouble during sanding and it is here that preventive action must be taken. Undercutting is the result of spots of different hardness abrading at different rates; the longer the sanding continues, the more likely are such spots to undercut. To solve this problem, a fast cutting cloth is needed to speed sanding and water is needed to wash off rock dust. Jade, for example, can be sanded on new cloth in seconds, but care is necessary not to distort the shape. During such a quick sanding job, the soft spots do not have time to undercut and the surface cannot help but be smooth. Recognizing this fact, some professionals use diamond powder on leather for sanding, finding the tremendously rapid cutting action of the diamond so effective that hard and soft spots alike cut

away with equal ease. Others sand undercutting materials on well worn and heavily loaded dry cloth, but the process is not reliable for all materials and great heat is generated because heavy pressure is necessary. Much time is wasted in dry sanding waiting for the stone to cool.

Wet sanding is successful for undercutting materials but the requirements are a new or nearly new cloth, a heavy supply of water, and a fairly high speed of rotation. The water tends to create a film which prevents the stone from contacting the cloth except upon sharp points of the abrasive grit. The high speed stiffens the cloth and speeds cutting. Taken together, these conditions practically eliminate serious trouble.

■ **FINE SANDING**

The same steps are used in fine sanding as in coarse sanding; simply substitute a fine grit cloth for the coarse one.

It is sometimes advantageous with very soft minerals to do all sanding on fine grit cloth; however, if a tendency to undercut is noted it may still be best to coarse sand as well.

When fine sanding has been completed, the surface should show an excellent glossy finish, covered with a multitude of minute scratches, all of the same size.

■ **POLISHING**

Preparations are simple. Wash all dopped stones thoroughly, to remove any loose grit. Be sure to scrub behind the gems also. Place a clean piece of newspaper near your work for powder and stones to rest on. If a tub type machine is being used, line the tub with fresh newspaper, clipped into position with clothespins.

Mix polishing powder in small lots only—just enough for the day's work. If an accident occurs and the powder becomes contaminated with dirt, only a little need be thrown away. Whatever buff is needed is now installed and wet thoroughly, a few drops of detergent having been added to the water. After the buff is damp, apply the powder solution with a small brush, dipping with a stirring motion from the pot. A thick paste is wasteful and tends to glaze the buff; it should be permeated with powder solution, not smeared. As in sanding and grinding, adopt a routine for completing the stone. Start with the bevel and finish this before going to the top. Well sanded cabs polish in seconds but if the polish is dull or pitted, you may have an undercutting material and a switch should be made to a leather or wood buff. Wipe the stone with a clean, soft rag or disposable tissue to inspect progress.

Rapid polishing requires firm pressure to build up the necessary friction; avoid being delicate with ordinary stones—use at least several pounds pressure. Grip the dop in such a way that the fingers support the underside of the stone, as shown in Figure 91. Try always to polish with the stone dragging on the buff to avoid catching an edge.

Fig. 91 A cabochon being polished on a felt buff. Note how the fingers support the gem from underneath.

Practically all polishing buffs work best when on the verge of drying. This is most noticeable with leather buffs, where powerful friction or "tugging" develops rapidly as the water evaporates. Although almost-dry buffs promote polish, they also generate heat, and this can build up so quickly that the inexperienced cutter is caught unaware until the stone loosens on the dop, or worse yet, cracks. The cure is not to avoid almost-dry polishing, but to do it in short spurts, checking frequently to see that the gem is not too warm. Jade, rhodonite, and a number of other gemstones, can be heated to the point where the dopping wax melts and they will remained unharmed, but most material will crack at that temperature.

Common polishing mistakes are: not enough pressure used, thereby prolonging the operation unnecessarily and promoting undercutting; failure to inspect the surface, leaving spots unpolished; use of too much powder in the mistaken assumption that if a little is good, more is better; and failure to recognize the "lemon-peel" finish of an undercutting material and not switching to another buff in time to prevent ruining the polish.

■ FINISHING

The bottoms of cabochons may be polished or simply smoothed on the flat sides of grinding wheels. If the material is transparent or highly translucent, a better effect is produced if the bottom is polished. If the stone is opaque or nearly so, polishing is simply gilding the lily. Whatever finish is settled upon, however, the bottom must be perfectly flat, for reasons which will now be explained.

When a cabochon is mounted in jewelry, it is encased in a ring of metal called the "bezel." Inside this ring is a ledge or step which goes completely around and which is put there for the stone to rest upon. When the stone is seated upon this ring, the bezel is bent over the edge of the stone to hold it securely. If the stone is perfectly flat it rests squarely upon the inner ring at all points and makes the jeweler's job easy and the finished mounting strong. If the stone is wavy-edged, slightly curved, or otherwise imperfect, the difficulties in setting are increased, as well as the chances for loosening or breaking the gem. It is essential that the bottom of the cabochon be flat and that the edge which rests on the inner bezel ring be beveled slightly to permit the stone to slip into the mounting without catching. Mountings and stones seldom match perfectly and a little adjustment is usually needed for a proper fit. Forcing a cabochon into a tight mounting without taking off the sharp edge of the gem results in chipping, which is sometimes bad enough to require recutting. Thus, to make the cabochon ready for setting, the finishing operation must provide a flat bottom and a very small bevel to take away the sharpness of the bottom edge.

To make the bottom flat, hold the undopped cab against the side of the rough grinding wheel until saw marks disappear; follow by smoothing on the fine wheel. Do not exert uneven pressure on the gem, as this results in grinding off more on one side than the other. A light, delicate pressure with the fingertips is best. If the cab is small, it is best to redop it backside out. If the stone is dopped in this manner, prevent lopsided grinding by holding the dop stick with the fingertips as near to the cabochon as possible, letting the stone find its own "seat" on the wheel. In most cases, polishing can be done directly from this stage but if the wheel marks are too coarse, they may be removed by lapping, the technique for which is described in Chapter 5.

After the base is flattened, the bottom edge generally is sharper than before because of removal of material. Switching to the fine sander, take a light cut all the way around in a smooth sweeping pass to create the tiny bevel wanted. Repeat if necessary, but be extremely careful not to make the bevel too wide. Strive for a width of $\frac{1}{32}$ inch or slightly less; this gives enough rounding and still allows the bottom of the cab to rest properly in its mounting.

There is nothing one can do to make an undersize stone fit a given mounting; if the stone is slightly oversize, it can be ground on the bottom in the manner described above to lessen its size uniformly. For this reason, errors in grinding to outline should lean toward oversize rather than undersize.

If the back requires polishing, the stone must be redopped. The same steps are used as in first dopping, but a little trick can be employed to make the job easier. Heat stones by holding them over the flame of the alcohol lamp until the wax begins to yield. If a glove is worn on the unoccupied hand, that hand can be used to remove the stone from the stick with an unscrewing motion. Being still hot, the stone is merely flipped around and stuck back on the stick, the wax shaped up and the whole set aside to cool.

Finished gems are cleaned off with alcohol to remove wax. If polishing powder has worked its way into crevices, brisk scrubbing with soap and water may remove it. Sometimes cracks are hairline in thickness, and removal of powder is impossible. The unsightly appearance of such gems can be vastly improved by rubbing in a bit of appropriately colored oil paint or India ink. The pigment soaks into the powder and disguises its presence.

■ **TREATMENT OF ODD-SHAPED CABOCHONS**

The methods just described take care of most cabochons that the amateur will want to cut; however, special shapes, such as hearts, crosses, hollow cabochons, and others, call for special tricks to finish them properly. In hearts and crosses, it is difficult to get into the deep recesses with ordinary wheels, sanders and buffs, but it can be done with care. For grinding the notches, square the edges of grinding wheels until right angles are formed. If possible, support the heart or cross on a steady-rest in front so that the gem is opposite the center of the wheel. In this manner, the edge of the wheel will cut a vertical notch in the angles of the cross or in the vee at the top of a heart. For the latter, it is then necessary to hold the heart freehand to the edge of the wheel and tilted downward at a 45° angle, to bevel the edges of the vee. Great care is needed to prevent overcutting. Sanding of the recesses is not practical except on a drum sander, and even then the tendency is to round the edges instead of leaving them sharp and clean. Some cutters avoid this by sanding the recesses with loose grit on the sharp edge of a hard wooden wheel; others cement sanding cloth to hard wood sticks and do the sanding by hand. Hearts, and even crosses, can be nicely finished by the tumbling process described in Chapter 16.

Hollow cabochons are handled as ordinary cabochons up to the point of finishing the backs. At this time they are dopped in reverse and the hollows ground upon a steel or copper ball-point tool operated in a drill press, lathe, or in a carving machine. Loose silicon carbide grit is used to do the cutting, the methods used being similar to those described in Chapter 17 for carving.

■ TREATMENT OF STAR AND CATSEYE GEMS

No special treatments are required for star or catseye gems once the rough pieces have been properly oriented, as described in Chapter 10. However, the hardness of sapphire, ruby and chrysoberyl prevent them from being ground, sanded and polished as readily as ordinary gems which are much softer. Most cutters find it necessary to use special equipment for these minerals, including separate sanders and polishers as described below.

If the very hard gemstones mentioned above are ground on ordinary silicon carbide wheels, wheel wear is exceedingly rapid while the gemstones seem hardly affected. For this reason, it is strongly advised that as much of the waste portions of such gemstones be removed beforehand by use of the trim saw. The rough gem is outlined with india ink, and the marks coated with a thin film of quick-drying lacquer or varnish to keep them from washing away. Take the gem to the trim saw, and with the gentle support of the fingers of both hands, proceed to saw notches into the stone as deep as possible without actually coming closer than about $\frac{1}{16}$ inch from the outline. The high spots between notches can be broken off or ground down with further touches to the saw blade. With care, a reasonably accurate "preform"

will result. Although there is danger that one or more saw cuts may accidentally be made too deep, the labor saved in rough grinding is easily worth the risk.

After trim sawing, the cabochon is taken to the rough grinding wheel and accurately outlined. At this point it is dopped and the top rough-ground to correct shape. Since polishing of hard gems involves generation of considerable heat which would quickly melt ordinary wax, it is a good idea to cement the stone to a clean dop stick with epoxy resin. This extremely strong cement can be ground off later or removed with a special solvent.

After rough grinding, the surface is made smoother by fine grinding, or it is finished upon sanding wheels of grit-impregnated rubber. The latter are very good and are recommended. However, care must be used not to let the gem rest in one position too long or else a flat spot will develop; keep the gem moving and twirling constantly in this and later stages. After these preliminary steps, all made necessary by the exceptional hardness of the gem materials involved, the stone is ready for polishing.

Figure 92 shows a clever device produced by the M.D.R. Manufacturing Company for grinding, smoothing and polishing hard star or catseye gems. The cups and cup holder fit upon an M.D.R. faceting arbor, and are interchangeable. Three cups are used: one for coarse shaping with 600 grit diamond powder, the second for smoothing with 1200 powder, and the last for polishing with 6400 diamond powder. The cups are made of copper, a metal which accepts diamond powder and retains it well. Similar steps can be performed on a special wooden lap in which three or more grooves are cut, each charged with its own grade of diamond powder. The innermost groove takes the finest grit, the middle ring takes the next coarser, and the coarsest grit is used in the outside groove. Thus any grit slung off while the wheel is turning will not contaminate the neighboring grooves. All diamond powders are applied as grease or oil mixtures, using the appropriate grit mixed with a very little oil or a

Fig. 92 Shaping hard cabochon star or catseye gems on special diamond-charged M.D.R. cups. An aluminum holder is attached to the lap unit of the M.D.R. faceting machine, and copper cups for grinding and polishing are attached in turn. (Courtesy M.D.R. Manufacturing Co., Inc., Los Angeles, California)

dab of vaseline. The mixtures are rubbed on in thin films with the fingertip; the diamond is imbedded automatically by the gem as it is being ground or polished.

Sapphire, ruby, and chrysoberyl gems demand hard pressure to grind, smooth, and polish, yet great care must be used to keep the stones moving, since metal cups or hard wood wheels do not possess the yielding surfaces used in ordinary cabochon sanders and polishers. There is no easy way to finish these gems, and time, patience, and hard work are required.

■ **CUTTING AND POLISHING CABOCHONS BY HAND**

Figure 93 shows a small kit assembled and sold by the Hobby Gems Company for those who would like to try their hand at cutting and polishing cabochons in the least expensive way possible. The principles used, and the raw materials, are the same as described before and only the electric motors used to provide the horsepower in the machine equipment are lacking. You must supply the effort yourself.

The dry method of making cabochons, as shown in Figure 93, is satisfactory because hand rubbing does not produce much heat in the gemstone, or raise much dust. However, others who have worked up cabochons by hand recommend wettable sanding paper or cloth used under water, or at least kept wet throughout the sanding steps. The same may be said for using a grinding stone. Water tends to wash away rock dust as soon as it appears, and to leave the stone and sanding cloth cleaner and faster cutting.

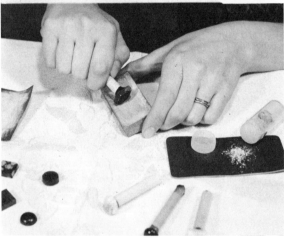

Fig. 93 *Top.* The Hobby Gems kit for making cabochons without machinery. *Bottom.* Close-up of grinding operation in which the gemstone is being given its rough shape. This inexpensive kit includes seven gemstone blanks, silicon carbide 80-grit shaping stone, sandpaper, and polishing pad of cowhide with cerium oxide as the polishing agent. Though patience is required, fine gems can be made. (Hobby Gems Co., Omaha, Nebraska)

Obtain pieces of gem material as slabs or flat chips. Chips should have their bases rubbed flat first to make the base of the cabochon. Mark out the profile on the base using a template or, if this is lacking, a bottle cap or some other object which will give a pleasing geometrical outline. Pliers should be used to nibble the blank in order to reduce grinding to the absolute minimum. For the first attempt, select some soft material such as calcite onyx, turquois, variscite, or other gemstone which

polishes well yet is not as tough as agate. Avoid material with inclusions, pits, or other irregularities which will be unsightly no matter how much effort is expended. Later, when softer materials are mastered, the hand cutter can go to agate and other quartz gemstones.

Using an 80 or 100 grit piece of discarded grinding wheel, or a small silicon carbide sharpening stone, rub the edges of the blank until the profile is shaped smoothly. Do not dop yet. Keep the grindstone wet by sponging with water. If the work is being done on a workbench, nail a strip of wood in front of the grindstone so that it cannot move when forward rubbing strokes are made. After outlining, shape the cabochon top, removing as much material as possible. Dop the cabochon now.

Sanding can be done dry or wet. For dry sanding, silicon carbide cloth or paper bought in a hardware store does nicely. Use a sheet of 100 grit for coarse sanding, followed by 220 and 400. These grades are marked on the back of sheets. Be sure it is silicon carbide abrasive. Garnet or sandpaper will break down too fast because they are not tough or hard enough. To prevent the paper or cloth from tearing, cement to a flat board or fold the edges and tack to the board. A piece of flat rubber sheet placed under the finer grades of cloth or paper allows the surface to yield and produces a more smoothly rounded cabochon. Go from one grade of cloth to another until all coarse marks are removed.

To sand wet, be sure to buy cloth or paper which can be used wet. The back of the sheet carries this information. Using contact cement —the peelable type sold in hardware stores for use with small electric hand buffers and drills— cement a strip of rubber sheet in the bottom of a shallow, flat-bottom dish, possibly a Pyrex pie dish, or a similar metal container. On top of the rubber, cement the coarsest grit paper or cloth. Pour in water to just cover the abrasive surface. Follow usual sanding procedures until the stone is ready for polishing.

The best material for the polishing buff is sole leather or a strip of thin flexible leather cemented to a wood block. The leather is kept moist but not sopping wet. After cementing in place, soak with water to permeate all fibers; later add a few drops of watery powder mix as needed. Heavy pressure brings up a polish in short order, depending on how well the sanding eliminated fine scratches. Use tin oxide or cerium oxide for most materials. Calcite onyx can be polished quickly by adding a drop or two of vinegar to the powder-water mix. For turquois and variscite, let the leather become almost dry to get the final polish.

Although hand cutting and polishing is tedious, it is still an excellent way of cutting many gemstones which are too fragile to stand regular treatment with power machines. Some like to treat opal by hand methods because there is much less chance of generating heat and cracking the gem. Other soft materials such as ulexite, cerussite, etc., can also be cut this way and also small areas of mineral specimens where it is desired to polish a "window" without going to the expense of getting a full set of power equipment. Finally, hand cutting is an excellent project for children since the initial cost is low and there is no machinery involved. As mentioned before, be sure to select gemstones which are fairly soft so that progress will not be discouragingly slow.

12 | *Faceted Gems*

A *faceted* gem is one in which the outside is covered with flat polished surfaces called *facets*. Faceted gems are usually cut from transparent material but some opaque material is also faceted. Reflections from the surface and from the interior of transparent faceted gems provide many twinkling patches of light which appear and disappear with the slightest movement and lend brilliancy even to gems which are quite colorless. The amount of brilliancy is dependent on optical properties of the gemstones themselves and the way in which the facets are cut. Perfectly clear gem material can be fashioned into lively sparkling gems by the skilled cutter or, conversely, can be made into dull and lifeless gems by ignoring the optical properties which make brilliancy possible.

■ REFRACTION OF LIGHT

When a light ray passes from the surrounding air into a transparent material, the ray is bent. How much bending occurs depends on the material itself. This is shown in Figure 94 where a light ray passes from air into a slab of glass. Refraction is shown at 1. Note that a vertical ray passes through without changing its direction; yet even a slight change in the path from the vertical causes other rays to bend sharply just as they enter the glass. After passing through, the rays again bend sharply and continue in the same direction they traveled before. The amount of bending depends on the angle at which the rays strike the glass.

This property of transparent materials has been known for years, not only for glass, but for other substances such as gemstones. The amount of bending is the same for every gemstone regardless of where it is found. Thus a piece of quartz, whether from Arkansas or Brazil, refracts a light ray in exactly the same way. This is true of every other gemstone except that impurities within the stone or changes in its chemical composition also changes the behavior of light a slight amount. A scientist many years ago interested himself in this property and found by tests and mathematical work that the amount of bending could

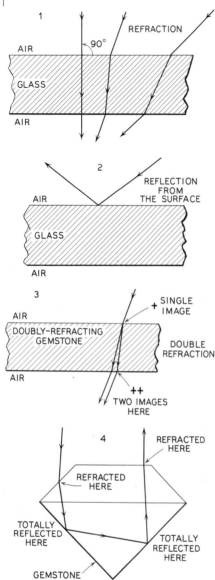

Fig. 94 Refraction and reflection. 1. Refraction of light through a piece of glass. 2. Reflection of light from a polished glass surface. 3. Double refraction in a typical gemstone. 4. Passage of light through a transparent gem, showing total internal reflection.

be stated in a formula and a number obtained which would indicate how strong the refractive power of any transparent substance is. This number is called the *index of refraction* and it is used by gem cutters as an indication of how they should cut the angles on faceted gems to get the best brilliancy. Gemologists, or those who study and identify gems, use a simple optical instrument called a *refractometer*

which measures the bending of light directly and gives a reading of refractive index.

What practical effect does the refractive index have on the cutting of gems? Refer again to Figure 94, this time to sketch Number 2. Here we see that if a light ray strikes the surface of the glass at a low angle, the light bounces from the gem or *reflects*. This property of polished substances is too well known to describe further, but the fact remains that a gem of *higher* refractive index reflects light much better than one of lower index. In the diamond, for example, this reflective power is so pronounced that very strong reflections from the surface of cut gems add a great deal to the total brilliancy and helps to make diamond gems as dazzling as they are. On the other hand, once light passes inside a cut gem, such as is shown in cross-section in sketch Number 4, it is bent when it first enters, or is *refracted*, then passes on to the back facets and is *reflected*, and finally leaves through the top. Again it has been proved that gemstones of higher refractive index can do a better job of refracting light and therefore appear more brilliant *providing they are cut correctly*. In any faceted gem the angles at which the facets are placed around the outside are designed to give the best brilliancy; they are *not* put on in haphazard fashion. This is where the skill of the cutter comes into play because he must know with what kind of gemstone he is dealing and how to place his facets so as to get best results in the finished gem.

■ **TOTAL REFLECTION**

Just as light is reflected from the surface of a gem, it is also reflected inside, as shown in sketch Number 4 in Figure 94. However, some light falling on the surface of the gem from the air is always refracted inside, but curiously enough, *all* of the light which strikes back facets within the gem is reflected and is therefore said to be *totally reflected*. However, the angle at which the light ray strikes the back facets is extremely important because if it is too steep, the light will leak out the back of the gem and will not reappear on top. This leads to the dull and lifeless gems mentioned before. Again the angles of the facets make the difference, and again the amount of inclination depends on the refractive index of the gem material. The angle varies but little from gem to gem, but is enough so that cutters take it into consideration when preparing faceted gems. Angles for the top and bottom of the gem are listed for each gemstone in cutting tables as in the table which appears in Chapter 14 where instructions for cutting faceted gems are given. For practical purposes, gems of higher refractive index can be cut slightly thinner than gems of lower index without losing brilliancy.

■ **DOUBLE REFRACTION**

Many gemstones have peculiar optical properties which cause light rays to split into two distinct parts when they enter a cut gem. This is shown in sketch Number 3 of Figure 94, and is called *double refraction.* Calcite, a very common mineral, is particularly noted for very strong double refraction, and, as the photo in Figure 95 shows, a clear piece placed over printed lettering makes it appear doubled. Only a few natural gemstones show strong double refraction, but synthetic rutile which is frequently cut by amateurs, is so strongly doubly refractive that special pains must be taken to orient the rough so that the finished gem doesn't look "fuzzy."

■ **LIGHT PATHS IN A GEM**

Now that some of the important optical properties of gemstones have been discussed, it is time to look at several gems in cross-section and see how their cutting either takes advantage of the optical properties or ignores them, to the detriment of the finished product.

In A of Figure 96, a faceted gem has been cut too shallow. Light rays entering from the top strike the back facets at an angle so steep

Fig. 95 Double refraction illustrated by a piece of clear calcite laid over print. Note the doubling. (Courtesy Smithsonian Institution)

that they do not reflect properly and are lost through the back. A gem cut this way is dull and lifeless.

In B, the gem is cut too deep and the light rays again escape even though they were totally reflected once.

In C, an example of a properly cut gem, the light rays are totally reflected as they should be, and come back out through the top of the gem to give the desired brilliant effect. In this sketch, the parts of a faceted gem are labeled and these names will be used from now on. The *girdle* is the widest part of the gem and is used by jewelers to grasp the gem in its mounting. It is usually made as thin as possible but not so thin that it breaks easily. The part of the gem above the girdle is called the *crown.* It consists of small facets surrounding one very large facet called the *table.* Most of the light which enters and leaves the gem passes through the table. The bottom part of the gem, called the *pavilion,* consists of many small facets which draw to a point at the tip. The pavilion facets must be cut at the proper angles if brilliancy is to be obtained but considerable latitude is allowed in crown angles without seriously lessening brilliancy.

Also shown in Figure 96 are *crown angles* and *pavilion angles,* or the ideal angles which will give full brilliancy. These are the angles previously referred to which are always given in cutting tables. The cutter sets these angles on his faceting machine to insure that the finished gem will be fashioned properly.

■ GEM ANGLES AND PROPORTIONS

In general, good brilliancy in transparent faceted gems is obtained by cutting the crown angles from 40° to 50°, and pavilion angles from 39° to 43°. The lower angles are used for gems of higher refractive index while the steeper angles are used for lower index gems. In other words, a gem of higher index can be cut somewhat shallower and still be brilliant. A table of recommended angles is given in Appendix 3; each gemstone described in Chapter 19 also has its proper angles given in the cutting instructions.

Proportions generally accepted for producing a pleasing gem are to make the table facet about 50 percent of the diameter. In the case of oblong step cuts, this is 50 percent of the narrower width of the gem. The depth of the top or crown is about one third the total depth, while the pavilion depth is about two thirds. These proportions change a great deal for step cut gems made for rings. In a ring, if the gem is too deep, the ring tends to tip over and causes much annoyance to the wearer. Trade cutters therefore cut large stones considerably shallower so they do not become too high. However, much of the reflective power of the bottom facets is lost since they have to be cut below the recommended angles. In general, for jewelry, it is not practical to cut large stones to best proportions, and only the smaller gems are so treated. Amateurs who have no intention of setting large gems in jewelry can and do cut them correctly of course.

■ THE IMPORTANCE OF SURFACE FINISH

The diamond is noted for clear, crisp brilliancy. This superior brilliancy is not due so much to its high refractive index as it is to the fact that a superior polish can be ob-

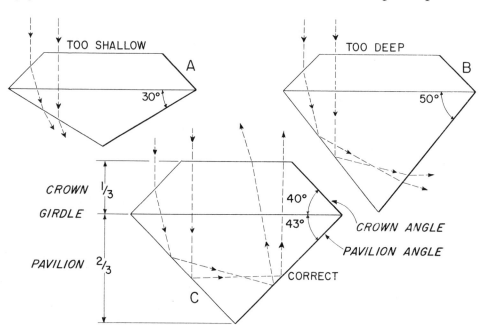

Fig. 96 Cross-sections of three faceted gems showing effects of cutting too shallow(A), too deep(B), and cutting correctly(C). Only in C do the light rays falling upon the gem reflect back through the top to give the desired brilliant effect. Also shown are correct proportions and angles for quartz.

tained on its facets. A good polish does two things: it allows maximum light to enter the gem, and the maximum amount to reach the eye, resulting in pronounced brilliancy. Any gem is greatly improved if its facets are polished perfectly flat, but unfortunately this is not fully appreciated by many cutters, with the result that their gems, although prepared with great care, fall short of being as brilliant as they could be. An imperfectly polished surface can have small pits or scratches, surface ripples or grooves left from the polishing lap, or rounded facet edges from using soft laps. Light striking such irregularities is scattered in many directions and much of it is lost. The importance of a good finish on faceted gems cannot be overemphasized.

■ COLOR

In many gemstones, color varies according to the direction in which the specimen is viewed. In green tourmaline which occurs in long, pencil-like crystals, the color through the sides may be bright bluish-green but a dingy brownish-green through the ends. Such gem minerals are called "dichroic" which means "two-colored." Dichroism varies considerably from gemstone to gemstone; sometimes strong, sometimes weak, and sometimes missing altogether. Figure 97 shows a typical Brazilian tourmaline crystal in which dichroism is pronounced. All sides of the crystal show an excellent bright green color, but through the ends, only an olive green is seen. A step-cut gem is properly oriented inside the crystal to show how it must be cut to put the best color "face up."

Dichroism should not be confused with *color zoning* or the occurrence of several differently colored areas in the same piece of rough. Color zoning and banding in a number of common gemstones are illustrated in Figure 98.

Since gemstones showing strong dichroism are often much better colored in one direction than another, the alert cutter studies each crystal to determine what the colors are and

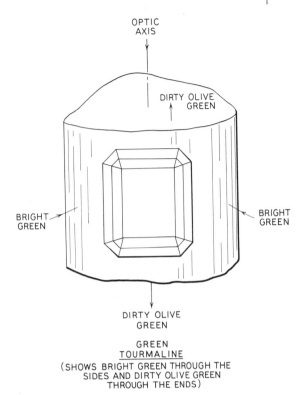

Fig. 97 Step-cut stone placed in a green tourmaline to show best dichroic color.

in which direction the gem should be cut to get the best color on top. Blue sapphire, for example, is often green through the sides and it is only through the ends that the prized blue appears. Other gems show this property to a degree that makes proper orientation worthwhile if not necessary.

Color is often distributed unevenly throughout a gemstone. It may be in bands, indefinite clouds, and sometimes in several colors at once. Although it is best to buy rough with even color distribution, there are certain gemstones which seldom show evenness, and the lapidary must make the best of it. When two colors are present, they may combine to give a third. Australian sapphire shows this effect when banded in dark blue and yellow, producing by combination, a shade of green.

Very dark colors prevent cutting of large stones even if the rough is otherwise suitable; a large stone only wastes the material, since it appears black. It should be cut into smaller stones, each capable of showing the color to

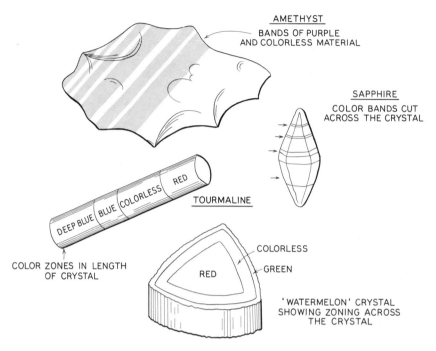

Fig. 98 Color zoning and banding in gemstones.

best advantage. Brazilian tourmalines, especially dark blue ones, seem quite black if cut in sizes larger than a carat or two. Australian sapphires suffer from this defect also and fail to show a good blue unless cut into very small gems. Sometimes a large gem can be cut from dark rough if it is cut shallow; however, this destroys the ability of the back facets to reflect light and the brilliance is seriously impaired.

■ **SELECTING FACETING ROUGH**

Buying rough for faceting is more difficult than buying cabochon material. Mistakes are more costly since the rough is far more expensive. Surface appearance does not always tell of the quality inside, and it is the inside, not the outside, which counts.

The shape of rough makes the difference between a small loss in cutting or a large one. Facet rough is usually sold in whatever shape it happens to be, therefore an awkwardly shaped piece costs just as much per gram as a piece already shaped like a preform. Tourmaline crystals, for example, are long, narrow pencils with triangular cross sections. Since

tourmaline is usually cut in emerald style, it is almost preformed by nature and little is lost in the cutting. On the other hand, citrine, amethyst, and beryl are sold in irregular chunks covered with concave fracture surfaces. If such pieces are spherical or cubelike, they can be cut with very little waste; but thin, elongated, or extremely jagged pieces are seldom economical, because nothing can be done but to grind off all projections, for which as much money has been paid as for the usable parts.

Flaws near the surface can usually be removed while preforming but beware of those that extend toward the center. Little can be done with such pieces except to save small clear areas. Always examine rough from all angles. Try to visualize what shape of stone could be cut. Estimate how much will be a total loss; if the amount exceeds 60 percent, think twice before buying because even more will be lost in cutting a gem from the good part. Flaws can often be seen by examination under a shaded desk lamp, as shown in Figure 99. Tilt the shade so that the light does not strike your eyes. Hold the rough just under the lip of the shade so that half is lit by the bulb

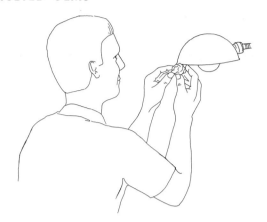

Fig. 99 Examining facet rough. The specimen is held at the edge of the light shade in such a way that the light shows flaws, cracks and inclusions. The eyes of the observer are above the lighted area in the shadow.

and half is in shadow. The light passing into the stone illuminates inclusions and other imperfections against a dark background. Inspect from all angles because some inclusions light up only at one point. The stone must touch the edge of the shade to prevent blinding surface reflections from confusing your view.

Examine next the distribution and quality of color. Many gemstones show sharp zones or bands of color which must not appear on top of the finished gem. If the banding is such that this cannot be avoided, look for another piece of rough. Where colors are in pleasant contrast, as in multicolored tourmaline, exceptionally handsome stones may be cut to show the contrasting hues, but, as a general rule, avoid rough with a pronounced color banding.

In gemstones with distinct cleavage planes, look to see if any appear in the rough piece. Such planes show themselves by silvery reflections or small rainbow-colored rings. If cleavage flaws are left in the preform, they may enlarge later and cause the gem to fall apart.

The size of faceting rough varies depending on what mineral it is. Some, such as pyrope garnet, are never found in large pieces, others, such as aquamarine, are commonly found in fist-sized pieces or larger. Therefore one cannot ask for large pyrope rough but can ask and get

aquamarine rough as large as wanted. Size of rough is also important in respect to color; the deeper the color, the smaller the gem must be cut to remain "lively" and colorful. Rough of large size is sold at top prices but if such pieces cannot be cut into one large stone because of color, it is better to buy smaller and cheaper pieces. A good rule of thumb in buying colored rough is: if you can see the back of the rough clearly while examining under a good light, that piece will turn out a gem sufficiently light in tone to be worthwhile; if the rough appears black and color is seen only by looking through it toward the light, it will not cut into a satisfactory single stone but may be acceptable if cut into several small stones.

■ IMMERSING GEM ROUGH

A better way to examine the inside of facet rough is to place pieces in a liquid which has nearly the same refractive index. Everyone has done this with ice, which when placed in a glass of water, seems to disappear except for the bubbles inside. This happens because the refractive index of ice is close to that of water. The same thing happens to gemstones when put in fluid with nearly the same refractive index; the exterior with all its confusing reflections magically disappears and only the flaws inside are visible. Immersing gem rough has the advantage in that the material is not harmed in any way. A flat spot, called a "window," could be polished on the rough to look inside, but since most rough is bought on approval, and must be returned to the dealer exactly as received, this is not permitted.

Immersion fluids can be of any kind providing that they are reasonably close to the index of the stone. If nothing else is available, kerosene, mineral oil, castor oil, oil of cloves,—almost any fluid is better than nothing, however, the closer the match, the clearer the results. The following table lists some fluids which can be used. Most druggists can order them for you if they do not have them in stock.

Table of Immersion Fluids

Fluid	Refractive Index	Gemstone	Refractive Index
Glycerine or turpentine	1.47	fluorite	1.43
		opal	1.47
Toluene or **xylene**	1.49	moldavite	1.48
		obsidian	1.50
Oil of cloves	1.54	feldspar	1.54
		cordierite	1.54
Anise oil	1.55	quartz	1.55
		scapolite	1.55
		labradorite	1.57
Bromoform	1.59	beryl	1.58
		brazilianite	1.60
		topaz	1.62
Monochloronaph-thalene°	1.63	tourmaline	1.63
		andalusite	1.64
		apatite	1.64
Monobromonaph-thalene°	1.66	spodumene	1.67
		peridot	1.68
		diopside	1.69
Monoiodonaph-thalene°	1.70	kyanite	1.72
		spinel	1.72
Methylene iodide°	1.74	pyrope	1.75
		chrysoberyl	1.75
		sapphire	1.77
		almandine	1.77
		zircon	1.90
		sphalerite	2.36
		diamond	2.42
		rutile	2.80

Notes:

1. °Denotes expensive.
2. Fluids printed in bold-face type are most useful.
3. Many of the above attack varnish and paint and are also poisonous. Avoid inhaling vapors and getting on skin or in mouth.
4. Higher than Methylene Iodide, no cheap fluid exists that can be used conveniently for immersion.
5. For closer matching, liquids may be diluted as follows to lower the refractive index: bromoform and methylene iodide diluted with toluene: monobromo-, monoiodo-, and monochloro-naphthalene diluted with benzene.

■ STYLES OF FACET CUTS

There are two basic styles from which all other cuts are derived, the *brilliant cut* and the *emerald* or *step cut*. As shown in Figure 100, the chief difference between the two is in the shape of the facets and their placement about the gem. In the brilliant cut, the facets are triangular or kite-shaped while in the step cut, all facets are more or less rectangular and arranged in steps.

The brilliant cut is particularly suited for colorless or faintly colored stones which, lacking hue, depend on clean, sharp, brilliant flashes of light for attractiveness. Step cuts may also be used for pale or colorless stones but find their greatest use in stones of decided color. No hard and fast rule governs the selection of a cut; the taste of the cutter as well as economic considerations determine which will be selected. Today's taste is toward simple step cuts for most colored stones, even for those only faintly tinged.

The step cut is less complicated than the brilliant, but because each facet is larger in area, grinding and polishing sometimes take longer. Slight inaccuracies in the step cut are easy to see, whereas in the brilliant cut, with its multiple reflections, large errors can go unnoticed. As a rule, small step cut stones are easier to do than brilliants of the same size, but step cuts on stones of about 30 carats are much more difficult.

Figure 101 illustrates a number of cuts used for various gemstones. The *scissors* or *cross cut* combines the rectangular outline of a step cut with the kite-shaped facets of a brilliant. This cut twinkles pleasantly but loses light through the bottom of the pavilion, where the last few facets must be cut at shallow angles to complete the pattern. The *hexagonal mixed cut*, as the name implies, is a mixture of the scissors cut on the crown and the step cut on the pavilion. This is very effective for light colored material. The *oval brilliant* is a variation of the standard brilliant with the facets being angled to fit the narrow elliptical outline. The *rose cut* is a simple pattern, being nothing more than the pavilion of a standard brilliant with an extra facet placed on each main. The bottom is perfectly flat. The rose cut is not brilliant but is useful for cutting dark gemstones which are to be mounted as side stones or as studs on metal surfaces. Very dark garnets and black gemstones are cut in this style. The *French cut* is popular for cutting very small gems since it combines brilliance with an interesting pattern. Many other cuts are employed but only the brilliant and step cut are used extensively.

The number of facets on a gem usually rises with size; thus the fifty-seven facets of a standard brilliant look well on gems up to about 10 carats but beyond that, this number gives too simple an effect. It is customary to add facets to larger gems by increasing the number of rows or by splitting single facets into double facets. Aside from the added sparkle, each facet is also easier to grind and polish.

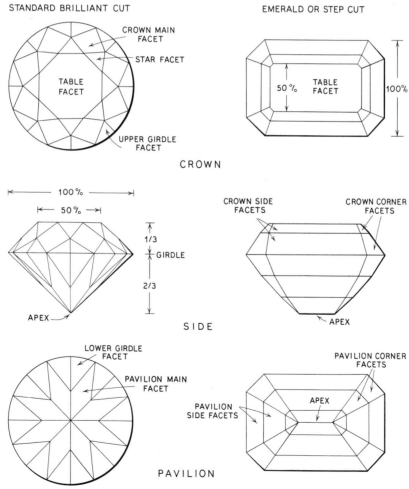

STANDARD BRILLIANT CUT

EMERALD OR STEP CUT

CROWN MAIN FACET

STAR FACET

TABLE FACET

UPPER GIRDLE FACET

50% TABLE FACET 100%

CROWN

100%

50%

1/3

GIRDLE

2/3

APEX

SIDE

CROWN SIDE FACETS

CROWN CORNER FACETS

APEX

LOWER GIRDLE FACET

PAVILION MAIN FACET

PAVILION CORNER FACETS

PAVILION SIDE FACETS

APEX

PAVILION

Fig. 100 The brilliant cut and the emerald or step cut.

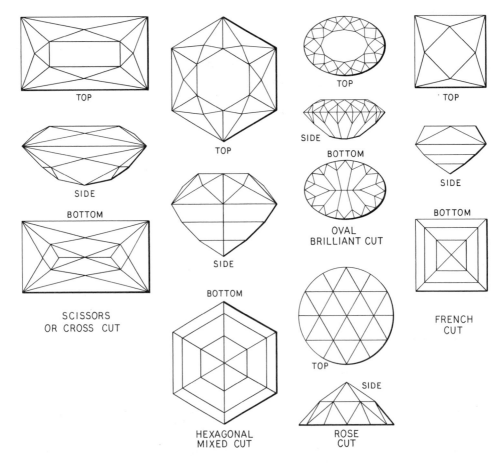

TOP

TOP

TOP

TOP

SIDE

SIDE

SIDE

BOTTOM

BOTTOM

BOTTOM

SIDE

OVAL
BRILLIANT CUT

BOTTOM

SCISSORS
OR CROSS CUT

BOTTOM

TOP

SIDE

FRENCH
CUT

HEXAGONAL
MIXED CUT

ROSE
CUT

Fig. 101 Common cuts for faceted gems.

13 | *Faceting Equipment*

Gems are faceted by cementing them to the end of a dop stick and holding the gem against a turning lap until a flat spot is cut away. After one flat area is made, the stick is rotated and another is cut. This is repeated until a circle of facets surrounds the gem. The position of the stick is shifted up and down to obtain other rows of facets, and in this way the top and bottom of the gem are covered completely. The facets are polished by repeating the procedure with a polishing lap substituted for the cutting lap. The gem is reversed on the dop stick and the facets on the remaining portion cut and polished in similar manner.

Traditional cutting follows the above method with the dop stick being held by hand. The end of the dop is propped against a board or "peg" to insure uniform angles. This is the "jamb peg" method which is still used by most commercial cutters, as shown in Figure 102. Since no measuring of angles takes place, much time and practice are needed to become skillful and to develop the versatility needed to make every kind of cut. Note that in

Fig. 102 Traditional "jamb peg" faceting in Idar Oberstein, Germany. The jamb peg board behind the hand is covered with small depressions in which the sharp end of the dop stick fits. The choice of hole, and of elevation angle, is done by eye while rotation angle is also controlled entirely by hand. (Courtesy Dr. Ing. W. Fischer, Rassmann Photo)

131

Figure 102 the jamb peg is propped against the board in the back which has a large number of holes in it to hold the pointed end of the dop stick. The operator has this much support to help him, but much training is required in placing facets around the gem and keeping a steady hand so that facets are not cut wrong. The elevation of the dop stick determines the elevation angle of each row of facets.

Today's faceting machines, designed for amateurs primarily but also used by professionals, hold the dop rigidly, and there is no chance for error once the proper setting has been made. Thus a long period of training is not needed and anyone can learn to cut faceted gems, after finding how the equipment works and following instructions for its use. For comparison, schematic drawings of modern faceting machines and the traditional jamb peg device are shown in Figure 103. Note that the principle of setting the elevation angles in each is the same except that the mechanical head

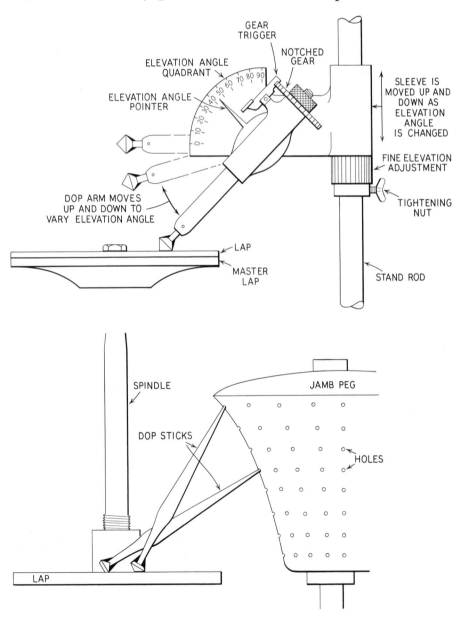

Fig. 103 The principle of the "mechanical head" and jamb peg.

reads off the angle in degrees while the operator of the jamb peg must estimate this angle.

There are a number of mechanical faceting machines on the market designed for amateur and professional use. The principal components consist of a stout *base plate* of metal which ties all parts together and establishes the accuracy of the equipment, a *master lap assembly* which provides a means for turning the cutting and polishing laps, and a *facet head assembly* which holds the gem and permits cutting and polishing at specific angles. Some machines use slightly different ways of setting angles, moving the head up and down, etc., but all work on the same principles. Faceting machines and accessories are most conveniently fitted into their own benches or desks, as shown in Figure 104.

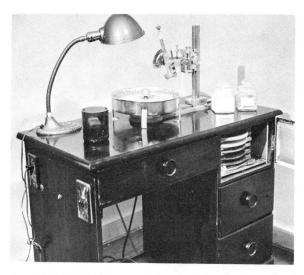

Fig. 104 M.D.R. facet machine and motor drive fitted into an inexpensive desk. All accessories, powders, etc., find storage space. Note polishing and cutting lap storage in top right drawer. (Courtesy Betty Campbell)

■ **FACETING HEADS**

In a modern faceting machine, the assembly used to hold and turn the gem while it is being cut and polished, is called a *faceting head*. Referring to Figures 105, 106, and 107, all of the components are labeled, including faceting heads. The separate components are described below.

The Stand Rod Assembly. This assembly supports the head and allows raising or lowering to any selected point. This change in height changes the angle at which the gem meets the lap, and establishes the angle of elevation. In most machines, the stand rod is a round steel shaft, but in the M.D.R. machine shown in Figure 105, it is a rack and pinion arrangement.

The stand rod is fastened to the base plate, usually by a method which permits it to be moved toward and away from the master lap assembly. This permits stones to be ground at low angles of elevation, or lets the gem be placed on other portions of the lap. Each head illustrated provides a height adjustment and locking feature to keep the head at the selected point. Stand rods must not only support the weight of the head, but must also resist the downward and sideways pressures during faceting. For these reasons, the rod must be strong and stiff.

The Quadrant Assembly. This part is attached to the head or, sometimes forms the support for other parts of the head. It is a quadrant of metal inscribed with an arc of 90° As the facet head is moved up and down on the stand rod, the pointer attached to the dop arm automatically points to the number of degrees in the *elevation angle*. This is the value at which the facets of the gem tilt in relation to the girdle of the gem.

The Dop Arm Assembly. The dop arm assembly is movable up and down. Running through its center is a bearing in which turns a metal shaft holding the metal dop stick at the lower end. This shaft is called the *dop arm*. The upper end of the dop arm is fitted with a gear wheel with a trigger to lock it in any selected notch. This establishes the *rotation angle*, or the placement of the facets as they encircle the gem. In the Lee facet head, shown in Figure 107, the movement of the dop arm backward disengages a pin underneath the

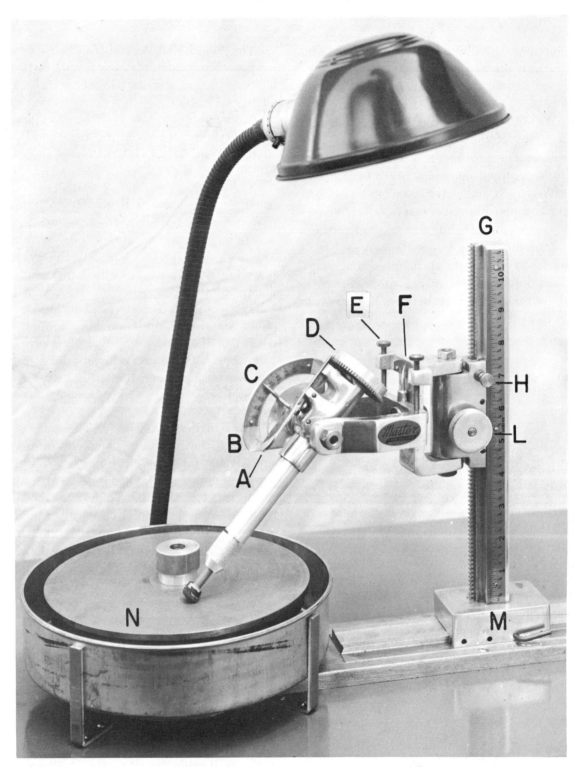

Fig. 105 M.D.R. master lap unit. A. Trigger. B. Elevation angle quadrant. C. Elevation angle pointer. D. Gear Wheel. E. Splitter adjustment screws. F. Splitter pointer. G. Mast (stand rod). H. Height locking screw. L. Height adjustment knob. M. Sliding mast base and lock. N. Master lap assembly. (Courtesy M.D.R. Manufacturing Co., Inc., Los Angeles, California)

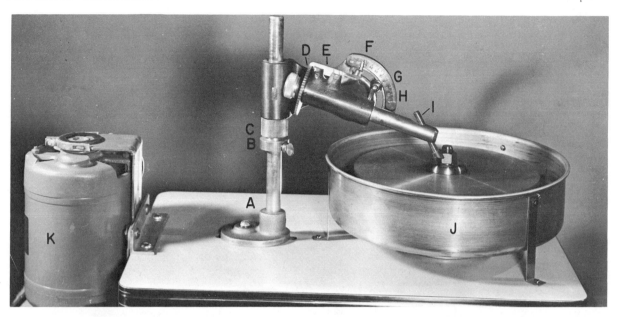

Fig. 106 Allen faceting unit. A. Stand rod and swiveling base. B. Coarse height adjustment. C. Fine height adjustment. D. Gear wheel. E. Trigger. F. Elevation angle pointer. G. Angle stop. H. Quadrant. I. Dop stick locked in 45° hole in dop arm. J. Master lap assembly. K. Motor. (Geoff Cook Studio. Courtesy Belmont Lapidary Supply, Belmont, California)

wheel and permits it to be turned to a new position. Returning the dop arm to the forward position re-engages the pin and locks the wheel in place. Note that the Lee device is not a gear wheel, but it works on the same idea.

The Pointers. There are two on the dop arm assembly, one for indicating angles of elevation, the other for angles of rotation. The latter is sometimes only a bench mark but again the idea is to point to the notch on the gear wheel, or to the pin setting desired.

Angle Stops. To prevent accidentally cutting a facet beyond the correct elevation angle, an *angle stop* is provided on many machines. It is a small locking device which rides in a special slot on the quadrant and can be tightened so the dop arm cannot go below the selected point. It is shown at G in Figure 106.

Dop Stick Locks. The method of locking the dop sticks into the dop arm varies. In the Lee and M.D.R. units, a friction chuck is used; in the Allen unit a setscrew is used.

Gear Wheels and Index Wheels. The movement of the dop arm within the sleeve bearing of the dop arm assembly is checked by engaging a trigger or pin in either a gear wheel or index wheel. Figure 108 shows the 64-notch and 60-notch gear wheels used to facet a variety of cuts. The diagrams illustrate how engaging the trigger in notch 64 cuts facet 64 on the brilliant gem. Both diagrams are drawn as if the reader is looking at the end of the dop arm to which the gem is attached. Gear wheels with 96 notches are available on some machines but none are available beyond this number. This is why a setting splitter must be used to get additional settings.

Setting Splitters. Many gem cuts, such as ovals, hearts, pears, marquises, etc., require settings which fall somewhere between those available on ordinary gear wheels. To get these "split" settings, makers of faceting equipment provide some means for slightly tilting the dop arm assembly, or the yoke holding this assembly. Figure 109 shows how the M.D.R. splitter is worked, while Figure 110 shows the

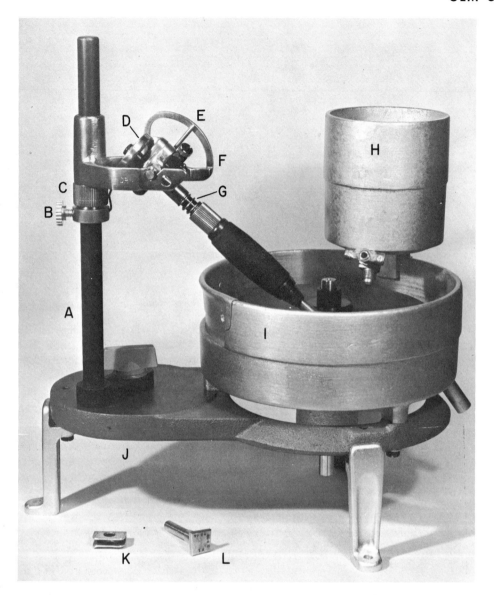

Fig. 107 Lee faceting unit. A. Stand rod. B. Coarse height adjustment. C. Fine height adjustment. D. Index wheel. E. Elevation angle pointer. F. Quadrant. G. Device for quickly changing index wheel settings. H. Water supply. I. Master lap assembly. J. Base plate. K. Girdle grinding attachment. L. Calibration plate for setting angle splitter device (shown to the left and below E). (Courtesy Lee Lapidaries, Cleveland, Ohio)

device on the dop arm assembly of the Lee facet head which is used for the same purpose.

■ MASTER LAP ASSEMBLIES

The *master lap assembly* is so-called because it is fitted with a dummy iron or aluminum "master" lap whose purpose is to support and drive the detachable laps which actually do the work. An accurate assembly is

necessary for accurate work, and the vertical shaft which supports the dummy lap, as well as the latter itself, must run true without wobbling. The lower part of the master lap assembly takes a pulley for a vee-belt to the motor.

The master lap assembly is mounted on the same base plate as the facet head stand rod. The ideal arrangement is a thick metal plate machined flat on top. Such a plate assures

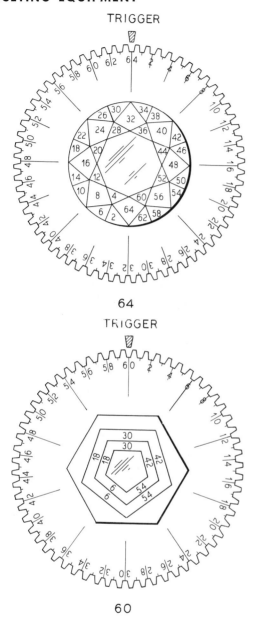

Fig. 108 The use of the 64- and 60-notch gear wheels. The 64-notch gear wheel cuts multiples of four, that is, rectangular cuts, octagons, and a variety of brilliant cuts. A standard brilliant is shown with each facet numbered to correspond to the notch which will be used to cut it. The 60-notch gear wheel cuts multiples of three and five, that is, triangles, hexagons, pentagons, etc. A pentagonal step cut is shown with settings needed to cut each row of facets. A hexagonal outline is shown also to illustrate how it too can be cut with this gear wheel.

alignment of the facet head to the master lap and is necessary for accurate cutting.

■ CUTTING LAPS USING LOOSE GRIT

Loose grit is used to cut facets on steel, lead, typemetal, or cast iron laps and is a fast, economical way to do the job. Its great disadvantage is the mess created by the loose grit particles, which are always troublesome unless carefully cleaned off. If the grit gets into moving parts of the machine or into the facet head assembly, serious wear will occur, while any grit left in the pan or perhaps splashed on the facet head may drop to the polishing lap and scratch the gem while it is being finished. If loose grit is used, all parts of the machine must be washed as well as the hands of the operator. Particular attention should be paid to washing the dop arm and dop stick. Some of these difficulties can be avoided by using silicon carbide grit with a lead lap. Lead is so soft that the grit can be rubbed into it while the lap is running and enough of it will remain imbedded to cut well. The surplus which does not imbed on the lap is washed off before the lap is used. Such laps cut well but like others using loose grit, are seldom used because of the disadvantages mentioned. The size of grit varies from 400 for coarse cutting to 800 for fine cutting.

■ DIAMOND CUTTING LAPS

Copper laps charged with diamond powder are cleaner and far more convenient to use than loose grit laps. Cold-rolled copper plate, ¼ inch thick, is generally used, but for accuracy, the disks should be machined flat and parallel on both sides before being charged with diamond. Lapidary supply houses furnish copper laps, charged or uncharged, but the expense of ready-charged laps leads many amateurs to charge their own. Because so little of the diamond comes off in ordinary handling, both sides of the same lap can be charged, one side with coarse diamond powder and the other with fine. In this arrangement, switching from coarse to fine cutting is merely a matter of stopping the motor and flipping over the lap.

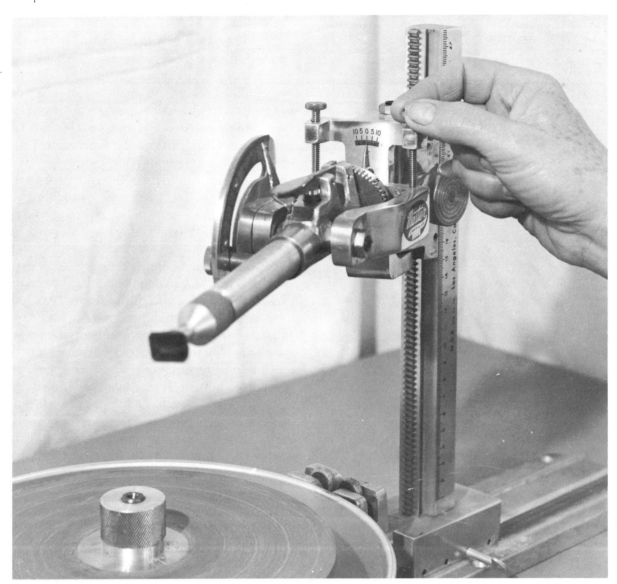

Fig. 109 Using the splitter adjustment on the M.D.R. facet head. The yoke holding the dop arm assembly can be tilted from side to side to "split" settings of the gear wheel. (Courtesy M.D.R. Manufacturing Co., Inc., Los Angeles, California)

■ CHARGING COPPER/DIAMOND LAPS

Two grit sizes are most convenient for all-around cutting, from the smallest and softest stones to the largest and hardest. For coarse cutting, 400 diamond grit combines rapid material removal with a finish smooth enough to go to polish for most stones. However, it is better to use another grit size, namely 1200 diamond, to "touch up" all facets which have been cut on 400 before going to polish. With this scheme, the polish not only comes up faster but there is less likelihood of rounded edges. Another advantage is that the slower cutting of the 1200 grit permits very accurate joining of facet junctions. For very soft stones, all cutting can be done on the 1200 side since material removal is fast enough yet not so rough that the stone is shocked or torn on its surfaces as could happen if 400 were used.

Diamond dust has a peculiar affinity for copper. Actually only the pressure of the thumbnail is needed to get particles to bite in, and trying to dislodge them only sinks them deeper. This is a warning not to let diamond dust fall on a dry copper lap accidentally! If it does, tip the lap and gently remove the dust

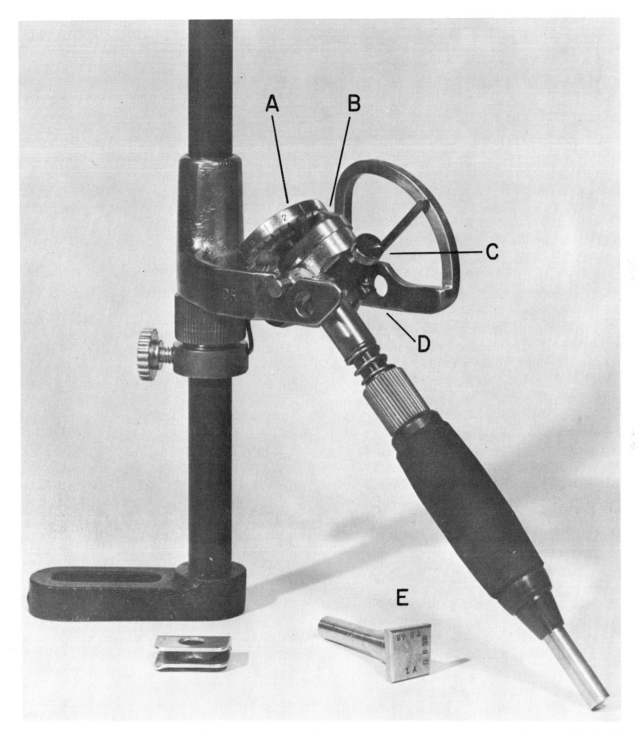

Fig. 110 Lee facet head setting splitter. A. Index wheel. B. Index wheel stop. C. Splitter adjustment screw. D. Splitter shift lever. E. Calibration plate for splitter adjustment. (Courtesy Lee Lapidaries, Cleveland, Ohio)

with a small soft brush. Do not use your fingers since the slightest pressure will cause the particles to stick and you will be in trouble. Too much powder at any point on the lap causes faster wear elsewhere and an uneven surface. This can happen through carelessness in applying the powder, particularly on a dry lap. Charging takes several steps: (1) oiling the lap, (2) spreading the powder, (3) driving in the powder, and (4) cleaning off the oil.

In order to spread the diamond powder evenly, the lap must be first coated with vegetable oil to suspend the powder and prevent it from sticking immediately. Any vegetable oil is about as good as the more expensive olive oil customarily recommended. Using an eye dropper, place about twelve drops of oil on the lap, spotting them evenly over the surface. Rub with the finger until the oil is spread in a uniform, thin film. If the oil is sloppy wet, take some off; the lap must be moist but not too much so. If too little has been put on, add a few more drops and re-spread. Run the lap for a few turns on the machine and spread the oil with the finger at the same time.

When the oil is properly coated, take a vial of diamond powder selected for the charge and tip it over the lap at a slight angle. Turn the vial from side to side to let the powder work its way to the mouth of the vial and dribble over the lip. Dribble tiny specks uniformly over the surface, being sure that each speck is no larger than a pinhead and that no more than about a dozen such specks are put on an 8-inch lap. Use too little powder at first until you get the knack. About ¼ carat in all charges an 8-inch lap. It is not the amount that counts but how well it is distributed. Using the fingertip, gently push the powder around in circular motions until it is as evenly spread as possible. Use the lightest of pressures to avoid sinking in the grains; this comes later. The purpose here is to get the grains in position. Do not put too much powder near the center of the lap and not enough near the rim; both are common faults. None is needed next to the center hole since this area is not used. Be sure, however, to run the powder to the rim.

The secret of success in driving in the diamond powder is the type of tool used. There is nothing better than hard compact agate. Brazilian agate is excellent. Cut a block as shown in the diagram in Figure 111. One of

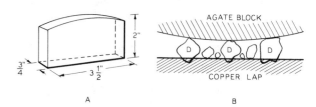

Fig. 111 A. Agate block used for diamond charging. B. Why it pays to get graded diamond powder. As you can see, you pay for the small particles but only the large ones are driven in.

the long narrow sides is then ground into rocker shape and it is this side which is used to imbed the powder. The rocker not only traps the powder as it is scrubbed across the lap but also imbeds it because of the very small area of agate which is actually in contact with the diamond and copper. A steel roller charging tool is shown in Figure 112, and works on

Fig. 112 M.D.R. steel roller designed for charging diamond powder into copper cutting laps. (Courtesy M.D.R. Manufacturing Co., Inc., Los Angeles, California)

the same idea except that the roller revolves as the device is pushed across the lap.

In use, the agate block is applied to the surface of the lap with a hard, scrubbing motion while the lap is motionless. All directions are used in scrubbing, and all areas covered and re-covered. Do this for at least fifteen minutes or until your arm is tired. Use about ten pounds of downward pressure; be sure that the lap is resting on a flat, nonskid surface. Remember not to rest it on the same work spot when charging another size grit; place a clean paper underneath first. After scrubbing, place the lap on the master lap and turn on power. Scrub again by letting the agate ride on the lap; keep it rocking to avoid grinding a flat spot on the curved agate surface. A few minutes of this "clean-up" operation will be enough. After charging, clean the lap with lighter fluid and it is ready for use.

Another excellent way of supplying diamond to cutting and polishing laps is to use commercially-prepared oily pastes containing suitable diamond grit. These pastes are usually color-coded so that the user can tell what size grit is being used from the color alone. The applicators are small plastic hypodermic-type guns in which the paste is already introduced. To use, merely squeeze out the required amount by pressing the plunger. These pastes are spread by the fingertip to cover all lap surfaces uniformly. They are also useful for charging wood laps for polishing hard star stones. The following sizes are commonly available:

Micron Range	Grit Size	Color Code
1–5	8000	yellow
4–8	3000	orange
8–22	1200	blue
20–40	600	red
30–60	325	brown

Courtesy Jack V. Schuller, Park Ridge, Illinois.

■ POLISHING LAPS

A polishing lap is used after all the facets have been cut on the diamond-charged lap. Naturally, a coarse finish on facets requires a longer time to polish, just as is true in cabochon work; but, instead of using two grades of sanding cloth, rough grinding in facet work is usually followed by smooth grinding.

Many cutters use only 400 or 600 grinding and go to polish. For small gems of a carat or so polishing is reasonably fast, but if gems are larger, it pays to cut with 400 and finish with 1200.

The variety of materials used for making polishing laps is endless. Many metals and alloys have been used as well as plastics, wood, cloth, and leather. However, most needs are satisfied by using two basic laps, tin and Lucite plastic.

■ TIN LAPS

Tin, like lead, is very soft and deforms easily. Because of cost, tin laps are usually made by pouring a layer of molten metal on a ¼-inch disk of aluminum. This sandwich lap is then turned on a lathe to make the faces smooth and parallel. The aluminum stiffens the tin and if it were not present, the tin lap would have to be at least ⅝ inch thick. Tin laps are expensive and some amateurs make their own from tin obtained in a junk yard.

To make a tin lap, melt the tin in a clean, cast-iron skillet somewhat larger in diameter than the finished lap. Be sure the skillet is level because a lopsided casting will have to be trued in a lathe with much loss in thickness. Leveling is done with a carpenter's level resting on the edges of the skillet. Tin melts at low temperature and the kitchen range will do for a source of heat. After the metal melts, skim off scum from the top and turn down the flame. After cooling, the casting must be turned in a lathe to finish the sides. If convenient, a slight recess of about 1½ inches in diameter should be turned about the bolt hole. This area will not be used anyway, and the recess makes it easier to scrape the top of the lap later when necessary.

■ LUCITE OR PLEXIGLAS LAPS

The above are trade names for methacrylate plastics. They are remarkably effective for polishing many kinds of gemstones.

They resist wear, are easy to keep in condition and, although rather expensive, last for a very long time. Lucite or plexiglas can be purchased in sheet form and made into polishing laps by anyone who has access to a lathe. It is again advisable to turn a slight recess, about $\frac{1}{16}$ inch deep, around the bolt hole in the center. If the surface is glassy, it should be dulled by sanding with coarse garnet paper.

Plastic laps must be at least $\frac{1}{2}$ inch or even $\frac{5}{8}$ inch thick, to prevent curling and deforming under polishing pressure. Thin sheets may be used but should be cemented together to a total thickness equal to that recommended above.

■ WOODEN LAPS

Several wooden laps are useful in faceting, one for polishing girdles of gems and another for polishing large facets. The one used for polishing girdles can be of any suitable wood and turned without much regard to accuracy or finish; the second, however, must be turned to size on a lathe and the surface carefully smoothed.

The girdle polishing lap is charged with a thin paste of alumina, crushed sapphire or Diamontine powder, cerium or tin oxide, or with Linde A. The latter is expensive and one of the others will do just as well.

The second lap is used to polish large facets which tend to develop scratches on metal or plastic laps. Table facets are particularly troublesome but may be polished to perfection with the use of wood. Tin oxide or Linde A, used sparingly, give good results. The table facet is polished by holding the dopped gem against the lap with the fingers. Exceptionally hard gems such as corundum and chrysoberyl may also be polished on wood using diamond powder.

■ DIAMOND-CHARGED TIN LAPS

A tin lap charged with 6400 diamond dust is also used to polish corundum and chrysoberyl and does a fine job. As an alternative, a plain copper lap can be used or, better still, copper plated on tin. Lead and mixtures of lead with tin, are also useful as well as typemetal. The diamond powder is mixed with Vaseline, oil, or grease, and smeared on in an extremely thin film. Only a small quantity is needed and you should experiment to determine the proper amount starting with a minimum quantity and adding more powder if polishing action is too slow.

■ WAX LAPS

Wax coated laps are marvelously effective for polishing very soft gemstones and touching up facets on ordinary materials which scratch or otherwise give trouble on standard laps. The wax lap is made by covering a stiff metal disk with cloth impregnated with beeswax. Perhaps the best metal to use is ¼-inch aluminum plate, but iron, steel, brass, or copper will do as well. If metals are not easy to get, ¼-inch composition board is suitable, but plywoods are generally too rough-surfaced.

When a metal disk is used, proceed as follows. Place the disk on a low flame or low setting on an electrical hot plate; it must become hot enough to melt beeswax but not burn it. Have ready a disk of cloth, preferably pillow ticking or similar close-woven fabric, well ironed to take out wrinkles. When the disk is hot, rub on beeswax until the top is coated with a uniform layer of melted wax. This layer should be just thick enough to soak the cloth but not so thick that the cloth floats on top. Use too little instead of too much. Take the cloth circle, hold opposite ends with the fingers, and place the sagging part on the metal disk near the center. Roll out to the edge to prevent trapping air in pockets. Shut off the flame, and while the disk is cooling, add a little beeswax on top by gentle rubbing. The idea is to fill all pores of the cloth. Let the disk cool.

When it is cold, cut out the hole in the center with a razor blade and place the disk on the master lap. Turn on the power. With a perfectly flat metal or stone block, rub down the wax. Now spray on some lighter fluid and rub again until the wax becomes tacky. The lighter fluid softens the wax and allows it to smear uniformly over the lap surface. By using lighter fluid carefully, and rubbing with the block while the lap is spinning, it is possible to get a perfectly flat surface.

The lap is made ready for use by smearing with Linde A and rubbing with the block. It can be used dry but moistened powder is preferred because using the lap dry eventually results in picking up wax on the gem. When badly worn, the lap is reconditioned by the lighter fluid treatment. Additional wax can be added by placing small pieces on the lap and remelting the entire top by brushing with the flame of a small blowtorch.

■ CONDITIONING POLISHING LAPS

Most polishing laps can be used "as is" but the smooth surface of a brand new lap is only good for polishing small facets as a rule. Larger facets polish on them with difficulty or develop scratches which are hard to remove. For these reasons, it is a good idea to condition new laps by a process known as *scoring*. Only soft metal laps are scored; Lucite, wax, wood, and others are not improved by this treatment. Copper, also, is always left smooth.

Tin, lead, and typemetal laps are scored by drawing radial lines with the tip of a knife. Heavy pressure is used, to make the scores at least $\frac{1}{16}$ inch deep. The pattern followed is shown in Figure 113, while the cross-section appearance of the lap is shown in the top illustration of Figure 114. After scores are made, the sharp ridges of metal on each side are removed with a smooth, flat, piece of agate or some other hard stone applied with heavy pressure while the lap is turning. The result looks like the middle illustration of Figure 114.

Because scoring leaves narrow ridges upon which the gem rides, as shown in the lower illustration of Figure 114, there is less suction and more pressure applied to the gem to promote polishing action. At the same time, the

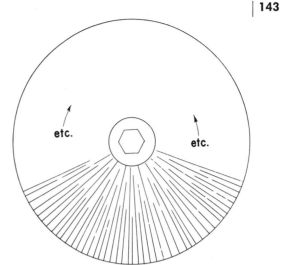

Fig. 113 Scheme for scoring a tin lap. The radial scores are from ⅛ to ¼ inch apart at the rim.

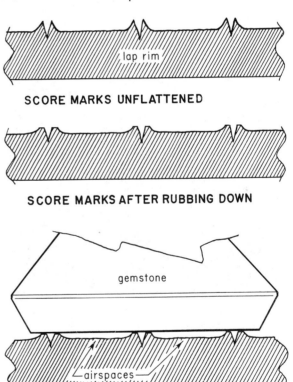

SCORE MARKS UNFLATTENED

SCORE MARKS AFTER RUBBING DOWN

GEMSTONE RIDING ON CONDITIONED LAP

Fig. 114 Cross-section of tin lap scored and rubbed down. The lower drawing shows how a gemstone rides upon the flattened ridges. Only the small areas atop the ridges contact the stone and effect polishing.

spaces between ridges serve to trap particles of powder or even minute bits of the gem itself and thus prevent them from causing scratching.

Small gems from ⅛ to ¼ inch in diameter may be polished on unscored laps; gems from ¼ inch to about ½ inch should be polished on laps which are scored about ⅛ inch apart; gems to 1 inch diameter, may be polished when the scores are about ³⁄₁₆ inch apart. Very large gems need scores about ¼ inch apart. However, scores which are too far apart cause trouble on small facets, and the rule is never to place the scores so far apart that any facet on the gem cannot straddle them.

Small fine scores may also be applied by a section of hack saw blade drawn firmly from the center of the lap toward the rim. Uniform fine scoring is done easily with the M.D.R. roller device shown in Figure 115. Another

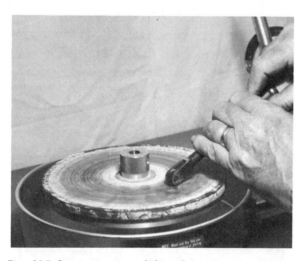

Fig. 115 Scoring a tin polishing lap using the M.D.R. hardened steel roller. (Courtesy M.D.R. Manufacturing Co., Inc., Los Angeles, California)

method is to use a razor blade to make many fine lines, or to let a sharp knife chatter on the lap as it turns. However, these are not very satisfactory methods. Extremely fine scoring is possible with a piece of coarse carborundum brick scrubbed criss-cross but there is danger of accidentally imbedding a piece of grit.

After a long period of use, a soft metal lap develops low places, usually about midway between the edge and the center hole. This part

of the lap tends to be used more than the inner or outer edges, and consequently gets more wear. Since the surface should be as flat as possible, it becomes necessary to remove the high areas. This is done by using a bearing scraper, as shown in Figure 116, or by sending the lap to a machine shop to be resurfaced. Another way is to rub down the lap by placing it face down on a large sheet of abrasive paper resting on plate glass or some other true surface. This is tedious but it works.

■ FACETERS TRIM SAWS

In principle, saws used for sectioning facet rough are exactly like trim saws used for cutting cabochon materials. However, because facet material is far more costly as a rule, the blades used are seldom over 6 inches in diameter and are made purposely thin. Such blades can also be used to saw cabochon slabs but it is better to reserve them for the use intended. Thin blades are far more delicate than ordinary trim saw blades, and naturally must be used with greater care.

There are several types of thin blades: notched-rim steel, notched-rim bronze or copper, and sintered-rim bronze or copper. The notched-rim kinds can be had as thin as .010 inch in 4-inch to 6-inch diameters. Although it rusts, steel is preferable because it is stronger and less likely to be damaged by inadvertent twisting of the rough. Unlike slabs which rest firmly on the flat saw table, much facet rough must be cut supported by the fingers alone, because its shape is such that it cannot rest flat. An excellent way of supporting irregular facet rough is shown in Figure 117, a photo taken in Idar Oberstein, Germany in a commercial cutting shop. The rough rests on two narrow metal ridges which fit close to the blade yet do not interfere with projecting points or irregularities of the rough gemstone. Despite all precautions, however, finger support sometimes weakens and allows twisting of the rough. If the saw blade is too soft, as in copper or bronze blades, it is possible that some of the edge may be torn off or actually cut off

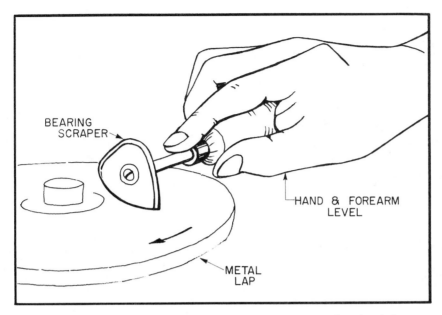

Fig. 116 Scraping a lap to remove surface impurities and to level the top.

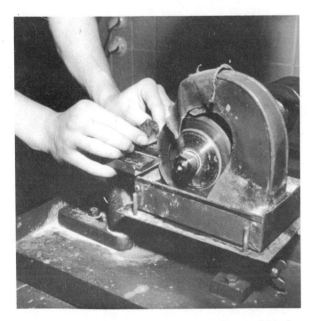

Fig. 117 Sawing facet rough on a thin diamond blade. The coolant used is water supplied by a damp rag above the blade. The gemstone is supported by two upright metal ridges just in front of the blade. Photo taken in Idar Oberstein, Germany. (Courtesy Dr. Ing. W. Fischer, Stuttgart, Germany)

Figure 118. Another kind with a transparent spray protector in addition to the regular hood, over the blade itself, is shown in Figure 119. Both can be used with oily coolants or water; however, water causes rusting and it is necessary to drain the tank and dry all parts as soon as sawing is finished. Open blade types such as the German machine shown in Figure 117, can easily be made with simple hardware store arbors. A folded piece of metal is needed just in front of the blade to support the rough stones being sawed. This can be made adjustable, up or down, to accommodate various sizes of rough. Water can be used and is not likely to cause much rusting because all parts are in the open. However, oily coolants, applied by brush, can also be used.

by a sharp projection of the gemstone itself when the stone twists. For this reason alone it is better to use steel.

A simply-made but strong saw is shown in

Fig. 118 Allen facet trim saw using a 4-inch blade. (Courtesy Belmont Lapidary Supply, Belmont, California)

Fig. 119 M.D.R. facet trim saw unit mounted on board for portability. The blade used is 4 inches in diameter. (Courtesy M.D.R. Manufacturing Co., Inc., Los Angeles, California)

14 | *How to Cut Faceted Gems*

THE following steps are needed to transform a piece of rough into a finished gem: *preforming*, which involves sawing and grinding, *dopping*, or cementing the preform to the dop stick, *grinding*, to cut the facets, and *polishing*, to smooth the facets. Dopping and subsequent steps must be done twice since it is possible to cut and polish only one half of the gem at a time. Some cutters dop the crown first so that the pavilion is finished first; others dop the pavilion and cut the crown first. There is not much difference.

Faceting is not difficult but is sometimes puzzling to the beginner until he learns how to use his machine. As with any other mechanical operation, it is necessary to know how the machine works before good gems can be cut upon it. Later in this chapter detailed instructions will be given for cutting a simple step cut, followed by the cutting of a brilliant. The step cut was chosen to be first because fewer settings of the facet head are needed and it is easier to understand the procedure.

■ PREPARING ROUGH FOR FACETING

The first step requires shaping of the rough to about the dimensions of the finished gem. The more closely the preform approaches the final shape of the gem, the less work will have to be done in cutting the facets. Some pieces of rough are small enough so that hand grinding is all that is needed to shape them into preforms; however, other specimens must be sawed first to remove unwanted material.

■ SAWING FACET ROUGH

Much rough is fragile and must be treated gently during sawing. Examine each piece carefully and note places inside where flaws or inclusions occur. Very small flaws can often be disguised by preforming the stone in such a way that they fall near the edge of a brilliant. The numerous overlapping facets break the light rays in a confusing manner and small reflections from the flaws themselves are scarcely noticeable. However, in step cut gems, the smallest flaws are immediately noticeable and for these it is far better to have flawless preforms. Under no circumstances should flaws be placed so that they appear directly under the table facet. No amount of faceting skill will disguise them and all of the painstaking work that went into the gem will come to nothing. Therefore, to be sure to avoid flaws, mark the rough with India ink, coating the marks with thin shellac to preserve them, and make saw cuts through those places where the cut will divide the rough into good and bad sections. Sometimes a large piece has flaws in its center; in this case, it is best to cut the piece in half and regard each section as a separate problem. Try to remove defective sections at once so that you will not forget them and accidentally leave them in the preform. Before sawing, consult Chapter 19 for information about the gemstone you are working on. Any peculiarities will be explained here and in the case of certain difficult gemstones, this information may save you expensive disasters.

Saw cuts often need not be taken all the way through. If a crack passes part way through the rough, saw the rest of the way, then snap between the fingers. Slender crystals, like tourmaline, can often be parted by nicking on opposite sides and breaking. After sawing, if you are not sure that all flaws have been located, re-dip the rough in an immersion fluid, or grind and polish the flat saw cut to make a "window" in the gem.

■ PREFORMING

Sawing can be used to remove most waste areas and to give partial shape to the preform, but generally it is necessary to shape the preform further on grinding wheels. For fragile or soft materials, the 220 wheel is satisfactory if it is well trued and smooth. Some cutters keep a special 400 grit wheel for delicate materials, since its cutting action is

gentler; however, the author has not found this usually necessary. Very large preforms of tough material such as beryl and quartz, can be preformed on wheels as coarse as 100 grit, but in this case leave a little material to be removed by another shaping on the 220 wheel.

Preforms for step cut gems are easy to make. Begin by deciding which part of the rough will be the table. Saw this carefully on the trim saw, making a flat cut. Dry the stone and mark the outline in India ink; brush lightly with liquid shellac to prevent washing off. Resaw or grind to profile. At this point a rectangular block will be the result. To permit cutting a gem with good proportions it is necessary that the depth of the block be about the same as its width. If the preform is too shallow or too deep, now is the time to correct it by more grinding. When satisfied, mark a line along the sides, one third of the distance from the top to bottom; this will be the girdle of the gem. Turn the block over and mark a midline on the bottom where the pavilion facets will draw in to a sharp apex. On the top, mark in a rectangle about half the width of the preform; this will be the table facet. Preserve all the lines with shellac. Now grind on the wheel to a little short of the marks, leaving the surfaces bulged a little. This is necessary to make room for the rows of facets which curve around the gem on top and on bottom. The shape is shown clearly in Figure 120. The better the marking and grinding, the easier it will be to cut the facets.

The circular brilliant preform is prepared as shown in Figure 121. Most cutters examine rough to find a flat area for the top of the gem and then grind this by hand on a cabochon grinding wheel until the area is approximately flat. It can be made quite flat by using the side of the grinding wheel. The rough is then held by hand and the sides ground to form a partial cylinder, as shown in Figure 121. However, if desired, the rough piece can be dopped at this time and preformed on the facet machine itself, as shown in Figure 122. This results in perfect roundness and insures that the cutting of the facets will be accurate. Some cutters always

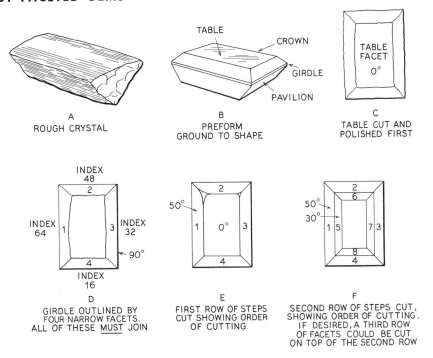

Fig. 120 Cutting the crown of a step cut.

use the preforming attachment, even for step cut gems, but with care and practice, a good preform can be made by hand grinding on silicon carbide wheels.

In using a mechanical preforming attachment, as shown in Figure 122, it is very important that as much material as possible be first removed by freehand grinding, so that the copper lap used for final shaping does not get too much wear, especially in one place. In time, such worn areas will be noticeably lower than the rest of the lap and may even be so bad that the lap surface has to be re-flattened. Mechanical preforming should only be used to make the gem girdle accurate. On the other hand, many cutters who have this problem, solve it by raising the dop arm to about 85°, holding it in position with the angle stop and grinding the preform as before but with the important difference that the entire lap surface can be used instead of only a small portion near the rim. This spreads the wear evenly. Other cutters keep a special lap which is used only for preforming. It is charged with 200 or even 100 diamond grit and can become rough and bumpy without doing much harm.

■ OTHER PREFORMS

Mechanical preforming is possible only with stones of regular outline. Gems of heart shape, pear shape, ovals, marquises, etc., cannot be efficiently or accurately ground except by hand on the grinding wheel. More will be said about this later in the chapter.

■ PREFORMING CLEAVABLE GEMSTONES

When preforming gemstones with good cleavages the easiest way to be sure that the cleavage planes do not coincide with any facet is to place the cleavage planes vertically in the stone or tilted about 5° to 10° from the table facet. Usually only one cleavage plane is prominent and is easily identified by its smoothness and transparency; its placement then becomes a question of orienting the table facet properly, and automatically other facets will not be cut upon it.

Figure 123 shows a rough topaz crystal and how it is oriented to prevent its one cleavage plane from coinciding with any facet.

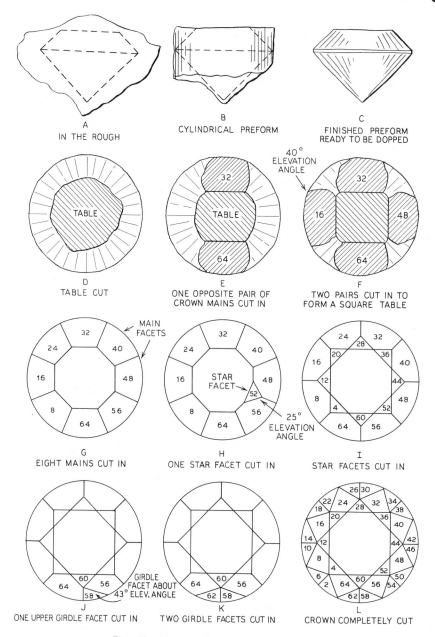

A
IN THE ROUGH

B
CYLINDRICAL PREFORM

C
FINISHED PREFORM
READY TO BE DOPPED

D
TABLE CUT

E
ONE OPPOSITE PAIR OF
CROWN MAINS CUT IN

F
TWO PAIRS CUT IN TO
FORM A SQUARE TABLE

G
EIGHT MAINS CUT IN

H
ONE STAR FACET CUT IN

I
STAR FACETS CUT IN

J
ONE UPPER GIRDLE FACET CUT IN

K
TWO GIRDLE FACETS CUT IN

L
CROWN COMPLETELY CUT

Fig. 121 Cutting the crown of a brilliant.

■ DOPS AND DOPPING

Dopping gems for faceting needs to be more accurate than is necessary for cabochons. Not only are smaller stones dealt with but the accuracy of dopping has a direct bearing on the accuracy of the finished stone. Facet dops are made of machined metal, and a special device called a *transfer jig*, as shown in Figures 124 and 125, is used to hold them during dopping. A set of dops is shown in Figure 126.

Transfer jigs are made from aluminum with a single, accurate groove on top for holding the dop sticks in perfect alignment. Two types are available: the kind illustrated in Figure 124, and another, in Figure 125, in which an additional leg is provided at right angles to the other two, for the purpose of centering the stone for dopping.

Preforms are heated in the same way as cabochon blanks and with the same tools, as

shown in Figure 127. However, only one stone is heated at a time because each must wait

Fig. 122 M.D.R. girdle grinder attachment in action. The attachment is located just under the fingers of the operator. Its top is fitted with rollers which permit the dop arm to be rotated and thus grind the girdle of the gem seen cemented in the dop stick. (Courtesy M.D.R. Manufacturing Co., Inc., Los Angeles, California)

Fig. 125 Gemlap three way transfer jig. The third arm supports a face plate dop which is used to insure that the gem is exactly centered. (Courtesy Brad's Rock Shop, Ferndale, Michigan)

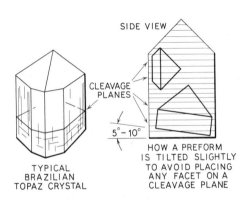

Fig. 123 Orienting an easily cleaved gemstone.

Fig. 124 Underwood-Allen transfer jig. Geoff Cook Photo. (Courtesy Belmont Lapidary Supply, Belmont, California)

Fig. 126 Allen steel dops for faceted gems. The conical dops are for brilliants, the vee-dops for step cut gems. The grooves are engaged by a set screw in the dop arm and allow dops to be interchanged in positive alignment. (Courtesy Belmont Lapidary Supply, Belmont, California)

Fig. 127 Dopping equipment for faceted gems. *Top.* Tin can oven with alcohol lamp at upper left. Various dops in different shapes and sizes at upper right. Transfer block with gem being transferred at lower left. Also shown are preforms in center, dopping wax at lower right, and minor accessories. *Bottom.* Heating gem and dops to make the transfer.

several minutes in the transfer jig while cooling. More stones on the dopping oven would get too warm while waiting their turn. Ordinary dopping wax is used unless the stone is heat sensitive, in which case pure stick shellac or jeweler's chasing cement is used because they stick at lower temperatures. Shellac melts at a lower point than dopping wax while the melting point of chasing cement is lower still.

When heating preforms, there is no way to tell by appearance alone whether a stone is hot enough to dop, but a little trick can be used to be safe. After the preform has been put on the dopping oven, heat a sliver of wax in

tweezers and stick it to the top of the preform. When the sliver begins to melt the stone is hot enough for dopping. Another way to heat preforms safely is to place them on a pad of steel wool in front of a heat lamp.

■ **45° DOP STICKS**

To cut and polish table facets, special dop sticks to hold regular dops vertical to the lap can be bought. Figure 128 shows one made by M.D.R. When properly aligned, the dop arm is at an angle of 45° to the lap; hence its name. The 45° dop is placed in the dop arm by its shank and locked loosely into position. The facet head is raised or lowered until the elevation angle pointer reads 45°. The dop is then twisted by hand until the beveled surface on the bottom finds its "seat" on the lap. The dop is tightened to prevent twisting while being used. Any regular dop stick inserted in the 45° dop will be vertical to the lap when the elevation angle reads 45°.

In the Allen machine, shown in Figure 106, a 45° hole is bored through the dop arm and serves the same function. A setscrew locks the dop stick in place. The Allen machine is aligned by inserting a face plate dop stick and loosening the nut at the top of the dop arm to allow the face plate to find its own seat on the lap. As before, the pointer indicates 45° while this is being done. When aligned, the nut at the top of the arm is tightened and a regular dop substituted for the face plate.

■ **DOPPING STEPS**

Insert and lock in place a special dop called the *face plate,* an example of which is shown in Figure 124 on the right side of the jig. The end of the face plate is round and flat, and the preform table presses against it while the wax is cooling. To prevent sudden cooling and cracking of the stone, paste brown wrapping paper or masking tape on the face plate prior to use. Then select a dop of the proper size and shape to fit the back of the preform. It should be smaller in diameter than the gem so

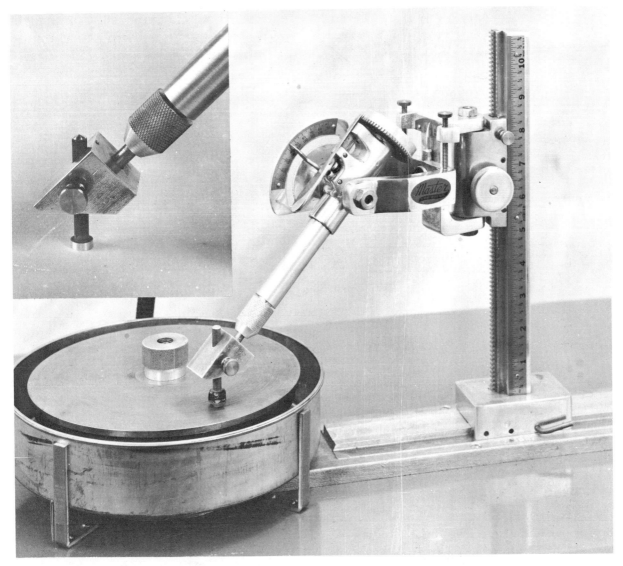

Fig. 128 M.D.R. 45° dop installed in dop arm. Note gem on bottom of dop being ground on diamond lap.

(Courtesy M.D.R. Manufacturing Co., Inc., Los Angeles, California)

that markings and facet junctions along the girdle can always be seen. Coat the dop with wax by heating in the alcohol flame and dipping up scraps of crushed wax, turning the dop to let the wax flow to all places in the dop interior. Press the dop over the back of the warm preform and use it to lift the preform from the warming oven. Insert the dop in the other side of the jig as quickly as possible and press firmly against the face plate, as shown in Figure 129. Enough pressure should be used to squeeze out excess wax and to be sure that the metal dop is actually in contact with the

preform. Be sure that the wax is soft during this step; if necessary, pass the junction over the lamp flame to keep the wax fluid.

While the preform is cooling, scrape surplus wax from around the girdle and shape the remainder to give support to the preform.

The above procedure is for dopping the back or pavilion first. This means that the top or crown will be cut and polished first. The author prefers this method because there is less chance for the preform to loosen, since more of it is cemented with wax. Other cutters prefer to flatten the crown first, then polish it

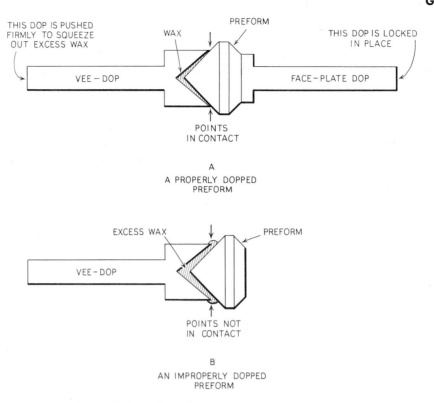

Fig. 129 Properly and improperly dopped preforms.

by holding the preform by hand on the polishing lap, and then dop this side.

■ TURNING THE STONE TO CUT THE BACK

Whichever way is used, crown first or pavilion first, it is necessary to turn the gem to cut its other half. The procedure here is for re-dopping after the crown is cut.

In turning a stone around, it is important that the gem be aligned perfectly so that all facets, top and bottom, meet accurately. Properly used, the transfer jig makes this a simple task. The lower illustration in Figure 127 and the diagrams in Figure 130 show the steps required. In A, of Figure 130, the dopped gem is locked tightly in position while the new dop, heated and coated with hot wax, is slipped quickly into the opposite side. In B, the new dop is pressed against the table facet of the gem and locked loosely in position. Although it may seem at this time that the union between wax and gem is satisfactory, this is seldom the case. Most often, the coldness of

the gem causes the wax on the new dop to congeal immediately and an excess amount of wax is trapped between the face of the new dop and the table facet of the gem. The contact between the new dop and the gem must be as close as possible to prevent the gem from shifting position. Accordingly, while the stone is still in the B position, the shank of the new dop is heated to remelt the wax. At the moment it becomes soft, the dop is pressed forward to drive out the excess wax.

In step C, the wax, still warm, is shaped with the fingers to give better support to the gem. When this is done, the dops, the wax, and the gem are allowed to cool. Finally, in step D, the old dop is removed by heating its shank. The flame of the alcohol lamp should be turned up to give strong heat; this warms the wax quickly and allows removing the old dop without heating the gem and disturbing its alignment in the new dop stick. To remove the old dop, gently bend the shank: as soon as the wax begins to yield, the old dop comes off easily. Step E shows how excess wax can soften and

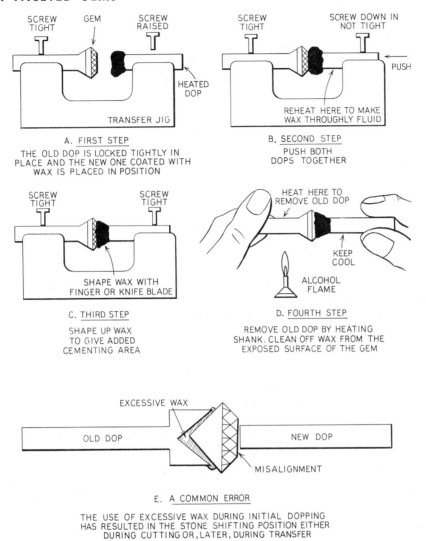

A. FIRST STEP
THE OLD DOP IS LOCKED TIGHTLY IN
PLACE AND THE NEW ONE COATED WITH
WAX IS PLACED IN POSITION

B. SECOND STEP
PUSH BOTH
DOPS TOGETHER

C. THIRD STEP
SHAPE UP WAX
TO GIVE ADDED
CEMENTING AREA

D. FOURTH STEP
REMOVE OLD DOP BY HEATING
SHANK. CLEAN OFF WAX FROM THE
EXPOSED SURFACE OF THE GEM

E. A COMMON ERROR
THE USE OF EXCESSIVE WAX DURING INITIAL DOPPING
HAS RESULTED IN THE STONE SHIFTING POSITION EITHER
DURING CUTTING OR, LATER, DURING TRANSFER

Fig. 130 Transferring a gem from one dop to another.

cause the gem to shift position. In all dopping of faceted gems, the best rule is to get as close a contact between gem and dop as possible.

Scrape waste wax from the back of the gem with a razor blade or knife. If the gem is soft, fragile, or cleavable, use the fingernail or wipe off the wax with alcohol. Be extremely careful near the sharp edge at the girdle—it may chip!

■ MAKING A STEP CUT GEM

The easiest cut is the step cut with rectangular outline and several rows of facets or "steps" on crown and pavilion. Begin with a preform as described previously. A good size is one about ½ inch in length and a little less in width. The depth should be about the same as the width to be sure enough material is in the pavilion to cut all the steps needed for brilliance. Rock crystal or smoky quartz will do nicely for the first attempt.

Have ready a small bowl of water and a piece of natural sponge about the size of a walnut for dipping up and applying water to the cutting lap. Cutting and polishing are improved if a few drops of liquid or a pinch of dry detergent are added to the water. Keep extra water handy in a milk bottle; add the detergent to that. Install the cutting lap with the coarse or 400 grit side up. Tighten in place with finger pressure only. If the gem has been dopped for cutting the crown first, the place to begin is with the table facet.

■ CUTTING AND POLISHING THE TABLE FACET

Insert the dop stick in the 45° dop or in the 45° hole, depending on what kind of machine is being used. Be sure that the dop stick is vertical, since the table facet must be at right angles to the axis of the gem. In the M.D.R. machine, this means resting the 45° dop on the lap, as described before; in the Allen type machine, it means raising or lowering the facet head so when the preform just touches the lap, the pointer reads 45°. Each machine is furnished with detailed instructions telling how to make the necessary adjustments.

When the dop is secure, the dop arm locked, and the index trigger engaged in the notch corresponding to one of the main settings, such as 64 or 32, start the motor and at the same time, wet the surface of the cutting lap with water. Lower the head very gently until the stone touches the surface and begins to cut. Be sure to keep the lap wet. *Never point the dop arm into the oncoming lap—always let the stone trail!* If the stone is pointed *into* the lap, a corner of the gem may dig into the copper and the gem will break out of the dop stick. Worse yet, the copper will be gouged and the lap will bump badly. The proper way to support the dop arm during cutting is shown in Figure 131.

As cutting continues, apply just a few ounces of pressure—no more—at least not until you see how fast cutting takes place and how well you are able to control it. About every ten seconds or so, lift the dop arm and inspect the surface of the gem. Wipe off the water to get a clear view. It will be easy to see which marks are due to the cutting lap and which are left from preforming. During all this, you must also watch the elevation angle pointer because as the gem material cuts away beneath, the

entire dop arm naturally lowers a little. This means that the original reading of 45° no longer shows up under the pointer and it is necessary to lower the facet head a little to compensate for the gem material being ground away, and to bring back the pointer to the 45° mark where it belongs. When all of the top is ground flat, the pointer should still read exactly 45°. If it does not, the table facet will be cocked a little to the axis of the gem and it will not look well when the gem is finished. Also when the time comes to reverse the gem for cutting the back, a tilted table facet will also tilt the gem and all remaining facets will be cut unevenly.

When the table is done, stop the motor and change to the 1200 side of the copper/diamond lap for the finish cut. The finish lapping continues only long enough to remove all traces of coarse lapping and to make all facet junctions meet accurately. The table is now ready for polishing.

■ POLISHING THE TABLE FACET

The cutting lap is removed and the Lucite polishing lap installed. If you refer to Chapter 19 you will see that this lap in combination with cerium oxide polishes quartz. Because the plastic lap is usually somewhat thicker than the cutting lap, the height of the facet head is adjusted by raising slightly until the pointer reads exactly 45° when the table facet touches the lap.

In a small bowl or dish, preferably one with a cover which can be put back as soon as polishing is finished, mix about one-quarter to one-half teaspoon of cerium oxide with several times its own volume of water. Use a small wad of surgical cotton for stirring and applying the watery mix to the lap. In case the cotton touches any dirty surface or dirt falls on the lap and is wiped off with the cotton, it can be discarded without losing much powder. Sponges are not as good as cotton and should not be used. Start the lap and apply the mixture, dipping up the cloudy water made by vigorous stirring. Too much powder is

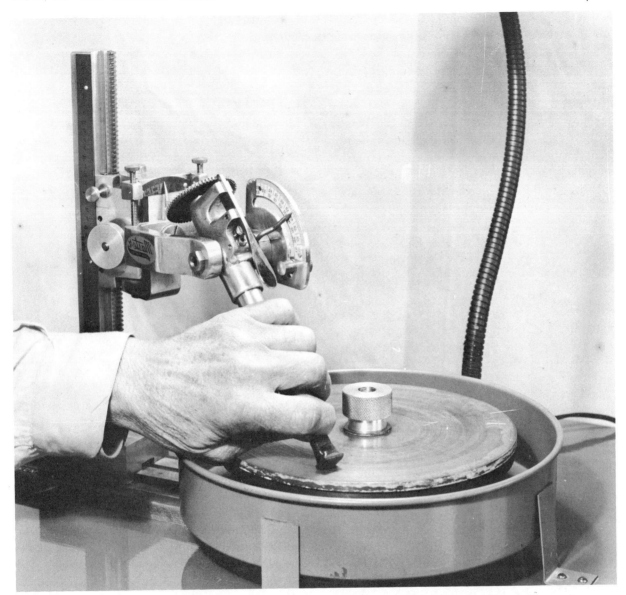

Fig. 131 Proper position for holding dop arm during cutting and polishing. The fingers and thumb are placed close to the gem to provide maximum support and better to "feel" the action. The lap turns clockwise so that the gem trails. (Courtesy M.D.R. Manufacturing Co., Inc., Los Angeles, California)

wasteful and also causes wavy surfaces on the facets. Lower the dop arm to the lap until the stone is in contact. Polishing begins immediately but you will find that a little more pressure is needed than during cutting to bring up the polish. The sign of polishing is feeling a definite "drag" or "tug" on the stone. As the polishing powder dries, the drag increases and this is the time to add a little more of the polishing mixture. Never let the lap run ab-

solutely dry because heat will be generated and cause the gem to crack. Lucite is apt to overheat any gem but tin and wood are less dangerous in this respect and are often allowed to run dry for short periods of time to bring up a better polish.

Because it is almost impossible to be absolutely accurate in placing the table facet on the polishing lap in exactly the same position it had on the cutting lap, it is necessary that polishing proceed for only a few seconds at first. Lift the dop arm and examine the table facet by wiping it off with tissue. You will usually find that a bright polished spot is present on one side of the facet, indicating that the facet is not really resting flat on the polishing lap. This is the time to adjust the height of the facet head a slight amount to make the facet lie flat. If one of the side edges of the table facet is polishing first, adjust the dop arm with the angle splitter to make the table facet level with the lap. Test by again applying the stone to the lap; lift and re-examine. When the polish begins over *all* of the facet at once, the adjustments are correct. Remember to do this with every facet whether it is being reground or polished. An improperly seated facet announces the fact by a sharp scraping noise instead of the quiet hum expected; whenever the scraping noise is heard, *immediately* lift the dop arm and see what is wrong.

■ POLISHING HINTS

A perfect polish shows no scratches or pits even under a ten-power magnifier. A poor polish is usually due to failure to smooth properly on the 1200 grit lap, or from not applying enough pressure to remove all scores and pits left by the diamond lap. To start the polish on a facet, it is often necessary to apply pressure, sometimes several pounds! The rule is this: have the right polishing lap and agent, be certain that the facet fits flush against the lap, then use enough pressure to get the job done as quickly as possible!

If a facet is slightly tilted on the lap, one edge only will show polish. The dop arm must be readjusted immediately to insure flat contact. Polishing on only one side removes enough material so that the facet may have to be recut to fit the rest. Facets which are slightly "off" can be repolished to accuracy, but it is a tricky operation because it is not easy to see what is going on. It is better to be sure that you are right the first time.

During polishing, keep the stone sweeping

back and forth across the lap to prevent polishing marks on the facet as well as to keep the lap worn evenly. If a gem is kept in one spot too long, the facet surface polishes away in shallow grooves and ripples and is less brilliant when finished. This is a serious problem in small facets which polish quickly.

■ OUTLINING THE GIRDLE

The next step is to cut the girdle by grinding the edges of the preform into a rectangular outline. This is done by taking the dop stick out of the 45° position and locking it into the dop arm in the regular position shown in Figure 131.

Turn the dop arm until the index number 64 is under the trigger; drop the trigger into the notch. If a different gear is used, drop the trigger in the highest number notch, whatever that may be. To understand how the gear wheel helps to put facets around the stone, refer to Figure 108 in the previous chapter. A 64 notch gear is shown at the top. Notice how each facet position corresponds to the opposite position of the gear wheel. Now turn to Figure 120 which shows the steps in cutting a simple rectangular step cut. Note how each facet is cut using the corresponding number on the gear wheel. When notch 64 is under the trigger, facet number 1 will be cut; notch 48 cuts facet number 2, etc. These same settings will be used to cut all of the steps on the crown since they are in the same position around the girdle of the gem. They will also be used when the time comes to polish each facet.

Install the coarse cutting lap. Have sponge and water ready. Lower the facet head, as shown in A of Figure 132. If the splash pan is in the way, go as low as you can or, if it has a removable section, take that off. In any case, go down to at least 70° elevation angle and, preferably, to 80° or 85°.

Start the motor and lower the dop arm gently until contact is made. Be careful: the preform is very narrow here and it is easy to cut too much. Stop cutting as soon as the facet

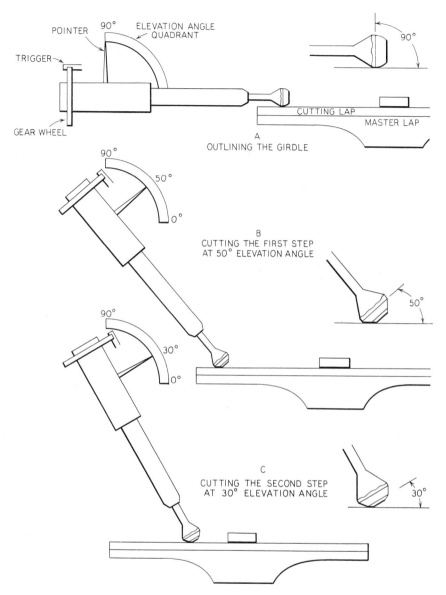

Fig. 132 Cutting steps on a crown.

reaches from one end of the stone to the other. Lift the dop arm, release the trigger and turn to the next setting of 48 for cutting the second facet; repeat for cutting the others using indexes 16 and 32. When all facets are cut properly, they will touch at the corners in a continuous narrow ring around the stone. If desired, they can be polished at this time or polished after all other facets have been finished. Some cutters do not polish the girdle at all since its lack of polish is scarcely noticeable after the gem is finished.

■ CUTTING THE CROWN

Cut only two rows of steps on the crown to begin with; these are enough to show the principles involved and to get the practice. Later, more steps can be cut on larger gems after you learn how to do it.

The first row of facets is next to the girdle and calls for a setting of 50° elevation angle. The position of the facet head for this step is shown in B of Figure 132. Unlock the gear wheel and again turn to notch 64; drop in the trigger. Lower the dop arm until the gem touches the lap. Raise or lower the facet head until the pointer reads 50°. Cut facet number 1 until it meets the girdle facet at all points from one end of the gem to the other. Do the same for the other facets, cutting each one until the edge of the girdle is ringed with a narrow, flat area. Be sure all corners meet exactly. Some adjustment is needed in elevation angle as cutting each facet causes the dop arm to lower a little past 50°. Use the fine adjustment on the stand rod as you cut so that the pointer stays on 50°. Very often, the facets do not meet exactly at the corners after cutting. Examine them carefully and decide which one or two are higher than the rest. Go back to their settings and recut them until the junctions meet exactly those of the other facets.

The second row is cut like the first, but a change in elevation angle is needed, as shown in C of Figure 132. When the second row is cut, the top of the gem should look like F in Figure 120.

After all facets have been cut on the coarse side of the diamond/copper lap, recut on the fine side. At this time you can correct any small errors as you go along.

■ POLISHING THE CROWN FACETS

Polishing goes from the top facets next to the table and finishes at the girdle, the reverse of the cutting procedure. Using the same polishing method described for the table, polish all facets on each horizontal row. When satisfied with the finish, remove the dopstick and lock it in the transfer jig for turning the gem around. Follow the steps shown in Figure 130.

■ CUTTING THE PAVILION

The pavilion facets are cut in the same way as the crown facets, except that there is no table facet. There is one place where difficulty may occur, and that is in lining up the back facets exactly with the corresponding facets on the crown.

Although the gem has been turned around

in the new dop stick, it is almost impossible to put it back in the dop arm and line up the facets by eye alone. A fairly correct alignment can be made but it is necessary to "cut and try" at least once to be sure. This is how it is done. Drop the trigger in notch 64 as was done for one of the long crown facets. Put the dop stick into the dop arm but do not lock tightly. Lower the dop arm to the lap as low as possible as shown in A of Figure 132 and twist the dop stick until it appears to lie flat on one of the long sides of the gem; now lock tightly in place. Raise the facet head to get an angle of 60°. The position is similar to B of Figure 132. This will be the elevation angle for the first row of steps next to the girdle. Turn on the motor and cut for a few seconds. Lift the dop arm and examine the cut. Figure 133 shows correct and incorrect cutting of the first facet on the pavilion (shown by the shaded area). In A, the trial cut shows that the first facet is slightly off; if this is not corrected, each of the remaining facets, as indicated by the dotted lines, will also be off. In B, the first facet is cut correctly because it is parallel to

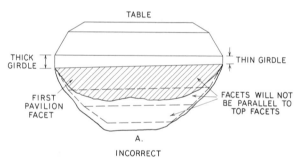

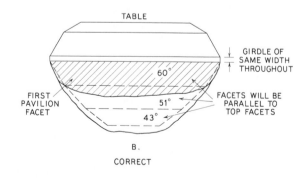

Fig. 133 Alignment of back facets on a step cut gem.

the top facet; therefore every other facet will be correct.

Continue cutting the first trial cut until it reaches over far enough to be sure there is or is not an error. As soon as you can see that the narrow girdle facet is lopsided, make a cor-

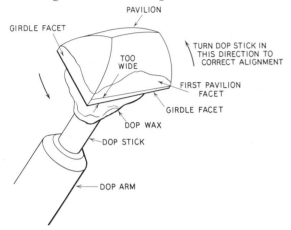

GIRDLE FACET
PAVILION
TOO WIDE
TURN DOP STICK IN THIS DIRECTION TO CORRECT ALIGNMENT
FIRST PAVILION FACET
GIRDLE FACET
DOP WAX
DOP STICK
DOP ARM

Fig. 134 How to align the back facets to the crown facets.

rection, as shown in Figure 134. In this illustration, the proper way to twist the dop stick is shown. To make the correction, unlock the dop stick just enough so that it can be twisted without slipping easily. Twist a *very small* amount and re-lock. Again lower the dop arm and re-cut the facet just enough to see what is happening. All trial cuts should be just long enough to prove that the facet is parallel or not parallel. If cut for too long a time, the trial cut may go so far that it cuts into the girdle and requires recutting a new set of girdle facets.

When trial cuts show parallel alignments, cut the pavilion facet until the girdle becomes a long narrow facet. Do not make it narrower than 1/16 inch. Later as you gain skill and confidence, girdles can be cut to half that width. Finish the trial facet and go on to the others. Cut them all to the same depth so that when you are through, the girdle facets are the same width all around the gem.

For facet heads which are fitted with setting splitters, the alignment method described above can be simplified. Proceed as before up to the making of the first trial cut. If only a

small adjustment is needed to make the trial cut parallel, use the splitter device, turning the dop arm in the direction noted in Figure 134. As before, several trial cuts may be necessary to remove all error.

■ **CUTTING THE REMAINING ROWS**

Set the facet head for an elevation angle of 51° for the second row; cut in each facet in turn. Use the same gear settings as before. Cut each facet until the facet next to the girdle is about one third as wide as the distance from the girdle to the tip of the pavilion. When all facets in this row are cut to the same width, and all join accurately at the corners, raise the facet head to an angle of 43° which will be used for the last row next to the tip. Cut these in. If your judgment of distance has been correct, the stone will have a dome-shaped pavilion with three rows of facets, each about the same width. This sounds difficult but in practice it is easy to do. Re-cut all facets on the fine side of the lap. The pavilion is now ready for polishing.

■ **POLISHING THE PAVILION FACETS**

Use the procedure described before, that is, polish the facets next to the tip of the pavilion first, then the next row, finishing with the row next to the girdle. When all are done, take out the dop stick and polish the girdle facets if these were not done before or, if desired, leave them unpolished. However, if they are to be polished now, proceed as follows. Remove the polishing lap and put on a wood one. In a band next to the edge, apply the same polishing powder. Turn on the motor. Holding the dop stick in the fingers, rest one of the girdle facets on the wood and press down with the forefinger of one hand. Use both hands to hold and steady the dop stick in case one of the sharp corners tends to dig into the wood. By raising or lowering the shank of the dop, you can adjust the angle enough to make the girdle lie flat on the wood. This method of polishing girdles is preferred by the author because it slightly rounds the girdle facets and makes them far less likely to chip in handling, particularly if the gem is being set in jewelry.

■ REMOVING THE STONE FROM THE DOP

It seems hardly necessary to give special instructions for removing finished gems from dops; yet—and this has happened to the author—carelessness at this stage may result in chipping or scratching. Stones which are not heat sensitive, can be warmed over an open alcohol flame, holding the stone 3 or 4 inches above the flame to soften the wax. When the wax begins to melt, take the stone in a bit of clean rag, pull from the dop and wipe off as much wax as possible. When the stone is cool, place in alcohol to dissolve the rest.

The safer way—and the one recommended until you know which stones are which—is to warm the shank of the dop stick and when the wax softens, remove the stone with the fingers. When the stone is cold, chip off as much of the wax as possible with your fingernails and soak off the rest in alcohol. Very soft stones should not be scraped at all. Keep your alcohol in a small wide-mouthed pill bottle. Line the bottom with some cotton to prevent gems from chipping as they are dropped in.

■ CONCLUSION

The instructions given above are the basic steps for cutting and polishing all step-cut stones. The simple four-sided step-cut rock crystal is the beginning of a variety of cuts based on the same principles. If, for example, an octagon is wanted, all that is necessary is to cut each of the four corners during girdling. In the same way, triangles, hexagons, and many other straight sided cuts can be outlined during the cutting of the girdle.

■ HOW TO ESTIMATE ANGLES FOR STEP CUT GEMS

Cutters have found that the best brilliance from a step cut comes when the angles between facets on the pavilion change gradually. Of course, any step cut can be made with just one row of facets but this would be an uninteresting gem to say the least. In very small stones, one, two, or three rows are all that there are room for usually, but for large gems it is the practice to put on as many as six. The resulting facets are very narrow and reflect light upward in slender ribbons; all in all, they make the gem much more attractive than it would be otherwise. However, the problem here is to decide at what angle each row should be cut. With experience, cutters learn what angle to begin with next to the girdle, and how much to change the angle for each row as they cut toward the tip of the pavilion, but the beginner needs some rule of thumb to avoid making mistakes.

To be sure of having a brilliant step cut, it is necessary that the preform be properly proportioned. One which is too shallow can never make a brilliant gem unless the girdle parts are cut down to thicken the gem. A preform which is too deep is all right, but calls for a lot of grinding later to remove excess material at the bottom. The best proportions for the step cut preform can only be obtained if you start with a block of rough which is nearly square in cross-section. The block can be longer in one direction, like a shoe box, but its cross-section must be nearly square. Thus, when it is marked off with one third of the depth for the crown, and two thirds for the pavilion, there will be room to cut a number of rows of facets on the pavilion and still get a brilliant gem. To get the best possible reflections of light from the pavilion, it is necessary that the row of facets at the very tip be cut at the recommended angles for the gem material concerned. This is not possible if the preform is too shallow. Some suggested proportions and angles for step cuts are shown in Figure 135. Steps of 5° and 10° between facets are standard, but steps as low as 3° can be cut if needed. However, very low steps widen so fast during cutting and polishing that it is easy to make mistakes. As a general rule, try

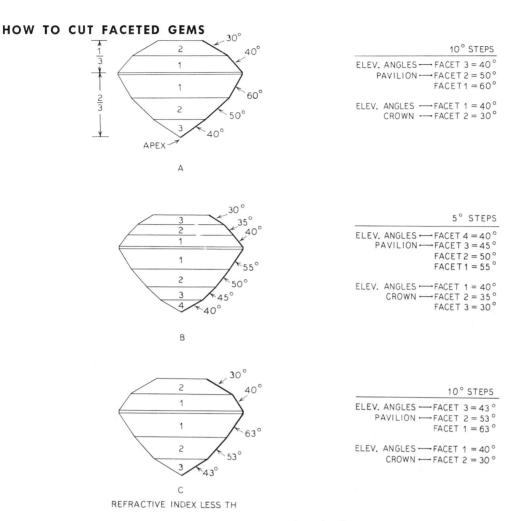

A

	10° STEPS
ELEV. ANGLES ⟶	FACET 3 = 40°
PAVILION ⟶	FACET 2 = 50°
	FACET 1 = 60°
ELEV. ANGLES ⟶	FACET 1 = 40°
CROWN ⟶	FACET 2 = 30°

B

	5° STEPS
ELEV. ANGLES ⟶	FACET 4 = 40°
PAVILION ⟶	FACET 3 = 45°
	FACET 2 = 50°
	FACET 1 = 55°
ELEV. ANGLES ⟶	FACET 1 = 40°
CROWN ⟶	FACET 2 = 35°
	FACET 3 = 30°

C

REFRACTIVE INDEX LESS TH

	10° STEPS
ELEV. ANGLES ⟶	FACET 3 = 43°
PAVILION ⟶	FACET 2 = 53°
	FACET 1 = 63°
ELEV. ANGLES ⟶	FACET 1 = 40°
CROWN ⟶	FACET 2 = 30°

Fig. 135 Proportions and angles for step cut gems.

to work with steps which range between 5° and 10° apart.

■ THE STANDARD BRILLIANT

The *standard brilliant* shown in Figures 100 and 121, is so-called because it is the basic brilliant style cut and is used far more than any of its numerous variations. It has thirty-two facets on top, with the table making thirty-three, while the pavilion has twenty-four, making a total of fifty-seven facets. In diamonds, it is customary to add one more facet, a tiny one on the very point of the pavilion called a *culet*. The purpose of this facet is supposedly to reduce the chance of splitting. Except on diamond, it is seldom used.

Figure 121, which shows the basic steps in cutting a brilliant, illustrates the simplicity of the procedure. Every facet has a corresponding notch on the gear wheel and makes cutting mainly a matter of going "by the numbers." See also Figure 108. For an initial attempt, make a quartz preform about ⅜ inch in diameter.

■ CUTTING THE TABLE FACET

The table is cut in the same way as for step-cut gems but polishing is postponed until after all crown facets are cut and polished. This is to provide a last minute opportunity to correct defects in cutting the small star facets which may often be restored to accuracy by cutting down the table slightly. Use the 1200 side of the copper cutting lap for all work on this gem.

■ CUTTING THE MAIN CROWN FACETS

Set the elevation angle at 40°. Turn and lock the dop arm in any major notch of the gear wheel as for example, 64. Set the angle stop on 40° to prevent cutting below this angle. Lower the head until the stone just touches the lap, and as before, start cutting. Cutting soon stops because the dop arm cannot go below the 40° position. Lower the head with the fine elevation adjustment to continue cutting; and repeat. Cut until the facet reaches from girdle to crown, as shown in E of Figure 121. Turn the dop arm to the opposite gear notch (32) and cut the opposite facet in the same way. Now cut another pair of mains exactly between the first two, giving four main facets all at right angles to each other. If the cutting has been done correctly, the crown will look like F in Figure 121. Each facet must be cut to the angle-stop position to be sure that the depth is the same all the way around.

Cutting the mains on a brilliant sets the accuracy of every other facet; for this reason, four facets are cut first on the crown to show a square on the table facet, as shown in F of Figure 121. The eye is sensitive to accuracy in a square and slight distortions are easily detected. If the figure is not a true square, it shows that one of the facets is a little too far out and should be recut slightly. When satisfied with the first four, cut in the other four to make eight. Do not overcut; one facet ground down too much will mean recutting all the rest to keep the pattern in balance. When finished, the eight crown mains should shape the table facet into an octagon, as shown in G of Figure 121, and all facets will be cut to the depth set originally on the angle stop.

A few words about the angle stop are in order because it is so useful in the cutting of brilliants. It was not used in step cutting because every facet was cut to join its neighbor at a well-defined junction point. In brilliant cutting there is no easy way of telling when a main has been cut down far enough. For this reason, the angle stop is used to be sure that each of the mains is cut to the same depth. If, after cutting all the facets to the depth deter-

mined by the angle stop, one facet still does not reach the girdle, this shows that that spot is the lowest place on the crown and all *other* facets must be cut down to it. Accordingly, lower the head with the fine adjustment, cut that facet until it does reach from the girdle to the table, then cut the rest to the new depth.

■ CUTTING THE STAR FACETS

Raise the facet head and set in an elevation angle of 15° less than the main angle, or 40° − 15° = 25°. Set the angle stop at this figure. Unlike the cutting of the mains, where the angle stop was used to be sure each facet was cut to the same depth, its use here is only to prevent serious overcutting. Each star facet is cut only enough to join its neighbor.

Set the trigger in one of the notches halfway between those used for cutting the mains. Bring the dop arm down to the angle stop and cautiously lower the head until the stone almost touches the lap; lower it the rest of the way with the fine adjustment until it begins to cut. *Immediately* check the tiny facet created by this first touch; if it is in the right place, continue cutting. Each star must be cut until its upper points appear to be about halfway across the two mains it straddles, as shown in H of Figure 121. If in doubt, undercut rather than overcut and go on to the next. If the stars are undercut, a section of the flat edge of the table facet will still be present between neighboring stars; looking at them will show which should be further cut to make them meet in a point.

The greatest care is needed in cutting stars because, being small, they cut rapidly, and because poor work is so obvious. They should just touch at their points, neither short nor overlapped.

■ CUTTING THE UPPER GIRDLE FACETS

A little judgment is needed to cut the girdle facets correctly. In general, these small triangular facets are cut at an elevation angle only 3° more than the crown main angle making them, in this case, $40° + 3° = 43°$. This angle varies and that is where the judgment is needed.

Place the trigger in a notch exactly halfway between those used for cutting the mains and the stars. To be sure which is which, study the diagrams in Figure 121 which give the settings. Lower the head gently and take a light trial cut. Inspect closely and try to judge whether the slope of the facet will make it touch the bottom of the star facet directly above it and still reach halfway to its neighboring facet along the girdle. If it looks as if it will reach the star first, the elevation angle is too low and the head must be lowered a little to correct. On the other hand, if the facet is too flat and stretches along the girdle without moving toward the star, raise the head to make it do so. Girdle facets, correctly and incorrectly started, are shown in Figure 136. Only the smallest trial cut should be taken to keep from overcutting in case the elevation angle was a little off.

To judge cutting girdle angles better, it

helps to mark the centerline on the girdle to serve as an aiming point. You will not be sure that these facets have been cut accurately until one pair is finished and they meet in the exact center as shown in Figure 121.

Figure 137 shows common cutting errors due to the stone shifting position or failure to use the angle stop correctly. Too much pressure results in the wax gradually warming and becoming slightly soft, which may result in the stone moving and losing its alignment.

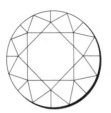

LOPSIDED CROWN

CAUSE: STONE SHIFTED POSITION
DURING CUTTING, OR, ANGLE
STOP NOT USED CORRECTLY.

LOPSIDED PAVILION

CAUSE: STONE SHIFTED DURING
TRANSFER, OR, ANGLE STOP
NOT USED CORRECTLY.

Fig. 137 Common cutting errors in the brilliant.

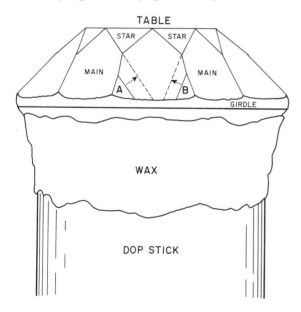

Fig. 136 Cutting girdle facets. At A the girdle facet is correctly started and when continued to the dotted line, it will meet the junction of the star facet and will also be centered at the bottom. At B, the facet has been incorrectly started and if continued to the dotted line will leave a large gap at the bottom.

■ **POLISHING THE CROWN**

Start polishing on the facets farthest away from the girdle and work back. This means polishing the stars first, then the mains, and finally the girdle facets. Since the facets are small, polishing is fast and enough material can be taken off to make small corrections if necessary. Sometimes, after all crown facets have been polished, the star facets show a small overlap. In small stones, polishing the table for a few minutes extra removes the error. If the error is large, it is worthwhile to recut the table on the copper lap to remove excess material which would take too long to polish away.

■ **TRANSFERRING**

This is done as described before.

■ **CUTTING THE PAVILION**

The greatest problem in cutting the pavilion is lining up the facets with those on the crown. This can only be done by cut and try methods.

Set the head to cut the bottom mains at 43° for quartz; be sure the trigger is in a major notch. At the place where the girdle of the gem is thickest, make a pencil mark directly below the center of the nearest upper main facet. Unlock the dop and turn until this mark seems vertical or, in other words, appears to be at the point where the stone will touch the lap when cutting begins. Lock the dop and lower the gem to the lap. Cut this facet partly, using the angle stop, then turn to the next main position and cut that facet to the same depth. Both are *light* cuts, only deep enough to meet each other sideways to make a junction. Wipe off for a good view and see how close the junction comes to a similar junction on the crown. If you are lucky, the junctions will coincide, but more likely they will still be off. Unlock the dop arm, twist slightly and relock. Recut both facets to get a new junction line; stop again and inspect. On this second try, the error should be so small that no more correction is needed. Once this alignment is correct, cut all eight pavilion mains, followed by the sixteen girdle facets, in the same way as for the crown. Be sure to use the angle stop for depth.

■ **POLISHING THE PAVILION**

Use the same procedures as described for polishing the crown.

■ **POLISHING THE GIRDLE**

If the girdle was accurately ground and dopped, it is uniform in width at all points, presuming, of course, that the cutting has also been well done. If this is not the case, the girdle must be trimmed to make it even all around.

If the facet head can be lowered to a nearly horizontal position, trimming is done while the dop stick is still in the dop arm, and followed immediately by polishing. If the head will not permit lowering all the way, remove the dop and hold in the fingers for trimming. Cutting is done on the fine lap using light pressure to avoid depressing the soft surface of the copper. Check frequently to avoid overcutting. Avoid catching an edge of the girdle since this could chip the stone and gouge the lap. A safer way is to do the operation on a wet sander with the added advantage of getting a slight rounding of the girdle at the same time. It is then polished on a wood lap.

Figure 138 shows properly and improperly finished girdles and the dangers involved in setting gems with extremely thin, sharp girdles.

■ **POLISHING TROUBLES**

Getting a perfect polish depends on using the right lap and the right powder for the right stone. For most gemstones, polishing is trouble-free unless scratches are left from grinding. These are easy to tell: they appear from the first and stay to the last, and their cure is obvious. Sometimes in spite of all care, scratches suddenly appear for no reason at all. These are most annoying and also the most difficult to get rid of. Often the polishing powder or the lap is blamed for becoming "contaminated," but actually this is seldom the case; more often the cause lies in the gem itself.

In many gemstones the crystal structure is such that polishing can not be done easily except in one direction. Like stroking the fur on a cat's back, there is only one way to get it smooth. When you get persistent scratching, change the direction of polishing by swinging the dop arm to another place on the lap. This makes the lap sweep across the facet from a

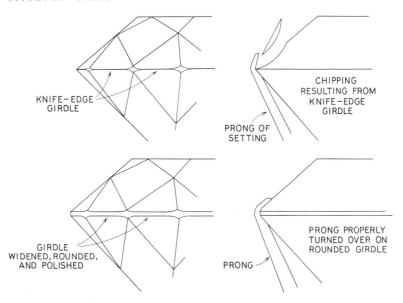

Fig. 138 Finishing the girdle of a brilliant.

different direction entirely. Also try changing the amount of pressure used to press the facet to the lap, varying from light to heavy. Experiment with different quantities of powder and different degrees of dryness on the lap. Sometimes a fine polish only comes when the lap is on the verge of drying out. If the lap speed can be changed, try a slower speed. If speed is fixed, try moving the gem as close to the center hole as possible, because here lap speed is slowest. When all else fails, switch to a wax or wooden lap. One of them is almost sure to bring up a perfect polish but either will also cause some slight rounding of facet edges.

The use of too much powder in the mix sometimes causes gems to wear away too quickly and to develop shallow depressions, especially behind sharp corners of small facets such as those on brilliants. Such shallow spots are smoothly polished but since they disturb the level surface of the facet, they make the gem appear less brilliant. Too many of them give the gem a "sleepy" look because the reflections are no longer sharp and crisp. The easiest cure is to keep the gem moving on the lap with a side-to-side movement which prevents depressions from forming and leaves the surface level.

■ FACETING OVAL BRILLIANTS AND OTHER ODD SHAPES

Modern faceting machines equipped with gear wheels for indexing are unsurpassed for cutting round brilliants, squares, octagons, and many shapes whose facets are placed at even angular distances. However, as soon as the shape of the gem departs from these ordinary shapes, it is found that there are not enough notches on any gear wheel to provide all the necessary settings.

This is made clear by referring to Figure 139, where a round brilliant is compared with an oval brilliant. Both cuts call for the same number of facets but in the oval brilliant, the facets must be stretched along the sides because the oval is a stretched circle. The gear wheel indexes needed for the round brilliant are shown on the left with radial lines which go directly to the center of the gem. Each of the facets can be cut accurately with these settings and those between on other notches of the gear wheel. On the right, where the oval brilliant is drawn, the story is different, and it can be seen that only the facets on the sides and ends can be cut with gear wheel settings while all the facets between must be cut with settings which may or may not be available on the gear wheel. Some will be available, if a

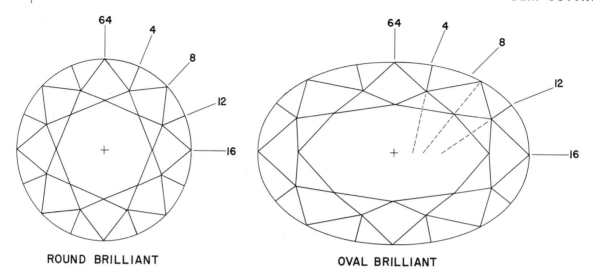

ROUND BRILLIANT   OVAL BRILLIANT

Fig. 139 Gear wheel settings for round brilliant compared to settings needed to cut an oval brilliant. Note that the settings between 64 and 16 cannot be obtained on the gear wheel. Each of the facets concerned has to be obtained by "splitting" or by hand adjustment of the dop arm.

little distortion of shape is not minded, but most of them will not be. The solid lines show the angles which correspond to gear wheel settings while the dotted lines show the angles at which the facets must be placed if the oval brilliant is to have its facets placed evenly and accurately around the girdle.

Some facet heads provide setting splitters which allow tilting of the dop arm or the assembly holding the dop arm so that any number of settings can be had between any adjacent notches on the gear wheel. In effect, by adjusting the splitters, it is possible to obtain an infinite number of settings. This sounds good but it is a nuisance to find the exact setting needed and an additional nuisance to keep track of them by writing them down on paper. Keeping track is necessary in order to go back to each facet for polishing.

The traditional cutter, using his jamb peg method, laughs at the trials and tribulations of the amateur who tries to cut any odd-shaped gem. Because the jamb peg dop stick is not fastened to anything and can be turned to any angle, the traditional cutter is able to find the right spot for the facet in a fraction of a second, and in several more, have it cut. Furthermore, he does not have to remember or record any gear wheel settings or splitter settings, and

can hit any facet for polishing even faster than it took him to find it for cutting. Granted that his hand methods in cutting ordinary gems do not usually give the accuracy so kindly put into mechanical heads by their makers, he still is able to make several acceptable gems in the time it takes the amateur to produce one. Furthermore, since the use of splitters in cutting odd-shaped gems is a matter of personal judgment in placing facets, the amateur will probably not make as accurate a gem as the professional even with the assistance of the mechanical faceting head.

Because of the enormous difficulties in producing acceptable oval brilliants, hearts, marquises, pendeloques, pears, and other unusual gems by using a mechanical head, amateur exhibits of faceted gems are conspicuous by the abundance of gems which can be cut easily on mechanical heads and the absence of odd-shaped gems which cannot. This is unfortunate because odd-shaped gems are fascinating. In many cases, an odd shape is a better cut to use with certain pieces of rough than a shape chosen only because it is easy to handle on mechanical faceting equipment.

Over the years the author has cut many odd-shaped gems easily by making a slight modification to his Allen facet head. Unfortunately, as simple as this modification is, it can not be made on many other machines because their design does not permit it. The modification consists of inserting a Neoprene garden hose washer under the locking nut on the end of the dop arm assembly. This nut is shown clearly just below and to the left of D in Figure 106. The knurled nut screws to the rotating dop arm and locks the gear wheel in place. The hose washer is inserted on the threaded part of the dop arm shaft between the nut and the gear wheel. The knurled nut is drilled and tapped to take a small set screw which can be used to tighten the nut on the threaded part of the shaft and keep it from backing off. The washer allows the dop arm to be slipped from any setting by merely twisting it with the hand. By adjusting the tightness of the knurled nut, and locking the nut in place with a small set screw, any degree of "give" can be obtained. For large gems where considerable pressure is placed on the dop arm during cutting and polishing, the tightness is increased, while for small gems, it is lessened. The large oval aquamarine shown in Figure 141 was cut on the Allen head modified as described.

In summary, the modification described offers these advantages: (1) it allows any setting whatsoever to be obtained almost as quickly as the jamb peg cutter can do it; (2) the setting obtained stays put and does not wander off if the hand holding the dop arm relaxes, a real danger in using a hand-held dop stick; and finally, (3) the accuracy of the gear wheel can *also* be used when desired. This last point becomes clearer when the instructions for cutting an oval brilliant are given.

■ CUTTING THE OVAL BRILLIANT

The oval brilliant was chosen because once it is learned how to cut this gem, many others such as pears, pendeloques, marquises, etc., can also be cut because the principles are similar. It is essential for accurate cutting that the preform be profiled as accurately as possible because the girdle of the

preform is marked with ink to show where the facets must go, and if the outline is lopsided, the facets will be too. Refer now to Figure 140.

In number 2 of this figure is shown a cardboard template, which is used for two purposes. Its first purpose is to help in grinding the outline of the preform accurately, while the second is to mark the placement of facets on the girdle of the preform. When the preform for an oval brilliant, as shown in number 1, has been ground, it is placed flat on a smooth surface and the girdle line inscribed in India ink. Use a small crow quill pen and rest it on several layers of thin cardboard until the point is at the right height. Now place the gem in front of the nib and rotate it while holding the pen steady. This insures a girdle line at exactly the same depth below the table facet at all points. Place the template on the girdle and mark the facet divisions, spacing them evenly around the gem. The result will be as shown in number 3. Coat the marks with shellac or varnish and let dry. Dop the gem on the pavilion to cut the crown first. At this time the table facet can be cut and polished either in the facet machine or by hand lapping.

Transfer the dopped gem to the facet machine and lock in place. Lower the facet head to its lowest point in order to place the preform girdle on the master lap. Set the gear wheel at 64; unlock the dop and rotate until one of the sides of the preform is resting on the master lap. Lock the dop stick. Rub a little red lipstick or grease pencil on the master lap and rub the side of the preform in it. Check to see if the red mark on the preform is exactly opposite the ink mark. If not, unlock the dop, twist the gem slightly and try again. The idea is to center the intended facet exactly on the mark and also on one of the major notches on the gear wheel.

When the marks coincide, switch to the other side and end marks and check these. Put on the cutting lap, and raise the head to the cutting position using a crown angle appropriate to the gemstone being cut. Start the lap and take a very light cut; lift the dop arm and check to see that this cut is opposite the ink

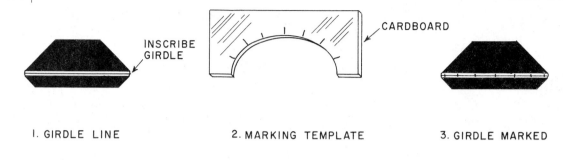

1. GIRDLE LINE   2. MARKING TEMPLATE   3. GIRDLE MARKED

INSCRIBE GIRDLE   CARDBOARD

4. SIDE AND END CUTS   5. CORNER CUTS   6. FACET CENTERS MARKED

Fig. 140 Steps in cutting an oval brilliant. 1. The gem is laid flat and the girdle inscribed in India ink. 2. A marking template is made which is also used for checking the preforming of the gem. 3. The girdle is marked in equal divisions. 4. The side and end cuts are made using gear wheel. 5. Corner cuts are put on. 6. All facets are marked in centers to help in cutting remaining facets.

mark. Make similar trial cuts on the other three facets. When satisfied that the cuts are accurately placed, cut each of the side and end facets to somewhat about the inked girdle line. Do not cut all the way down as yet until you are sure that these facets are placed correctly. After cutting, the preform will look like number 4 in Figure 140. These cuts, made with the gear wheel, establish the basic accuracy of the oval. That is why it is important to take as much trouble with them as has been described.

To cut the corner facets, turn to a setting which appears to coincide with the ink mark on the girdle between the marks just used. Make a light cut and see if it is centered directly above the ink mark. If not, slip the dop arm or use the setting splitter to make the correction. Take another light trial cut, extending it only far enough to remove the previous cut. By this method of taking trial cuts and adjusting, it is surprising how easily one gets the knack of placing facets. When one of the corner facets is placed correctly, cut to the same depth as the side and end facets; note the gear wheel setting and turn to the notch directly opposite.

This will enable cutting the opposite facet at exactly the same angular distance away. Repeat this process to cut the other two facets until the preform looks like number 5 in Figure 140.

The tendency in cutting ovals is to stay at the same position of the faceting head without changing elevation angle from facet to facet. This is a mistake because it will result in a table facet which is not properly centered within the oval outline of the gem as a whole. The elevation angle must be reset for each of the main facets as you go along.

After the eight main facets have been cut, mark the centers of each with India ink, as shown in number 6 of Figure 140. This is to give aiming points when cutting the star facets and girdle facets. The stars are cut first.

Raise the facet head to give about 15° less elevation angle than was used for cutting the mains. Slip the dop arm, or use the setting splitter to place one of the main facet junctions opposite. Lower the head and with the gentlest touch possible, cut an extremely small star facet. Examine to decide which way the dop arm must be adjusted to make the star stretch to each of the ink marks and still go

halfway down toward the girdle. Again several light trial cuts and adjustments will be neces-

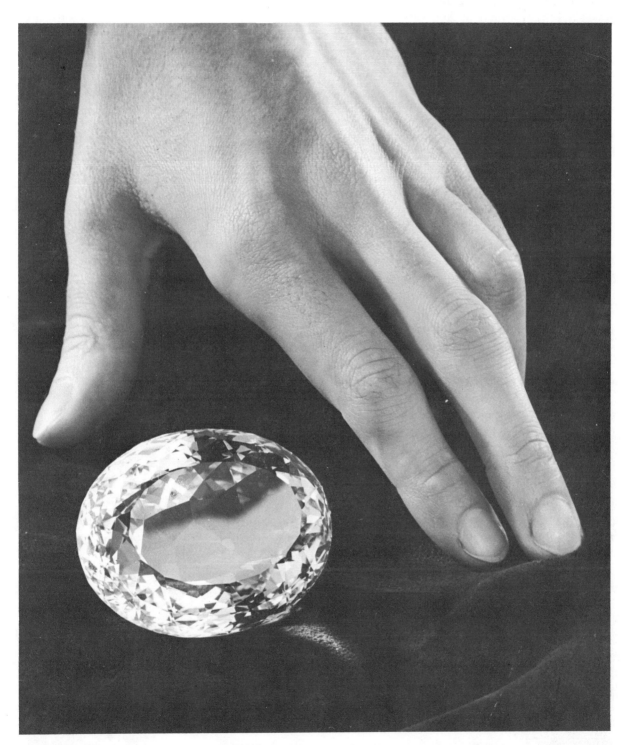

Fig. 141 Oval aquamarine of 578 carats cut by the author for the Smithsonian Institution. It is 2⅜ inches long and 1⅞ inches wide. The color is yellowish-green. This gem was cut without using numerical settings on the facet machine; all facets were positioned by eye. (Courtesy Smithsonian Institution)

sary. When the correct setting has been obtained, cut down to size. Next jump over to the position on the opposite side of the gem and cut that corner, since at least the elevation angle will be correct. Then cut the other two stars which also use the same elevation angle. Using the same procedure, cut the other four stars.

In similar manner, using an elevation angle about 3° more than the main facet angle, cut the girdle facets. These are far more difficult to do than the star facets because very slight changes in angle of rotation cause a fast change in the position of the facet. If slight errors are made, they may often be corrected in polishing, particularly in small gems.

To polish, return to the mains, polishing them first, then the stars, and finish with the girdle facets. Make corrections as you can. In polishing, the way to get "on" to any facet is to touch the gem to the lap for only a second. A rasping noise announces the fact that a corner is being polished and not a flat facet. Make a correcting adjustment immediately. Note where the point of impact occurs on the gem since this will tell you which way to twist the dop arm to seat the facet on the lap. For the four side and end main facets, stop the lap, set in the proper elevation angle, and twist the dop arm until you feel the facet fall flat on the lap. Start the lap and polish for a second or two. Examine to see if a correction is needed.

The pavilion of the oval brilliant is usually cut to a knife-edge ridge, as shown in Figure 101, but may also be cut to draw to a single point. Stout ovals are suitable for the latter style but long narrow ovals should be cut in the ridge fashion to get better brilliance. The pavilion main facets present few problems and are easily cut, again adjusting elevation angle to be sure each of them is at the same angle. The girdle facets are difficult but can be cut more easily if ink marks are used as before and another set of ink marks placed below the girdle to about one third the way to the apex of the pavilion to mark the terminations.

Although cutting of odd-shaped gems is certainly more difficult on a faceting machine,

it is not so difficult that it cannot be done except by a select few. After you have learned how to cut standard styles, begin experimenting with oval brilliants and learn how to solve their problem. The sooner this is begun, the sooner you will become expert.

■ FACETING LARGE GEMS

Gems up to 500 or 600 carats can be cut on ordinary machines if certain modifications are made. Since such gems are far deeper than smaller gems, it is necessary to raise the stand rod at least 2 inches. The simplest way to do this is to obtain a 2-inch thick billet of metal—iron, brass, or steel all do nicely —and have it machined flat and parallel on two sides. Bore a hole of the same diameter as that in the base of the stand rod. Obtain a long bolt for fastening the stand rod base to the billet and into the base plate of the facet machine. When installed, the stand rod rests on the billet while the long bolt fastens the stand rod base and billet to the bed plate.

Ordinary dops are completely useless for large gems and it is necessary to have some made. Face plates of at least ¾ inch in diameter are necessary as well as large vees and conical dops corresponding in shape to those shown in Figure 125 but on a grander scale. They can be made of any metal but soft steel is probably cheapest and best. Unless you have access to a machinist's lathe, you must get the dops made in a machine shop. On the other hand, if you can use a welding torch, or have a large blow torch, the dops can be made from steel drill rod with tops welded or brazed on. Some inaccuracies can be tolerated in all dops except face plates. It is extremely important that these have the flat surfaces which touch the gems as close to right angles to the dop stick shank as possible.

Since much larger facets are going to be cut, ordinary cutting laps are far too slow to be useful, even the 400 grit coarse lap tends to glaze facets instead of cut them. A good cutting lap for several-hundred carat gems is copper charged with 200 diamond; for larger gems, a 100 diamond lap is very useful for rapidly removing material. Since both laps are severe in their action, careful recutting of all facets with 400 is essential before going to polish.

As an alternative to getting special roughing laps, the regular 400 lap can be used if the stone is preformed so accurately ahead of time that very little material has to be ground off in the cutting. It is also a good idea to design facets that are not too large if only the 400 lap is to be used. For example, in step cut gems, make the steps more numerous and narrower. In brilliant gems, double the number of facets or split the rows. The 578 carat aquamarine shown in Figure 141, was cut with a 400 lap. However, it was preformed very carefully and none of the facets were made large except the table facet, and the latter was cut and polished by hand lapping rather than using the facet machine.

■ PREFORMING LARGE GEMS

The size of large gems automatically keeps them from being preformed easily on small trim saws or grinding wheels. The latter can be used but must be trued absolutely smooth to prevent bumping. Waste material is most conveniently gotten rid of by sawing preforms upon a small slabbing saw, using 10- to 12-inch blades. Larger saws are fine but the thicker blades make more wasteful cuts. Even spodumene can be cut on slabbing saws, and indeed the job is done better because the power feed is smoother and more uniform than feeding the rough by hand, as would be necessary if a trim saw were used. Blanks must be marked exactly with India ink, coated with shellac to prevent washing off. Set in the slabbing saw clamp and adjust as carefully as possible to put the cuts where they belong. Remark with ink as needed—do not guess! By judicious use of the saw, the greatest part of the rough will be removed and much time saved in grinding. The large beryl shown in Figure 142 was preformed on a 16-inch slabbing saw.

When the sawing is finished, again mark

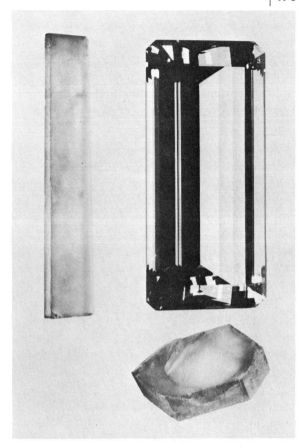

Fig. 142 Large step cut yellow beryl measuring 4¾ inches in length and 2 inches wide, cut for the Smithsonian by the author. The weight is 2,054 carats. The remaining sections of the large clear hexagonal crystals from which this gem was cut are shown at the left (base) and below (termination). (Courtesy Smithsonian Institution)

the gem accurately, and take to the grinding wheel to eliminate more material. Every part taken off here saves time in later operations. If grinding wheels of 10-inch diameter are available, use those in preference to smaller sizes. Soft bond wheels are preferable to medium bond. Be sure water is generously supplied to prevent burning.

■ DOPPING

Because of the size of the gems involved, internal stresses due to heating are more likely to cause cracking than in the case of small gems. It is not a good idea to try to heat the entire gem to dopping temperature and take a chance on getting one portion so hot that it cracks. The following schemes have been used successfully by the author.

Place a piece of thin cardboard on top of the regular dopping oven; rest the gem on top, table facet down, and surround it with a circular piece of cardboard, like a stovepipe, to keep away drafts. Use the regular small alcohol lamp and trim its flame to about ½ inch tall. This does not warm the stone nearly enough for dopping but it warms it safely and evenly and is better than trying to cement it cold. Select a dop of proper size and shape to fit the pavilion and heat in another flame. Coat it heavily with stick shellac. Place a clean piece of cardboard on the workbench and transfer the warm preform to this. Use gloves when handling the warm gem. Apply wax to the back of the preform by melting stick shellac in the alcohol flame and letting the droplets fall on the back until a layer about ⅛ inch thick is formed. A knife blade is used to shape the wax. Heat the dop stick and apply to the preform, screwing down firmly to get the metal as close to the stone as possible. Drip on more wax until a supporting cone is built around the back of the stone and within and over the dop. Turn up the alcohol flame to full height, and picking up both gem and dop stick, twirl in the column of hot gases which rise above the flame. Let the wax melt where it is thickly layered to get it to flow and spread evenly; continue until the wax is uniformly distributed and almost fluid. Place the gem back on the cardboard, keeping the dop stick upright and centered as best as you can until the wax begins to stiffen. Check to make sure the shank is vertical by resting a carpenters or machinists square alongside and glancing past the edge. Do this on one side and then on another to be sure the dop stick is squared in two directions. Very accurate alignment is possible with this method but it calls for some juggling.

Another method of alignment is to use the facet machine. The idea is to insert the dop stick in the 45° dop. The master lap, covered with a thin piece of cardboard to prevent its coldness from cracking the gem, is used to support the preform, table facet down, and to slide it under the dop stick installed in the 45° dop. The pointer on the dop arm has to be at 45°. When the gem is placed under the dop stick, the stick is allowed to slide down on top of it to make the join. Still another way to do the job is to get a machinist to make a jumbo transfer jig, like the one made for the author shown in Figure 143. In attaching dop sticks it helps to mark the gem along the girdle edge with India ink to show where the

Fig. 143 Dopping accessories. Normal size dops are shown at center while jumbo dops and transfer jigs are shown at right.

center of the gem is. The dop stick shank can then be aligned with these marks to center it.

For dopping gems over 1,000 carats, the author has lately used an alcohol blowtorch instead of a dopping lamp because the flame can be directed better. The intense flame is always applied to the dop stick and to the shellac, but never to the gem itself. Enough heat is transmitted by this method to warm up the gem gradually so that a good bond is possible.

■ DOPPING TABLE FIRST

If the pavilion of a large gem is irregular and its apex is not exactly in the center of the preform, it is better to attach the dop to the table facet first and cut the pavilion first. It can be centred accurately according to India ink marks along the girdle and running across the table facet.

To dop the table, wipe it off with alcohol to be sure it is clean; do not touch it afterwards with the fingers. Coat the table with a thin layer of liquid shellac; let dry. Place on the stove to warm as described before, but rest the preform on its side so that the shellac coating on the table facet does not stick to the cardboard. Heat a face plate dop stick and smear a very thin coat of stick shellac on its surface; too much will cause tilting of the gem and incorrect alignment. When the preform is warm, take the face plate and stick to the table facet. Transfer to the workbench and set the gem in a bed of steel wool to hold it upright. Heat the dop stick shank and at the same time, drip on stick shellac, building up a puddle around the face plate. The small blow torch is useful here because it can be directed against the shaft of the dop stick. When the wax is almost fluid, shift the dop stick to center it; let cool.

■ CUTTING AND POLISHING LARGE TABLE FACETS

The tables of large gems are almost impossible to cut and polish on standard machines. Few machines are built strongly enough to withstand the severe wrenching created by the friction of cutting and polishing. For this reason, these facets must be cut and polished by hand using lapping techniques similar to those described in Chapter 5.

After preforming, lap the table with 220 grit on a regular lapping machine, or if the table is reasonably smooth and level, start with 400 grit. If a lapping machine is not available, use a flat piece of steel or plate glass and rub the gem back and forth by hand. As soon as the surface is perfectly flat, switch to 400 grit or to 1200 as the case may be. Do not use a rotating lap for 400 or 1200 grit because no matter how carefully you use them, deep scratches are almost certain to result. It is far safer to lap by hand. Wipe the stone dry and examine under a strong light to see if there are

any circular marks which indicate that a grain of grit has been dragged across the surface. Such marks *must be eliminated* by additional hand lapping because invariably there are deep cracks beneath them. When the surface is lapped correctly, it will be frosted with absolute uniformity everywhere. The final lapping is always with 1200 grit.

To polish, use Pellon sheet cemented to a hard lap for quartz and beryl gems. The polishing agent is cerium oxide although others will do. There will be some rounding of the edges of the table facet after polishing but since the edges will be cut off when the crown facets are put on, this is of little importance. Continue polishing until the entire surface is flawless. *Caution:* if at the beginning of polishing scratches appear, go back immediately to the 1200 grit lap and get rid of them. It is almost impossible to polish out scratches in a reasonable time; time is saved by re-lapping.

For extremely large facets, going directly to Pellon may be rather slow and some time can be saved by pre-polishing on a well-scored tin lap. *Caution:* the lap must be deeply scored to be effective; if it is not, it may cause severe scratches which will require lapping all over again. After polishing on the tin lap to the point where the surface is practically finished, switch to the Pellon and remove the last few pits, ripples and other surface irregularities.

■ POLISHING OTHER FACETS

The only lap recommended for polishing facets of large gems is well-scored tin. The author has found no others satisfactory. The scores should be deeper than usual, at least ¹⁄₁₆ inch, and drawn from center to edge with shorter scores between, as shown in Figure 115. A flat block of clean agate is used to rub down the ridges after scoring. For very long facets, that is, from about 1 to 3 inches in length, the scores should not be less than ⅛ inch apart and no more than about ³⁄₁₆ inch apart. This provides enough air space under the facet to prevent suction and to permit enough pressure to be exerted to get swift polishing. Larger areas will require scores as far apart as ¼ inch. Use Linde A for polishing, in a moist but not wet paste. A deeply scored lap of this kind polishes large areas of topaz, as in the 3200 carat blue topaz which is shown in Figure 144.

■ LARGE FACETING MACHINES

The author had built a special large machine for cutting and polishing faceted gems up to about 5,000 carats weight. This machine is shown in Figures 144 and 145. It reproduces the Allen design, for which permission was graciously given by Mr. Gene Allen. It is larger by a factor of 1.5 but some dimensions were changed slightly for reasons of strength and greater flexibility. The base plate is a casting of aluminum, machined flat on top, and rigidly supporting the master lap assembly and facet head. A locking mechanism under the facet head permits sliding toward and away from the master lap. Special laps of 12-inch diameter were made for the author by Mr. Allen and consist of copper cutting laps, a lead cutting lap, a steel cutting lap and tin and Lucite polishing laps, as shown in Figure 146. Several aluminum laps were also obtained to use in making a wax lap, Pellon lap, wood-surfaced lap, etc.

This machine has been used to cut an 1800 carat spodumene for the Royal Ontario Museum, a 2050 carat beryl for the Smithsonian, as shown in Figure 142, and a 3,200 carat blue topaz also for the Smithsonian Institution. The last is shown during cutting in Figure 144.

Fig. 144 Cutting a 3,200 carat blue topaz. *Top.* Preform with table polished, resting on a 12-inch tin polishing lap. *Center.* Polishing the back facets after cutting in the steps. The dark strips along the edge are facets which are finished. *Bottom.* The crown facets are completely polished. This gem weighed over 3,200 carats when finished. It is now in the Smithsonian collections.

Fig. 145 The author's large faceting machine made after the Allen model and enlarged 1.5 times. The master lap unit takes 12-inch laps. The stand rod is 16 inches tall and made from 1-inch diameter steel rod. The dop arm is about 10 inches long. It is estimated that gems up to 5,000 carats can be cut easily on this machine.

Fig. 146 A series of 12-inch laps for large faceting machine. *Top,* left to right: copper charged with diamond, tin lap, teak en-grain blocks cemented on aluminum, and cloth-covered wax on aluminum. *Bottom.* Pellon cemented to a Lucite lap.

15 | *Spheres and Beads*

Among the most fascinating objects which the lapidary can make are spheres of gem material, such as those shown in Figure 147. Ground to perfect geometrical form and polished to a glistening luster, they never fail to excite wonder and admiration.

The making of spheres, and also of beads, is not as difficult as one imagines. By taking advantage of certain mechanical principles which have been known and used for many years, even the beginner can turn out satisfactory work. The making of spheres will be taken up first, followed by a discussion on the making of beads.

■ SELECTION OF MATERIAL

One of the difficulties of sphere making is finding and selecting good raw material, particularly for large spheres. Any cracks, flaws, or other defects show very plainly on a finished sphere, and no amount of artifice will disguise their presence. Those experienced in making spheres advocate the closest examination of rough blocks. Many have been broken from larger blocks, and minute cracks, often too small to see easily, radiate from points of hammer impact. It pays to examine rough with a magnifying glass in strong light to see if cracks can be detected. Even more difficult is the problem of finding flawless material in transparent gemstones, since here internal defects will certainly show after the final polish is applied.

A test for absence of cracks is to soak the rough block in water or oil for a few hours. If soaked in water, wipe off afterwards and note if discolored lines appear on the surface. These are often places along cracks where water is working its way out. If soaked in oil, clean with detergent solution, dry, and observe the surface an hour or so later. By this time oil will also work its way out and easily show those places where cracks are located. In any event, it pays to be careful in selection of material because making a sphere involves much work and it would be a pity to waste it all on poor material.

Fig. 147 Paul A. Broste of Parshall, North Dakota with part of his extensive collection of spheres which he made himself. Years of searching for flawless material suitable for these spheres is matched by the great care which has gone into their cutting and polishing. (Courtesy Paul A. Broste)

■ BLOCKING THE SPHERE

A sphere is always begun from a cube, and the object in preliminary sawing of rough is to reduce it to this form. Clamp the stone into the slabbing saw and cut one face which will do as a face of the sphere. Remove and mark with a perfect square for the other cuts. If possible, place the rough in the saw so that two parallel cuts can be taken during the first sawing, the distance between them being equal to the thickness of the cube. If this is not possible, then each of the six faces of the cube will have to be cut separately. Mark and cut the cube, finishing by grinding off any sharp projecting corners.

■ MAKING A TEMPLATE

To help in sawing excess material from the cube, make a template. Find the smallest cube face on the roughed-out block. Place this face down on a piece of cardboard and draw the outline with a sharp pencil. Cross the square with pencil lines from opposite corners. Where the diagonals intersect, place the point of a compass and draw a circle within the square. Do not go *over* any side line. This circle represents the cross-section of the future sphere. Draw tangents across each of the diagonal lines to indicate where the edges of the cube will be sawed off. When the tangents are drawn, the figure will be an octagon. Cut this out with scissors.

■ THE SAWING GUIDE

Figure 148 illustrates a clever device which greatly simplifies the sawing of the

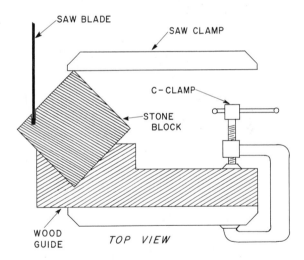

Fig. 148 Wooden guide for sawing sphere preforms.

cube corners. The device is shown installed in the carriage clamp of a slabbing saw. By its use, the cube can be sawed accurately and conveniently without a great deal of juggling and chance for error. The device is made of any close-grained hardwood sawed with an accurate 90° vee on one end to receive the stone cube, as shown in the illustration. It is moved in and out of the carriage clamp to approximately the right position, then clamped firmly with the C-clamp. Exact adjustment laterally is made with the cross-feed screw on the carriage. Once this adjustment has been made and the saw blade cuts exactly along the line marked on the stone cube, any other cut is merely a matter of opening the jaws, turning the cube, closing, and making a new cut.

Small cubes can be handled by making two clamps of the same type and holding the stone between them clothespin fashion.

■ SAWING CUBE EDGES

When ready to saw off the edges of the cube, clean the stone carefully and apply the template to each face, marking along the edges with easily visible pencil. India ink or white ink are useful depending on the color of the stone, the idea being to get contrast so that lines can be seen clearly. Protect the markings with a brushing of shellac which will not be affected by the coolant oil of the saw.

Set the block in the guide and lock in place. Move the saw carriage over until the blade is just outside of the mark. Great care must be taken not to cut even a little inside the marks because this will mean that the finished work will have one dimension smaller than the rest and will require extra grinding later before a perfect sphere can be obtained. Feed the carriage forward very slowly to prevent the saw blade from being deflected by the sloping side of the stone. When the blade has cut a notch exactly along the edge of the line, allow the carriage to go forward on slow feed to complete the cut. Open the carriage clamp, remove the stone and flip over for another cut. If the stone is nearly perfect as a cube, no further lateral adjustment of the saw carriage will be necessary.

The first series of edge cuts will remove narrow triangular strips of stone from four sides of the cube. The next set of cuts will take off the edges at right angles to these, and finally a third series of cuts will remove the last few sharp projections. At this time the stone will show six small square faces corresponding to the faces of the original cube, plus twelve faces on the former cube edges. The sphere-to-be is now ready for grinding.

■ PREFORMING THE SPHERE

A word of caution is in order here in respect to grinding the sawed block: do not attempt to make a sphere larger than your grinders are capable of shaping. In general, spheres of several inches in diameter cannot be handled comfortably on grinding wheels of less than 10 inches in diameter. If your grinding wheels are 6 or 8 inches in diameter, you should not try to use them for shaping a sphere larger than about 2 inches in diameter. However, as will be explained later, it is sometimes possible to use smaller wheels if a steady-rest for the sphere is carefully rigged. The problem in grinding heavy objects on small wheels is the setting up of disastrous bumping which can easily ruin a wheel and even crack the stone itself, especially if the stone is held freehand to the wheel face.

The first step in grinding off the projections of the sawed block is to grind away one set of edges which are parallel to each other. There are three such sets on the sawed block; start at any one. However, before doing any grinding, mark the exact center of each cube face with a black or white dot about ¼ inch in diameter to remind you not to grind these off and lose track of what you are doing. These marks represent the proper thickness of the future sphere and by *not* grinding them off, you will be prevented from grinding the preform into some lopsided shape. Protect each mark with a coating of shellac or varnish.

The first grinding of the sphere will result in a rough cylinder. Turn this and grind off another set of edges intersecting the first; then do the same with the third set until the cube is rounded. Grind off the sharp corners which are left until an approximate sphere results.

At this time, set up a steady-rest in front of the grinding wheel. If your grinder does not have one already installed, obtain a heavy block of wood, stone, or metal, and put it in front of the wheel in proper position so that the sphere can rest on top and be rolled forward to contact the grinding face. Cover the top of the steady-rest with a piece of sole leather on which the sphere can rest. Take the sphere in the hands, with fingertips placed opposite each other, and turn the sphere slowly. Let only the high spots "tick" on the face of the grinder. In this way all high spots will be taken off in succession. Change the position of the sphere frequently and be sure to check the cube face marks to be certain that they are not being ground off. Places which are obviously high can be marked with pencil for special attention. The rough sphere is now ready for final shaping.

■ SHAPING THE SPHERE

The principle of all sphere shaping is shown in Figure 149. The preformed sphere is placed between two segments of pipe, one of which is tilted at an angle to the other and held by hand. The lower pipe is screwed

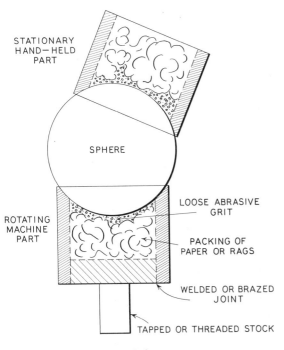

STATIONARY HAND—HELD PART

SPHERE

ROTATING MACHINE PART

LOOSE ABRASIVE GRIT

PACKING OF PAPER OR RAGS

WELDED OR BRAZED JOINT

TAPPED OR THREADED STOCK

Fig. 149 Sphere cutters.

to the shaft of a vertical or horizontal lapidary unit and turned at slow rpm. By sweeping the upper section of pipe in a rotary motion, and at the same time making the sphere turn also, the loose abrasive soon cuts away all high spots until a perfectly round shape is generated. Obviously, the better the sphere is preformed, the more likely it is to turn easily in the pipes and to achieve its final form faster. This is why careful attention to preforming pays.

Pipes for cutting spheres are available from manufacturers of all-purpose units such as those discussed in Chapter 8, or they can be made at home. The pipe attached to the shaft of the machine should be fairly accurate and some care is needed in making it if one decides to assemble his own. However, the job is not difficult if a lathe is available to turn out the stock to which the pipe is fastened. Prior to use, the pipe sections should have their inner edges shaped to a 45° angle to fit the surface of the sphere more closely. Always avoid placing sharp edges on the pipes and, during cutting, remove the sharp edges which eventually develop. Serious cuts to the hands can result otherwise. Sphere cutters should be about two-thirds to three-quarters the diameter of the sphere. Speed of rotation is from 150 rpm to 500 rpm, lower speeds being better for larger spheres and vice versa.

■ LAPPING

Install the proper sized cutter on the machine; have ready a wide-mouthed jar partly filled with 100 silicon carbide grit, and a brush to apply the watery grit mixture. Turn on the machine and brush the cutter with a heavy mixture of grit; apply the sphere and keep turning it, replenishing the grit frequently. Do not ever allow the sphere to stay in one position for more than a few seconds! This can quickly result in lapping a deep ring around the sphere which will take much additional work to remove. The idea is to keep the sphere constantly turning in every direction at all times.

When the sphere has some of the high spots

taken off, apply the top hand-held cutter and press down upon the sphere and cause it to move about. Apply grit frequently. For large spheres, it will not be necessary or even very comfortable to use an upper pipe since both hands will be needed to keep the sphere moving about, while the weight of the sphere will provide all the downward pressure needed.

Some cutters have found that loose packing inside the cutters, as shown in Figure 149, is useful for storing grit in contact with the sphere and therefore calls for less to be applied by brush. Others do not use any packing at all and claim equally good results.

After lapping has continued for some time, remove the sphere, wash and inspect. If you are not certain that the surface is uniformly ground, draw wax-pencil lines around the sphere and return to the machine for brief, additional lapping. Low spots will still show pencil marks and indicate that additional work is needed. A similar trick is to spray the sphere with colored lacquer and re-lap; any low spots will show instantly. When the sphere is finished, clean the sphere, remove and clean the cutters, and repeat the entire process using 220 grit followed by 400, and finish with 1200. Hard gemstones such as agate, rock crystal, etc., can be polished directly from the 1200 stage. Some cutters advocate a sanding step for softer gemstones such as calcite onyx, rhodochrosite, etc., stopping at the 400 grit stage and sanding by hand with small squares of very fine abrasive paper or cloth. The sphere is turned in the clean cutter and the sanding done on top, shifting the position of the sphere from time to time to cover the entire area.

■ POLISHING

Two methods of polishing are possible, the first by hand, holding the sphere against a polishing buff as with other lapidary projects, or the second, where the sphere cutter attached to the machine is covered with polishing material and the sphere polished in the same manner it was cut.

In the first method, the sphere may be held directly against any vertical polishing buff suitable to the gemstone being polished, and the surface of the sphere systematically covered until it is all done. It can also be propped against the buff by using a steadyrest, again covered on top with a piece of leather on which the sphere rests. If the leather is wetted, the sphere will slide upon it and actually spin under the friction created by the polishing buff. During the process, the hands are used to control the speed of the sphere to prevent it from twirling too rapidly. A thick buff can be allowed to wear on its face until its curvature approximates that of the sphere. This gives greater contact area and expedites polishing.

In the second method of polishing, the cutter is removed after lapping, carefully cleaned and replaced on the machine. The top is covered with stout canvas or thin leather, soaked to give pliability. The material is folded with as few wrinkles as possible and secured by wrappings of strong twine. The center is allowed to sag somewhat so that more contact area will be obtained with the sphere during polishing. If leather is used, an excellent pre-polish can be obtained on certain gemstones by coating the leather with 1200 grit. The resulting finish is in the nature of an extremely fine sanded surface. Gemstones which can profit by this treatment are indicated in Chapter 19, and before any kind is treated as a sphere instructions for its cutting should be consulted in this chapter.

■ SPHERE MAKING MACHINES

Several firms now manufacture machines designed to remove much of the tedious effort formerly necessary in the shaping and polishing of spheres. A machine of this type is illustrated in Figure 150. All of the machines work on the same principles used to cut spheres by hand and show arrangements similar to those noted in Figure 150. The heart of the machine consists of two arms supporting the cutters. Each arm is fitted with a pulley

Fig. 150 Victor sphere making machine. A machine of this type takes much of the work out of shaping and polishing spheres. The right hand arm assembly is movable to accommodate spheres of various diame- ters. Shown installed are sphere cutters covered with polishing cloth and gripping a sphere in the process of being polished. (Courtesy Victor Valley Gem Shop, Fallbrook, California)

which is turned by a vee belt from a motor below. The cutters turn in opposite directions, and when the sphere runs freely, cause it to rotate in all conceivable directions. Both hands of the operator are free during the process, but he must keep the sphere supplied with grit or polish, as the case may be. Pressure upon the cutters is adjustable, and by selecting the proper amount, the sphere can be made to spin readily with efficient cutting action. Polishing is done on the same machine by attaching polishing cloths to the cutters. Various size cutters are furnished to enable cutting a variety of spheres from as small as several inches to as large as 10 or 12 inches.

■ BEAD MAKING

In jewelry, the term "bead" can refer to small gems of any form, provided that they are strung on a cord, but for our purposes we will discuss how spherical beads are made, particularly those meant to be bored with central stringing holes. Very satisfactory beads can be made entirely by hand using cabochon techniques; however, where a considerable number must be made it pays to shape them automatically. Only recently has it been possible for amateurs to buy a specially-designed bead-making mill, as shown in Figure 151. This machine is simple in construction and use and is designed to be operated in a standard home workshop drill press.

■ PRINCIPLE OF THE BEAD MILL

The Crown bead mill shown in Figure 151 consists of a base with four uprights. Within the uprights fits a stout metal tank pressed upward by the four stout springs shown in the first photograph. In the bottom of the tank is a metal plate with a shallow groove of circular cross-section which runs in a circle, while above, and attached to the drill press chuck, is another metal plate with a matching groove. At the top is a cover which reduces splash and noise while the machine is running. Approximately spherical beads of gem material are placed in the groove in the bottom of the tank, along with a watery charge of silicon carbide grit, and the top assembly is lowered over them as shown in the right-hand photograph of the illustration. When the motor is started, the upper plate presses on the beads causing them to roll around the groove and wear to spherical shape. Since the tank contains enough abrasive mixture to keep the beads covered, no special attention is needed except to keep downward pressure on the drill press spindle. From time to time the beads are inspected to see if they are perfectly round. Beads of various size are made by slabbing gem material into slices of varying thicknesses, and re-sawing to get cubes of different thicknesses. These are shaped to approximate spherical form on the grinding wheel and a batch of all the same size processed at once in the bead mill.

To save time in preforming beads, slabs of proper thickness can be core drilled to provide cylindrical sections, which then require less work than if the slabs were sawed into cubes.

The bead mill will not polish beads and this must be done either by hand or in a tumbler.

■ OTHER METHODS OF MAKING BEADS

Beads of fairly large size, say over ½-inch diameter, can be made as spheres are made. However, smaller beads are difficult to handle and it is almost impossible to make a series of beads by hand and have them turn out exactly the same size as can be done when using the bead mill just described. Nevertheless, acceptable work can be done by hand without use of either a bead mill or sphere cutters, as will be described below.

To make a set of fairly uniform beads, obtain gem material of good quality and slice into slabs equal in thickness to the desired bead diameter. Cut into strips and cross cut into perfect cubes. If many beads are to be made, slice a number of slabs, trim off projections, and cement together with stick shellac or resin glue. When the cement has set, place the stack of slabs in the saw and cut off sections equal to the slab thickness. Careful sawing will not jar the slabs loose. Each of the resulting slabs will now consist of a series of stone strips cemented together. Re-cement these slabs, let the glue set, and again saw through them, this time cutting across the strips. Dissolve the cement and recover many small cubes of great uniformity which can now be ground to make bead preforms.

To give final shape to the preforms, it is necessary to make a holder which will support the preforms as they are presented to the face of the grinding wheel. An excellent holder consists of a section of bamboo, about 16 inches long, one end of which is cut away inside at a 45° angle. The bead is placed in this end and held by the tips of the forefingers of each hand with the other end of the bamboo tucked under the arm and pressed against the side of the body. A steadyrest is installed in front of the grinding wheel and the forward end of the bamboo rested upon it. To grind the bead, move the bamboo stick forward until the bead contacts the grinding wheel. Rotate the bead with the forefingers much as you would in making a sphere. With some practice it is possible to spin the bead in all directions and generate a fairly accurate spherical form.

As an alternative to the bamboo, a piece of dowel rod can be used to support a piece of metal tubing which is also beveled on its in-

Fig. 151 The Crown bead mill. This simple device is designed to be operated in a home workshop drill press as shown. *Above left.* Bead mill unit showing tank supported on springs between four uprights. The shaft at the top is meant to be fastened in the chuck of the drill press and is the only part that rotates.

Above right. Bead mill installed in a drill press with upper grinding race and cover lifted out of the tank. *Below.* Upper bead race lowered into position ready to run. (Courtesy Crown Lapidary Equipment, Los Angeles, California) side forward edge. Various sizes of scrap tubing can be used for various sizes of beads, but obviously there is a limit to how small a bead can be made by this method because of lack of room for the fingertips to guide the bead.

The supporting tubes are also used for sanding and polishing, or polishing can be done by placing the beads in a tumbler as recommended before.

■ BEADS OF NON-SPHERICAL FORM

Beads do not have to be spheres, in fact, many interesting necklaces are made of beads which are faceted, tumbled to irregular form, or comprised of small sections of polished gem material fastened with metal clamps or wires. There is considerable variety possible and the amateur need not feel that spherical beads are the only kind that should be made.

■ BEAD DRILLING

Figure 152 shows a drilling guide which is very useful for spherical beads. The initial drilling is done by using only the top part or the centering jig. The bead is slipped into the conical depression and clamped in place with the metal clamp on the side. The latter is slotted so that it can be moved up and down, and locks in position with the screw. The assembly is then placed under the drill point, centered carefully, and fastened

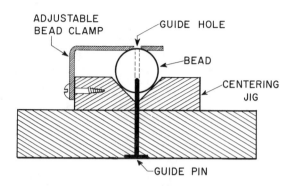

Fig. 152 Guide for drilling holes in beads.

so that it cannot move during drilling. The drill hole is run about halfway only to prevent an unsightly crater at the end of the hole where the gem material is very likely to break through. The bead is unclamped and the centering jig placed on top of the base which contains the guide pin. This is moved about underneath the drill point until the pin is directly beneath and then fastened. The partly drilled bead is slipped over the guide pin and clamped in place and the remainder of the hole drilled. Any slight raggedness of joining will not be noticeable because it will occur in the center of the bead.

If it is desired to smooth the bore holes of the drilled beads, this can be done by stringing the beads on a wire which is stretched until it it taut. Silicon carbide grit in water is applied to the wire and the beads rubbed back and forth until the bore holes are smooth.

16 | *Tumbling*

Tumbling is a method of mass producing gems by placing rough pieces of gem material in a barrel, adding abrasives and water, and turning the barrel over and over until the stones are perfectly smooth. Once the charge has been put into the barrel and the power turned on, very little attention is needed. This, plus the fact that resulting gems are beautiful yet curious in shape, makes the tumbling process very attractive. It is also attractive from the standpoint that many small bits of gem material which cannot be otherwise used to advantage, are perfect for tumbled gems. At one time, the only practical way of mounting such gems was by grooving them with a thin diamond saw and "caging" them with wire which ran around the gem in the sawed slot. Making the slot was a tedious and time-consuming process, and hence did not have much appeal. However, with the invention of super-strong epoxy cements, anyone can cement bell-caps, eyes, and rings to the gems, and the use of tumblers by amateurs has taken great strides forward. Thousands of tumbling machines are sold every year, and the production of tumbled gems both by amateurs and professionals probably amounts to many millions of stones.

■ PRINCIPLES OF TUMBLING

The name "tumbling" is misleading because gemstones are too brittle to be tossed about and knocked against each other without chipping or breaking. In industry, large tumbling barrels actually do "tumble" metal parts since the impact of part against part is desired, however, in gem tumbling, it is more truthful to say that the gemstones "slide" against each other rather than "tumble." The principle in all gem tumbling is to turn the barrel at such speed that the stones are carried up one side of the barrel where they flop over as they near the top, and then slide to the bottom. In effect, each stone keeps making innumerable round trips, up and down, wearing off its rough corners, and those of its neighbors in the process. If kept up long enough, all formerly rough bits of gemstone will be worn perfectly smooth. The action within a tumbling barrel is shown in Figure 153.

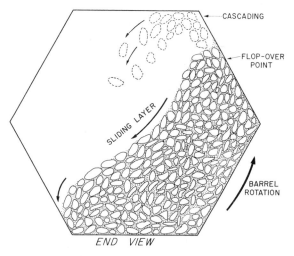

CASCADING

FLOP-OVER POINT

SLIDING LAYER

BARREL ROTATION

END VIEW

Fig. 153 Abrasive action within a tumbling barrel. At the proper speed, the rough gems at the bottom and right side of the barrel are carried upwards to the flop-over point. Here they turn over and slide downward in a layer, as marked. If the barrel turns too fast, the gems cascade and fall, rather than slide, to the bottom. This results in severe chipping and prolongs the length of time required to finish the charge.

To shorten the process, it is customary to use coarse abrasives at first, then clean out the barrel and wash the charge, and use finer abrasives as a second step. The final step is polishing.

■ BARREL SHAPE AND SIZE

Tumbling barrels are usually hexagonal since this shape is supposed to carry the pieces upward better and give a more positive flop-over at the top. However, a number of successful commercial producers use round barrels exclusively and seem to have no difficulty turning out excellent quality gems, while many amateurs also use round barrels and obtain similar results. Thus it seems that the shape of a barrel is not too important; however, it is important to consider size since this has a direct bearing on how quickly abrasion occurs.

Referring to Figure 153, it can be seen that

if the barrel is deep, more gems will press upon each other and those underneath will be subjected to greater abrasive action. This means that if a deeper barrel can be bought, it will be possible to grind faster than with a shallow barrel. Most amateurs are content to wait as long as necessary for results, and are satisfied with smaller barrels, but for commercial operators it is probably more economical to use barrels as large in diameter as possible. The most popular tumblers for amateur use carry barrels from about 6 to 12 inches in diameter. Larger ones can be had, of course, but since they do not work well unless about half full of charge, far too many gems will be turned out and it becomes embarrassing to dispose of them. There is a limit to what one can do with tumbled gems, and it is wise to consider this when deciding on the size to buy.

■ BARREL CONSTRUCTION

Practically every kind of container imaginable has been pressed into service as a tumbling barrel. Amateurs have used small cans with tight-fitting or screw-top lids, glass jars, automobile tires, paint cans, oil cans, steel drums, etc. All of them are more or less satisfactory if they do not spill or leak, or, in case gas develops inside as sometimes happens, if the lids do not blow off or the container explode. To avoid explosions, it is helpful to stop the tumbler every few days and take off the seal to let the gas escape. Some tumblers are fitted with an automatic valve which allows gas to escape yet does not permit leaking. Open front tumblers, such as shown in Figure 154, present no problems in this respect.

Barrel linings are important for several reasons, not the least of which are preventing the wearing out of the barrel and reduction of noise. The best liners are rubber or plastic; both prevent the charge from rubbing against the inner walls of tumbler barrels and cushion gems so that noise is reduced. Since such liners provide more friction, they aid also in bringing gems up to the top to the flop-over point. Homemade barrels may be lined with rubber sheet-

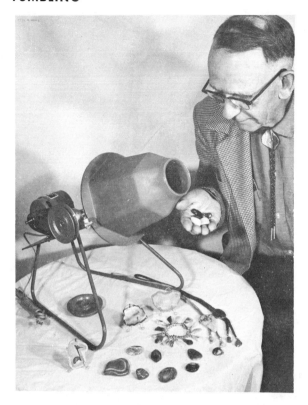

Fig. 154 The 7-lb. capacity Slik midget tumbler. The barrel is made of fiberglas with a liner of polyvinyl. The open-front design permits gases to escape and to inspect progress of work. Some tumbled gems are shown mounted and unmounted in jewelry. (Courtesy S. E. Landon Company, Joshua Tree, California)

obtain a range of sizes which will fit many tumbler barrels. The entire charge enclosed in the tube, is then slipped into the barrel and tumbled as a whole. Another idea, which is useful to reduce noise is to place the charge in an inner barrel and to put this barrel inside a larger barrel, filling the spaces between with sawdust. This insulation practically eliminates all objectionable noise.

■ BARREL SPEEDS

For any given diameter of barrel, only one speed is best. This speed is just enough to carry the charge up the inner wall of the barrel and turn it over at the top, as shown in Figure 153. Faster speeds result in "cascading," or flipping of stones, which then separate and fall with considerable impact upon each other. Some claim that this action is good to begin with since it promotes knocking off sharp corners rapidly and reduces the length of time needed to do the entire job. However, with fragile or easily cracked gem material such as obsidian and quartz the resulting gems may be too flawed to be worth much, no matter how well subsequent operations are carried out. Still faster speeds merely result in centrifugal force plastering the charge against the walls of the barrel with practically no motion within the charge. Needless to say, it would take forever to obtain grinding at such speeds.

ing, usually about 3/16 to 1/4 inch thick, but great care is necessary to cement the rubber properly and to make a close-fitting joint. A poorly made joint will soon tear up and roll, and the job will have to be done over again. Some amateurs use wood or Masonite sheet for liners, sawing out staves which just fit snugly against each other when slipped into the barrel. When wet, the staves expand slightly and tighten themselves in place. Professionally-made tumblers, such as those shown in Figures 154 and 155, are fitted with complete seamless liners which last for a long time and do not tear or roll back.

A clever idea when using unlined metal barrels, is to place the charge in a length of rubber automobile tire inner tubing, pinching off both ends tightly to prevent leaks. By using old car or truck inner tubes, it is possible to

On the other hand, speeds which are too slow are just as bad as speeds which are too high. Slow speeds result in the charge being carried only part way up the walls of the barrels, and then sliding back instead of flopping over and sliding in layers as is wanted. The noise made by a tumbling barrel indicates which action is taking place. Speeds which are too fast may result in practically no noise since the charge is hugging the walls and not rubbing, or may be extremely noisy and clattering because cascading is taking place. Slow speeds may manifest themselves by an on-and-off swishing sound as the charge rises part way up the side of the barrel and slides back. The

ideal speed causes a sound which is best described as a steady swishing or murmuring noise.

Professional equipment is already made to provide the best tumbling speeds, and one needs only start the motor to operate the tumbler. However, for those interested in making homemade machines, the following speed table will be helpful since it will govern pulley combinations needed to get the proper speed for the size barrel being used.

Table of Tumbling Barrel Speeds

Diameter of Barrel	Rpm
6 inches	35 to 55
10 "	25 to 40
12 "	15 to 25
16 "	5 to 15

Some operators recommend changes in barrel speeds from higher rpms during grinding to lower rpms during polishing, about half the speeds given in the above table being recommended for polishing. Speeds which are somewhat too slow during grinding may result in flattening of stones, particularly when softer gemstones such as obsidian, turquois, lapis, etc., are being handled. If the finished gems are wanted for pendants, then this may be desirable; on the other hand, if the gems should be more rounded, then it may be necessary to increase the speed slightly to provide some rolling as well as sliding in the top layer of the charge. It has also been found that a more rapid grinding action is promoted and more flattish stones are produced, when the mixture is thin and watery. Conversely, a thick mixture produces "chunky" stones but the total grinding time is increased.

Fig. 155 (*Opposite*) Scott-Murray Hy-Pol tumbler being prepared for tumbling. *Top.* Adding abrasive charge to rough gems. Note detachable rubber liner. *Bottom left.* Loaded barrel placed on rollers of machine. *Bottom right.* Examining some of the finished gems after final polish. (Courtesy Don Bobo's Lapidary Products, Seattle, Washington)

■ SELECTION OF MATERIAL

Too many persons take low quality material and tumble it in the hope that stones too poor to cut as cabochons will somehow be transformed into beautiful gems. Tumbling performs no feats of magic, and poor material placed in a tumbler will always give poor tumbled gems. Tumbling rough must be solid, hard material, without cracks, pores, cavities, or soft inclusions. Although shallow depressions are scoured out and polished in the tumbling barrel, deep holes are inaccessible and will still be there when the rest of the gem is finished. Furthermore, it is almost impossible to remove coarse grit from deep holes and the grit carries over to contaminate the next step. For these reasons, considerable care must be used in selecting material.

Ideally, the charge should consist of gemstones exactly alike since all will behave exactly alike. However, it is possible to mix sizes and get good results, although it sometimes happens that when the proper finish appears on one size of stone, it will not on a smaller or larger size. The most important rule is not to mix stones of greatly different hardness or toughness. Tumbling very soft or very brittle gemstones with those which are much harder or tougher results in rapid wearing away of the weaker materials, sometimes to the point where they completely disappear! Tough minerals, such as jade and rhodonite, take considerably longer to smooth than minerals which may be just as hard but more brittle. Thus, at the finish of a run, you may find one kind of gemstone nicely smoothed while the other is still pitted and obviously needs far more running time to finish.

Very large stones are difficult to tumble without their receiving numerous small fractures and surface cracks. The principle here is that small stones when thrown against each other are not usually moving fast enough to cause cracking, but not much speed is required to cause cracks to appear in large stones, for they weigh a great deal more and therefore strike each other with greater force. Some operators prevent damage to large stones by tumbling a few at a time in batches of smaller stones. Usually they must be sent through several batches before they are finished. Quartz, obsidian, and other brittle materials, in sizes of 1 inch or more in diameter, are particularly likely to develop rough edges or many small curved cracks just under their surfaces. If enough large material can be gathered for a complete load, it can be tumbled successfully, providing the speed is carefully adjusted to allow only sliding within the charge.

■ PREPARATION OF ROUGH FOR TUMBLING

After suitable material has been selected, it is prepared for tumbling by breaking into fragments of about the same size. Some use a hammer and anvil to break chunks of rough; others saw pieces into thick slabs and then break them. Skill is needed to avoid waste. Fragile or brittle materials, especially quartz and obsidian, produce sharp splinters which easily cut the fingers or fly about endangering the eyes and face. For this reason, gloves and goggles *should be worn.* Commercial tumblers often use small rock-crushers for mass production of suitable rough, while some dealers who own such crushers sell broken pieces ready for tumbling at so much a pound above the basic cost of the rough.

A device used by mosaic workers is good for breaking tumbling rough. A thick chisel is imbedded in a heavy block or log of wood, butt down and point up. A rock hammer with chisel point is used for striking. The rough is placed over the lower chisel point and struck lightly with the hammer; both chisel edges should be opposite each other. In most cases the rough stone will be cleaved along the line desired.

Because crushing involves the creation of fractures, and pieces containing them will not look well after tumbling, these should be culled out and either rebroken or discarded. Fine quality material such as richly colored amethyst, colored tourmaline, beryl, etc., should have defective places removed on the rough grinding wheel. Many operators claim that this

step, though troublesome, pays off in the lessened time required to tumble such gems. There is also a considerable loss of material if the batch has to be tumbled to the point where all defects are removed.

■ CHARGE SIZE

Most experts advise filling the barrel to half or slightly more of its volume with stones and abrasive, the spaces between stones and grit being filled with water until the level is just at the top of the charge. Too light a load of stones promotes slipping and very slow abrasion, but too much prevents the proper sliding action from developing. A wetting agent, usually a household detergent such as Tide, is added in the amount of 1 tablespoon per 10 pounds of charge. Adding more water until the mixture is very thin promotes rapid grinding; some commercial operators claim it is impossible to use too much water.

■ ABRASIVES

Silicon carbide is used almost exclusively for grinding. The first grind is done commonly with very coarse grit, usually 80 mesh, while the second grind is with 400 or 600 grit. Some operators use more than two grinding steps but the majority get excellent results with two.

If available, broken chunks of silicon carbide from discarded grinding wheels may be used in the first grind to hasten the process, and some operators make a practice of going to shops of gem cutters and other users of grinding wheels to obtain discards. These are broken into pieces about 1 inch in diameter and added to the initial batch of stones and abrasive. As the solid pieces of silicon carbide wear, the grains of grit add their abrasive action to the loose grit originally placed in the tumbler.

Since broken grinding wheels are not always available when wanted, small blocks of solid abrasive made especially for this purpose may be bought. These are quite cheap and equally effective in obtaining rapid grinding action.

The ratio of grit for the first grind is about 1 to 3 pounds of abrasive to 10 pounds of stones. The lower amount is used for softer stones and the higher amount for hard and tough gemstones. Faster grinding action is obtained if the charge is dumped and washed every day or two, and fresh grit added. However, this is costly and many operators let the first grind charge stay in a longer period of time. Theoretically, it is possible to keep the tumbler running on a single charge of grit and, as the grit breaks into smaller and smaller particles, the surface smoothness of the stones becomes correspondingly finer until the same quality of finish is obtained as would be the case if several grind steps were taken.

For the second grind, the ratio of fine abrasive is less, that is, only about one half to one pound for ten pounds of stones is needed. *Caution:* Do not wash grits and rock dust down household drains as it will eventually settle and clog the plumbing.

■ TUMBLING TIMES

With 80 grit for the first grind, three to four weeks of continuous tumbling are needed to make perfectly smooth surfaces. With second grinds, about one week is necessary. These times vary according to shape and properties of rough gemstones, size of tumbler, and other factors and, as is so true of tumbling as a whole, hard and fast formulas cannot be given. In any case, the test is to look at the batch and see if stones are worn as much as they should be during the first grind. If they are, then there is no point in going further; however, if small pits remain, or surface cracks are present, then the operation must be carried on longer. In examining the batch, it is wise to wash and thoroughly dry a generous sample. All stones look better when wet, especially as water creeps into surface cracks and disguises their presence. A similar inspection should be made during the second grind. A clever test to see whether this grind is finished is to take a stone at random and see if it will polish quickly on a polisher. If so, it means that the surface scratches are fine enough for the polishing step. Prolonged grinding tends to create flattish stones.

■ POLISHING

Practically everything has been advocated for polishing, from a simple mixture of water and detergent to complicated formulas involving a witches' brew of ingredients. Again it is impossible to set specific formulas which are sure to work. Some operators find that adding a little detergent to water alone results in a splendid polish when the gemstones are all of the same material. Others add artificial "polishers" by placing small squares or cubes of hardwood, Masonite, cork, or leather scraps in the polishing mix with the idea that these will carry the polishing agent and rub it against the gems. Fine-grain additives include sawdust, clay, ground nut shells, corncob, ground cork, etc. In addition to acting as polishers, additives cushion the gems to keep them from striking each other directly and causing chipped or worn spots along sharp edges. All seem to work, although the most popular additives appear to be pegs of wood, 1-inch squares of Masonite, or scraps of sole leather.

The ratio of polishing agent to charge is about 1 pound of agent, plus 5 pounds of additive "polishers," to each 20 pounds of fine-ground gems. Popular agents are tin oxide, tripoli, levigated alumina, cerium oxide, rouge, and chrome oxide; in other words, the standard agents used in other lapidary operations. Tripoli and levigated alumina are the least costly, but tin oxide, although more expensive, works well with many types of gem material.

Polishing ordinarily takes from four to five days, or perhaps a week. Check progress as before by examining samples of washed and dried gems. Inspection of the surface under a ten power glass helps to reveal signs of any remaining frostiness indicating that additional polishing time is needed.

The polishing step will not overcome mistakes made in grinding steps. If inspection of gems after several days of polishing, shows them to be badly frosted or pitted, they have not been properly smoothed during fine grinding, and should be reground rather than wasting more time on polishing them.

■ TUMBLING HINTS

Whatever you do, keep a log book of your tumbling operations. Include such items as weight and size of all materials used, types of materials, polishes, grits, additives, and, of course, how long any step was carried on.

Stones with rough or dirty surfaces, such as agate nodules, can be pre-tumbled with clean sand and water.

Some permanent anti-freeze added to the tumbler water will permit operation outdoors in below freezing weather.

Always clean barrels and lids *thoroughly* between steps.

After first grind, remove duds and stones which need further grinding; add these to future batches. Repeat for fine grind and for polish. Also remove stones with deep holes because these will carry grit into the polishing stage.

Since tumblers run continuously, the power consumed can be considerable, particularly if the machine has poor bearings, excessively heavy parts, etc. All sources of friction take their toll without adding to the tumbling. Since a heavily loaded ¼ hp electric motor can use dozens of dollars of power in a year, it pays to consider this cost seriously before deciding to make your own machine. Most commercially made tumblers are carefully designed to run with the minimum of friction and without overloading the motors recommended for use.

Some noise is unavoidable in tumbling; therefore select a work area which will give least annoyance to you and your neighbors. Cleaning out and washing is a dirty job, and again, the choice of work place should take this into consideration. An open-bottom box covered with suitable screen is handy for washing and selecting stones.

Since coarse grits are cheapest, carry on the first grind until stones are perfectly smooth; do not depend on later steps to remove imperfections.

Gems difficult to polish perfectly in a tumbler may be "touched up" by hand on a polishing buff; this may save much tumbling time in the long run.

■ HOMEMADE TUMBLERS

The principles of a tumbler are so simple that many amateurs make their own. However, when one must buy the necessary rollers, pulleys, belts, and other parts, it is doubtful if much money can be saved, and the finished product may not be as efficient as a machine specifically designed to do the job. Nevertheless, there are simple ways of making tumblers, and some ideas for them are given here.

One idea which has the merit of being simple and cheap, is to rig a steel rod in a pair of greased wooden blocks in which it turns, and to suspend an automobile tire over each end. A pulley or belt running over the rod turns it and also turns the tires. Charges are placed in each tire and eventually the stones are tumbled. There are many drawbacks to this scheme but it will work.

Another idea advanced by an amateur with a steady supply of wind near his house, was to fasten a can to a wooden propeller hub and let the wind keep turning it over. Still another attached his tumbling barrel to a water wheel. All of these schemes are novel but few work as well as machines designed to do the job right.

The simplest design which provides satisfactory results is to use two steel rollers fitted into pillow block bearings on a stout base of wood planks. The distance between roller bars is governed by the size barrels used. The barrels are generally steel paint or grease cans fitted with clamp-on lids. The rollers can be long and supported with additional bearings,

Each barrel is fitted with a pair of rubber tires or with flat strips of rubber to provide the necessary friction against the rollers. Rubber garden hose has been used for this, also flat rubber or leather belting carefully spliced. The other alternative is to cover the rollers with rubber strips or sections of hose. Motive power is applied by a large pulley fitted to the end of one roller rod, and connected by vee belting to the motor or to another set of pulleys to reduce the speed still lower.

Another rig, also simple to make, has a single shaft tilted upward and fitted with a steel-strap basket on the end in which an open-end barrel fits snugly. The shaft is supported by two ball bearings, one of which is a thrust bearing to take the downward load. Since the shaft must be fairly strong and stiff, it may be difficult to find a drive pulley for its lower end with a hole large enough to fit the shaft.

■ **WHAT MACHINE TO BUY**

In the last several years at least a dozen tumblers have appeared on the market and there is no end in sight to the designing and manufacturing of new models. Some are small, some are large, some use round barrels, some hexagonal barrels; there seems to be an endless variety in types and details of construction. However, for all models, the following points should be looked for when buying, once you have settled upon the size that you need. Size is important too, but it must be remembered that although larger units generally work better because heavier charges give faster grinding action, smaller units are less noisy, more portable, and produce small numbers of gems—which may be all that one can use.

A good tumbler runs smoothly and with very little friction. This can be tested by turning the motor shaft by hand. If considerable effort is needed, it indicates that the motor may be overloaded and will be expensive to run in terms of electrical power consumption. Vibration should be at a minimum. The barrel must be easy to seal and foolproof against leaks. Tumblers with up-tilted open ends, like minia-

ture cement mixers, are very convenient to use because there is no sealing problem and no danger of gas pressure build-up. All barrel parts must be smoothly lined, without crevices, to facilitate washing out between steps. It is best to pay more and obtain tumbler barrels with rubber or plastic one piece liners; these are quieter, less shocking to the stones, and last a long time. Avoid plain metal barrels, which are noisier and wear faster. A tumbler fitted with cheap, easy-to-get can barrels may be satisfactory, since replacements can be obtained. Avoid glass jar barrels which may break with handling or may be more dangerous than metal if pressure inside causes them to explode.

All machines have been tested numerous times by manufacturers to obtain successful tumbling results on a variety of gem materials. Operating instructions and formulas are furnished and should be followed.

■ **USES OF TUMBLED GEMS**

The principal use of tumbled gems is in jewelry, but the problem has always been how to fasten the stones securely in their mountings. The smoothly rounded and polished exteriors provide no easy grip for conventional mountings, and attempts to set them in cabochon type mountings usually result in awkward designs. Early fastenings used wire fitted into narrow grooves which were painstakingly cut with a thin-blade diamond saw. The wire was wrapped around the stone and twisted into a suspending loop. With the advent of strong cements, especially the epoxy resins, it was found that small metal caps or terminal fittings could be cemented to the stones directly. In one style, called the "bell" cap, the separate prongs are spread apart until the cap fits snugly over the stone on a pointed end. It is then cemented in place. In another style, a small flat area is ground on the gem and the fitting cemented to that. The latest method of fastening involves slotting one end, or opposite ends, with a thin diamond saw blade, and inserting a metal ring which is ce-

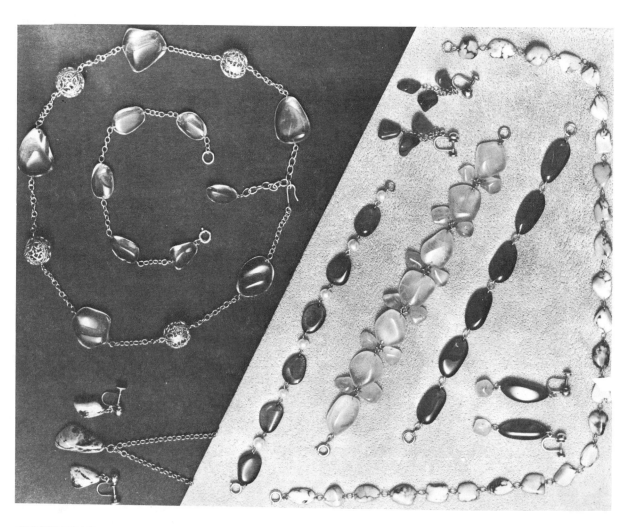

mented in place. Assembled pieces of jewelry using tumbled stones with ring fittings are shown in Figure 156.

The greatest problem, and also the stumbling block for most beginners in using cements on gem surfaces, is making certain that the gem and metal fittings are spotlessly clean. The slightest trace of finger oil is enough to prevent the cements from adhering properly and, in time, the stones will fall from their mountings. To prevent this, wash the gems and fittings in clean solvent such as acetone or others which dissolve grease and oil. Lighter fluids and gasolines are not good enough since most of them contain additives which leave thin films of foreign material on the surfaces after drying. After cleaning, stones and fittings should not be touched wherever the cement is to be applied. Other precautions to insure a good job are to work in a warm dry room and to set assembled gems into clean sand so that rings or other fittings will not tip during drying. In particular, the directions for mixing cements should be carefully followed, since proportions are critical.

■ OTHER USES OF THE TUMBLER

Although the majority of tumbled gems begin as raw bits of material, the tumbler is useful for finishing a large variety of forms which normally have to be finished by hand work in other ways. In general, if it is properly operated so that the speed is just right, a tumbler will do the equivalent of sanding and polishing of cabochons, small carvings without deep recesses, slabs, crosses, rings, buttons, profile forms such as fish, flowers, let-

Fig. 156 (*Opposite*) Tumbled gems. *Top.* At left are shown raw gemstones crushed to uniform size and including rose quartz, tigereye, and obsidian. At right are shown the same materials after being tumbled. *Bottom.* Treasure Crafts ringed gems assembled into jewelry. Each gem is carefully slotted on the ends and a ring inserted and permanently cemented into place with epoxy resin. (Tony Ricca Photo, courtesy Treasure Crafts, Ramona, California)

ters, faces, etc. There is no limit to what can be done, providing objects are not too heavy and do not have deep recesses which cannot be reached by the particles of grit. Where rings and other objects with holes or depressions are to be tumbled, it helps to add many small bits of gem material which can fit into the depressions and scour them out during the process.

Referring to Figure 153, it is necessary to be sure that the tumbler speed is adjusted so that only sliding action takes place at the flopover point if slabs and other flats are to be finished. Any degree of real "tumbling" results in nicked or frosted edges on slabs or flats, cabochons or buttons. A certain degree of rounding of sharp edges is inevitable but, by careful selection of the speed, the major abrasion on flat objects will be on their faces where it is wanted. Thin slabs of agate no more than ⅛ inch thick and up to 4 inches in diameter, have been polished successfully in tumblers and the author has seen cabochons, buttons, rings, and many other objects, polished perfectly by tumblers; in some cases, where difficult material was involved, they were polished better than could be done by hand.

■ TREATMENT OF SPECIFIC GEMSTONES

Cryptocrystalline Quartz. Included here are the chalcedonies, jaspers, agates, and other varieties of quartz which the amateur is most likely to use as grist for the tumbling mill. The extremely fine structure of gem materials in this class results in beautiful polishes but their great toughness requires a very long first grind to get rid of surface blemishes. It is difficult to break up rough into suitable chunks, and it pays to select only those pieces which are fairly uniform in size and without holes or deep depressions. Sharp edges should be snipped off with nibbling pliers, and pieces with deep cracks should be discarded or rebroken. Cherts and flints are more troublesome than ordinary chalcedonies because they contain small pores and places where minute crystals of quartz tend to break out and leave pits. For these it is sometimes necessary to spend more time in the second grind operation to insure a finish smooth enough to go to polish.

Crystalline Quartz. Rock crystal, amethyst, citrine, and others in this group are noted for brittleness and a tendency to develop small circular cracks on surfaces and sharp edges. Cracked rough also tends to break up during tumbling, and should be culled out beforehand. More cushioning or slower speeds are required to prevent marring this material during all steps. Quartzites, such as aventurine, are tougher than other varieties but contain numerous pits where inclusions reach the surface. Again a longer period of fine grinding is necessary. Tigereye is tough but presents problems because chunks of rough will split with the "grain," resulting in many sliver-like instead of blocky fragments. Sometimes long slivers can be broken across the middle to shorten them, but at other times the only recourse is to saw the slabs through the center of the band and thus obtain two flat pieces, which are then broken into smaller blockier chunks.

Obsidian. This cheap and abundant material is easy to grind but difficult to finish. It is extremely brittle and requires that the tumbler charge be filled with cushioning material and the speed adjusted so that only sliding takes place. Most mistakes are made in the fine grind step where deep chipping occurs due to overly-vigorous tumbling action and surfaces are therefore not smooth enough to be polished.

Feldspar. Subject to easy cleaving and also much softer than any quartz gems, feldspars must be carefully selected before putting them in the tumbler. However, they grind quickly and easily, and many surface defects are removed in a short time. Fine grind must be gentle and the charge should be inspected frequently to see if chipping or peeling is occurring on cleavage planes. If roughness is noted here, additional cushioning material is needed or the tumbler should be slowed slightly.

Tourmaline, Beryl. Both minerals are hard and tough with no cleavages. They are brittle however, and must be treated in the same way as crystalline quartz to prevent chipping and rough edges.

Rhodonite, Jadeite. These are finished beautifully in tumblers despite the fact that they are difficult to polish well by hand. They tolerate considerable rough tumbling action because of their toughness and do not crack easily. However, many small surface pits may remain unless the fine grind step is carried on long enough. Check frequently during this step to be sure that enough time is given to insure a good job.

Nephrite. Some varieties tumble well but others undercut and develop a gloss instead of a polish. The problem is to adjust the speed of the tumbler during fine grinding to the point where sliding occurs since it is this rubbing action which tends to prevent undercut spots. Cushioning agents should not be used and the final fine grind should be with fresh grit and stones alone. A good polish is obtained on more or less granular material, but fibrous types tend to gloss only. It may be possible to obtain a finish on such types by tumbling with leather scraps plus almost-dry powder.

17 | *Carving and Engraving*

MORE and more amateurs are turning to carving and engraving, for these branches of the lapidary hobby offer a greater chance for self expression and creative satisfaction. True artistry is possible because carving and engraving of gemstones is really miniature sculpture, and sculpture has always been classed as one of the fine arts. To provide inspiration as to what to carve or engrave, the work of a number of skilled amateurs as well as professional lapidaries in famous carving centers of the world are shown in this chapter. However, these are but a few ideas, and the beginner needs only to look about him in the world of nature to find many more which he can copy. If he is inclined toward making jewelry, no better and no more attractive carvings can be made than those of graceful leaves, flowers, and other forms of vegetable life, which can be set later in suitable mountings. Miniature carvings of animals, including household pets such as cats and dogs, are always a challenge. Carving need not be in great detail, since the purpose is to suggest the form and spirit of the animal without bogging down in futile attempts to depict every wrinkle or hair on the skin. Indeed, some of the most successful sculptures are those in which form and proportion are *suggested*, with the details left to the imagination of the onlooker. On the other hand, there is no denying that the realism of a carving such as is shown in Figure 157 is extremely attractive.

■ RAW MATERIALS

The best gemstones for durable carvings and engravings are also, unfortunately, the hardest. However, the beginner who may be discouraged at the prospect of spending a great deal of time on hard stones can practice on softer materials such as amber, jet, coral, shell, and ivory, and at the same time learn important lessons in designing and executing projects which will serve in good stead when harder or more expensive materials are treated.

Gemstones and certain organic materials usually classed with gemstones are listed in the following table, along with some important characteristics. The list is not complete but

Fig. 157 A magnificent example of lapidary work from the former Tsarist lapidary shops at Ekaterinburg in the Urals of Russia. This compote of realistic gem-stone fruits is made entirely of stone. The base is gray jasper, turned on lathes, and assembled in sections. (Courtesy Chicago Natural History Museum)

does include the materials most likely to be available. Generally speaking, it is easy to get small flawless pieces of gem material but dif-ficult to obtain large pieces suitable for carv-ings over several inches in diameter. Even common agate and chalcedony are seldom free of cracks when over about 4 inches in diameter and some carvers who have tried their hand at larger works claim that finding such material is quite a trick. Again the beginner is advised not to worry about this. He can gain a sense of accomplishment in a shorter period of time by trying a small project first.

Carving and Engraving Raw Materials

WORKABLE WITH STEEL TOOLS

Meerschaum (Sepiolite)	White, porous, not brittle; favored material for pipe and cigar holder carving; takes only dull polish.
Gypsum	Alabaster variety compact; translucent; white to pale pink, yellow, etc.; often attractively banded, takes good polish.
Talc	Massive rock-like types (soapstone) sometimes suitable for larger carvings; uniform pieces free of inclusions difficult to obtain; dull dark colors.
Amber	Pale yellow, golden yellow, red, brown; opaque to transparent; pieces seldom over several inches diameter; brittle, chips easily; takes fine polish.
Anthracite	Dead black; brittle but works easily and polishes well.
Jet	Dead black "hard" coal; very brittle but works easily and polishes well.
Ivory	Not very brittle; works easily and takes fine polish.
Shell	Not brittle; favorite material for cameos and low relief carvings; polishes well.
Calcite	Marble and calcite onyx much used for carvings.
Coral	Less brittle than rock-like varieties of calcite; extremely fine-grained; takes excellent polish.
Aragonite	Massive varieties handle similarly to massive calcite but somewhat harder; uncommon.
Lepidolite	Difficult to obtain without much harder inclusions; never polishes well.
Howlite	Compact and fine-grained; polishes well; white, opaque.

EASILY WORKABLE WITH SILICON CARBIDE POINTS OR GRIT

Malachite	Fairly tough; difficult to obtain in flawless pieces.
Azurite	Difficult to obtain in pieces larger than an inch in diameter; often porous.
Rhodochrosite	Fragile; inclined to part along bandings; takes fine polish; bright pink with white markings.
Serpentine	Pure material easily worked but many types contain hard inclusions; polishes with difficulty; usually dark green.
Smithsonite	Compact and tough; difficult to polish.
Fluorite	Brittle, inclined to disintegrate; difficult to polish.
Variscite	Difficult to obtain pure pieces over an inch in diameter; compact; not brittle.
Lazulite	Rare in other than small pieces.
Lapis Lazuli	Due to admixture of calcite and pyrite must be handled with care to obtain smooth surface; difficult to polish; fairly tough.
Obsidian	Very brittle; easily obtained in large blocks.

CARVED SLOWLY WITH SILICON CARBIDE WHEELS AND GRIT

Feldspar	Obtainable in large masses; easily cleaved.
Opal	Very brittle; heat sensitive.
Turquois	Inclined to be brittle.
Rhodonite	Obtainable in large pieces but these inclined to separate readily along black veining; very tough.
Nephrite	Obtainable in large pieces; very tough; difficult to polish to high gloss.
Idocrase	Very tough; difficult to polish.
Jadeite	Obtainable in large pieces; very tough; difficult to avoid "lemon-peel" surface but polishes easily.
Quartz	Crystalline varieties brittle; cryptocrystalline varieties very tough; all polish well; abundant.
Garnet	Tough but sensitive to heat; seldom obtainable in large pieces; massive varieties handle like idocrase.
Tourmaline	Brittle; takes very fine polish; small sizes only.

Beryl	Tough; capable of taking considerable detail; sometimes obtainable in solid pieces several inches in diameter.

Carved Only With Diamond Wheels or Grit	
Corundum	Massive varieties obtainable in pieces to several inches in diameter; also in large crystals; gem varieties seldom obtainable except in very small crystals or fragments.

Note: The above divisions are not fixed and the lapidary often saves much time by using harder abrasives for materials which are listed in a softer class. For example, if diamond grit is available, it permits cutting beryl much faster than silicon carbide grit. Further information on characteristics is given in Chapter 19.

■ DESIGN VERSUS MATERIAL

The professional sculptor working in marble can draw a design and after determining how large his finished work is to be, can order a block of flawless marble with confidence that it will be delivered. Unfortunately, the sculptor in gemstones has to work the other way around most of the time. He must keep looking for fine gem material and only after finding it, is he free to think about what can be made from it. Some of the most ingenious carvings have been made because the lapidary wanted to use most of his valuable raw material. The Chinese carvers are especially noted for this and the author recalls a number of small objects of Chinese origin in his collection in which the shape and size of the raw material dictated what was to be done with it.

Several examples may be mentioned to show how this was done. A pink California tourmaline crystal was carved into a Kwan Yin goddess, but since tourmaline crystals are inclined to be clearer near their tops, and more flawed at their bases, the carver placed the feet at the base of the crystal and made the head of the goddess fit into the almost flawless material at the top. Thus the body, draped in folds of clothing, appears translucent, while the head and exposed flesh appears transparent. A small nephrite pebble from Khotan is carved as a gourd of translucent "mutton fat" jade, nearly white in color, but a small cricket is left perched on the gourd and stands in sharp and humorous contrast because it is part of the original brown rind of the pebble. In still another example, an exceptionally skilled Chinese carver had fallen heir to a small agate nodule in which a translucent white interior was covered with a thin black layer. The black layer was carefully cut away to show several crickets, bats, and Chinese script characters sharply outlined aganst a much lighter background. In effect, this piece is not only an example of sculpture but also of cameo work, where the object is to cut away a dark layer to expose a light layer beneath. A beautiful example of adapting a design to the rough is shown in Figure 158.

Many irregular pieces of rough, or those which seem too thin, are easily and tastefully carved into such things as leaves, flowers, or free-form shapes which can be used as trays or bowls. For example, malachite often comes in rather thin shells which may be only ½ inch thick though quite broad in area. By careful hollowing and by cutting shallow depressions to give some character to the surface, extremely beautiful trays can be carved. Some Italian Renaissance cups, usually mounted in jewel-studded gold work, have been carved from solid agate nodules. The nodule interior was hollowed and polished, then the outside carefully carved to display the colorful bandings. Much Mexican agate can be handled in precisely this way.

■ THE USE OF MODELS AND SKETCHES

Practically every sculptor is taught that the place to make and correct mis-

Fig. 158 Carving in massive Mozambique ruby corundum by R. S. Harvill of Sinton, Texas. Called "The Good Samaritan," this carving is shown below the rough piece from which it was painstakingly prepared. The rough piece weighed 4,500 carats while the finished piece weighs 3,400 carats. Harvill's ability to achieve grace and dignity in his carvings is well shown in this example. (Courtesy R. S. Harvill)

takes is on the model, not on the final sculpture itself. Even the Chinese carvers seldom trusted to bench-side inspiration, and it was the practice among them to keep large design books in which numerous patterns were depicted by an artist and from which the supervisor of the cutting establishment selected a design appropriate to any piece of rough. The use of a model in a carving shop in Germany is shown in Figure 159. Although it may be argued that

Fig. 159 Carving of gemstone figurines in a cutting establishment in Idar/Oberstein, Germany. Electric motors drive small arbors whose cutting points are interchangeable. Note the small tank over the arbor in the foreground which holds water for cooling and washing the cutting point. The dachshund model in the foreground is being copied in gem material. (Rassmann Photo, Idar/Oberstein, courtesy Walther Fischer)

this is likely to result in the carving of many pieces which are nearly the same, nevertheless a model or pattern is vital even for a completely original piece. This is less important where leaves, flowers, or free-form objects are being carved since considerable latitude in design is permissable without offending the sensibilities of the viewer, but if the human or animal anatomy is being portrayed, any slight error is likely to be glaringly evident. Most of us may not be able to put our finger on the exact place on the sculpture where the error

has been made but we still know that someplace, it is wrong.

A model should be the exact size of the finished object if possible. It is shaped until satisfactory and kept close at hand during all stages of work. Exact duplication is made possible by using a pair of dividers to measure the important dimensions and then to transfer them to the stone. Marks are made in India ink and protected by a coating of varnish. At first these serve as guides for the removal of major portions of waste material in the process known as "blocking out." New marks for important features are made as the work goes on until the sculpture has progressed to the point where shaping by eye will not harm the final design.

Models may be made of clay powder, available in art supply stores, mixed to a thick pasty consistency for easy shaping. Knives, spatulas, and curved pieces of wire mounted in wooden dowels serve to shape the figure. Smoothing can be done by wetting the fingertip and lightly rubbing the surface. Soft bar soap is also useful for modeling material but should be used fresh since it becomes too brittle when dried out.

Flat carvings such as trays and dishes, leaves and flowers, need not be modeled "in the round" but can be patterned after sketches. Place a piece of strong paper over the rough material and clip with scissors to the approximate outline of the useful gem material. Be careful to exclude porous, cracked, or otherwise defective areas. Place this rude pattern on clean paper and trace the outline lightly. Experiment with soft pencil to achieve a pattern which fits within the outline of available rough yet gives a pleasing effect. Make as many sketches as needed until something worthwhile is obtained. When ready for carving, keep this pattern at hand and copy from it as needed. Marks made upon the rough in India ink will again serve as useful guides.

■ THE PRINCIPLES OF CARVING AND ENGRAVING

As in other lapidary processes, the method of removing material is by the use of abrasive grains, whether used alone or mounted in solid wheels or in saws. Preliminary shaping is always done as much as possible with a power saw since this is the fastest way to take off unwanted portions of the work. Soft material can be sawed with hack saws, jeweler's saws, or coping saws, but harder materials must be sliced with diamond saws or with mud saws using loose abrasive.

Because of the recesses which are characteristic of carvings and engravings, it is necessary to obtain the final shape by the use of many small rotary tools, abrasive points, miniature saws, and others which have both the proper curvature to provide the surface wanted and the small size to enable them to get into recesses. Few of these tools are purchased ready to use; most carvers make their own, as will be described later. Surfaces are smoothed by the use of wood or leather wheels with loose grit, and polished with similar wheels using standard polishing agents.

■ THE CARVER'S EQUIPMENT

Prior to the discovery of the wheel, ancient carvers used abrasive points of stone or pieces of wood charged with loose abrasive to cut away their carvings. The motive power was back and forth stroking with the hands. Curiously enough, this method, somewhat modified, is still used to carve cameos in shell at the famous cameo carving center of Torre Del Greco near Naples, Italy. Here the apprentices are taught how to use sharp steel engravers to scrape away the shell and small sticks of hard wood to rub pumice powder against the miniature carvings to smooth surfaces.

The earliest fully-skilled carvers were the Chinese, who used the principle of the wheel to speed abrasive action. The same tools and methods, scarcely modified by the passage of thousands of years, are still employed. Figure 160 shows Mr. Sheu-Tse Koo demonstrating the operation of the ancient Chinese lapidary machine. He learned his art in China and has retained his skill here in his adopted land.

Figure 161 shows him demonstrating his skills before a rapt audience at a California show. The basic components of this machine are depicted in Figure 25 in Chapter 3. The rude but extremely effective machine has certain advantages over power-driven machinery. Since the motive power is supplied by foot pedals which run the leather strap back and forth to rotate the spindle, any speed is available to the operator. This flexibility is extremely difficult to obtain in a modern machine using a standard alternating current motor. Slow speed permits delicate work and allows placing the carving points at any spot without fear of overcutting. Slower speeds also permit grit to adhere better to the edges of the cutters while the alternate back and forth motion of the wheels also promotes grit retention. In any event, the effectiveness of this machine is proved by the superb carvings produced by Mr. Koo and by countless forbears.

■ MODERN MACHINERY

Modern carving machines generally utilize simple ball- or sleeve-bearing arbors such as those shown in Figures 162 to 165. In Figure 162, the arbor is mounted in a rigid stand with the arbor tilted downward toward the table top. The threaded end of the shaft takes a Jacobs chuck which accommodates shanked tools of various sizes. The author uses a similar arrangement except that the arbor is mounted on heavy plank which is hinged to the front edge of the workbench. This allows the arbor to be used in a level position or tilted to any downward angle wanted. Depending on the tools used, the downward angle is often more convenient since it permits looking down upon the work and being better able to see what the tool point is doing. Needless to say, a strong light, such as a desk lamp bent close to the work, is essential for good vision.

The rig shown in Figure 163 uses a double-ended arbor, which adds versatility and permits switching the work quickly from a tool at one end to a tool at the other. One end is fitted with a chuck for small carving tools, while the other is fitted with a small grinding wheel.

Another horizontal arbor arrangement is shown in Figure 164. Here the arbor shaft is extended a considerable distance to one side in order to permit working upon large or long carvings without running out of space. This same arrangement is to be noted in Figure 165, where the arbor shaft is made purposely thick to allow the operator to exert a great deal of pressure upon larger objects.

The alternative to a fixed arbor and shaft is flexible shafting, as shown in Figure 166. Instead of bringing the carving to the machine, the work is held steady, or even fixed upon the bench if need be, and the tool point of the machine brought to the work. There are many advantages to this method, but the fixed arbor is capable of using larger tools and a greater variety, since a larger chuck can be used. It is also easier in using a fixed arbor to exert more pressure on the work without as much chance of slipping, since both hands can be used to hold the object steadily. However, the flexible tool shaft is excellent for detail or very delicate work since both hands can adjust themselves to the most desirable position and do so automatically. Another advantage of flexible tools, such as the type shown in Figure 167, is that kits of points useful for shaping softer gem materials can be obtained from almost any hardware store. ·

Also useful to a limited extent, are small hand-held electric motor tools, shown in the background of Figure 183. However, since the operator must carry the weight of the tool at all times, there is a tendency to slip and make mistakes. Also there is the problem of suppying water to the points without accidentally shorting out the motor or possibly getting a severe electrical shock.

■ **SELECTION OF AN ARBOR**

For complete versatility, it is a good idea to obtain both a fixed or swinging arbor, and a flexible shaft tool. Very good work

can be done on the arbor alone however, and it is recommended that this be the first piece of equipment obtained. Inexpensive, rugged arbors, fitted with sleeve- or ball-bearings, can be obtained in hardware stores with one end threaded and the other meant to take a pulley for the vee-belt to the motor. Double-ended arbors are also available with the drive pulley in the center and both ends of the shaft available for accessories. In any case, obtain an arbor with a shaft threaded at one end upon which can be screwed a chuck. Buy the chuck at the same time and screw it on; test for true running by spinning the shaft as rapidly as possible while the store clerk holds the arbor securely to the counter. Cheaper arbors are often made carelessly and it may prove that the threaded portion of the shaft is far from true. This will instantly become apparent upon spinning because any drill or piece of metal shafting inserted and locked in the chuck will wobble at the end. You may to try several arbors before you find one which does not wobble very much. Although it is possible to straighten the arbor shaft by screwing on the chuck, closing its jaws tightly, and tapping with a hammer, this is a delicate operation and one which is better avoided. For extremely delicate work, such as engraving, the best arbors are fitted with sleeve-bearings, since all ball-bearings require a little play in order to roll easily and they do not run as smoothly.

At home, mount the arbor on a piece of hardwood 2- by 6-inch lumber, and attach this to the edge of the workbench with a pair of

Fig. 160 (*Opposite*) Sheu-Tse Koo of San Francisco, California, demonstrating the operation of the ancient Chinese lapidary machine. Wooden bearings support steel mandrels of various sizes and shapes (*see also* Figure 25). The points are easily interchanged by slackening the leather drive belt and lifting off the mandrel and substituting a new one. Abrasive grit is supplied by the right hand while the left holds the stone beneath the disk. In the foreground is a tub of water which is used to wash the stone for frequent inspection of progress. (Vano Photo, courtesy Sheu-Tse Koo, and *Lapidary Journal*)

Fig. 161 Sheu-Tse Koo of San Francisco, California, demonstrating the carving skills learned by apprenticeship in the jade carving shops of China. Behind him, on the left, are numerous spindles which afford a variety of carving, slitting, and grinding points for use in the machine at which he is shown working. On the right in the foreground is a bow used for wire-sawing. (Courtesy Sheu-Tse Koo and *Lapidary Journal*)

strong hinges. The pulley end of the arbor should be fitted with a pulley of the same size as on the motor, thus giving an rpm of 1725. This is a good speed for efficient work without being so fast that grit and water are splashed excessively. The motor should be ¼ hp, or perhaps somewhat less, but a motor which is too small will not permit work on any except the smallest carvings. The motor is fitted to the top of the workbench on a sliding board so that as the plank holding the arbor is tilted up or down, the motor can be slid back and forth to take up the slack in the vee belt.

In this connection, the author's arrangement consists of a washing machine motor mounted vertically. The belt makes a half twist from the motor pulley to the arbor pulley and eliminates the need to readjust the position of the motor every time the arbor is moved. Splash guards consist of pieces of roofing tin attached to projections from the bench in such a way that they cover the plane in which the carving tools spin.

■ DENTAL DRILLING MACHINES

Very fine carving work on smaller objects is possible with the older style cord-driven dental machines in which motor speed is regulated by a foot pedal rheostat. Straight and offset handles are available and allow great flexibility (as well as the extreme delicacy of touch with which almost every reader is familiar in another sort of carving). One skilled amateur carver has discarded all other carving machines in favor of a dental machine, claiming that the work that can be done with it is far better and far more quickly done. The advent of super high speed turbine dental drilling machines has meant that conventional machines are now available on second-hand, and some models can be bought for far less than a new machine would cost.

■ THE DRILL PRESS

For hollowing carvings, especially in making bowls, boxes, or caskets, a drill press is extremely useful. Core drills are used to excavate the major portion of waste material in a process shown in Figure 168. A narrow hole is drilled first. The core is then tapped with a piece of soft iron or brass rod and broken away at the bottom. Another hole somewhat larger is drilled around the first and the cylinder of stone removed by undercutting

with a diamond or abrasive grit saw mounted on a steel shaft long enough to reach. This weakens the cylinder next to the bottom and insures that it will break off at that point. If it does not, the undercutting must be repeated with a disk of slightly larger diameter.

The drill press can be used for making gemstone rings, as shown in Figure 169 where a blank of jade has been processed into a drilled blank, then shaped on the outside as if it were a round cabochon, and finally smoothed and polished. Core drilling is described more fully in Chapter 9.

The drill press is also useful for smoothing the bottom surfaces of cavities. For example, after the cavity shown in Figure 168 is widened to the desired point, the bottom is smoothed by inserting an iron flat-faced tool, applying grit and water, and exerting downward pressure until the surface is level. The same surface can be sanded with wooden dowels and polished the same way. In the event the bottom is curved into a spherical section, the spherical tool used to grind the shape can be coated with cloth and used to sand and polish the surface.

Fig. 162 Gem carving as practiced by Don MacLain of Compton, California. *Top.* Sawing gem material. *Center.* Jacobs chuck mounted at the end of an arbor provides motive power for a variety of small abrasive tools. *Bottom.* Grinding a vee in a jade leaf using a small steel rotary cutter charged with abrasive grit. (Photo by Jim Carnahan, Whittier, California)

Fig. 163 Carving as done in the workshop of Ed and Leola Wertz of Caldwell, Idaho. The Wertz' use a horizontal double-ended mandrel, one end of which can accept larger accessories such as grinding wheels and polishing buffs, while the other, shown in the foreground, is fitted with a small chuck to take fine carving tools. A leaf carved from gem material is shown in the process of being veined. (Courtesy Ed and Leola Wertz)

■ USE OF LATHES

Accurate machinist's lathes can be adapted to shape stone objects of circular cross-section as those shown in Figures 170, 171, and partly in Figure 157. The principles used are nearly the same as those employed in mak-

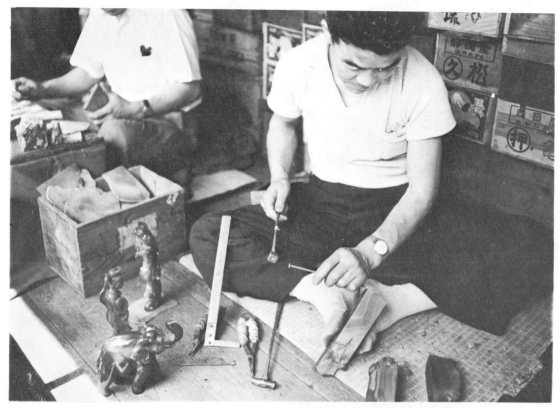

Fig. 164 Carvers at work in a cutting shop in the famous lapidary center of Kofu, Japan. *Top.* Much of the waste from a large block of agate meant for a carving is removed by carefully administered chiseling. A narrow steel rod is used as a blunt point chisel and is struck by the small hammer held in the right hand of the operator. *Bottom.* Carving with abrasive grit on metal points inserted in a horizontal arbor. The lose grit is supplied by the right hand while the left hand manipulates the object. The tub is used to rinse off the object, save it from damage in the event it drops from the hands, and to collect the grit, which is re-used. (Courtesy Donald Parser, New York, New York)

ing wood or metal objects, but due to the greater hardness of stone, it is necessary to remove the bulk of the material by a clever process of sawing and chipping before launching on the actual smoothing of the surface. The block of stone is prepared by flattening both ends and cementing the broadest flat to a steel face plate with a stem meant to fit in the lathe chuck. The other end of the stone is brought against a small core drill and a hole drilled. The

core is carefully knocked out and reamed with a steel point sharpened to a 45° angle until a conical cavity results. This is then carefully cleaned, lined with a bit of thin, heavily greased leather, and the steel point reinserted. The work is now clamped securely by the face plate at one end and the steel point at the other.

Saw cuts are made into the stone by mounting a diamond saw next to the lathe bed so that it can be moved back and forth. Piping must be rigged to supply water to the edge of the blade. The stone is cut by advancing the saw blade into the side of the stone column and rotating the work by hand into the saw blade. The sawing is begun upon the highest points and the saw assembly fed forward as necessary to deepen the cut. A series of cuts is made along the length of the stone object, each being carefully measured in depth as work progresses against a template design kept handy. Cuts must be no more than about $\frac{3}{16}$ inch apart in order to simplify breaking off the numerous stone flanges between cuts.

After sawing and removal of waste stone, the object is smoothed by hand against a silicon carbide wheel, or spun in the lathe and smoothed with pieces of silicon carbide

Fig. 165 Carving gemstone bowls in Idar-Oberstein, Germany. Very strong mandrels mounted in ball bearings enable the operator to exert great pressure and thus save time in grinding away the interior of a gem bowl. The actual grinding is done by ball-shaped silicon carbide points. The strip of carpeting above the point is supplied with a drip of water. (Courtesy Walther Fischer, Stuttgart, Germany)

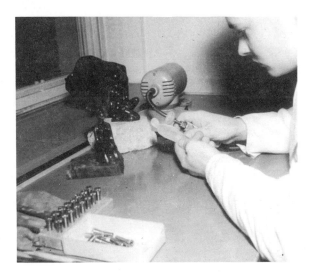

Fig. 166 Flexible shaft hand tool being used to shape a rock crystal figurine. Photo taken in lapidary apprentice's school in Idar-Oberstein. (Courtesy Walther Fischer, Stuttgart, Germany)

held firmly upon steady rests. Water must again be supplied. Final smoothing is similar to methods used for metals and woods, that is, strips of abrasive cloth are passed around the object and pressed against the surface to remove grinding marks. Strips of cloth or leather can be used for polishing, or the work can be removed from the lathe and polished on an ordinary buff.

As shown in Figures 170 and 171, the Russian lapidaries were not content with simple lathe work and used the machine only to prepare some parts of the pattern and to rough out others. The rough areas were hand carved later, as for example the flutes in the rhodonite vases of Figure 170. It is also known that such objects were seldom made of one piece of raw material, and it is therefore likely that the vases and the candlestick were made of several sections, recessed and doweled to fit together with cement.

■ **USE OF SLABBING AND TRIM SAWS**

The principal use of conventional diamond saws is to block out carvings. When a design for a particular piece of gem material has been settled upon, the major portion of waste material can be cut away by skillful sawing if the design outlines are transferred to thin paper and pasted to the stone block. If this is not convenient, then the outlines can be drawn directly upon the block with India ink or white ink, and the marks coated with shellac to preserve them. As an example, let us say we are to carve a lion in erect posture with head raised. The side profile is transferred to paper and straight lines representing saw cuts are drawn just outside the profile, as shown in Figure 172. The block is now placed in the slabbing saw and clamped in proper position for any of the cuts. Adjustments of position are made by inserting small wedges of wood between the block and the carriage clamp. As many outside cuts are made as possible in this way but there will be recessed areas where a slabbing saw cannot be used. In this case, the block is taken to a trim

saw and numerous smaller cuts made into recesses, and intervening sections of gem material broken or wedged off with a thin chisel.

A small diameter trim saw is also used in hollowing bowls, trays or dishes. The area which is to be depressed is carefully and plainly marked to avoid making wrong cuts. The trim saw table is removed or swung back out of the way and a temporary splash guard of cloth rigged over the blade to prevent coolant spray from being thrown out. The block of stone is carefully applied to the blade and fed very gently without twisting. After the cut is started, the piece is taken off and inspected for progress. Some practice is needed to develop enough steadiness in the hands to hold the piece so that it does not twist and seize the blade. Two methods of cutting can be used: the first, a series of parallel cuts leaving thin flanges of stone between cuts; the second, a series of radial cuts which cross each other in the center of the depression. The second method is useful for the hollowing of objects with spherical depressions. Both methods are shown in Figure 173. Because the web of stone between cuts in the radial method grows thicker toward the outside, many more cuts are usually necessary than are shown on the drawing. A conventional trim saw is awkward for this work, and it is better to mount a saw blade on a swinging arbor which can be lowered upon the work as necessary.

Another excellent use for a diamond saw in carving is to use the edge as a miniature grinding wheel, especially when the material to be ground is exceptionally hard. The carving is held to the exposed edge and numerous small depressions are made at every angle possible. Later these are snapped or wedged off, and the

Fig. 167 (*Opposite*) *Top.* Foredom Model GG-8D power tool being used to grind a small fragment of gem material. *Bottom.* Model 2 buffer-grinder being used to polish a gemstone. Electrical tools of this type are extremely useful for carving and can handle a wide variety of accessories. (Courtesy Foredom Electric Company, Inc., Bethel, Connecticut)

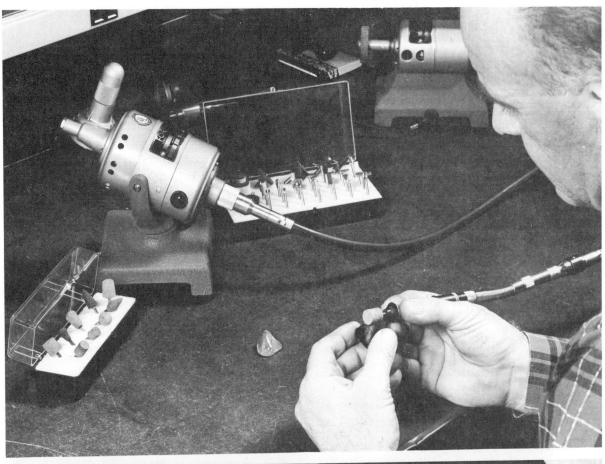

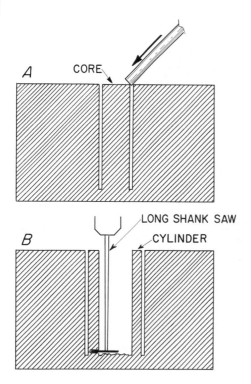

Fig. 168 Hollowing stone by core drilling. At A the narrow core left by the drill is knocked loose with a metal rod struck by a hammer. At B a long shank saw tool is inserted in the hole and used to undercut the cylinder left by the second core drilling. This process is repeated until the cavity is as large as is wanted.

process repeated as necessary. The work of removing excess material is also aided by the use of the metal rod tapped with a small hammer, as shown in the upper photograph of Figure 164. By sawing and knocking off unwanted material, most of the drudgery of waste removal is eliminated. Also the shallow depressions left by saw cuts make surface grinding go much faster than if a smooth surface were being ground.

The standard slabbing saw can be used as a lathe for the shaping of stone objects of circular cross section. The stone piece is flatted at both ends and blocks of wood cemented to them with epoxy resin. The centers are marked and conical bearing holes bored part way into the wood. The stone object is then supported in a wooden box between two bolts whose points, protruding inward from the ends of the box, fit into the recesses at each end of the stone

object. By making the bolts adjustable, any degree of tightness can be obtained. The box is clamped into the carriage vise by one end and the object presented to the edge of the saw blade. The carriage is moved forward to the proper point and a saw cut made in the stone which is carried all the way around by turning the stone object by hand. *Caution:* do not ever allow the stone to spin! It will severely damage the saw and will wrench itself loose from its fastenings! A series of cuts can be made along the length of the object by using the carriage cross feed crank. The author has used this device successfully for shaping a block of quartz into an egg.

■ USE OF STANDARD GRINDING WHEELS

Ordinary cabochon making grinding wheels are very useful for the removal of considerable waste material from carvings, and should be employed whenever possible to minimize the amount of later tedious fine grinding. If possible, a special double-ended arbor should be set up to take small grinding wheels of 4 inches in diameter or less. In some cases, regular wheels which have worn too small to be effective on the cabochon grinder are excellent for carving purposes, but they may have to be bushed to fit snugly on the shaft of a small arbor. If regular wheels are too thick to be useful, they may be sliced in half on the slabbing saw to make two wheels, each of the same diameter but only half as thick. Thin wheels of this type are valuable for all sorts of carving, especially since their cutting edges can be readily shaped to round-nose, vee, or any other shape which the carving calls for.

Discarded grinding wheels in 100 and 220 grit can be sliced into thin sheets of from ⅛ to ¼ inch thickness from which very small wheels can be made. The sheets are cross-cut into squares and made roughly circular on a standard grinding wheel. The centers are bored by using a sharpened three-cornered file or a small diamond-impregnated tube drill. The disks are then mounted in small mandrels. If much carv-

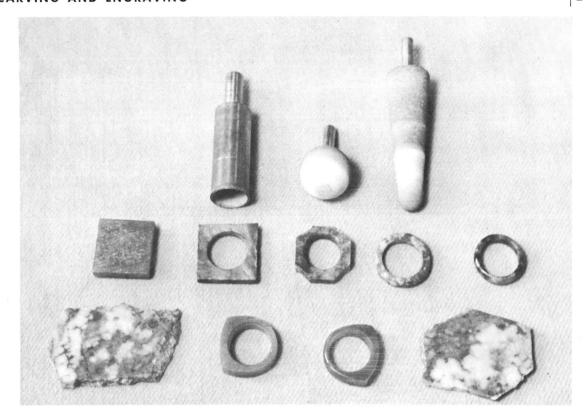

Fig. 169 Making a gemstone ring, showing steps and tools used to do the job. At the top are a hole saw for cutting out the centers, a reamer (right) for sizing the holes, and an abrasive ball point (center) for rounding the edges of the holes. A series of jade rings in various stages of completion is shown below. Photos taken in the workshop of Helen Stiles Burton. (Courtesy *Lapidary Journal*)

ing is to be done it pays to make a supply of such miniature grinding wheels and keep them at hand.

Additionally, small carving wheels are useful on the bench carving arbors described before but it is generally necessary to buy special mandrels from the hardware store to handle them. Such mandrels consist of a metal shaft with a flange in the center against which the wheel is tightened by a washer and nut. The other end of the shaft is left plain for insertion in the gem grinder chuck. Larger hardware stores also carry small grinding wheels made from silicon carbide or aluminum oxide, the latter usually pigmented an orange-red color. Unfortunately such wheels are designed to abrade metal and are not as soft in grade as would be desirable for gemstone carving. Nevertheless they are very good for many purposes and a variety of sizes and shapes will

prove helpful, particularly for the shaping of softer gemstones.

Another use for discarded standard grinding wheels is to make files from them for hand-smoothing of carved surfaces. A wheel is sliced in the slabbing saw into ½ inch square strips, or less, depending on the size of the carving. Edges are shaped on the grinding wheel to make vees, rounds, or any other profile needed to get into the proper places. Because of the porosity of grinding wheels, much coolant oil will be absorbed by them during sawing unless pores are filled first. Before sawing, soak the wheel in water to which a small amount of detergent has been added. Wait at least one half hour to allow the water to penetrate. Take the wheel out of the water, wipe dry and saw immediately. Remove the pieces from the saw as soon as they are cut and place in a bucket filled with boiling water to which considerable

Fig. 170 Rhodonite objects from the former Imperial lapidary workshops at Ekaterinburg in the Urals of Russia. The flower bud vases and candlestick show how carving was frequently combined with lathe turning in the same object. This was a favorite treatment of the old Russian lapidary masters. All objects shown are assembled, that is, the bases and tops were made separately and then cemented together. (Courtesy Chicago Natural History Museum)

detergent has been added. Unless this is done, the sections of wheel will continue to exude oil in annoying quantities for a long time and may interfere with carving or stain the material should it happen to be a porous type of gemstone.

■ **AUTOMATIC HOLLOW GRINDING**

Figure 174 illustrates the essentials of a machine which can be made at home to perform automatic hollow grinding of bowls. After a stone has been partly hollowed by sawing as just described, it is cemented to the bottom of a coffee can or other suitable container, and the container attached firmly to the center of a turntable which rotates at very slow speed. A cast iron or mild steel grinder attached to a long shaft is lowered into the depression and held in a lightly-touching position by a wedge placed beneath the grinder mount and the adjustable sliding base. A hinge is provided to allow the grinder to be lowered or raised at will. The grit pan (coffee can) is filled with a slurry of silicon carbide and both motors are turned on. The grinder is gently lowered until it barely contacts any projections of stone in the bottom of the bowl. It is allowed to grind until these are worn off. When the noise indicates no further grinding, the wedge is moved slightly to allow the grinder to descend a little more. This process is continued until the bottom of the bowl is fairly smooth. At this time, the grinder can be permitted to rest with its own weight bearing upon the bottom of the bowl.

Fig. 171 Rock crystal seal and compote from the Imperial lapidary workshops of Ekaterinburg in the Urals of Russia. Work of this kind is no longer being done in the U.S.S.R. (Courtesy Chicago Natural History Museum)

The principle of this grinder is such that a perfect spherical hollow will be ground in the bowl. Action is fairly rapid since there are no "dead centers" where the grinder rotates almost to a stop, as is the case with solid drills or with shapers applied directly from above. The purpose of the turntable is to insure that all portions of the cavity are ground evenly by the grinder. Various tools can be substituted for the grinder to permit polishing after finish grinding.

By making the machine adjustable in height as well as along the base, smaller or larger bowls can be handled, and the lips of bowls can be flared at any angle desired. It is also possible to grind the exterior of the same bowl by turning it over and carefully centering it atop the turntable in a grit pan. A hollow-faced grinder can be used for the grinding, or a straight-faced grinder which is adjusted in angle to cover all areas. However, the usual method of finishing the exterior is to cut away as much waste as possible on the saw and grind to final dimensions, checking thicknesses of web frequently to avoid variations. Figure 175 shows part of the extensive collection of Ashley

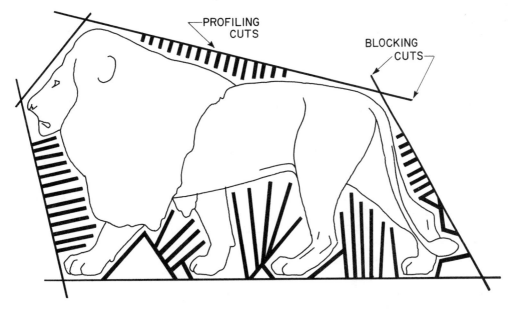

Fig. 172 Blocking out a carving. The long cuts are made on a slabbing saw, and the numerous short cuts are made on a trim saw with the carving held in the hands. The flanges of stone between cuts are broken off by wedging with a chisel.

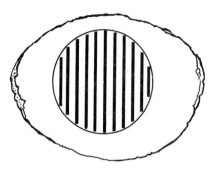

PARALLEL CUTS

RADIAL CUTS

Fig. 173 Saw cut patterns for hollowing bowls. *Top.* Parallel cuts of varying depth. *Bottom.* Radial cuts to the same depth. This figure is simplified for clarity and usually many more cuts are necessary than are shown.

bowls carved on a machine employing similar principles.

■ SMALL CARVING TOOLS

The final details of almost all carvings are created by grinding with small tools. The clothing folds, facial details, and hair of the Kwan Yin in Figure 176 were cut with small tools. Except for the very soft gem materials, ordinary steel cutters, or "rotary files" as they are called, are completely useless. However, steel, iron, or copper points used in conjunction with loose grit are satisfactory though not as fast in their cutting action as diamond-charged metal points. Most carvers and engravers make their own metal carving points and there is no reason why the amateur cannot make his own too. Excellent points are easily shaped from a variety of nails, from broad-head roofing nails to ball points formed from finishing nails, bolts, screws, door hinge pins, etc. The metal part selected is inserted in the chuck of the carving machine and shaped with a machinist's file to the profile wanted. If

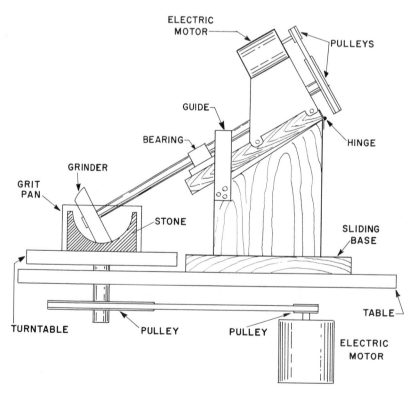

Fig. 174 Schematic drawing of an automatic hollow grinding machine.

Fig. 175 A series of bowls carved from American gemstones by George Ashley of Pala, California. The large bowl in the center is rhodonite, lower left is petrified wood, the others are agate. The inside curvature was generated by semi-automatic machine methods. (Courtesy George Ashley)

a supply of nails and other fasteners is kept handy, any desired form can be shaped at a moment's notice and used immediately thereafter for carving.

Larger metal carving points, perhaps up to 1 inch in diameter, are more difficult to obtain. Probably the best solution is to go to a machine shop and have a variety of points turned from soft iron bar stock. Figure 177 shows a number of shapes which will prove useful in all sizes, from very small to large. Extremely small points patterned after those shown in Figure 177 are used in engraving of cameos and intaglios. Tube drills are also useful for carving. One particular application, outside of the obvious one of drilling holes, is for making rounded knobs or bosses, such as appear upon the raspberries in Figure 157. This is done by sinking the drill a short distance into the gemstone surface, cutting away the exterior material, and rounding the cylindrical projection which remains raised above the surface.

■ USE OF LOOSE ABRASIVES

Small metal carving tools cannot cut by themselves and must be supplied with loose silicon carbide grit which actually does the cutting. The usual method of applying grit is to scoop up a small quantity (prepared beforehand as a thick watery paste) and apply with the fingers to the place being carved. As the tool rotates, additional paste is supplied to keep the cutting action proceeding efficiently. For very small work, many professional carvers use a sheet metal cup, about 1 inch in diameter, fitted with a clasp arrangement on the bottom, and worn as a ring on a convenient finger. The cup is filled with a pasty mixture of grit and vaseline or, if an oily mixture is not wanted, a mix of grit, clay, and water. With this device, the carving point can be immediately replenished with grit by touching it with the paste in the finger cup. The finger selected is usually the left hand forefinger with the cup

Fig. 176 Figurine representing Kwan Yin, Goddess of Peace, in tigereye quartz. Modern Chinese work. (Courtesy Chicago Natural History Museum)

Silicon carbide in 100 grit size is generally used for roughing, in 220 size for fine details, and in 400 size for sanding. Finer sizes impart an extremely fine glossy finish, as on areas in a carving which cannot be easily reached for polishing. Light pressure is a *must* with coarser grits, since the object is to sweep the grains under the carving point and this cannot be done if too much pressure is exerted. On the other hand, finer grits are more likely to be caught under the points and more pressure can be applied. In any case, a little experience will soon show the proper degree of pressure to use in order to obtain fastest material removal.

■ **DIAMOND TOOLS**

There is no question that sintered diamond tools are vastly superior to any others for removing hard gem material from a carving. However, the great cost of diamond

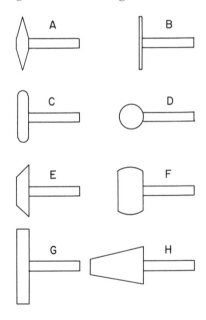

Fig. 177 Carving tools. A is used for fine lines and cross-hatching. B is used similarly but is also useful for leveling small surface areas. C is used for small curved areas or for finishing the bottom of folds as in clothing. D for curved areas. E for undercutting and surface leveling when tilted over. F for flattening of broad areas and removal of material from exteriors. G for flattening and for 90° creases or folds. H for hole reaming. Many other variations in shape are also useful.

placed so its open end is on the palm side of the hand.

Loose abrasives are also used for sanding, a process which will be described shortly. In addition, loose diamond grit, mixed with vaseline, is the standard mix for engraving and for cutting details on sapphire and ruby carvings.

as compared to silicon carbide makes it impossible for many amateurs to buy the considerable variety of points needed for even elementary carving. Nevertheless, such points cut so well that it often pays to buy several shapes, reserving them for use in places where ordinary grinding with loose grit is troublesome, or where the material is too hard for cutting with silicon carbide, as for example, the sapphire carving shown in Figure 178. Several lapidary supply houses now offer a variety of such tools in standard shapes. To get the best from them, they should be used with a *very light touch* to keep from breaking out and losing the diamond grains. They should not be used dry because this results in overheating and loosening of the diamond. Dental supply houses also offer a variety of points but these are naturally of very small size and their use must be confined either to very small carvings or extremely fine details on large carvings. However, they are very good for roughing out cameos and intaglios.

Sintered diamond carving tools have been made successfully by amateurs who have access to certain tools which are needed for forming the points and soldering them to steel shanks. The process will be described briefly for the benefit of those who would like to try making some.

Sintering metal is a special granular form of nickel or copper. This powder is mixed with diamond powder (usually 100 grit) in the proportion of three quarters sinter powder to one quarter diamond powder by volume. The thoroughly mixed powder is poured into a cylindrical metal die and stamped with a close-fitting plunger until it is thoroughly compacted. The cylindrical die is fitted with a detachable base so that the compressed powder disk can be pushed out. The stamping causes the metal grains to flow slightly and to interlock. The disk is heated to cherry red in a *reducing* atmosphere, that is, an atmosphere which removes oxygen from the surface of the metal grains. Unless this is done, the metal grains will not fuse to each other and the disk will have no strength. Commercially, sintering is usually done in a

hydrogen atmosphere since hydrogen combines very readily with the oxygen found in oxides on the surface of the metal grains. At home, a fair degree of oxygen removal can be obtained by placing the disk in powdered char-

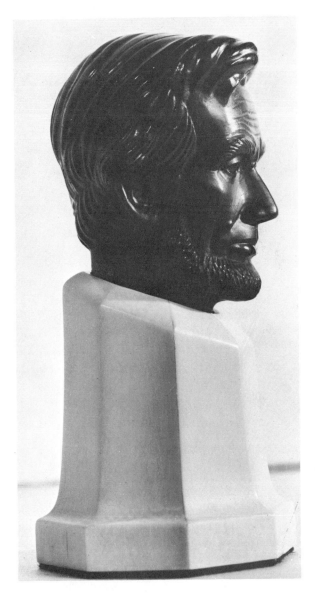

Fig. 178 Lincoln head carved in dark blue Australian sapphire. This magnificent miniature began from a piece of rough weighing 2,302 carats and finished weighing 1,388 carats. It was carved for the Kazanjian Brothers of Los Angeles by Norman Maness. The height of the carving is $2\frac{9}{16}$ inches. A flexible shaft tool powered by ¼ hp motor was used for the work. The rpms varied from 1,500 to 3,000, while the diamond grits used ranged from 120 to 1100. (Courtesy Kazanjian Brothers)

coal, tamping the charcoal firmly about the disk, and heating in a closed oven until fusing takes place. After fusion, the disk is silver soldered to a steel shank of desired diameter. Two places in the making of sintered disks are crucial: (1) extremely high compression must be used to press the powder mixture together, and (2), removal of oxygen from the metal grains by heating in a reducing atmosphere is absolutely necessary.

The classical diamond carving point, used for hundreds of years for engraving, is made from soft copper soldered to a shank of steel. Diamond powder is charged into the copper by rolling the point on a piece of agate over whose surface has been spread a thin paste of grease and diamond powder. The diamond is imbedded by pressing the point against another piece of agate while rotating at slow speed. In order to cut well, points of this type must be used with an extremely light and delicate touch, since more pressure merely tears out the diamond grains. All in all, this method is only satisfactory for extremely fine work such as engraving, and is not very good for carving of larger objects where large areas must be worked. For engraving cameos, professionals use a wide variety of points as shown in the background of the photographs of Figure 179.

■ SURFACE SMOOTHING

As in other forms of lapidary work, the rough surface of a carving must be smoothed before it can be polished. There are several ways of doing this, depending on the hardness of the material. For soft materials, smoothing is easily accomplished by hand sanding or by the use of loose grit applied to small felt or leather wheels. Difficult-to-reach recesses are smoothed with loose grit or minute squares of sandpaper cemented to the beveled end of a small stick of wood. For hard materials, it is usually necessary to follow rough grinding by smooth grinding to remove coarse scratches. Even so, the surface will still be quite irregular and further smoothing will be necessary. Small ripples, dips, and scores can often

be taken out by rubbing with a file made from a piece of grinding wheel. One end is cut at a 45° angle and the stick is applied to the work much as one rubs paper with an eraser on the end of a pencil. It is important to note that surface waviness is *not* removed by sanding, because the sander point, whether a wheel or a piece of cloth or paper, tends to ride each dip and hollow without rubbing off the high spots. Broad surfaces can be made reasonably level during grinding by first rubbing with a small block of wood coated with some brightly colored wax crayon. High spots which need grinding will be apparent at once and can be

Fig. 179 Cameo cutting in the lapidary apprentice's school in Idar-Oberstein, Germany. A small, carefully-designed and smooth running arbor is supplied with a large variety of interchangeable points, which are visible in the background. (Courtesy Walther Fischer, Stuttgart, Germany)

systematically cut down. This treatment is then followed by rubbing with abrasive block as before described.

An abrasive block is useful for getting into all manner of creases and deep depressions. The block is shaped on a grinding wheel to fit the depression; it is then rubbed briskly back and forth with a little water supplied to assist in the brasive action. The work should be wiped frequently to inspect progress. For extremely small areas, such as those at the bottom of a cavity or next to a corner, the abrasive stick should be shaped almost to a point with the very tip flattened to the 45° angle recommended.

Sanding is best accomplished with hardwood dowels of various diameters inserted in the chuck of the carving machine and shaped with a wood rasp to the proper contour. Loose moist grit is applied to the points and the surfaces gone over systematically until a good gloss has been achieved. Dowels of birch may be bought in almost any hardware store or lumber yard. Those from ¼ to ½ inch in diameter will prove most useful. Sections can be cut as long as wanted in order to reach awkward places without having the work bang against the chuck of the carving machine. Do not use too much water with the dowels because the wood becomes soft and disintegrates quickly. Disintegration can be slowed by first soaking the dowels in hot melted paraffin or beeswax. If available, very hard and compact woods such as lignum vitae, ebony, or ironwood will prove more durable then birch. Also useful are bakelite resin plastics such as Micarta.

Sanding wheels of leather are very good for smoothing of flat or slightly curved surfaces. They can be made from disks of walrus hide or ordinary sole leather cemented together to give any thickness or diameter. Like wood, their surface softness tends to grip abrasive grains readily and sweep them against the stone with great efficiency. Thin leather disks mounted on mandrels should be backed on both sides by metal washers to support and stiffen the disks. As the disks are used, the edges mushroom and cover the metal washers. Felt disks are made in the same way but due to softness, wear rapidly and offer few advantages over leather.

Another type of sander is made from ordinary wet or dry cloth cut into a number of small disks and mounted on a mandrel. If a series of disks is cut, each slightly smaller than the one before, a tapered edge can be obtained which will be quite stiff. Otherwise it is necessary to back the disk with a piece of rubber sheet which, in turn, must be backed with a washer to provide the desired stiffness.

To get into awkward places, it is frequently necessary to use sticks of hardwood charged with loose grit or covered with small bits of sanding cloth. Strips of sanding cloth passed over the work and rubbed briskly back and fourth—like shining a pair of shoes—are also excellent; even shoe laces, impregnated with moist abrasive, are of great help in finishing hard-to-reach grooves and recesses.

■ SHELLAC-ABRASIVE WHEELS

The superior finish of Chinese jadeite carvings is largely due to the use of special sanding wheels made of shellac and powdered abrasive. Before silicon carbide was in common use, powdered corundum or emery was the abrasive employed, however, silicon carbide is now used almost exclusively. These wheels are remarkably tough yet soft enough on their surfaces to impart a fine glossy finish when used after loose-grit grinding. They are simple to make.

The materials are flake shellac, bought in a paint store—or, failing that, stick shellac—and loose abrasive grit. The abrasive is generally 400 silicon carbide. The shellac is powdered and mixed with grit in the proportion of two thirds abrasive to one third shellac powder by volume. The abrasive powder alone is placed in a pan and heated over a flame until hot enough to melt the shellac readily. The shellac powder is now added bit by bit and stirred thoroughly. The thick mass is removed and placed upon a flat metal or stone surface and folded a number of times, like bread dough, to mix the ingredients thoroughly. It is finally rolled flat or portions poured into molds of desired shape. Holes are drilled by piercing with a hot iron rod. Wheels made from this mixture are used in the same way as other abrasive wheels.

Small batches of the above mixture can be used to make carving points. Dip up the mixture with a steel rod, twirl to form a ball, and as the mixture cools, shape with the fingers or roll upon a metal plate. When it is hard, insert the shank in the chuck of the carving machine and turn to finished form with a silicon carbide stick.

■ POLISHING

Soft materials are polished with soft buffs and ordinary polishing agents. Felt wheels in various sizes, cotton wheels, strips of flannel, and other soft fabrics can be used. Felt strips cemented to sticks, like those jewelers use for polishing metal, are also useful. For hard stones, however, it is better to use hard buffs, particularly those made of leather or wood. Leather is successful most of the time, even against sapphire, but then it must be charged with fine diamond powder. Linde A, cerium oxide, tin oxide or chrome oxide are all satisfactory, but the last agent should be used with caution because it discolors the work so badly. Small wooden wheels or balls turned on the ends of dowels are very good but must be employed almost dry. Vigorous hand rubbing with wooden sticks or bits of sole leather may be necessary for spots where power tools cannot reach. Some soft materials polish well with wet powder, but others, such as malachite and azurite, will not achieve a high gloss unless the agent is nearly dry. Almost dry polishing is also necessary for nephrite, jadeite, rhodonite and other gemstones notorious for undercutting.

In the event that polish is slow in coming up, it is often helpful to pre-polish with the shellac wheels described before, or to use an almost dry leather wheel charged with 1200 silicon carbide grit. Chinese carvers bring up a splendid polish on jadeite with the shellac

wheels, and the author has found 1200 grit on leather equally effective.

■ HIGHLIGHTS AND SURFACE TEXTURES

The final finish of any carving is not always a perfect glassy polish. Indeed there are many instances when such finishes are actually harmful rather than helpful. A brilliant polish over every detail of a carving often reflects flashes of light which are visually disturbing and detract from appreciating the form and grace of the sculpture itself. In other instances, carvings are part sanded and part polished to give texture or to simulate differences—as flesh compared to cloth, hair compared to flesh, etc. In the statuettes of Figure 180 for example, the bust of Turgenev is finished by sanding all surfaces except the base and the lapels of the jacket, which are polished to suggest velvet. The horse is also matte finished, with hair suggested by numerous very fine vee-shaped grooves. In Figure 181, only partial glossing of the human frame is attempted, but the bald area on the head is made somewhat mor glossy to provide contrast to the hair itself. Th tree and soil are rightly left dull.

A sanded or matte finish is obtained by the use of loose abrasive. The character of the surface is similar to that left by ordinary loose grit lapping and is caused by the same abrasive effects. However, as the grit size becomes smaller, the carving tools tend to sweep the grit against the stone in an action more closely akin to that of sanding cloth. This results in surfaces showing directional lines. To get more uniform textures it is better to use coarser grits which tend to roll under the tools rather than to rub. Soft tools, that is, leather, wood, cloth or felt, promote directional lines, while hard tools like iron points promote matte finishes.

■ SAND BLASTING

Propelling a high velocity jet of abrasive grit against a stone surface is a modern technique much used by makers of monuments for "raising" letters against other-

Fig. 180 Rock crystal carvings from the former Imperial lapidary workshops of Ekaterinburg in the Urals of Russia. On the left is a lifelike bust of Turgenev; on the right a beautifully executed head of a horse. (Courtesy Chicago Natural History Museum)

wise smoothly polished surfaces. The entire area is polished first, since this is easiest to do, and the parts to be sandblasted are cut away from a rubbery masking material which is then stuck to the surface of the stone. The rubbery material bounces the abrasive grains and protects the stone beneath from the pitting action. Amateurs have engraved plaques and spheres by this method, using a machinist's oil can partly filled with 100 silicon carbide grit, through which high pressure air from an air compressor is supplied. When ready to blast, the can is turned over to let the grit dribble into the nozzle opening and be propelled out the nozzle tip at great speed. Ordinary masking tape is used to protect the stone with the designs cut out with the sharp tips of broken off razor blades. The work is done inside a large cardboard box which is fitted with hand holes and plastic windows. This arrangement pre-

vents grit from flying about or being inhaled by the operator.

■ CHEMICAL ETCHING

Carbonates, such as calcite in its numerous varieties, can be etched to matte finishes upon selected areas by the use of dilute hydrochloric acid (HCl). Silicates, such as opal, quartz, chalcedony, feldspars, etc., can be etched with hydrofluoric acid but extreme care must be employed in using this dangerous acid not to inhale its fumes or let even the slightest drop fall upon any part of the body. Dangerous and painful burns will result. The method of preparing the stone for etching follows the procedures used for etching of metal. The design to be etched is drawn upon the surface and asphaltum paint, thinned to a runny consistency, is painted over all areas ex-

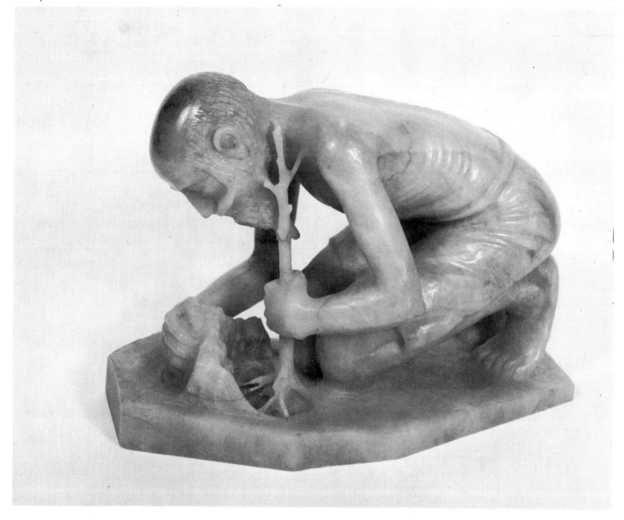

Fig. 181 "Old Man Planting A Tree" An exceptional carving in gray-green jadeite by R. S. Harvill of Sinton, Texas. Perfect proportions, posture, and strong feeling are portrayed in this simple yet extremely effective piece. (Courtesy R. S. Harvill)

cept the design. If asphaltum is not available, melted beeswax can be used but the stone must be warmed to allow the wax to spread evenly. As an alternative, the design can be cut out of masking tape and applied to the stone and the entire object dipped in asphaltum or wax. When the coating has hardened, the tape is carefully stripped off. The acid can be applied by brushing or dipping. Dipping is generally more satisfactory but must be done in a pan or tray of polyethylene plastic, since other containers may be affected by the acid. Rubber gloves must be worn, and when the agent is hydrofluoric acid, wooden tongs of several feet in length must be used to place the object in the bath and to remove it later. This is necessary to prevent any accidental splash from contacting the body. Also, with hydrofluoric acid the work must be carried on under a laboratory hood or must take place outside the house. A supply of running water should be kept handy to wash the object or to rinse off any acid which is accidently spilled or splashed.

■ THE TREATMENT OF SOFT MATERIALS

Many beginners, and indeed some advanced students of carving, like to carve the softer gemstones and organic materials, because ordinary wood-working tools can be used and progress is faster. Hack saws, jewelers saws, and silicon carbide slitting disks such as dentists use, are excellent for sectioning. Blocking out is done with the same tools, followed by shaping with a variety of rasps, machinist's files, and riffling files. Surface smoothing utilizes bits of sandpaper, dry or wet types, wrapped about dowels or slivers of wood shaped to fit recesses. Fine sanding is accomplished with loose silicon carbide grits or pumice, applied with pieces of limp, moist leather. The final polish can be put on with leather, cloth, or felt, used by hand or made into small buffing wheels.

Figure 182 shows a few of the simple yet effective tools which are used to carve jet. Figure 183 shows how coral is fashioned by hand methods and by the use of a hand-held power tool, shown in the background. Although the work is simple and progresses rapidly, the softness and brittleness of the materials requires some delicacy of touch to prevent serious mistakes or breakages. Additionally, polishing is sometimes a problem because the organic materials overheat easily and may crack. The cure for this is to be careful and thorough in final sanding stages so as to reduce polishing to the minimum required.

■ FORMS OF CARVING

Carvings vary from those in which the entire figure is depicted in all dimensions and is viewable from all sides. This is full sculpture or sculpture "in the round." This, and other forms of sculpture, are shown diagrammatically in Figure 184. High relief sculpture shows figures and objects protruding from the background but attached to it. This form

Fig. 182 Simple tools used for carving jet, coral, amber, and other very soft gem materials. Shown are several small saws, files, sanding blocks, and a polishing block, along with samples of jet. (Courtesy H. H. Cox, Jr., Palatine, Illinois)

Fig. 183 H. H. Cox, Jr., shaping and smoothing red coral on a sanding board. The pieces of coral shown at the right have been cut from a larger branch using a jeweler's saw. Note files and hand electric tool also used for carving. (Courtesy H. H. Cox, Jr., Palatine, Illinois)

of sculpture is used a great deal in wood carving. Low relief is familiar in the mural carvings which the ancient Egyptians executed upon their temples. Pattern or design was perhaps more important in this style of carving, but some attempt was made to portray depth. Low relief is used for cameos. Intaglio reverses low relief by carving the objects as if they were impressed in the stone. In fact, carvers of intaglios use wax impressions during work to check upon progress; when the wax is removed from the cavity, the design stands up in low relief, like a cameo.

Sculpture in the round demands the most work, and probably the most care in execution since the object must look well no matter from what position it is viewed. High relief and low relief, though calling for less work, cause prob-

lems because it is difficult to give the effect of depth in a shallow layer of material. An example of relief carving in ruby corundum is shown in Figure 158. Note that an excellent effect of depth was obtained even though the layer of ruby in which the carving was executed was not very thick.

■ **BASIC CARVING STEPS**

The process of transferring designs to the rough gemstones and blocking out have already been discussed. The latter step is beautifully illustrated in the series of photographs in Figure 185 where a block of Wyoming nephrite jade was carved by Donal Hord and his assistant, Homer Dana. The processes used by Mr. Hord will, on a smaller scale, be those which the beginner must use to shape his rough into the finished object. Note how material was removed by sawing intersecting cuts into the block. Where the cuts met or nearly met, the wedge of waste stone was broken out. As many cuts as possible were made before the tedious task of grinding with abrasive wheels was begun. As grinding progressed, the saw planes were obliterated until the statue was covered entirely with rounded areas and began to show promise of final form. Delicate grinding later deepened creases and folds, and otherwise developed detail. The dull finish in one of the photographs shows actual shaping completed and sanding finished. The final photograph shows the work polished and ready for exhibit.

■ **REFERENCE TO THE MODEL**

To avoid serious mistakes in blocking out, the carver must constantly refer to the model. If blocking outlines are carefully put on the rough, the resulting profile serves as a series of points of reference. When one set of blocking cuts has been made and the carving reduced to the desired profile, the stone is turned to the side and another profile pasted on for the side blocking cuts. At this time, the parts of the carving which stand highest are ground to almost final dimension. How much to grind is checked by measuring distances across the model with a pair of dividers and using the dividers on the sculpture to check progress. When a few points have been established, they are clearly marked with ink protected by shellac. These points should not be ground further until most of the work is complete.

In similar fashion, depressions in the block of stone are cut, using measurements from the model to tell how much. Eventually, the stone is reduced to the form where a recognizable likeness appears, and from this point, detailed shaping takes place.

Boldness in carving is a fine attribute, but few beginners develop it because they worry so much about making a cut too deep that they tend to nibble away at their work and prolong it unnecessarily. Wherever considerable material must be taken away, the fastest method should be used. For example, if the space between the legs of an animal is to be removed, several deep cuts should be made with a small diamond saw mounted in the chuck of the carving machine and the intervening stone wedged out. This is better than slowly and painfully grinding away the material by use of loose grit or an abrasive wheel. Speedy progress should always be the carver's aim, since enthusiasm wanes with tedious work and he may finally become so discouraged that he will tend to shortchange the all-important finishing touches.

Final shaping is done with loose grit applied to steel or diamond tools. As before, the deepest parts of the design should be sunk first to help develop the sculpture faster and, at the same time, make it easier to shape the material on each side of the depression. The bold form of the carving should be brought out with wheels or points as large in diameter as possible. Switch points frequently to fit curvatures needed. As the carving takes shape, begin using smaller points. Deep grooves, clothing folds, or places where the design is undercut should now be attacked with vee tools, smoothing off and fairing the sharp cuts into the curves of the surrounding areas.

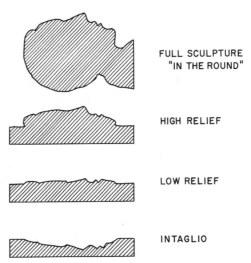

FULL SCULPTURE "IN THE ROUND"

HIGH RELIEF

LOW RELIEF

INTAGLIO

Fig. 184 Cross sections of various forms of carving.

When as much material as possible has been removed with coarse grits or coarse wheels, go over the work with finer grits, developing even finer details as needed. Be certain that no part is ignored since these will plague you later when you begin sanding and polishing. The work should be rinsed in water often and dried to examine the luster of the surface. Places which are not smooth enough are marked with wax pencil for more attention. Broad flat or slightly curved areas must now be filed with slices of grinding wheel to eliminate bumps and shallow spots. Particular care must be paid to exposed skin areas of human figurines or to the surfaces of flower petals or fruits. Folds of cloth, hair, twigs or branches, or other coarse texture areas may be left alone.

Fine grinding, as described before, is really the last chance to change or regulate the shape of the carving, and for this reason, any part not previously well done should be sought out now and corrected. When you are satisfied, clean the work and prepare for sanding.

Sanding is done with hard wood dowels placed in the chuck and shaped on their points to proper curvature. To make the dowels stiffer and less likely to bend and snap off, use somewhat larger diameter sections than actually needed, and taper the shanks by filing with a wood rasp. The point is then shaped to fit the work. Be certain to use sections of dowel long enough to prevent the work from banging against the chuck. During sanding, use considerable pressure and plenty of grit. Select one area at a time to sand; stay with it until it is finished perfectly before moving on to another. In this way, cover the entire area and inspect for spots which need further work. Broad, flat, or nearly flat areas may again be treated by hand-sanding with strips of abrasive cloth cemented to blocks of hard wood. This helps to make such surfaces smooth and pleasing in form.

The final step is polishing, and it is done with either leather wheels, fresh wooden dowels, or with wood sticks or leather cemented to sticks for hand rubbing.

Perfectly flat areas on the outside of carvings should be lapped and polished as described in Chapter 5. Interior flat surfaces, as the bottom of trays or bowls, should be lapped with a flat steel tool held in a drill press; sand and polish with wood plugs. Uniformly curved interiors of bowls can be polished by casting opticians pitch in the cavity, after inserting a metal stem. This stem is later inserted in the jaws of the drill press to provide the necessary rotary motion. The inner surface of the bowl must first be coated with a watery film of polishing agent to prevent the pitch from sticking. To be certain that the metal stem is centered, place the bowl beneath the drill press chuck, insert a long narrow metal drill in the jaws, and lower until it is exactly over a center mark at the bottom of the bowl. Secure the bowl in place and substitute the metal stem for the drill. Fill the bowl with pitch, lower the stem into the pitch, and hold steady until the pitch is hard. When the pitch is solidified, it forms an exact replica of the bowl interior. As with flat pitch laps, score the outside as described in Chapter 5.

■ BASES FOR CARVINGS

Almost any carving is set off and made more important looking if furnished with a suitable base. The Chinese always fitted wooden bases to their carvings, keeping special wood carvers employed for this purpose. Bases varied according to the style and spirit of the design. Complex carvings with many convolutions were most often supplied with bases of simple form, sometimes being merely blocks of dark brown or reddish-brown wood with an inlay of silver wire in scrolls. Conversely, vases or figurines of extreme simplicity of line usually called for ornately carved bases.

Suitable bases can be made easily from any good cabinet wood. Mahogany, rosewood, teak, and others, are eminently suitable and should be used whenever possible. Rectangular, circular, oval or contoured bases can also be made from stone, but the color and pattern must not clash with the material of the carving nor be so

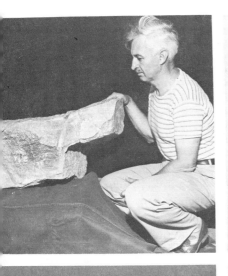

Fig. 185 Steps in carving "Thunder," a Wyoming jade statue carved by Donal Hord and his assistant, Homer Dana, of Pacific Beach, San Diego, Calif. The statue is now in the San Diego Museum of the Arts in Balboa Park. *Top to bottom, left to right.* Mr. Hord with the rough block of jade. Blocking out cuts made by diamond saw reduce the figure to approximately final dimensions. Grinding begins after the saw cuts, followed by finer and more detailed grinding. The next to last photo shows shaping completed and smoothing begun. The last photos show the finished work. (Photos by Homer Dana)

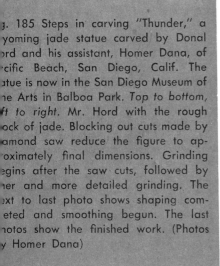

conspicuous that the eye is drawn to the base at the expense of the carving itself. In general, darker tones in either wood or stone are best.

■ RELIEF CARVING

Relief carving, as so beautifully exemplified in Figure 158, must be laid out with considerable care before the stone is touched. If the objects in the design are all in the same plane, such as leaves and flowers growing upon a bush or spreading from a vase, only two levels of the stone must be cut away, that is, the level for the objects, and the background level. If the objects occupy several planes, that is, some in the foreground and some in the background, then at least three levels must be cut away to strengthen the illusion of depth. In high relief carving, objects are made to stand out more conspicuously by undercutting along the edges. In cameos, the thinness of the shell or onyx from which they are carved prevents deep carving but the illusion of depth is preserved by overlapping the subjects, cutting deeply only where one subject meets the next. This creates a shadow and makes it seem that one object is closer to the eye than the other. This trick is used a great deal in medals and coins which, as everyone knows, are thin and flat yet which give the illusion of depth very nicely. For those who would like to try their hand at low relief carving, no better examples for study can be had than freshly minted coins. They should be studied under magnification to see how the artist who created the original model achieved his effects. A fine low relief carving in precious opal is shown in Figure 186. Figure 187 shows a magnificent rock crystal screen carved in low relief.

Low relief carving, also known as engraving when the work is minute and detailed, is the method employed in the making of cameos. The artist obtains either shell or agate with layers of contrasting colors in order to contrast the design, usually in a lighter color, to the background, usually of a darker color. Most shell cameos show only two colors, a light one for the design and a darker one for the background, but agate cameos may exhibit several colors, as shown in Figure 188. In these carvings, the agate had at least four layers of material in various hues. The carver placed his design in such a way that the foreground hair of the subjects was brown, the faces white, the remainder of the body still another hue and the background very dark. Suitable cameo material is obtainable from the common Florida conch shell, which provides white upon pink, and from the helmet shells of Far Eastern waters, which provide white upon brown. From the mineral kingdom, agate onyx in contrasting color bands is furnished by Brazilian and Uruguayan agate nodules, especially the kind in which the central cavity is filled with perfectly straight bands of contrasting color. Ordinary banded agate, usually gray with opaque white bands, is also cut into blanks and dyed to provide the necessary strong color contrasts. In such agate the gray portions accept the dye while the white portions remain in their original colors. Most agate cameos currently produced in Germany (see Figure 179), are made from dyed South American agate.

■ INTAGLIO CARVING

Intaglio is the exact reverse of low relief carving, the design being sunk into a flat surface, as shown in Figure 184, instead of carved to stand above. Miniature intaglios are extremely common in ring stones, many of which are carved with family crests, mottos, or other designs. Seal rings carved intaglio produce a cameo-like raised design when impressed into hot sealing wax. Intaglio carving is also used to decorate flat panels, as shown in

Fig. 186 (*Opposite*) Low relief precious opal carving prepared from Australian material. This photograph is greatly enlarged to show detail. Similar work in the nature of cameos is sometimes done upon precious opal seams in boulder matrix, in which event all the opal is carved away except for the high portions of the design itself. (Courtesy Ward's Natural Science Establishment, Rochester, New York)

Fig. 187 A splendid example of low relief engraving in transparent rock crystal. Engraved in Vienna, this screen is entitled the "Finding of Moses" and is re- puted to be the largest of its kind known. Dimensions of the screen are 6 by 7 inches. (Courtesy Chicago Natural History Museum)

Figure 189, or to lend interest or texture to the surfaces of carvings as shown in Figure 190.

■ CARVING AND ENGRAVING OF SHELL

Many amateurs have success- fully tried carving and engraving of shell, since this material is soft and can be worked easily with steel tools. The raw material is conch or helmet shell, the latter preferred because the inner layer is rich brown and provides a better contrast to the outer layer which is creamy white. Fresh shell is softer and less brittle than shell which has aged or weathered for a con- siderable period of time. The steps in carving are as follows.

A section of shell about 1 inch to 2 inches in diameter is cut away by using a small cir- cular steel saw mounted in the carving machine chuck. The edges are trimmed to get rid of sharp projections. A block of wood about 2 inches thick is cut into a circle about 2 inches

Fig. 188 A pair of fine antique cameos, carved with special attention to obtaining color contrast from the vari-colored onyx. The example on the right shows a number of dark and light layers and the carver has skilfully utilized them to make the face of the subject stand out clearly. (Courtesy Chicago Natural History Museum)

in diameter. The top is warmed and coated heavily with chaser's cement or, lacking this, a mixture of dopping cement to which some beeswax has been added. The layer is made about ¼ inch thick. The shell section and the cement layer atop the block are warmed together; when the cement is quite soft, the shell is pressed into it and moved about to be sure that its underside is prefectly supported by the cement. The wood block now serves as a convenient hand hold for the carving work.

The shell surface is cleaned of wax, and smoothed with files until it is uniform in texture and free of any cracks. The design is now placed on, either free hand or traced, using India ink to trace over and preserve pencil marks. To hold the work, rest the block of wood flat on the workbench, gripping it firmly with one hand. With the other hand, apply the selected engraving tool to the surface, placing the thumb *against* the block so that any inadvertent slip will not cause the point of the engraver to jump over the carving and stab the hand holding the block. This is the basic position for the work, and you will soon discover that the thumb not only prevents accidents, it also lends great delicacy of touch because it regulates very exactly the forward movement of the engraving tool.

As is true of carving in general, the design is blocked out first and the several levels of waste material cut away. Outlining is done with a narrow round nose or vee graver, the kind used by engravers of silverware and jewelry. Work a deep groove around the outline, being careful to cut up to but not *into* the outline. The shell outside the design is cut away with careful strokes of a flat graver until the design portion stands considerably above the remainder. Do not cut away all the background as yet.

At this time, begin developing the features of the design itself, using the vee and other shapes of gravers as necessary. Strokes should be light; any attempt to take away all the material at once will only bury the point and possibly chip off shell. Keep a small Arkansas white hone at hand to sharpen the gravers frequently. Enlarge cuts and shape forms with small jeweler's riffling files. When much of the design has been modeled, cut away more of the background material and then return to the design to deepen it and make its curves and hollows more pronounced. Work the foreground and background alternately until the design is finished and needs only to be smoothed. At this time, the remainder of the background can be cut away until the dark shell layer is exposed.

All surfaces are minutely inspected and gone over with flat gravers and files to smooth them as much as possible. Pumice or fine silicon carbide grit applied to an orange stick, cut on its end to a 45° angle, is used to sand all surfaces. For hollows, shape the end of the stick to suit. The background may now be polished and the foreground left matte as preferred. When the work is finished, warm the shell carefully and unstick from the wax; clean, and trim edges to a suitable outline.

Excellent carvings and engravings upon mother-of-pearl and abalone are also possible with the above techniques. This is a popular form of art work in the Orient, where pearl shell is used to decorate furniture and to make decorative screens. Flat plaques, meant for setting in jewelry, are frequently engraved with a host of very fine lines made with vee-point gravers. In such work, there is little attempt to achieve sculpturing; the effect of the piece depends solely upon the lines.

Fig. 189 Venetian jewel box, measuring 5 by 7 inches, exemplifying the use of transparent rock crystal panels engraved intaglio. (Courtesy Chicago Natural History Museum)

■ CAMEOS IN HARD GEMSTONES

The carving of agate and other hard gemstones into cameos demands all of the artistic sense required by larger works and an even greater degree of delicacy. The methods of securing the work and lay out designs are similar to those used for shell cameo work but the tools are vastly different. The professional cameo carver uses a larger variety of diamond charged points, as can be seen from the background of Figure 181. Each tool is made specially to cut a certain line or depression, with each pattern being available in several sizes. Professionals, who must work rapidly, need a wide assortment, but amateurs, can usually take their time and improvise tools as work goes along.

Because cameo cutting is more delicate than ordinary carving, the carver must have a smaller arbor, smaller tools, and a means of magnifying the work. The arbor should be fitted with sleeve-bearings, which allow it to run with less vibration than would be the case if ball-bearings were employed. Large hardware stores sell steel shafting and bronze bearings to suit, and after a little shopping around, the beginner will be able to assemble a small arbor using ½-inch shafting, with one end

Fig. 190 Warrior in rock crystal, a fine example of Russian lapidary work from the Imperial workshops of Ekaterinburg in Tsarist Russia. The lapidary has decorated the surface with shallow engraving, and, in places, polished highlights and left other areas with a matte finish. (Courtesy Chicago Natural History Museum)

threaded to take a small chuck and the other to take a narrow pulley. The threaded end should be prepared by a skilled machinist, to make sure that when the chuck is screwed on it will run absolutely true. Avoid the use of vee belts; instead, try to get round leather belting which runs with less vibration. Mount the arbor about 6 inches above the workbench, thus providing a good height for resting the forearms and bringing the work to the tool point with firmness and delicacy. A large magnifying glass on an adjustable stand should be interposed between the eyes and the work. As an alternative, use a set of forehead-mounted magnifiers which can slip over the eyes and provide the necessary magnification. A strong light placed close to the work is also essential. The engraving tools generally used for

cameo work are copper points soldered to steel shanks. However, a variety of nails, turned to shapes suitable to the contours of the work, will do almost as well when used with loose silicon carbide grit.

To make copper-tipped tools, obtain a supply of ⅛- to ³⁄₃₂-inch steel drill rod and cut into sections about 2 inches in length. Turn one end of each to a tapered point. From pure copper bar stock, saw slices ranging from ⅛ to ¼ inch thick, and resaw into cubes. Drill or punch a hole in each, then tap the tapered steel drill rod into the hole to provide a close fit. Remove the copper; coat both copper and steel with silver solder flux. Heat the steel on charcoal with a jeweler's blowtorch and apply silver solder to the tip of the steel rod. Slip on the copper with a pair of iron tweezers; heat strongly until the solder flows. When cool, place the tool in the chuck and turn the copper tip to desired shape with files. The copper tips may now be charged with 100 to 40 diamond grit suspended in vaseline. Smear the diamond-vaseline mixture on a flat piece of agate, using another piece of agate, roll the tool point between them with considerable pressure to drive the diamond into the copper. For vees and disks, the diamond must be driven in by applying the agate block to the tool point while it is spinning in the chuck.

The methods of cutting the cameo are similar to those described under the cutting of shell cameos except for the difference in tools. Since the diamond dust is never deeply imbedded in the copper points, only the lightest pressures can be employed. As the tools are used, they are recharged from the diamond mixture on the agate block.

■ **INTAGLIOS**

Intaglios and other forms of sunken work, are carried out with exactly the same tools as are used for cameo work. It is the practice of professionals to check their work frequently by pressing wax into the work and inspecting the raised cameo-like form which appears on the wax after it is lifted off.

18 | *Mosaic and Inlay Work*

■ MOSAIC WORK

T HE ancient art of imbedding small bits of colored material in cement to cover and decorate walls, floors, and other surfaces, is called *mosaic*. The small pieces of colored material are called *tesserae*. Mosaic work using gemstones is popular among amateur gem cutters since it is both decorative and utilitarian. Surplus gem material can be used to advantage in ordinary mosaics, while exceptionally fine mosaic projects can absorb better material which is too small or not quite good enough for cabochons or faceted gems. The world of gemstones provides colors and patterns without end, and the only limits to what can be done by the amateur are his own skill and patience.

■ MATERIALS FOR MOSAICS

Professional mosaicists use mostly ceramic or glass tiles, either alone or broken into smaller pieces. Unglazed tiles, commonly used on floors, are dull in luster because they lack the glassy coatings; richer colors and effects are produced when the materials are glazed. The same can be said about gemstones; undoubtedly sections of gem slabs which are unpolished will provide considerable color and contrast but better effects will be obtained if surfaces are smooth. Successful and colorful mosaics have been made from small tumbled gems, pieces of polished slabs, and cracked bits of gem material such as those produced for use in tumbler charges. In respect to tumbler rough, it is often possible to obtain many small bits of attractive material which are too small to be tumbled. Crystalline minerals, particularly members of the quartz family, are excellent because the fracture surfaces are smooth and bright. Crushed chalcedony, agate and jasper, tend to be dull but this may be just the effect needed for some special mosaic design.

Glass and tile tesserae are broken into smaller bits with stout nipper pliers or, if large and thick, by cracking upon a hardened steel chisel imbedded in a heavy wood block with the point upward. A hammer with a similar chisel point is used to tap the pieces and to cause them to split where desired. Thin slabs of gem material can be broken in the same way. Because of the danger of flying splinters, protective goggles should be worn.

In general, gem slabs as they come from the diamond saw are too dull in color to be useful. To heighten color, they should be coarse-sanded or, better yet, fine-sanded to a good gloss. Polishing heightens colors still more and should be seriously considered if a small but fine mosaic is wanted as for an inset in a wooden box or table top. Reasonably good gem tesserae can also be obtained by making slabs about ½ inch in thickness, resawing into strips, then cracking across into square sections. Many of the pieces will be irregular, but corners and sharp edges can be taken off with nippers. If the geometric regularity typical of professional mosaics using square tesserae is wanted, then sanded or polished slabs can be sliced into squares, rectangles, or triangles on the trim saw. Slow feeding will prevent ripping the edges.

The size of mosaic stones depends on the size of the project. The general rule is that if the mosaic is less than 1 square foot in area, the individual bits should not be over about ⅛ to ¼ inch in diameter. Large mosaics, several feet or more in length, may use bits up to several inches across. Another rule is that mosaics appear neater and more workmanlike if all the pieces are about the same size. Therefore refrain from using large pieces of material with smaller bits. These are not fixed rules, however; attractive large pieces of just the right color and pattern may find tasteful employment in the proper design.

■ **BASES FOR MOSAICS**

Bases may be of several kinds of material, depending on the size of the project and where it is to be used. Panels meant for walls are best made with waterproof plywood bases, ½ inch thick for areas of about 2 square feet or less, ⅝ inch thick for areas up to about 16 square feet, and ¾ inch thick for larger panels. Concrete bases, properly reinforced with imbedded wire, may be made as thin as ½ inch for small mosaics, up to about 2 inches in thickness for very large projects. Concrete reinforcing wire or expanded mesh should be used, however, strong stiff wire, criss-crossed and bound at the joints, will also do. The wire holds the concrete together and prevents small cracks from developing into major fractures.

Small mosaics of less than 1 square foot in diameter, may be assembled upon Masonite or similar hard pressed wood materials. However, large panels of this material are seldom available in sufficient thickness to prevent warping or bending. Since wood products are never waterproof, it is necessary to cut the plywood base exactly to size and carefully paint with water sealing compound over all areas including the edges. Several coats are necessary to be sure that water from the cement will not be absorbed.

Wood bases are rimmed with aluminum, copper, brass, or sheet iron, which serve to outline the mosaic and prevent the cement and tesserae from overlapping the edges. Strips are cut extra long, then bent around the wood form until the edges overlap. The overlapped part is carefully trimmed to make a flush joint. Thin hardwood strips are suitable for rimming but should be waterproofed along inner edges where they will be in contact with the cement. Metal and wood strips may be fastened with small round head nails or screws.

Concrete bases are so heavy that they are seldom used by amateurs for anything more than floor pavings, decorative stepping stones, concrete bench tops, etc. They are not rimmed, except by the wooden forms used to enclose them during the time the concrete is poured. The forms are prevented from sticking by lining with heavy wax paper which is peeled off later. If decorative rims are required these can be installed later or provisions made for them by inserting bolts through the wooden forms, leaving threaded portions outside. When the mosaic is finished, the wooden forms are removed and metal or wood strips attached with nuts.

■ BASE REINFORCEMENT

Because all cement bases tend to expand or shrink slightly, it is important that the cement layer be reinforced with wire screen or with metal wires or rods. Expanded metal mesh, such as is used by builders for plaster or stucco work, is good material to use, but ordinary ¼- to ½-inch mesh galvanized screening is easier to get and more rigid. For small mosaics up to several square feet in area, the mesh is cut to about ½ inch short of the rims and stapled to the wooden base. When cement is applied, it is forced through the mesh with a trowel or spatula until the mesh in completely enclosed. For larger projects, support the mesh on small pieces of stone so that it passes about midway through the concrete layer. Very large works call for iron reinforcing rod, used much in the same way as in laying roads, floors and other broad expanses of concrete. On the other hand, very small projects of less than 1 foot in area do not need reinforcement at all, and many mosaicists use neither wire screen nor a base layer of cement.

■ CEMENTS

The standard cement for larger projects is one part portland cement to three parts clean washed sand. Only a little water is added at a time, until the mixture is smooth and pasty; it must not be runny. An alternative is mortar mix, such as is used for cementing bricks. Cover all cements with a damp cloth and keep damp for about a week to let the cement cure slowly. This helps eliminate cracking and at the same time allows the cement to develop maximum strength.

For small projects, spackle compound, used for home repairs of plaster, is fairly good but is weaker than portland cement. It may be used directly on wood and the bits of gem material imbedded in it to build the design. However, if larger mosaics are made, the regular cement or mortar is better.

A useful glue for mosaic work is white polyvinyl glue, sold in plastic squeeze bottles in various sizes. The glue is prepared with water, and when it dries out, a hard, tough, translucent and almost colorless film is left. This glue is only water-resistant after drying, and is therefore suited for mosaics which will not be subjected to repeated wetting. However, it is convenient to use, and is especially valuable for preparing crushed-stone grouts for repairing or filling spaces in the finished mosaic. The proper color of stone is crushed to a powder and then mixed with enough glue to make a paste. This is then forced into cracks or holes and left to dry. It can be carefully leveled and burnished later to put on a finish gloss. If the mixture contains too much glue, it will shrink; for this reason only enough glue should be added to make it fluid enough to apply.

Small mosaics are successfully put together with epoxy cements, but all epoxies are expensive, and when mosaics become larger it is cheaper to use portland cement. The epoxy is mixed according to directions, a little at a time, as needed. It is applied to the base with a small spatula or flat piece of wood. The pieces are imbedded and left to set. As with all epoxies, better adhesion is obtained if no grease or oil whatsoever is present on the mosaic base or on the tesserae. The mosaic should be placed on a level area until the epoxy sets, since there may be a slight tendency for the bits of stone to move from their positions if the base is tilted.

Other mosaic glues which have been used are casein, tile mastic cement, stick shellac to which has been added colored crushed stone, etc., caulking compound, and roof repair compound. Tile mastic, caulking compound, and roof repair cements are generally slow in drying, and tend to shrink and develop cracks unless filled with crushed stone powder. Crushed brick is good, also crushed tile, powdered quartz, or gemstone materials. Their function is to prevent contraction of the cement and to make it harder and less liable to wear or weather. Since many of these compounds dissolve easily in gasoline or lighter fluid, finished mosaics must not be cleaned with such fluids.

■ ASSEMBLING THE MOSAIC

After a design has been settled upon, it is transferred to the mosaic base by freehand sketching or by carbon paper tracing. The various colored bits of gem material are put in separate containers to be near at hand when wanted. Mix a little cement or mortar, and place over a small area of the design in which the color is the same; set in the bits of material leaving spaces of about 1/16 inch between tesserae. When satisfied with the result, mix more cement and apply to another small area. In this way the work can proceed in small steps, and can be interrupted at any time without waste of cement or the need to chip out cement that hardened before the job could be finished. Do not skip about in the assembly but work in a small area near the center and go outward toward the edges. If portland cements are being used, lay a damp cloth over the work when finished.

For small mosaics it is possible to place the base layer of cement and cover immediately with tesserae. It is not necessary to lay a bed of cement and wait for it to harden before proceeding with the actual setting of the tesserae unless the base layer is needed for strength, as in large mosaics.

■ GROUTING

In general, no attempt is made during setting of tesserae to imbed them so deeply that the base cement rises to the upper level of the stones. Deep spaces are left deliberately between tesserae so that they can be filled with grout later. Grout is cement which is fluid enough to flow or force easily between tesserae. It is applied by smearing a layer over the entire surface and forcing into spaces with a spatula. The surplus is then scraped off, and as much more as possible taken off by wiping. If the separate stones are smooth and flat, this technique is satisfactory, but if rough bits are used, too much grout will be left no matter how carefully it is cleaned, and the result may be dull and dirty looking. In such cases, it is

better to use rolled up cones of wax paper to inject the grout. Roll the paper until the opening is about 1/16 to 1/8 inch across, put in several tablespoons of grout, fold back the edges to prevent leaking, and squeeze the grout into crevices between the stones.

Portland cement grouts can be cleaned from tesserae with weak muriatic acid solution, applied with a small brush. However, grouts made from asphaltic materials, polyvinyl glue and others, are not easily cleaned at all, and great care must be used in applying them in the first place to prevent soiling. If the entire top of the mosaic is to be lapped level and polished, grouting need not be so careful.

■ INTARSIA MOSAIC WORK

A variation of classical mosaic work is called *intarsia*, or sometimes *pietre dure*, or Florentine mosaic work. In this style of mosaic, flat pieces of stone are fitted together as closely as possible to make designs and pictures, much as pieces of glass are joined to make stained glass windows. However, intarsia is never transparent; pieces are always cemented to a base of stone, wood, or other hard material. Some kinds of intarsia are inlaid into stone panels which are then flattened to a common level and polished.

The beauty and effectiveness of intarsia depend on the skill used in making designs and selecting various kinds of stone to cover areas of different color and texture. An inkstand of intarsia in possession of the author is made of a black slate bordered along the edge by wreaths of pinkish ivory flowers and malachite leaves. Near the center is a floral design of wild roses with brownish-green serpentine leaves. Flowers, leaves, stems, petals, and even the very fine pollen filaments, were all carefully inlaid into shallow recesses cut into the surface of the soft slate. This technique is understandably more difficult to execute than the more common intarsia work where no inlaying is required. Examples of modern intarsia executed in Florence, Italy, are shown in Figure 191. Note particularly how much in-

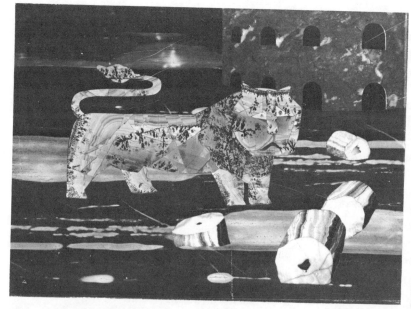

Fig. 191 Florentine intarsia work, a form of mosaic. (Courtesy *Lapidary Journal*)

terest is added to areas of the designs by selecting patterned stones for some and plain stones for others.

The raw material for intarsia is sawed into slabs ranging in thickness from ⅛ to ¼ inch, depending on the size of the work. Thinner slabs are suitable for inlays and for projects not over several inches across. Larger slabs should be used for larger projects, since they must be strong enough to withstand lapping and polishing. It is important that materials selected be of approximately the same hardness; it is easy to undercut soft materials when both are used together. Intarsia workers in Florence lean heavily upon marble, serpentine, and other

stones of similar hardness, texture, and workability. Before use, all slabs are trimmed to remove sharp projections left from sawing. Do not use slabs which show deep saw marks or waviness due to improper sawing. All slabs must be nearly flat to avoid excess lapping later.

■ **DESIGN OF INTARSIA MOSAICS**

Until you have gained some experience, stick to simple designs such as those shown in Figure 191. To begin, turn to the field of nature for inspiration. Many handsome projects can be based upon flowers, leaves, simple landscapes, or simplified birds and animals. Since each section of the design must be cut to exact outline, avoid complex small curves whose matching with adjacent slabs presents severe problems. The reasons for simplicity will be evident when the time comes to cut patterns from the slabs.

In selecting any design, color is of great importance, as is the relative lightness or darkness of the color. Slabs which show shadings of color are useful for indicating shadows in the object being portrayed. In the better classes of Italian work, the artisans seldom used solid colors for flower petals for example, but tried to cut sections of stone which shade from edge to edge. When fitted into the work, the petals stand out clearly and realistically from their neighbors. This trick is also used in leaves to simulate the shadings which occur naturally from one side of the leaf to the other. Slabs with mottlings, dendritic patterns, bandings and other distinctive markings, suggest designs where such characteristics can be cleverly utilized. The tiger shown in Figure 191 has been made from a dendritic material.

■ TRANSFERRING THE DESIGN

When a design is selected, preferably no more than several inches across to start with, it is divided into sections, like a jigsaw puzzle, each section calling for its own piece of slab. Make a carbon tracing on a fresh piece of paper. The original will serve as a guide when assembling the pieces, while the carbon copy is cut up into separate pieces. Make all cuts as smoothly contoured as possible; avoid zigzags or waviness. Paste the separate cutouts on selected slabs with waterproof cement. Later, when the slab has been cut, scrape off the paper with a razor blade.

■ CUTTING SECTIONS TO SHAPE

Cut along outlines of each slab with the trim saw, leaving at least $1/16$ inch of material along the edges. Watch for chipping; if any occurs you are cutting too close.

Inside curves are roughly shaped by making numerous saw cuts toward the pattern edge and breaking off the sections of stone between cuts. On the grinding wheels of the cabochon unit or, better yet, a small grinding wheel placed in the chuck of the gem carving rig, trim all edges exactly to the edges of the pattern, making the ground surfaces as close to right angles to the slab surface as possible. Try to make all curves smoothly faired and all straight edges perfect by judicious grinding on the side of the grinding wheel or upon a lap. The better the edges, the better the fit in the finished work. Be gentle in grinding or lapping since any chipped edges will plague you later when the time comes to flat the entire intarsia surface.

■ ASSEMBLING THE PIECES

Assemble the intarsia on a piece of plate glass or a flat sheet of stone, such as slate blackboard. To prevent any possibility of cement sticking to the slate or glass, lay down a piece of wax paper first and the sections of stone on that. Keep the original drawing handy to refer to when assembling, particularly if the design is complex. Fit all pieces together tightly. If serious gaps exist between pieces, check to see if delicate regrinding can make for a better fit. Sometimes a better match can be made but at other times taking away material from one section only adds more error to another. Enclose the pieces with edgings of metal secured in place on the bench by pieces of wood nailed against the sides. The slab sections must not be allowed to shift position during backing.

■ BACKINGS

Perfectly satisfactory backings are made in the same way as described under mosaics and using the same materials. However, the backings are applied directly upon the intarsia instead of the sections of stone being imbedded into the backing, as is the case with mosaics. If epoxy resins are used, be very certain that all slabs are perfectly clean. Some workers in intarsia prevent separation of slabs from backings by scoring the slabs with a trim saw. This gives "tooth" to the slabs and helps the cement to hold better.

■ FINISHING

When cements are thoroughly set and cured, the entire assembly is lapped flat and polished, as described in Chapter 5. If the backing is of Masonite or some other thin material, care must be used not to flex the intarsia at any time during lapping.

■ INLAY WORK

The Italian method of inlaying intarsia is to carve out flat-bottomed recesses in soft slate to receive thin slabs of gem material. The edges of the recesses are carefully trimmed to make them square and to avoid unsightly chipping. Paper is pressed over the cavities or stretched over the surface and rubbed with graphite crayon to delineate the edges. The paper is cut up to make patterns, and pieces of stone are shaped to fit. Since black slate is used, it is not necessary to try for a very exact fit because any slight gaps will be filled with an asphaltic mastic cement which matches the slate color. The mastic is applied to the cavities and brushed to cover all surfaces; a slight excess being used and squeezed out later when the pieces of stone are forced into the recesses. Warming of the slate helps to keep the mastic more fluid and easy flowing. When the cement is hard, the entire piece is lapped and polished to a dull gloss; the final polish is applied by waxing and hand rubbing. A truly perfect polish is not practical with this method because the heat generated will make the mastic flow and allow sections of stone to shift. However, a well-moistened pitch lap should overcome these difficulties and allow application of an excellent natural polish.

19 | *Treatment of Gemstones*

MANY gemstones in this chapter are so rare and so unusual that this is the first time that instructions on how to cut them have been given. Strictly speaking, all are not "gemstones" in the usual sense of the word because they are not durable enough for jewelry. Yet the well-advanced amateur is sure to experience deep satisfaction in discovering and cutting rare minerals even though the finished gems may never become anything except collector's items. Mineral names are used as much as possible, with variety names appearing in the index. If in doubt about a name, consult the index.

■ PHYSICAL PROPERTIES

The first figure at the top of each gemstone description is the specific gravity range of the gem material. Next is hardness, with two values—the first being standard *Mohs Hardness*, as found in mineralogical textbooks, and the second, the *apparent lapidary hardness*. These are not always the same, although the differences are seldom great. Hardness must not be confused with toughness. Hardness is defined as resistance to scratching, but toughness relates to how easily or with how much difficulty, a gem material can be broken. Remarkable degrees of toughness are noted, that is, if the material is very tough, very weak, etc. The last set of figures is the average refractive index for singly-refractive gemstones, or the range of indexes for doubly-refractive stones.

Within each description also appear remarks on cleavage, sensitivity to heat, dichroism, color ranges, and other items of information helpful to the cutter.

■ TREATMENTS

Successful methods for cutting each material are given but they are not, by any means, the only methods. Space does not permit telling every combination of powder and lap which can be used, or other ways of cutting and polishing which cutters have tried and found workable. However, it is believed that the best ways are described.

■ LOCALITIES

Only noteworthy localities are given without any attempt to be specific as to location of deposits.

ACTINOLITE

G. 3–3.2   **HM** 5–6   **HL** 6   **R.I.** 1.61–1.64

Color slightly grayish-green. Ends of crystals show a yellowish color. Glassy luster and perfect transparency. The sides show four, very lustrous, flat, cleavage surfaces. Cleavage is very easy; great care must be used in sawing to prevent shattering. Crystals can be broken easily by nicking on opposite sides and snapping with the fingers.

Not heat sensitive to ordinary dopping temperatures. Because of easy cleavage, preform carefully and always with the grain. Grinding across ends of the crystal is likely to result in shattering and should not be attempted. For cutting facets, use 1200 copper cutting lap. Cutting across the ends of the crystal is slow, while across or with the sides, is fast. Crown facets 40°, pavilion facets 40°. Polish with Linde A on tin.

The only source of suitable faceting rough is Madagascar and then only in small quantities. Mineral specimen dealers may at times be able to furnish suitable material.

ALGODONITE AND DOMEYKITE

Algodonite:	**G.**	8.4	**HM**	4	**HL**	same
Domeykite:	**G.**	7.5	**HM**	3–3.5	**HL**	same

Both minerals occur as irregular masses along with other ores in the copper mines of the Keeweenaw Peninsula, Michigan. Cabochons and polished specimens are occasionally prepared from suitable masses, but because of rapid tarnishing soon become unattractive unless coated or sprayed with lacquer.

Algodonite shows a bright steel-gray color and metallic luster when freshly broken but quickly becomes dull on exposure. Domeykite

is similar but tarnishes to yellowish and then to dark brown. Attractive specimens of domeykite forming silvery masses and veinlets in white quartz come from Ahmeek and Mohawk but polishing such material is difficult due to the greater hardness of the quartz matrix. Neither mineral is difficult to saw or grind but each chips badly along saw cuts and upon ground surfaces. The pits left behind are often very deep and require prolonged fine sanding to remove. Somewhat heat sensitive, particularly in large pieces; heat slowly and carefully and dop with stick shellac. After coarse and fine sanding, a fine surface is produced by sanding on damp leather using 1200 silicon carbide. Polish on leather with Linde A. Clean, dry, and spray surfaces with lacquer. Large flats are lapped with 1200 silicon carbide and finish-lapped with 1200 on a wood lap. Polish on wax or wood with Linde A.

AMBER

G. 1.05–1.10   **HM** 2–2.5   **HL** same   **R.I.** 1.54

Amber is a fossil resin found along the eastern coast of the Baltic Sea and elsewhere. Many other fossil resins similar to amber are found throughout the world but seldom offer the quantity and quality of material characteristic of Baltic sources.

Generally yellow but verges toward brown and red also. Transparent to translucent. Despite its softness it is not particularly brittle, making it useful for carving. Softens at 150° C.; melts at 250–300° C. Burns readily. Slowly attacked by alcohol and other organic solvents. Crown angles 40°–50°, pavilion angles 43°.

Ordinary steel implements such as jeweler's saws, files, knives, etc., cut amber with ease; finishing is done with successively finer grades of sandpaper. Sand with water to prevent heating. Polished quickly with flannel, felt, or flexible leather impregnated with tripoli powder or tin oxide. Leather used damp is preferred. Depressions in carvings are smoothed with paste abrasive using medium hard sticks of wood shaved to fit. Similar sticks are used to polish.

Found in irregular rounded masses which

sometimes enclose insects and other organic remains. Specimens with insects are expensive; those offered at ridiculously low prices should be regarded with distrust because clever falsifications are frequently attempted. Aside from the Baltic, excellent amber comes from Sicily, Rumania, and Burma. The Sicilian and Burmese amber often occurs in a number of colors. Amber has been found in Mexico, along the Atlantic Coast of the United States, and in Canada. Fine pieces have been found infrequently in the marl pits of southern New Jersey.

AMBLYGONITE

G. 3.11   HM 5.5–6   HL 5.5   R.I. 1.61–1.64

Formerly only from the Lower Pit on Plumbago Mt., Newry, Maine, in faceting grade and then only in very small fragments; lately in very fine, pale straw material from Minas Gerais, Brazil, and from Sakangyi, Burma. Clear, flawless fragments from both sources yield gems up to 20 carats. The author's collection includes a Brazil gem of 14 carats. This material is now difficult to get because supplies were small and were quickly bought up.

Specimens from Brazil and Burma handle with equal facility in all stages of cutting. Sawing proceeds smoothly with only a slight tendency to fray on the edges of cleavage planes. Grinding is also smooth and material is removed quickly, however, surfaces are left slightly rough due to break-out of small angular fragments. There is little tendency to shatter or to develop cracks. Dop with stick shellac. Although amblygonite is a phosphate, it is more heat resistant than apatite. Due to softness, fine lapping on a 1200 diamond/copper lap is usually enough to shape the gem but even so, slight chipping is noted along sharp facet edges. Polishing is very fast using Linde A on tin but serious furrowing or grooving is likely to occur and it is necessary to swing the facet arm back and forth to level the facet. A better finish is obtainable using Linde A on wax but with the usual penalty of slightly rounded facet edges. Cerium oxide also polishes. Crown angles 40°, pavillion angles 40°.

ANALCIME

(Analcite)

G. 2.3   HM 5   HL same   R.I. 1.49

Although common in cavities in pillow basalts, analcime is seldom found in clear colorless crystals suitable for faceting. Those which are, seldom exceed ⅛ inch in diameter. Brittle; not particularly heat sensitive; grinding and lapping normal; polish with Linde A on tin or with tin oxide or cerium oxide on Lucite. Crown angles 40°–50°, pavilion angles 43°.

ANATASE

(Octahedrite)

This rare mineral is seldom transparent enough to cut. It has very high refractive index and therefore was once mistaken for diamond, with which it is found in the gravels of Brazil.

ANDALUSITE

G. 3.2   HM 7.5
HL 7.5 (facet material)   R.I. 1.63–1.64
HL 3.5–4.5 (for chiastolite)

Occurs in two cuttable forms—clear faceting material and translucent crystals with crosslike black inclusions (chiastolite) which, when cut through and polished, sometimes make unique stones. Facet gems most attractive when properly cut; finished gems show reddish reflections in green body color. Not all specimens exhibit these colors however; many are pinkish in tone and show little contrast. Found as stream pebbles of small size showing traces of the rectangular crystal form. Mostly transparent but many crystals flawed with small, wispy inclusions which, if numerous, may cut into catseye gems. Cleavage planes are present but developed with difficulty and may be disregarded for all practical purposes. Strong, tough, and not heat sensitive.

No precautions need be taken in cutting except to orient specimens which show red and green in such a manner that finished stones show alternating patches of red and green on top. To do this, examine rough and determine direction of red color; grind table parallel to this direction and not across. If one of the red ends is brought uppermost, the finished stone appears red only. Crystals usually elongated with the long way showing the red color; in such cases, rough is already suited for octagon step cuts and, when finished, will show green in the middle and flashes of red at each end. Polish with Linde A on tin. Crown angles 40°, pavilion angles 40°.

Andalusite is found in Brazil; similar material from Ceylon. Madagascar has provided some small, intense green, water-worn fragments in sizes not exceeding a few grams. Brazilian gem crystals reach 80 carats.

CHIASTOLITE

Chiastolite is much softer on the grinding wheel, with estimated lapidary hardness of only 4. Crystals are sliced across to show patterns within, which vary from one end to the other. Undercuts; polish with Linde A on leather, preceded by careful wet sanding on 400 cloth.

In gravels near Chowchilla Crossing and near Daulton's Ranch, Madera County, California. In rock at Sterling and Lancaster, Worcester County, Massachusetts.

ANGLESITE

G. 6.38   **HM** 2.5–3   **HL** same   **R.I.** 1.88–1.89

Fine clear colorless crystals from Tunisia in Africa provide material for small faceted gems. Finished gems are attractive due to high refractive index but because this mineral is soft and fragile, it is a test of skill to finish a gem. Very heat sensitive and should be cold dopped. Grinds easily and smoothly; laps rapidly on 1200 grit diamond/copper lap; polishes with Linde A on wax. Crown angles 40°, pavilion angles 40°.

ANHYDRITE

G. 2.9–2.98   **HM** 3–3.5   **HL** 3.5–4   **R.I.** 1.57–1.6

Mostly colorless, but fine purple has been found. Transparent to translucent. Three directions of very easy cleavage, all at right angles

to each other. Quite sensitive to heat. Found in massive form in salt and gypsum beds in Europe and the United States. Beautiful, transparent, violet specimens from the Simplon Tunnel, Switzerland. Ordinary saws, no matter how fine, reduce crystals to shreds. If sawing is necessary, a fine jeweler's saw with some oil, will do. Do not preform on a grinding wheel. In dopping, use chaser's cement and apply heat cautiously. Avoid sharp corners in cutting as these will fray. Crown angles 40°–50°, pavilion angles 43°. Polish on a wax lap using Linde A. An extremely difficult stone to cut in all respects.

ANTHOPHYLLITE

G. 2.9–3.4   **HM** 5.5–6   **HL** same

Sometimes displays the schiller effect of bronzite or iridescent colors similar to labradorite. Lapidary treatment is the same as for enstatite.

ANTHRACITE

Aside from its far greater brittleness, anthracite coal is cut and polished like jet. Principal sources of suitable material are deposits in eastern Pennsylvania.

APATITE

Gem Varieties

Asparagus stone, originally from Murcia, Spain—yellowish-green.

Moroxite, from Arendal, Norway—blue or greenish-blue; yellow; purple.

G. 3.17–3.23   **HM** 5   **HL** 4–4.5   **R.I.** 1.63–1.64

Transparent to translucent. Extremely brittle and weak; sensitive to heat, requires low melt dopping wax such as stick shellac. Specimens must be carefully examined as most are flawed. Sawing, grinding, and preforming must be done gently. Thin phosphor-bronze blade is best for sawing; preform only on 400 or 220 grit wheel. Dop slowly and carefully, using stick shellac, and with preform resting on a slip of cardboard to lessen heat shock. Facet on

1200 diamond/copper lap. Prepolish all facets on tin using Linde A; then polish on wax using Linde A, cerium oxide, or tin oxide. Crown angles 40°, pavilion angles 40°.

Splendid yellow crystals from Cerro Mercado, Durango, Mexico, may reach several inches in length and an inch across but large ones are seldom flawless. Smaller crystals provide the majority of gems from 5 to 15 carats; flawless gems to 30 carats reported. Mexican apatite heat treats to colorless. Small but fine, purple to violet crystals once found in Maine at Mt. Apatite near Auburn and at other Maine localities. Olive-green material comes from open-pit mines in Wilberforce, Haliburton County, Ontario. Crystals range to several feet in length but are shattered and clear stones of only 1 or 2 carats may be cut. Facet grade purple from Saxony and western Bohemia; moroxite from Norway; asparagus stone from Jumilla, Murcia, Spain. Burma occasionally produces pale green and blue waterworn crystals often of large size; also, rarely, catseye material. Recently, small green facet and catseye material from Brazil; also from Madagascar.

APOPHYLLITE

G. 2.3–2.4   **HM** 4.5–5   **HL** 4.5   **R.I.** 1.53–1.54

Occasionally cut to take advantage of the strong pearly luster in crystals. Mainly white to colorless. Transparent material may be faceted. Brittle and weak; grind only on 220 or 400 wheel and never into the cleavage. Polish on leather with Linde A or felt with cerium oxide. Faceting material preformed on 220 wheel and cut on 1200 diamond/copper lap. Polish on tin with Linde A. Crown angles 40°–50°, pavilion angles 43°.

Often found in cavities in basalt. Fine material from trap rock quarries in northern New Jersey, Connecticut and Massachusetts. An area several miles south of Oregon City, Oregon, produces massive apophyllite with clear areas suitable for faceting. The silver mines of Guanajuato, Mexico, produce fine snow-white crystals suited for cabochons but extremely fragile. Also in Nova Scotia at Bay of Fundy,

Cape D'Or, Partridge Island, Haute Island and Swan's Creek above Cape Blomidon. The Faroe Islands, Iceland and the Isle of Skye off the northwest coast of Scotland are famed for excellent material. India produces exceptional crystals from basalts south of Bombay.

ARAGONITE

G. 2.9–2.95   **HM** 3.5–4   **HL** 4   **R.I.** 1.53–1.68

White, grayish, yellowish and greenish; luster glassy, inclining toward resinous; seldom transparent. Brittle; somewhat sensitive to heat but ordinary dopping temperatures, carefully applied, prevent breakage.

Grind facet material with care on 1200 diamond/copper lap. Polish with Linde A on wax or wood. If scratching occurs, use tin oxide. Crown angles 40°, pavilion angles 40°. Cabochon material polishes on leather with tin oxide or on felt with cerium oxide.

Beautiful clear material comes from European sources and is sometimes obtainable from mineral dealers. Colorless prisms about ¼ inch across from Herrengrund, Czechoslovakia; pale yellow crystals from Horschenz, near Bilin, Bohemia, cuttable to 10 carats; also small transparent places in crystals from Agrigento, Sicily and Guanajuato, Mexico. Cabochon material in beautiful blue from Chili and from Laurium, Greece; brown striped massive material from Karlsbad, Germany. Excellent white fibrous material from Rice's Cave, Dubuque, Iowa and from Wyandotte Cave, Indiana. "Satin spar" type from Bridger Buttes, Wyoming. Blue massive, banded with circular patterns, from Pauli, Peru.

ARGILLITE

A soft gray material from Slatechuck Mountain, Graham Island, British Columbia, has been used for carving for many years by the Haida and Thlingit Indians of the Pacific Northwest. It is carved and incised with ordinary steel tools and then sanded through increasingly finer grit grades until smooth. The final polish is obtained by rubbing with wood shavings and stove polish.

AUGELITE

G. 2.5–2.7   **HM** 4.5–5   **HL** 5–5.5   **R.I.** 1.57–1.59

One perfect cleavage fairly easy to start; very brittle; not sensitive to ordinary dopping temperatures. Polish with Linde A on wax. Crown angles 40°–50°, pavilion angles 43°.

Small gem material reported from New Hampshire; from Champion Mine on the west slope of White Mountain, Mono County, California in colorless crystals up to ¾ inch in diameter.

AXINITE

G. 3.3   **HM** 6.5–7   **HL** 6–7.5   **R.I.** 1.68–1.69

Predominantly grayish-brown showing strong directional changes of color: material from Luning, Nevada, shows pale brown to almost colorless in one direction, deep brown in another, intense brownish-red in the third direction. Most material some shade of brown although gray, blue-gray, yellow and greenish-yellow are known. Seldom free of flaws or inclusions but more or less transparent. One distinct cleavage present but not troublesome. Brittle; not heat sensitive.

No difficulties in cutting but a great variation in hardness noted depending on crystal direction. Polish with cerium oxide on Lucite or Linde A on tin; if scratching occurs, change direction of polishing. Crown angles 40°, pavilion angles 40°.

Finest crystals hitherto from St. Cristophe near Bourg D'Oisans, Isère, France; recently in magnificent large and flawless crystals from Coarse Gold, Madera County, California. Transparent waterworn crystals up to ¾ inch in length from Feather River gravels in Yuba County, California; also near Fallbrook in San Diego County. Bladed material sometimes yielding small clear sections near Luning, Nevada.

AZURITE

G. 3.8–3.9   **HM** 3.5–4   **HL** same   **R.I.** 1.73–1.83

Intense blue; massive material opaque; some crystals transparent. Massive azurite is less compact and hard than malachite, with which it is often associated. Not heat sensitive in massive form but single crystals suitable for faceting are very sensitive. Rough for cutting should be as solid and compact as possible to avoid ingraining with polishing powder.

Grinding very rapid; use fine wheels and sanders only. Polish on leather after prolonged gentle wet sanding on 400 cloth. Linde A best but chrome oxide will do. After mechanical polishing, apply fine gloss by gentle hand rubbing with a piece of moist, clean leather dipped in a very thin solution of chrome oxide. Transparent crystals can be faceted with Linde A on wax. Crown angles 40°, pavilion angles 40°. Polish is speeded by adding a drop or two of dilute hydrochloric acid to about a tablespoon of water mixed with Linde A. This method may etch adjacent facets. Slight additions of acid to polishing agents used for massive material often beneficial.

Seldom found in quantity; most localities are extinct. Formerly in splendid specimens with malachite from Bisbee and Morenci in Arizona and Kelly, New Mexico; such specimens, polished or unpolished, occasionally turn up at mineral dealers. Small nodules from Arizona currently available but many have hollow centers and are inclined to be porous. An extremely porous, soft and fragile mixture of cuprite, azurite and malachite is sold under the name of "burnite"; it polishes with difficulty. Splendid, intensely colored, transparent crystals from Tsumeb, South West Africa. These are facetable but gems must be cut very small to show color.

BANDED RHYOLITE

(Wonderstone)

Porous and variable in reaction to lapidary treatment. All types are soft and easily treated until final sanding and polishing at which time surfaces refuse to become acceptably smooth despite careful treatment. Cabochons will polish with Linde A on leather. Flat specimens are polished to exceptional luster using Linde A on wax or rouge on pitch.

TREATMENT OF GEMSTONES

BARITE

G. 4.3–4.6   **HM** 2.5–3.5   **HL** 3   **R.I.** 1.64–1.65

Colorless, pale blue, and rich brown in well formed crystals from ½ inch in length to as large as several inches in faceting grade; a massive variety from England is brown with a slight chatoyancy. Very heat sensitive. All operations must be done with extreme care. Sawing invariably starts cleavages and should be avoided. Preform on true 220 or 400 wheel. Dopping very troublesome; heat must be applied very slowly and gently. Rest preform on slip of cardboard while heating, warm dop and face-plate also and dop with chaser's cement. Polish on wax lap with tin oxide or Linde A. Crown angles 40°, pavilion angles 40°.

Suitable facet material near Sterling, Logan County, Colorado, in flattish crystals of blue tint; often with colorless cores; crystals and cleavage fragments up to ½ pound come from Silverband Mine near Knoch, Westmoreland, England, and are commonly available from mineral dealers. Small, almost flawless, rich yellow to brown crystals in concretions in Pierre shales along Cheyenne River and Elk Creek, Meade County, South Dakota. These crystals seldom show traces of cleavage and are stronger than other varieties. Colorless crystals to 1½ inches in Beaver Junior Mine, O'Connor Township, Thunder Bay District, Ontario; fine large pale brown crystals to 4 inches in Rock Candy Mine at Kennedy Creek, north of Grand Forks in British Columbia.

Massive material from Pillar Point, opposite Sackett's Harbor, Jefferson County, New York; interestingly banded, brown massive material resembling petrified wood from Middleton, near Youlgreave, Derbyshire, England.

BAUXITE

The variety containing numerous spherical nodules of hard material cemented together in conglomerate-like masses, is sometimes polished to show internal structure. Due to great variations in hardness, it is impossible to obtain a uniform finish, however, final lapping with 1200 grit helps, followed by polishing on pitch or wax with tin oxide or Linde A.

BAYLDONITE

This relatively rare, bright yellow-green mineral is found in massive form in Tsumeb, South West Africa. It polishes on leather with Linde A to a fine finish and a peculiar semi-metallic luster.

BENITOITE

G. 3.65–3.69   **HM** 6.2–6.5   **HL** 5   **R.I.** 1.76–1.8

Found only in San Benito County, California, near the headwaters of the San Benito River. Facet grade material from crystals which are small though occasionally 1 inch or more in diameter. Generally dark blue but also colorless. Uneven color distribution common with centers pale to colorless, exteriors intensely blue. Best color in finished gems obtained by orienting to place table facet at right angles to sharp edges of crystals. Since most crystals break off along edges, ordinary rough is usually well suited to this orientation as the pavilion of the gem can be placed to coincide with the vee-shaped corners of crystal edges. Most specimens badly flawed with tight cracks; pieces useful for faceting, very rare. The largest cut gem is only 7.5 carats and is in the Smithsonian Institution.

Not heat sensitive. Polish on Lucite with cerium oxide or on tin with Linde A. The latter produces a polish so quickly that it is necessary to guard against creation of polished grooves or deformed facet edges. Very small facets are cut and polished on the polishing lap directly. Crown angles 40°, pavilion angles 40°.

BERYL

Gem Varieties

Emerald—bright bluish-green.
Aquamarine—pale greenish-blue or various tints of blue.
Morganite—pink or purplish-pink.
Golden Beryl—yellow.

Goshenite—colorless.

Green Beryl—yellowish-green.

G. 2.63–2.8   HM 7.5–8. .   HL 7   R.I. 1.56–1.6

Also pale orange, pale reddish-orange; dark brown star material from Brazil. Greenish aquamarine is most common gem quality beryl; often found in very large pieces as complete crystals, stream-rolled fragments or rough broken bits. Morganite often occurs in large fragments also. Goshenite rare; most material classed as goshenite shows traces of color. Golden beryl and green beryl occur in pieces large enough for 50 carat gems. Emerald is usually found in rough crystals weighing only several grams. Greenish and bluish beryls show better color looking down upon tops of crystal prisms; orient table facets accordingly.

Emerald usually flawed; other varieties remarkable for high degree of transparency. Inclusions left in finished gems are repeatedly reflected and result in disfigurement. Inclusions noted are minute tubular cavities, indefinite veils of small bubbles, and, rarely, small crystals of other minerals. Numerous slender tubes create fine catseyes scarcely less distinct than chrysoberyl catseyes.

Easy to handle at all stages. Tough and remarkably heat resistant. Polish on tin with tin oxide or Linde A, or on Lucite with cerium oxide. For emerald, which is often fissured, tin is best because any metal and powder forced into cracks during polishing can be removed later with nitric acid. Crown angles 40°–50°, pavilion angles 43°.

Cabochons polish quickly on leather with Linde A; felt with cerium oxide is acceptable but much slower. Chrome oxide can be substituted for Linde A providing gems do not have open cracks into which this brilliantly-hued powder can creep. Most catseye material contains very fine tubes into which no powder can enter, but morganite is always penetrated by coarse cavities through which agents pass readily under polishing pressure. Seal holes by heating stone and dipping in warm liquid shellac; upon cooling, shellac draws into holes and seals them. Remove later by boiling in al-

cohol. Dipping in hot paraffin also accomplishes same result.

Almost all gem beryl comes from Brazil; emerald is mined intermittently in Colombia. Fine beryls also from Madagascar but not abundant on American market. Natural blue rare. Recent experiments prove deep greenish or olive-green beryls turn blue upon heat treatment. Not all beryls change, pale greenish-blue varieties stay the same or become paler. Morganites from Brazil seldom more than pale reddish-pink; a cut stone must be large to be colorful; Madagascar morganite stronger in color. Madagascar also noted for intensely blue aquamarine.

Excellent blue aquamarine formerly obtained from feldspar quarries near Portland, Connecticut, also on summit of Mount Antero, Chaffee County, Colorado; gem-quality aquamarine and morganite from San Diego County area, California.

BERYLLONITE

G. 2.81   HM 5.5–6   HL same   R.I. 1.55–1.56

Colorless; glassy luster; perfectly transparent in facet grade. Hairlike, tubular inclusions sometimes noted. Cleavages troublesome and must be avoided. Brittle and somewhat heat sensitive. Usual fragment size ¼ to ½ inch. Cuts with a "catchy" drag, like zircon. Easy to overcut because some directions cut much faster. Eliminate all cleavage cracks during preforming to prevent enlargement. Polishes with scratching on tin using Linde A but polishes smoothly with cerium oxide on Lucite. Do not let Lucite lap run dry. Crown angles 40°–50°, pavilion angles 43°. Found only in a decayed pegmatite vein at the base of McKean Mountain near Stoneham, Oxford County, Maine.

BORACITE

G. 2.91–2.97   HM 7–7.5   HL 7   R.I. 1.66

Seldom spoken of as a gem possibility yet it has all the essentials. Fairly common in Germany where it is found in gypsum and salt deposits. Mostly pale green; peculiar cross-hatching effect noted in transparent crystals due to variations in optical properties. Finished stones exhibit a curious soft or "sleepy" look. No cleavages but slight pitting experienced in grinding; eliminate by changing direction of grinding. Rough in fine cube-like crystals about ¼ to ½ inch in size, clear but deeply pitted on exteriors. Linde A on tin produces a quick, fine polish. Crown angles 40°, pavilion angles 40°.

German localities are Stassfurt, Douglashall, Leopoldshall, Solvayhall near Beroberg, and Hildesia near Hildesheim, in Saxony. Also from Hanover at Kalkberg, Schildstein, Enne, and Hohenfels. Rarely available from mineral dealers.

BORNITE

G. 5.06–5.08 **HM** 3 **HL** same

Compact bornite difficult to process because of brittleness and tendency to develop pits. Cabochons are finish-sanded on leather using 1200 grit. Polish with rouge on cloth buff or with Linde A in very thin solution on leather. Flats are best lapped on lead using 400 grit and polished on wax with watery Linde A. Linde A on Pellon is very effective but takes time to develop a good finish.

BRAZILIANITE

G. 2.94 **HM** 5.5 **HL** 6.5 **R.I.** 1.6–1.61

Color resembles deep yellow of chrysoberyl and Mexican apatite. Transparent, but often filled with fine flaws. Brittle, separates easily along a perfect cleavage plane which is always apparent in rough. Not heat sensitive. Most rough is small. Orientation is necessary to avoid the one excellent cleavage; aside from that, no trouble is experienced. Grinding is "catchy" and considerably slower than one would expect from the Mohs hardness. Polishing is fast and smooth on tin with Linde A. Furrows tend to develop and are counteracted by swinging the dop arm back and forth while polishing. Crown angles 40°, pavilion angles 40°.

In quantity, only from Minas Gerais, Brazil; also small facet-grade crystals from the Palermo Quarry near North Groton, Grafton County, New Hampshire. Brazilian rough yields gems up to 30 carats.

BREITHAUPTITE

G. 8.23 **HM** 5.5 **HL** same

Associated with massive niccolite, cobaltite, and smaltite in ore veins of Cobalt, Ontario, and sometimes polished as cabochons or flats. Treatment is same as for Algodonite.

BROOKITE

Frequently mentioned in gem literature, brookite seldom occurs large enough to be cuttable. The author has never seen a transparent cut specimen.

CALCITE

G. 2.71 **HM** 3 **HL** 3 **R.I.** 1.49–1.66

Transparent to translucent to opaque massive in wide color range but often yellow or colorless. Perfect, easily developed cleavages in three directions cause much trouble during faceting. Fairly sensitive to heat. Because of cleavages, grinding on diamond laps is unsuccessful; use lead lap with loose 400 silicon carbide grit. Polishing must be on wood or wax; it is impossible on tin, marginal on Lucite. Polishing agent not important, but tin oxide or Linde A are as good as any. Brilliant cuts should be avoided. Crown angles 40°–50°, pavilion angles 43°.

Massive material easier to handle because of compact, granular structure. Grinds and sands very quickly; cuts and shapes with ordinary steel tools. Polish with tin oxide. Action of tin oxide is speeded by dissolving a few crystals of oxalic acid in powder-water mix. *Caution:* oxalic acid is poisonous. Oxalic acid *must not* be used in faceting.

Facet quality abundant: from copper deposits of Michigan; Joplin, Granby, and other mines in Missouri; Gray Cliff, Montana; fine large brown crystals from Rosarita Beach, Baja California, Mexico, yielding splendid rich reddish-yellow gems. Commonly available from mineral dealers. Massive forms include the stalactites and stalagmites of limestone caverns, numerous varieties of marble, and calcite onyx as used in inkstand bases. Excellent calcite onyx from many localities in the United States, Mexico, Argentina, and abroad.

CANCRINITE

G. 2.42–2.5   **HM** 5–6   **HL** 5   **R.I.** 1.49–1.52

In bright orange to lemon yellow masses associated with sodalite in the Canadian occurrences; very rarely yields clear areas suitable for faceting minute gems. Treated in the same manner as sodalite but contains a greater number of hard inclusions which tend to leave rough surfaces unless very carefully sanded in the case of cabochons, or lapped in the case of flats. Seldom occurs in pieces larger than several inches across.

CASSITERITE

G. 6.8–7.1   **HM** 6–7   **HL** 6 (massive)   **R.I.** 1.99–2.1
HL 7 (facet material)

Occurs in two forms of interest to the cutter: transparent faceting material and massive banded nodules, or "wood-tin," which can be cabochon cut. From black to colorless and shades of brown. Massive material often shows yellow, sometimes red and green, but always in grayish tones. Remarkably tough in all forms. Unaffected by heat. Facet quality material in glistening crystals and crystal fragments; massive forms nodular with fine circular markings, often of different hues. Crystals usually clear only in outside layers; the detection of transparent areas is difficult, the dark interiors giving the impression that entire crystals are black and opaque.

Saws with great difficulty; all but freshly charged blades tend to glaze. Saw off pieces parallel to crystal faces to salvage transparent outer zones. Polishes on tin using thick mixture of Linde A; run lap fast and almost dry. Crown angles 30°–40°, pavilion angles 37°–40°. Cabochon material must be carefully sanded on 400 wet cloth and polished on leather with Linde A.

The most famous locality is Bolivia where the Araca Mine, at Viloco, La Paz, Quimsa Cruz, produces fine crystals. Good material

also from New England, New South Wales, Australia and from the Stiepelmann Mine, Arandis, South West Africa. Cabochon material abundant in gravels of Arroya Carrizal, Tierra Blanca, Guanajuato, and from other states in Mexico and from the Maragua District and Ocari, near Colquechaca, Bolivia. Wood tin occurs in nodules up to several pounds; faceting material seldom exceeds several grams.

CELESTITE

G. 3.95–3.97   **HM** 3–3.5   **HL** same   **R.I.** 1.62–1.63

Crystals mostly small, seldom more than ½ inch. Blue, colorless, red, orange. Soft, fragile, and with several cleavages; very heat sensitive. Grinds fast; Linde A on wax. Never quite perfect polish. Crown angles 40°, pavilion angles 40°. Faceting material: Put-in-Bay, Strontian Island, in Lake Erie; fine blue crystals on Mt. Bonnel near Austin, Texas; bright orange from Forks of Credit, Ontario, Canada; Glen Eyrie near Manitou, El Paso County, Colorado.

CERUSSITE

G. 6.5–6.6   **HM** 3–3.5   **HL** 3   **R.I.** 1.8–2.08

Occasionally found sufficiently large and clear for gemstones. Extremely soft, brittle and sensitive to heat. Scarcely suitable for cutting except as a curiosity. Pale yellow, brown, colorless. Transparent to translucent. Literally explodes in direct contact with flame. Rough in crystals seldom exceeding several grams of clear material. Extreme care needed in all operations. Polish with tin oxide on wood or wax with latter preferred, good polish almost impossible to obtain. Crown angles 40°, pavilion angles 40°.

Exceptional material from Tsumeb, South West Africa; fine catseye rough from Mammouth Mine at Tiger, Arizona.

CHLORASTROLITE
(Pumpellyite)

Occurs only as small nodules weathered from basaltic rocks with the best material found on Isle Royale in Lake Superior. Color ranges from pale gray-green to green-black. Gems of ¾ inch are now considered large.

Varies greatly in hardness according to how decomposed the material may be; if fresh from rock, it is quite hard; if badly weathered, it may be so soft that it refuses to polish. Hardness ranges from 5 to 6. Polish on felt with cerium oxide. Care must be taken not to over-grind pebbles in the desire to develop a better pattern; if the pattern is poor to begin with, it probably will not improve.

CHONDRODITE

G. 3.1–3.2   **HM** 6–6.5   **HL** 5.5–6   **R.I.** 1.59–1.64

Facet material once found in considerable quantity during operation of the old Tilly Foster Iron Mine, near Brewster, Putnam County, New York. Deep brownish-red gems resemble almandine garnet. Weak and brittle; take care in all stages of cutting. Scratchy, difficult polishing with all powders on Lucite or tin, however, Linde A on wax or wood produces a fine finish. Crown angles 40°, pavilion angles 40°. Stones exceeding one carat are very dark and should be cut shallow.

CHRYSOBERYL

G. 3.5–3.8   **HM** 8.5   **HL** 8.5–8.8   **R.I.** 1.76–1.77

Transparent varieties provide faceted gems; finely fibrous material yields excellent catseyes. Usually transparent; often flawed by inclusions and many fine cracks. Mostly in crystals but also in stream-worn pebbles. Very tough, not heat sensitive. Rough seldom large, stones of several carats are all that can be expected ordinarily. Brownish material often available in larger pieces. Catseye rough is rare. Prized colors are pale lemon-yellow to yellow for faceted gems, honey color with bluish eye for catseye. Highly translucent catseye material is very valuable as is the alexandrite variety.

Rough grinds well on ordinary wheels despite hardness. Facet in the ordinary way but polish on tin, zinc, or typemetal with very fine (6400) diamond dust. Some workers prefer copper with diamond. Small faceted gems sometimes polish on tin with Linde A. Sand cabochons through two grades of grit, finish sand on a hard wood lap with 1200 diamond dust. Polish on hard wood with 6400 diamond dust. Considerable heat is generated and must be checked as it forms to prevent loosening of dopping cement. Crown angles 40°, pavilion angles 40°. High crowned cabochons are needed to produce a sharp eye.

From gem gravels of Ceylon, also from various localities in Minas Gerais, Brazil. Also found in the United States but seldom in gem grade. Alexandrite is found in the Ural Mountains and in Ceylon. In daylight, alexandrites appear to be some shade of green (olive green for Ceylon stones and bright emerald green for Russian). Under artificial light, the green color disappears more or less completely and a purplish-red replaces it. Such stones are very rare and rough is unobtainable.

CINNABAR

G. 8.09   **HM** 2–2.5   **HL** 2.5–3   **R.I.** 2.91–3.26

Large transparent red crystals from China; small clear crystals from Mexico and elsewhere. Heat sensitive. Despite softness, cinnabar withstands cautious grinding and lapping. Clogs diamond/copper laps and is better lapped on lead with 400 grit. Polish on wax with Linde A. Polish is seldom perfect and often shows very narrow furrows. Crown angles 30°–40°, pavilion angles 37°–40°.

CLINOZOISITE

G. 3.25–3.5   **HM** 6   **HL** 6   **R.I.** 1.72–1.73

A member of the epidote-zoisite series and treated in the same manner as epidote. However, since it is somewhat more fragile and cleavages are developed more easily, it must be treated with greater care. Crown angles 40°, pavilion angles 40°.

Clear material suitable for faceting from near Gavilanes in Baja California.

COBALTITE

Sometimes polished because of attractive reddish metallic color. In fairly large masses in silver mines near Cobalt in Ontario. Some rough is veined with quartz and calcite and makes interesting cabochon material. Grinds normally but finish sanding is done on leather with a thin slurry of 1200 silicon carbide grit to remove numerous small pits left after grinding and coarse sanding. Polish with Linde A on leather.

COLEMANITE

G. 2.42   HM 4-4.5   HL 5   R.I. 1.6-1.61

Clear crystals are cut at times as curiosities. Transparent, often with minute inclusions. Colorless. Very brittle, weak. Grinds smoothly and easily. Polishes with some difficulty on Lucite with cerium oxide; better with tin oxide. Changes of polishing direction are needed to eliminate scratches. Crown angles 40°, pavilion angles 40°. Found at Boron in the Calico District near Yermo, San Bernardino County, California. Crystals may reach ¾ inch.

COPPER RHYOLITE

Altered rhyolite impregnated with native copper and copper minerals occurs in abundance in a number of places on South Mountain, Adams County, Pennsylvania. General coloration varies from green in several shades to grayish-pink, depending on the presence or absence of epidote. Rock structure shows its metamorphic origin because it contains small masses of quartz which may be circular, oval, or stretched into narrow oval streaks. In places native copper is found associated with various colorful copper minerals such as malachite, azurite, and cuprite. Cuprite imparts lovely red to reddish-orange hues to the compact material, especially in patches surrounding veinlets of native copper. This material often occurs in large blocks, suitable for many lapidary projects such as book ends, pen bases, spheres, etc. Commonly the South Mountain

copper rhyolite is misnamed "cuprite." Although the better specimens do contain this colorful mineral, it is a very small part of the whole. Saws and grinds easily but, being composed of many minerals of varying degrees of hardness, it requires jade-polishing techniques to prevent undercutting. Careful wet sanding with 400 cloth followed by polishing with Linde A on leather produces an excellent polish. Large flats polish well on wood or pitch but require prolonged treatment.

CORAL

The precious coral of the jewelry industry is fished from beds along the north coast of Africa in the Mediterranean, and from Japan. A peculiar variety of black coral comes from beds along the coast of southeastern Alaska and from the Hawaiian Islands. This black coral does not contain the stoney calcium carbonate skeleton of the precious coral.

Ordinary coral is essentially calcium carbonate with little organic matter and is cut and polished in the same way as massive calcite. Steel carving tools are frequently used to make figurines, perforated and carved beads, etc. Sanding is done by hand using a succession of finer grit papers and finally buffing on cloth wheels with tripoli followed by tin oxide. Polish black coral with jewelers rouge.

CORUNDUM

Ruby—dark red.
Sapphire—all colors except dark red.
Adamantine Spar—brown, showing schiller.

G. 3.96-4.05   HM 9.0   HL same   R.I. 1.76-1.78

Corundum occurs in all colors. The most expensive and highly prized varieties are dark red, as in true rubies, also deep blue, orange, and a fine green. Below these rank purple, yellow, pink, and lastly colorless. Colors must be definite and intense; grayish, mottled, or pastel tints are less valuable. Much corundum contains numerous fine, silky inclusions and is cut into star stones. As inclusions increase in quantity, stronger and sharper stars result.

Remarkably tough in all transparent varieties; practically unaffected by even white heat. Schiller varieties and massive forms split readily and are sometimes almost impossible to cut on this account. Gem crystals seldom exceed a few ounces at most and the majority are small bits scarcely larger than peas. Much rough is waterworn and should be examined in immersion fluids to check for flaws; often banded in color and also filled with tiny platelets which, in gems, reduce brilliancy, particularly in Montana river sapphires.

Corundum is difficult to cut and polish because of its hardness. Ordinary silicon-carbide wheels are quickly worn during shaping of rough. Faceting on copper results in breakdown of diamond powder into smaller particles, leaving the lap in poor condition and less sharp than before. Large stones are trimmed to approximate shape by nicking on the trim saw in many places, leaving small projections that can be more easily removed on grinding wheels. Sanding on coarse grit cloth only; fine grit does little abrasion. Rubber sanding wheels are useful for smoothing of cabochons prior to polish. For faceted stones use care in cutting, since different directions in the crystal are of different hardness; the direction across the base, for example, is particularly slow in grinding. Polish on copper, bronze, or tin, useing 6400 diamond grit with oil. Tripoli can be used on bronze or type metal, but is slow and apt to groove facets. A good combination: polish first with diamond, follow with tripoli to considerably improve the finish. Crown angles 40°, pavilion angles 40°. Cabochons are polished on wooden laps with 1200 diamond first, followed by 6400. Leather will do, but a firmer surface is better. Considerable heat is generated, and care should be taken to cool the stone by dipping in cold water from time to time.

Commercial cutters of star sapphires and rubies claim that far more brilliant finishes are obtained if fine grinding is done upon copper laps, followed by polishing on laps of the same metal. This treatment is aimed at eliminating the numerous small pits which fre-

quently result from rough grinding and which are not completely eradicated by ordinary methods. However, though very effective because it results in severe "point" pressure upon the curving surfaces of cabochons and thus removes material very quickly, this method requires that the dop stick be twirled constantly to prevent formation of flat spots upon the gems. This must be done also when polishing upon copper laps using 6400 diamond grit.

Synthetic star sapphire or ruby boules may be troublesome in orienting unless carefully examined first. Older star boules had the needles arranged in the outer layer of the boule while the center was practically clear material. In these examples the apex of the star was actually on the side of the boule and it was necessary to slit the boule along its length, and from each half, cut more or less square sections. These were then rounded to establish the cabochon profile and finished on top in the normal manner. The trick was to be sure that the boule was not slit in just the *wrong* way because then nothing but the very smallest gems could be obtained. Boules are now being grown so that needles occur throughout the boule, and further, are arranged so that the boule can be sliced across, like a sausage, and from each slice, a star stone is obtainable. Thus the latest star ruby or sapphire boules are exactly like natural crystals in this respect.

Principal sources of fine facet and star rough are Ceylon and Burma. Australian sapphire fields produce dark brown star material, occasional fine pieces of yellow and green material, and even more rarely, crystals of good blue color. Most Australian blue sapphire is worthless unless cut into very small gems. The so-called "star ruby" from India is more accurately classed as red corundum since it scarcely compares at best with the poorer grades of star ruby from either Burma or Ceylon. Yogo Gulch, Montana, sapphires are very fine but unfortunately always small and seldom obtainable. River sapphires from Montana sometimes produce very good gems but most are pale in hue and often filled with inclusions which severely restrict development of brilliance in faceted gems. Amateur cutters are very unlikely to obtain good corundum rough because the best class of material is cut in the lands of origin and seldom sold to dealers from abroad.

COVELLITE

G. 4.6–4.8   **HM** 1.5–2.0   **HL** 2.0–2.5

Occasionally, splendid massive covellite is obtained from Montana or Alaska and, when cut, takes a fine polish. During treatment, covellite is seen to be gray-yellow in color but tarnishes almost immediately to rich blue-purple. Treatment is conventional but because covellite is soft, sanding must be done carefully to avoid destroying the proportions of cabochon gems. Polish on leather with Linde A.

CROCOITE

G. 5.99   **HM** 2.5–3.0   **HL** same   **R.I.** 2.3–2.7

Although none of the beautiful red-orange crystals from the Dundas District in Tasmania, Australia are very large—seldom more than ¼ inch in diameter—some provide facetable material from clear areas. It is possible to facet crocoite despite its softness but the greatest care is needed in all stages to prevent crumbling. Dop with cold cement; chasers cement will also do, since the crystals can stand some heat without breaking. Crocoite grinds readily and easily on the 1200 diamond-impregnated copper lap and polishes with some minute scores, on wax with Linde A. It will chatter and crumble on tin or any other hard lap. Crown angles 30°–40°, pavilion angles 37°–40°.

CUPRITE

This relatively common copper mineral sometimes occurs in small crystals clear enough to facet. No information on cutting is available.

DANBURITE

G. 3.0   **HM** 7.0–7.25   **HL** same   **R.I.** 1.63–1.64

Fairly tough and not heat sensitive, danburite handles with ease. Polish with Linde A on tin. Crown angles 40°, pavilion angles 40°. A brilliant cut is recommended to take advantage of the remarkable clarity.

Fine, colorless crystals from Obira and Bungo in Japan; from the gravels of the Mogok gem tract of Burma in pale to deep yellow etched crystals, sometimes of large size; from Mt. Bity and Imalo in Madagascar; splendid crystals from mines near Charcas, San Luis Potosi, Mexico. A large quantity of colorless to faintly pink facet grade material has been produced from the latter locality in the past few years. Some crystals are large enough to provide flawless gems of six carats or more.

DATOLITE

G. 2.8–3.0   **HM** 5–5.5   **HL** same   **R.I.** 1.62–1.67

Crystallized datolite is mostly pale yellowish-green. Massive material is opaque white, pink, orange, and reddish, often veined, and with specks of native copper. Luster of crystals glassy, that of compact material is very much like the surface left by broken china. Crystals brittle, massive material tough. Insensitive to heat. Nodular datolite is found in irregular lumps reaching 5 inches across; crystals seldom exceed 1 inch and are mostly flawed.

Because of differences in hardness, datolite must be faceted carefully. All edges should be finished particularly well because they tend to crumble. If cutting shows traces of surface pitting, change direction. Polish on Lucite with tin oxide, but change polishing direction at any sign of roughness. Crown angles 40°, pavilion angles 40°. Cabochon material handles without difficulty but requires a smooth surface in fine sanding. Polishing is done with cerium oxide on felt or Linde A on leather.

Fine crystals reported from Habachtal near Salzburg, Austria and from other Alpine areas.

Very fine facet material obtained from time to time at Lane's Quarry, Westfield, Massachusetts, and in smaller crystals from basalt quarries in northern New Jersey. Massive datolite comes from several copper mines on the Keeweenaw Peninsula, Michigan.

DIOPSIDE

G. 3.27–3.31 **HM** 5–6 **HL** 5–7 **R.I.** 1.67–1.7

Facet quality from colorless through pale green to drark green, sometimes so intense that fragments look black. Lighter colors are more desirable. Glassy in luster, crystals clear but some minutely cleaved, others filled with straight silk capable of making exceptionally fine catseyes. Several cleavages exist but are initiated with difficulty and not of great concern. Remarkably insensitive to heat. Rough usually in single crystals or clear cleavage fragments. Best color appears through the sides of crystals, ends showing a rather disagreeable yellowish-brown tinge. Rough often large enough to cut stones of 3 to 10 carats and sometimes larger.

Sawing is easy across crystals but should not be rushed. Sawing with the grain usually results in splitting the crystal. Preform gently. Cutting of facets is fast in all directions except across ends of crystals where it is very slow and facets tend to glaze. Polishing very troublesome due to scratching. Linde A or tin oxide on tin are satisfactory for small facets but exactly the right polishing direction is needed to get a smooth surface. It is better to use wood or wax laps with either tin oxide or Linde A. Dark material, cut in large sizes, will appear black. Crown angles 40°, pavilion angles 40°. Lesser angles may be used for very dark material.

Splendid diopside from colorless to dark green from various localities in the Alps. Fine dark green fragments from Madagascar but too dark for stones larger than 5 carats. The best catseyes come from Burma and command a fancy price. Vivid green chrome diopside yielding small clear areas for faceting from Otukumpu, Finland. In the United States, ex-

cellent light colored material yielding gems up to 10 carats, was produced many years ago near De Kalb, St. Lawrence County, New York. Unique massive diopside, intense blue to violet (violane), from St. Marcel, Piedmont, Italy.

DIOPTASE

G. 3.3–3.35 **HM** 5 **HL** 6 **R.I.** 1.65–1.70

Suitable facet material only from extreme ends of crystals. Pieces of good material seldom larger than 3/16-inch diameter. Three cleavages, like calcite, and extremely troublesome. Brittle; not heat sensitive. Little preparation of rough is needed; a fragment of crystal is dopped directly and worked on from there. Cut gently on 1200 grit, avoiding development of sharp corners which easily break off. Polish on Lucite using cerium oxide. Crown angles 40°, pavilion angles 40°. Sometimes massive dioptase can be used for cabochons. Grind on 220 grit and fine sand on 400 grit cloth wet. Polish on felt with cerium oxide. The only localities producing single crystals large enough to cut are those in the Congo.

ENSTATITE

G. 3.25–3.3 **HM** 5.5 **HL** 6 **R.I.** 1.66–1.67

Occasionally clear crystals are faceted into gems. Bright green material of small size comes from diamond mines near Kimberly in South Africa; brown etched crystals from India. Both are tough, insensitive to heat and with little tendency to cleave but considerable differences are noted in hardness. Across ends of crystals is very hard as compared to that parallel to the length. Faceted gems are polished with Linde A on tin. Crown angles 40°, pavilion angles 40°. Indian material often dark brown; shallower gems are indicated. Massive enstatite displaying metallic reflections is called *bronzite* and is very fragile. Break pieces to get fragments for cabochons as attempts to saw usually result in shattering. Grind with care on 220 grit wheel and polish with cerium oxide on felt or Linde A on leather.

Indian enstatite is often large enough to cut 10 carat gems, while the handsomer green material from Kimberly yields gems no larger than a carat or two. Bronzite is not common; some comes from Webster, North Carolina and from several European localities.

EPIDOTE

G. 3.25–3.5   HM 6–7   HL same   R.I. 1.74–1.76

Intense brownish-green color but sometimes yellowish or greenish-yellow. Glassy luster; crystal faces often brilliantly smooth. Clear crystals display dichroic colors: deep green, brown, sometimes red. One easy cleavage but not of importance. Not heat sensitive. Polish using cerium oxide on Lucite or Linde A on tin. Changes of polishing direction may be necessary. Most stones are dark and must be cut thin in order to show color. Crown angles 40°, pavilion angles 40°. Cuttable material mainly from Untersalzbachtal in Austria. In the United States, facet quality from the McFall mine near Ramona, California. The famous Prince of Wales Island locality in Alaska produced very small cuttable epidotes of a yellowish tinge. Good crystals in several deposits in the Greenhorn Mountains of Kern County, California. The best epidotes seen by the author were several small, light yellow-green crystals from Brazil.

EUCLASE

G. 3.05–3.1   HM 7.5   HL 6.5–7.5   R.I. 1.65–1.67

Described repeatedly by all authorities as difficult to cut, euclase is really fairly trouble-free. Sharply pointed transparent crystals, colorless to pale violet, pale blue, blue, and straw yellow. Never found massive. Avoid placing the perfect cleavage on a facet, orient to take advantage of the best color. Not heat sensitive. Cut on 1200 and polish with Linde A on tin. Polishes very fast with removal of considerable material. Great differences of hardness exist; exercise care not to overcut

facets in soft direction. Crown angles 40°, pavilion angles 40°.

Gem quality material only from the Urals of Russia and from Boa Vista and Capao da Lana, Minas Gerais, Brazil.

EUXENITE

Compact masses and crystals of this radioactive rare earth mineral are sometimes cut into faceted gems. Good material comes from Minas Gerais, Brazil. Fairly tough and insensitive to heat. Saws with difficulty and grinds and laps scratchily. Polishes easily on heavily scored tin lap with Linde A.

FELDSPAR

Gem Varieties: Moonstone, peristerite, sunstone, amazonite, labradorite.
Also transparent, affording faceted stones.

Mineral Species: Albite—blue moonstone, colorless facet material. Oligoclase—colorless facet material, sunstone. Orthoclase—pale yellow facet material, sunstone, moonstone. Microcline—amazonite. Labradorite—labradorite, also pale yellow facet material.

G. 2.54–2.67   HM 6   HL 6   R.I. 1.52–1.57

Rarely in crystals; mostly massive, often badly shattered. Transparent to translucent. Most varieties show pronounced cleavage. Not heat sensitive at normal dopping temperatures. Polishes smoothly and easily with cerium oxide on felt for cabochons, and with cerium oxide on Lucite or Linde A on tin, for faceted gems. Crown angles 40°–50°, pavilion angles 43°.

Moonstone and Peristerite

Finest moonstones from Ceylon and Burma. Almost transparent gems with a strong blue light are most highly prized; next are those displaying silver reflections.

Excellent colorless albite in flawless pieces from Rutherford Mine, Amelia, Virginia; also white massive showing blue adularescence. Fine white moonstone showing silvery reflections from Mitchell Creek Mica Mine, Upson County, Georgia. Beautiful moonstone from New Mexico. Peristerite showing blue and other colors obtainable from various localities in Canada.

SUNSTONE

Best material from Tvedestrand, Norway, in small masses several inches across of deep reddish-orange color; cut gems produce gleaming golden reflections. Other sunstones compare poorly to Norwegian material. Fair sunstone, occasionally fine, from Alan Wood Iron Mine, Mine Hill, New Jersey. Some Canadian peristerite shows sunstone reflections. Labradorite also shows sunstone effect at times. Sunstone occasionally noted in yellowish, transparent feldspar from Modoc County, California, and from Oregon.

LABRADORITE

Fine material from Labrador coast in individual crystals as large as a foot across. Most is badly shattered and seldom capable of making sound cabochons greater than 1 inch across but excellent for polished slabs and blocks. Splendid uncracked material from Finland. Also fine from Madagascar. Found extensively in eastern Adirondack Mountains of New York in Essex and Lewis counties, in fine grained masses but not in the solid sheets of splendid unbroken color typifying Labrador material. Pale yellow, transparent, facetable labradorite in small grains capable of cutting gems of several carats from Clear Lake, Millard County, Utah; similar material from Modoc County, California, also from Oregon and Texas.

AMAZONITE

Finest dark green and blue-green from several mines near Amelia, Virginia. Formerly in considerable quantity from Pike's Peak region of Colorado. Excellent material from Ontario and Quebec. The finest is translucent.

MISCELLANEOUS FELDSPARS

Colorless to pale greenish oligoclase at the Hawk Mica Mine, Bakersville, North Carolina, producing small, very brilliant gems. Beautiful, transparent, yellow orthoclase from Madagascar, large enough to cut 10 to 20 carat gems exceptionally free of inclusions.

FERGUSONITE

Many crystals of this radioactive mineral are solid and are suitable for faceting curious if valueless gems. No special precautions are needed in preparation. Insensitive to heat. Grinds scratchily on diamond/copper laps; behaves better with 400 silicon carbide grit on lead. Polish with heavy paste of Linde A on deeply-scored tin lap.

FIBROLITE

(Sillimanite)

G. 3.25 HM 7.5 HL same R.I. 1.665

A common metamorphic mineral receiving its name from the fibrous appearance of its usual massive form. Very rarely, transparent pale blue crystals which cut small faceted gems are found in gem gravels of Burma and Ceylon. Fibrolite is hard and tough except in crystals, where toughness is greatly tempered by a very easy cleavage. Not heat sensitive. Tremendous differences in apparent hardness according to crystal direction, the hardest cuts across the edges of cleavage planes. Flat fragments are almost impossible to facet because of easily developed cleavages and only the rounded crystals are strong enough to withstand lapidary abrasion. Crown angles 40°, pavilion angles 40°. Preform on perfectly smooth 220 wheel; avoid direct grinding on edges. Grind on lead with 400 silicon carbide grit and polish with Linde A on tin. Fibrous and catseye material requires gentle treatment, especially catseye material from South Carolina. Cabochons are polished with Linde A on leather.

Common fibrous material from Idaho has been polished for its weak chatoyancy. Excellent dark reddish-brown catseye material in much fractured crystals from Oconee County, South Carolina. Facet grade crystals from Mogok, Burma; also Ceylon.

FLUORITE

G. 3.01–3.25   **HM** 4   **HL** 4   **R.I.** 1.43

Mostly transparent but seldom free of bubbles, inclusions, or strong color zoning. Predominant colors are purple, green, blue, and yellow. Red and pink are rare. Cleaves easily along four directions yielding characteristic octahedrons seen commonly in mineral collections. Brittle. Very sensitive to heat. Rough often in pieces weighing a pound or more. Massive forms granular and only translucent. Handle with care in all stages of cutting, particularly in dopping. Avoid cleavage planes by placing tables of faceted gems somewhat off a cleavage surface. Grind only on 1200 diamond/copper lap and polish only on wood or wax lap; harder laps cause serious scratching. Crown angles 40°–50°, pavilion angles 43°.

Faceting fluorite from many mines in western Kentucky and southern Illinois. Colorless crystals from Madoc, Ontario. Fine specimens from England. Deep emerald green from Africa. Splendid green from Westmoreland, New Hampshire and Jefferson County, New York.

FRIEDELITE

A rare mineral, only cuttable from translucent masses found sporadically in the zinc mines of Franklin, New Jersey. Finest form is orange-red, highly translucent, and fine-grained. More commonly reddish or brownish. Cerium oxide on felt or Linde A on leather polishes cabochons; Linde A on tin for faceted stones.

GADOLINITE

G. 4–4.5   **HM** 6.5–7   **HL** 6.5

Black to blackish-brown rare earth mineral, sometimes cut into faceted gems as a curiosity. Fairly hard, inclined to be brittle,

saw carefully to avoid excess chipping. Not heat sensitive. Normal grinding followed by polishing with tin oxide or Linde A on tin or typemetal. Common in some pegmatites, notably in the extinct Barringer Hill locality in Texas; also from various localities in Sweden and Norway.

GARNET

Almandine—reddish, purplish, brownish, mostly dark but sometimes light.

Pyrope—red to brownish-red, usually very intense.

Grossularite—colorless to white, green, yellow, brown, red, reddish-brown, massive and in crystals.

Spessartite—orange, dark red, brownish-red.

Rhodolite—pale reddish-purple.

Andradite—brown, bright green (demantoid).

G. 3.41–4.2   **HM** 6.5–7.5   **HL** same   **R.I.** 1.74–1.89

Physical constants vary in the several species. Most gem garnet is transparent except for grossularite which, in massive forms, is translucent. No pecularities and no directional effects in cutting or polishing. Brittle except in massive grossularite which is remarkably tough. Fairly heat sensitive but withstands ordinary dopping temperatures. Cut garnets are never large, partly because rough is badly shattered and partly because darker varieties appear black. Light colored grossularite and spessartite rarely produces gems larger than 10 carats. Almandine may cut into very large cabochons.

Grind with care to prevent chipping. Avoid dry sanding. Preliminary sanding with 1200 grit on leather is helpful in preparing cabochon surfaces for polish. Polishing is fast on leather using Linde A or chrome oxide. Faceted stones trouble-free in all respects. Polish on tin with Linde A. Crown angles 40°, pavilion angles 40°, but dark material requires a shallower cut.

ALMANDINE

From Madagascar in small irregular broken

pieces of dark brownish-red to lovely pale purplish-red. Ceylon; Jaipur, Kishangarh and Rajputana in India; Minas Gerais, Brazil; also Australia and Tanganyika. From North Creek, New York; also South Dakota, Montana and Georgia. Star material from Idaho.

PYROPE

From Arizona and nearby areas in New Mexico; of superior quality but seldom over 2 grams, in small rounded pieces. The famous "Bohemian Garnets" occur in a considerable area near Trebnitz in the northeastern part of Bohemia. Excellent pyropes also occur with diamond in South Africa. Also from Australia, Southern Rhodesia, Brazil and Mexico.

GROSSULARITE

Massive, associated with "californite" idocrase at many localities in California; also Oregon. Pink crystals, sometimes clear in small areas, from Xalostoc, Morelos, Mexico. Splendid green massive "Transvaal jade", from South Africa.

SPESSARTITE

Splendid orange, red-orange, and red facet grade from Amelia, Virginia; Ramona, California; and Ceara, Brazil; also from Madagascar.

RHODOLITE

In gem quality principally from Cowee Creek, North Carolina; also from Ceylon and Madagascar.

ANDRADITE

Splendid transparent yellow-green to emerald green crystals of small size (demantoid) from the Urals; greenish-brown facet material and chatoyant cabochon material from Stanley Butte, Arizona; also from Italy.

GLASS

Man-made glasses are frequently cut and polished into gems and ornamental items, as well as into lenses, prisms, and other objects of scientific value. Glasses are created in a large range of compositions, with accompanying wide variations in physical and optical properties. As a rule, all handle with equal facility in lapidary operations. Chief characteristic of ordinary glass is heat sensitivity and brittleness. High-silica glasses, such as Pyrex, are not heat sensitive but are brittle. Glass must be dopped with care and ground and lapped through a succession of grits to avoid development of many deep sub-surface cracks which later cause trouble in polishing. Glass flats and curves, such as employed in lens and prism work, are ground with silicon carbide, emery, or aluminum oxide grits or, as is more the practice in the case of curved surfaces, ground with special diamond-impregnated or sintered bronze laps. Gems are cut satisfactorily with diamond/copper laps. Crown angles 40°–50°, pavilion angles 43°.

Glass can be polished with tin oxide but most is now polished with cerium oxide. Pitch laps are still used for final polishing of large flats and lenses but Pellon with cerium oxide is also successful. For faceted gems, use cerium oxide on tin or Lucite. Exercise care using Lucite not to let the lap run dry and overheat.

GOETHITE

G. 3.3–4.3   HM 5–5.5   HL 6

Massive fibrous goethite is sometimes compact enough to polish but considerable care during sawing is needed to avoid splitting. Cabochons are ground and sanded normally. Not heat sensitive. Polish on leather with Linde A. Grind flats on lead with 400 grit and polish on wax with Linde A. Well-scored tin polishes also.

GRANITE AND GRAPHIC GRANITE

The United States is blessed with many quarries furnishing handsome examples of granite. Some, like the Red Waupaca Granite of Wisconsin and the mottled green and pink unakite of the Appalachian Mountains are very handsome and worthy of making into larger lapidary projects such as book ends, ink stands, spheres, etc. Due to the granular nature, rough treatment during sawing, grinding, or lapping is likely to dislodge grains or create pits which take much time to eliminate in subsequent work. In sawing, set the feed at the lowest rate, to prevent excessive chipping and pitting. Similarly, in preparing flats, carry all lapping steps to the point where pits are eliminated. In cabochon work, similar precautions are necessary during sanding to avoid undercutting during polishing. Polish cabochons using Linde A on leather; flats are finished almost perfectly by polishing on pitch or wood. Soft buffs, like felt, result in undercutting.

GYPSUM

Alabaster—granular translucent in a variety of pale colors.

Satin spar—fibrous, brilliantly chatoyant material; white to pale pink or orange.

A favorite ornamental for many centuries; lends itself to carving with ordinary steel tools and finishing with successively finer grades of sandpaper or sanding cloth. Bowls, vases, dishes and the like, are turned on lathes much like wood, while statuettes and other carvings in the round are executed with carving chisels and files. Despite its very great softness, satin spar is often made into beads which are very handsome as long as they last. Normal lapidary treatments prepare gypsum but all abrasive steps require the greatest care to prevent too-rapid removal of material. Only a few seconds inattention during sanding may result in a lopsided cabochon. Gypsum is polished with almost any agent on soft buffs or on leather. It is better to put the final polish on by hand with a piece of felt cloth, wool cloth, or a strip of damp leather impregnated with polishing agent.

Excellent grade gypsum from Michigan, Colorado, and elsewhere in the United States. Good satin spar primarily from England.

HAMBERGITE

G. 2.35   **HM** 7.5   **HL** 6.5–7.5   **R.I.** 1.55–1.63

Very rare, only from Madagascar in transparent facet grade. Colorless, glassy luster, usually transparent except when filled with numerous partly developed cleavages. Brittle.

Two easily developed cleavages at right angles to each other and parallel with the long dimensions of crystals. Crystals crude or deeply etched, usually showing traces of cleavages. Avoid placing any facet upon a cleavage. Girdles of faceted gems should be left fairly thick to prevent crumbling. Considerable variation in hardness according to direction; the hardest is across the ends of crystals. Saw carefully to avoid furring edges and causing many minute cleavages. Cut only on 1200 diamond/copper; do not cut rectangles or corners will crumble. Polish on Lucite with tin oxide or with Linde A. Crown angles 40°, pavilion angles 40°. Difficult to handle at all times.

HEMATITE

Hematite is the red oxide of iron and the principal ore of the metal. Small quantities are regularly consumed in cutting intaglios and faceted gems, the latter sometimes called "Alaska diamonds." Material is principally supplied by iron mines in Cumberland, England; good material also from Arizona and Minnesota. Seldom cut in this country because of the cheapness of the product and the mess created by the intensely red powder. Can be faceted or cabochoned on ordinary equipment. Tough and insensitive to heat and shock; however, examine rough carefully to detect radial partings in the kidney-like masses along which the rough separates easily. Cabochons are polished best on cloth buffs, leather, or wood, using cerium oxide, levigated alumina or Linde A. Pre-polish cabochons on leather with 1200 silicon carbide grit used wet. Faceted gems polish with Linde A on tin, or upon other soft metal laps, or upon wax; brilliant and flawless polishes are difficult to obtain. In Germany, it is polished with magnesium oxide on cloth buffs or upon laps covered with cloth.

HODGKINSONITE

G. 3.90   **HM** 4.5–5   **HL** same   **R.I.** 1.76–1.79

Small pieces sufficiently clear to facet are occasionally found with other minerals in the zinc mines of Franklin, New Jersey. Color pinkish to purplish-pink. Pieces seldom exceed ¼ inch. Splits readily along one perfect cleavage plane but this is not troublesome in polishing. Polish with tin oxide on Lucite. Crown angle 40°, pavilion angles 40°.

HOWLITE

G. 2.53–2.59 **HM** 3.5 **HL** 3–3.5

Carving and cabochon material occurs in characteristic "cauliflower heads" in borate deposits, each nodular mass consisting of multitudes of minute interlocked crystals which give the material a certain degree of toughness despite low hardness. Can be carved with steel tools and smoothed with files and sandpapers. Material from California is black-veined, which adds attractiveness, although the dark veinings are inclined to be softer due to clay fillings. Grind and sand cautiously to avoid removing material too quickly. Polish with tin oxide on felt. If undercutting is noted, switch to Linde A on leather. Avoid cerium oxide and chrome oxide which stain badly.

Splendid large masses from Tick Canyon in California; similarly from Nova Scotia.

HYPERSTHENE

Displays a metalloidal sheen similar to bronzite in massive form; occasionally clear facet grade. Handle in the same way as enstatite.

IDOCRASE

Californite—massive translucent; white, green, greenish-yellow.
Cyprine—massive blue granular.
Also facet material in various colors.

G. 3.4–3.5 **HM** 6.5 **HL** 6.5 **R.I.** 1.71–1.73

Abundant is massive material but rare in clear crystals suitable for faceting. Californite used extensively for cabochons and large lapidary projects, and in many respects resembles nephrite jade. A very translucent variety of fine yellow-green color from Pulga, California is capable of being faceted into small but not

brilliant gems. Massive material extremely tough, like jade. Likely to contain soft inclusions which badly undercut during sanding and polishing; polishes well on leather with chrome oxide of Linde A; felt must not be used. Flats polish on wood. Facet angles for transparent material are: crown angles 40°, pavilion angles 40°.

IOLITE

(Cordierite, Dichroite, Water Sapphire)

G. 2.60–2.66 **HM** 7–7.5 **HL** 7 **R.I.** 1.53–1.55

Mainly purplish-blue and very intense in one direction, changing to pale grayish-blue to nearly colorless or yellowish as the stone is turned. Transparent to translucent; inclusions very common and sometimes abundant. Inclusions of hematite sometimes cause reddish aventurescence; other inclusions cause stars and catseyes. Rough in massive form, usually as waterworn pebble. Faceted gems seldom exceed one or two carats but flawless examples up to ten carats are known. Cabochons may be cut to much larger sizes but are blackish in appearance due to intensity of color.

Orient rough to put blue color face up; grinds, sands, and otherwise handles with no unusual characteristics. Polish with cerium oxide on Lucite, or Linde A or tin oxide on tin. For cabochons, use Linde A or chrome oxide on leather; avoid latter if rough contains open crevices. Crown angles 40°–50°, pavilion angles 43°.

Facet rough from Connecticut, Wyoming, Ceylon and Madagascar. Red aventurescent from the last two places and also from Norway.

JADEITE

G. 3.3–3.5 **HM** 6.5–7.0 **HL** 6.5 **R.I.** 1.65–1.67

Highly prized by the Chinese, this compact and tough material is one of the minerals classed under the general term "jade," the other being nephrite which will be discussed later. Because of its toughness, jadeite lends itself readily to the most delicate carvings.

Massive, very fine granular to coarsely granular. Translucent to almost transparent in the finest varieties. White when pure, but other colors common, such as green in various shades, yellow, red, orange, blue, lavender, etc. A very deep-green variety which appears black is called *chloromelanite*. Some colors are superficial, being natural staining by mineral substances. Very tough but not as tough as nephrite. Freshly broken surfaces present a sugary appearance, twinkling with reflections from individual crystals. Rough often in large sizes, but strong hues occur only as small patches. Often seamed and fractured. Exceptionally clear pieces sometimes faceted.

Jadeite undercuts badly unless properly treated. Fine sanding must be done with copious water to give gentle cutting. Polish on leather using Linde A; the final gloss appears when the lap is on the verge of drying out. Insensitive to heat. Colorful examples may be faceted to a high luster using a thick paste of Linde A on a well-scored tin lap.

Only two places—upper Burma and Japan —supply acceptable jadeite rough material. The jadeites of California, and the recently-discovered material from Guatemala are dull in color and uninteresting on the whole.

JET

Jet is fairly tough and takes a fine polish, but its softness militates against its use in hard-worn items of jewelry. Like amber, it is carved with ordinary steel tools and abrasive papers and finally polished on cloth, felt, or leather, with cerium oxide, Linde A, or tin oxide. Leather buffs are preferable.

In the United States jet occurs in coal seams of south-eastern Colorado and in Utah, also New Mexico. The best jet comes from Whitby, England.

KORNERUPINE

G. 3.28–3.34   HM 6.5   HL 6.5–7.5   R.I. 1.67–1.68

Yellow, brown, or greenish. Glassy luster. Transparent. Two directions of perfect cleavage easy to start in Ceylon material but diffi-

cult to initiate in Madagascar rough. The latter shows only one cleavage well and in all respects appears much harder than the assigned Mohs number of 6.5. Not heat sensitive.

Rough is found as water-rolled pebbles in Ceylon and in glassy fragments from Madagascar. Polish on tin using Linde A. Crown angles 40°, pavilion angles 40°.

KYANITE

G. 3.56–3.67   HM 5–7.5   HL same   R.I. 1.71–1.73

Colorless, pale to medium blue, grayish-blue, greenish-blue, pale green, bluish-green. Transparent; pearly luster on faces parallel to best cleavage direction. Often badly flawed due to many partially developed cleavages; also with peculiar step-like inclusions across crystals. Not heat sensitive. Rough mainly in narrow to flat blades, usually with best cleavage plainly exposed. Examine rough for freedom from cleavages because these enlarge during cutting. Sawing is precarious because of tendency to rip and split. Crystals are brittle; part by nicking on opposite sides and breaking with fingers.

Grinding must be most gentle and always with the grain. Avoid grinding across ends of crystals. Cut on 1200 lap following same precautions. Do not grind parallel to the length of the crystal on the side containing the best cleavage plane or crystal will immediately tear and be ruined. Polish along same directions; use Linde A on tin. Crown angles 40°, pavilion angles 40°.

From Machakos District, Kenya, in large, flattish crystals banded green to blue to colorless. Fine sapphire blue from Brazil; pale green from Yancey County, North Carolina.

LAPIS LAZULI

G. 2.50–2.90   HM 5.5   HL same

Intense blue, fine-grained lazurite usually with calcite; pyrites almost invariably present. The best lapis is intense ultramarine blue verging toward purplish. Some regard pyrites as lessening its value, but others feel that a small quantity uniformly sprinkled throughout the mass adds value. Poorer qualities are lighter in color or dingy because of grayish impurities; also, mottled white and blue material is not highly prized. Lapis is quite tough, although soft. Not heat sensitive. Careful grinding required to control shape due to softness. Final sanding must be done well to prevent pyrite inclusions of considerably greater hardness from protruding during polishing. Polish on leather with Linde A or chrome oxide. Polish faceted gems on tin with Linde A.

Finest material from Afghanistan, Lake Baikal in the USSR, and Bokhara, Turkestan; pale blue from Chile in the Andes of Ovalle, Coquimbo. In the United States, from San Bernardino County, California, and Italian Mountain, Colorado.

LAZULITE

Soft but cuttable into fairly attractive cabochons. Rare; seldom in large masses of solid color. No unusual problems except undercutting due to soft impurities. Somewhat heat sensitive; grind cautiously on 220 wheel. Lap with 1200 grit for flats. Polishes with Linde A on leather or wax. Chrome oxide can be substituted for Linde A.

Largest masses from Champion Mine, White Mountain, Mono County, California; also elsewhere in California. Small crystals from Graves Mountain, Georgia, but not suited for cutting. Massive lazulite of fine blue color in Palermo Quarry, North Groton, New Hampshire. Facet grade crystals as small, water-rolled pebbles, in diamond washings of Minas Gerais, Brazil.

LEPIDOLITE

Yellow, gray or pink to purplish lithium-bearing mica often in fine-grained masses taking a fair polish. Used for ashtrays, small dishes, paper weights, etc. Soft. Turned and worked with steel implements. Undercuts badly; polish obtained on leather with cerium oxide or Linde A, fair polish obtained with felt but considerable undercutting occurs.

Compact masses common on dumps of

feldspar quarries in Maine, particularly in Oxford County. Gem mines of San Diego County, California, provide much richly colored, fine-grained material.

LEUCITE

G. 2.47   **HM** 6   **HL** 6   **R.I.** 1.51

Comparatively rare in clear form; most crystals opaque white and unsuited for cutting. Transparent crystals up to ¼ inch in lavas of the Alban Hills near Rome, Italy, provide only known faceting material. Heat resistant, tough, cuts well and polishes readily on Lucite with cerium oxide. Crown angles 40°–50°, pavilion angles 43°. Finished gems show peculiar color flashes due to interference films.

MAGNESITE

G. 3   **HM** 3.75–4.25   **HL** 4.5–5.5   **R.I.** 1.51–1.7

Usually massive and translucent, but locality at Bom Jesus dos Meiras in Brazil produces transparent, colorless crystals which cut faceted gems of 10 or more carats. Perfect, easy cleavage in three directions, as in calcite, but not easily started. Heat sensitive, explodes in direct flame, however, by careful heating and the use of stick shellac, it can be dopped. Grinds with considerable variation in apparent hardness but much care must be used to avoid starting cleavages. Lap only on lead impregnated with 400 silicon carbide grit. Polishes slowly but surely with Linde A on wax; harder laps polished some facets but abraded others. Crown angles 40°, pavilion angles 40°.

MALACHITE

G. 4   **HM** 3.5–4   **HL** same

Treasured for ages because of its intense green color and interesting circular markings, malachite is easy to work but difficult to polish. Crystals are exceedingly small and it is only the massive material which is of interest to the lapidary. Many localities furnish malachite but very few produce material thick enough for cutting. At present, copper mines in the Congo, Rhodesia, and South West Africa furnish the bulk of the meager quantities available. Some material comes from the copper mines in Mexico but this is even more scarce than material from abroad. Alternate bands of pale to dark green indicate places where malachite varies in density; darker portions are denser and easier to polish, lighter are less compact and more difficult to polish. Because it breaks readily along the fibrous grain, cabochons are cut somewhat thick to lend strength. Heat sensitive but care in dopping prevents fractures.

Grind cautiously to avoid lopsided stones. Fine sand on 400 cloth using plenty of water to produce high gloss. Polish on leather with Linde A or chrome oxide. Undercuts on felt or cloth. Finish polish by hand with clean leather dipped in a very thin suspension of water and chrome oxide, to which a little soap is added. Hand finishing is tedious but results are worth it. Polishing is speeded by adding a drop or two of weak acid to the polishing suspension; vinegar or dilute muriatic or oxalic acid, are suitable. To prevent marring when using acid-polish solutions, keep surfaces wet and as soon as work is completed, dip entire piece into clean, pure water. Touch up surface with acid-free polish suspension.

MARCASITE

Treated in the same manner as Pyrite.

MESOLITE

G. 2.29   HM 5   HL 5

Often confused with natrolite but distinguished by much finer, needle-like crystals. Compact masses suitable for cutting and polishing into handsome chatoyant cabochons. White to pale pink or yellow, grinds and sands rapidly, polishes quickly and perfectly with cerium oxide on felt. Somewhat heat sensitive. Cuttable mesolite from Oregon, Nova Scotia, and New Jersey.

METEORITES

Metallic meteorites which must be sectioned and polished are extremely difficult to handle. Diamond saws clog and glaze and eventually stop cutting. Also, since the material rusts, care must be taken during polishing to avoid fingerprinting since this leads to development of corroded spots. The most successful sectioning method uses a steel band saw or steel disk, charged with abrasive mud, usually silicon carbide, to which boron carbide is added to speed cutting. Supply abrasive generously to the cut. Grits should be suspended in a mixture of grease and oil to prevent rust. Steel disks should turn about 120 rpm. Meteorite may be held in a clamp or embedded in a block of plaster of paris. Some specimens cut using metal-cutting band saws; others, containing very hard constituents, must be cut with abrasives. Lap with silicon carbide grit in kerosene, or hand lap using successively finer grades of sanding paper or cloth, placing abrasive sheets on hard, absolutely flat, surfaces. Final polish with diamond paste on flat buff covered with petrographic laboratory polishing cloth or Pellon. Linde A on Pellon will polish but must be suspended in light oil, kerosene, or similar water-free liquids to avoid rusting.

MICROLITE

G. 5.9–6   HM 6   HL 6   R.I. 1.98–2.02

Occurs in small quantities in granitic pegmatites but seldom transparent or in crystals larger than ⅛ inch. Rutherford Mine near Amelia, Virginia, is the only known locality to provide facet grade material. From this mine, the author obtained a clear crystal which cut into a flawless, red-brown gem of over three carats. Not heat sensitive. Preforms quickly and easily on silicon carbide wheels but cuts scratchily on diamond/copper lap. Polishes easily and smoothly on tin with Linde A. Crown angles 30°–40°, pavilion angles 37°–40°.

MIMETITE

G. 7.24   HM 3.5–4   HL 3.5

Occasionally, rounded masses of yellow-orange color lend themselves to cabochon treatment. The color is unusual and the luster of finished gems is brilliant. Treatment is normal; take care in dopping not to overheat. Cabochons must be cut thick. Polish with tin oxide or Linde A on leather. Faceted stones are polished on tin or wax with Linde A.

MORDENITE

Rare zeolite mineral occuring in nodules comprised of minute felted white crystals. Treated in the same manner as thomsonite.

MUSCOVITE

Occasionally massive pink in pegmatites as in the Harding Mine district, Taos County, New Mexico. Treated in the same manner as Lepidolite.

NATROLITE

G. 2.2–2.25   **HM** 5–5.5   **HL** 5   **R.I.** 1.48–1.49

White to colorless, coarse, prismatic crystals. Two perfect cleavages parallel to the length. Fairly sensitive to heat (whitens with excessive heat). Crystals rarely more than ⅛ inch in diameter. Polishes readily with cerium oxide on Lucite, less readily on tin with Linde A. Crown angles 40°–50°, pavilion angles 43°.

Facetable crystals from Ice Valley region of British Columbia; fine, large crystals from Poona, India; large crystals from Brevig, Norway; excellent material from near Livingston in Montana, and from Summit, New Jersey. Lovely, massive radiated yellow material occurs in cavities and seams near Hohentwiel in Hegau, Württemberg Germany.

NEPHRITE

G. 2.9–3.02   **HM** 6–6.5   **HL** same   **R.I.** 1.6–1.65

Exceedingly tough ornamental material customarily classed as jade (see Jadeite). Composed of either actinolite or tremolite in the form of minute, fibrous crystals. Found in a range of colors, but most is green or white. Whites can be very pure in hue but greens are generally yellowish, brownish, or blackish.

"Spinach Jade" is an appropriate Chinese designation of a typical color.

Grinds easily but causes difficulty in sanding and polishing due to undercutting. Careful sanding is the secret of success and the exact method employed varies from material to material. Sometimes wet sanding will give the smooth gloss needed; sometimes dry sanding will. If pitting is seen, some change of technique is needed. Polishes fastest with Linde A on leather but chrome oxide will do. If polishing on leather is unsuccessful, try a soft wooden lap with tin oxide. Heavy pressure is applied and the lap allowed to become almost dry. Nephrite can be handsomely faceted on tin using Linde A while larger, flat areas can be polished on wooden laps using chrome oxide. Only uniformly textured material can be so treated however.

Nephrite of excellent quality known as "greenstone" or "Maori jade" occurs in New Zealand. The best quality is intense green, uniform in texture, and sometimes available in large boulders. Similar material occurs in a wide area in Wyoming but is less common than olive-green types, some of which appear black when polished. Good material also from alluvial deposits along the Fraser River in British Columbia and in the Jade Mountain district of the Kobuk River Valley in Alaska. A number of localities in California produce good material but the best does not compare to New Zealand, Wyoming or Alaska material. Also from Europe and Asia but rough material rarely sold in the United States.

OBSIDIAN

G. 2.3–2.5   **HM** 5   **HL** 5   **R.I.** 1.5

A glasslike volcanic lava. Black, red, or brown, sometimes greenish, and at other times transparent to translucent, often with small inclusions which reflect light. In very large masses except in the so-called "Apache Tears," which are small nodules of translucent to transparent brownish obsidian rarely exceeding the size of walnuts. Heat sensitive and very brittle. Easily recognized by well-developed conchoidal fracture. Thin slabs can be cut using an ordinary glass cutter. Considerable care is required in fine sanding to get a high polish later. Wet sanding is indicated because of the ease with which obsidian is cracked by heat. Polish on felt with cerium oxide. Faceted stones are polished on Lucite with the same powder, but the lap must not be allowed to run dry. Rough blocks containing inclusions must be oriented properly to show iridescence or sheen. Inclusions often in perfectly flat bands, slight deviation from correct direction results in sheen appearing on sides of stones instead of the tops. Crown angles for faceted stones are 40°–50°, pavilion angles 43°.

Widespread throughout the Western States. The most prolific locality is Glass Buttes in Oregon, 50 miles east of Bend. Striped translucent material from Montgomery Pass in California has been used to make beautiful doublets and triplets. Slabs are cut very thin and then polished to show alternating strips of clear and dark material. When sections are crossed at 90° or three sections at 60° apart, very interesting effects are obtained. This material has also been used to make translucent lamp shade panels.

OPAL

Gem Varieties

Precious Opal—any variety displaying the characteristic pure and brilliant hues known as "play of color."

White Opal—precious opal of white or near-white body color.

Black Opal—precious opal of black or gray body color.

Fire Opal—transparent to translucent red to orange opal with or without play of color.

Jelly Opal—highly translucent precious opal of almost colorless body hue.

Hyalite—colorless transparent opal.

Common Opal—any variety lacking play of color.

Wood Opal—opal replacing wood.

G. 1.9–2.2   **HM** 5.5–6.5   **HL** 5–6   **R.I.** 1.43–1.46

Opal is a widespread and abundant mineral but of the enormous amount available, only a small percentage is of the precious variety and it is rapidly vanishing. Common opal, which frequently replaces wood and is abundant in other geological situations, is perhaps most often cut and polished by amateurs. Colorful varieties are scarce, however, and much opal is not worth lapidary treatment. As is true of many other gemstones, high quality precious opal, whether from Australia or Mexico or from other sources, is seldom available upon the market. Most of the Australian material sent to the American market is trash, because good grades are much too expensive for most amateur lapidaries to consider; such material is murky white with small irregular patches of precious material.

The play of color in Australian white opal generally occurs in thin seams within a sandwich of common material known as "potch." Unfortunately the most vivid coloration is usually seen "edge on," as shown in Figure 76, and it is therefore necessary either to settle for a large flattish gem of indifferent quality or to saw the band of precious material into small cross-sectional slices to obtain several much smaller gems of higher quality. Almost all precious opal shows better coloration in certain directions and it pays to immerse rough specimens in glycerine, or water, if glycerine is not available, and to examine them under a strong light to determine how the gem should be oriented. Australian black opal frequently shows extremely vivid play of color when one looks down upon the thin seams in which it usually occurs, and because of this feature, it is commonly cut in very thin slices and cemented to backings of common opal, obsidian, or black glass. Such assembled gems are called "doublets." More recently, doublets have been made into "triplets" by cementing an additional lens-shaped colorless section of quartz atop the opal face.

Mexican opal also displays directional properties in respect to color as does much of the black, white, and jelly opal of Virgin Valley,

Nevada. None of these varieties present much difficulty in orienting properly.

Saw with very thin steel or bronze diamond-charged blades but nick seam fragments on opposite sides and snap in the fingers instead of sawing all the way through. Commercial cutters of opal use very thin roofing tin blades charged with a slurry of 400 silicon carbide and find that cutting is rapid enough for all practical purposes. Heat sensitive but by careful elevation of temperatures during dopping, cabochons and facet preforms can be dopped with stick shellac or even with ordinary dopping waxes. Sanding and lapping must be wet and no heat allowed to develop at any time. Polishing is rapid and perfect using cerium oxide on felt in the case of cabochons and the same agent on Lucite in the case of faceted gems. Cracking likely to occur on Lucite, however, and great care must be exercised not to let the lap run dry. Crown angles 40°–50°, pavilion angles 43°.

Australia is the premier locality for white and black opals of commerce but fine opals also come from several states of Mexico, notably Queretaro. San Luis Potosi in Mexico and Waltsch in Bohemia provide colorless transparent hyalite suitable for faceted gems. Transparent faceting material also from Mexico in a variety of reds, oranges, and yellows; also from Brazil. Jelly opal from Australia is often faceted. Recently, precious opal has been produced in small quantities from Honduras. Virgin Valley in Nevada has been productive and numerous examples of black to nearly colorless precious opal are now available. Although much of the Nevada material cracks, as does precious opal from other sources, a large number of specimens do not. Common opal in the form of petrified wood from the states of Washington and Oregon is often cut and polished into slabs, book ends and other ornamental objects.

PEARL AND MOTHER-OF-PEARL

Fine-quality fresh-water pearls and shell are recovered from clear streams and rivers in the eastern United States and the Midwest. They occur in several varieties of shellfish which are locally called "mussels" or "clams." Much of the shell of these mollusks is suitable for decorative purposes, including inlay work on boxes and jewelry. Abalone shells of Southern California are particularly colorful. Australian pearl oyster shells may be used for making fine ash trays. The outside is ground away, sanded, and buffed with tin oxide. The treatment of all shell follows generally that employed in the fashioning of coral (q.v.). It is reported that inhaling the dust of abalone shell during dry sawing, grinding or sanding, causes severe nausea and other ill effects. This material should be abraded in water to avoid this danger.

PECTOLITE

White, compact, fibrous forms take a fine polish and display an excellent silky sheen. Treat gently during sawing and grinding to avoid furring of fibers. Polish with Linde A on leather.

Suitable material has come from Lake County, California and in trap rock quarries of New Jersey and Connecticut.

PERICLASE

(A synthetic)

G. 3.67–3.90   **HM** 6   **HL** 7.5   **R.I.** 1.74

Synthetic material has been cut but unless preserved in air-tight, moisture-free containers, the fine polish deteriorates and all surfaces become dull. Colorless; fragments with one very good cleavage difficult to start; tough. Hardness considerably above Mohs figure. Polishes slowly on tin with Linde A. Not heat sensitive. Crown angles 40°, pavilion angles 40°.

PERIDOT

(Olivine, Chrysolite)

G. 3.3–3.5   **HM** 6.5–7.0   **HL** 6.0–6.5   **R.I.** 1.65–1.70

Usually yellow-green to brownish-green; prized colors are distinctive deep yellow-greens of great uniformity. Transparent but often filled with small inclusions which may be minute black spinel crystals (Arizona) or platey or needle-like negative crystals (Burma). Sometimes platelets and needles are so abundant that polished cabochons yield fairly effective catseyes or moonstones. Fairly tough and insensitive to heat. Rough specimens occur as shining crystals (St. Johns), etched crystals (Burma), or irregular nodules (Arizona).

Sawing, preforming, and cutting normal; polishing is troublesome. Preparatory to polishing cut all facets on 1200 diamond-copper noting if pits develop. If pits do occur, shift lapping directions to eliminate. To polish, use thick paste of Linde A to which a drop or two of muriatic (hydrochloric) acid has been added; apply to tin lap. Polish in an almost dry condition. Large facets may have to be polished on wax lap with Linde A-acid mixture. By using this method, the author recently repolished a fine 189 carat Burma gem which had its large table facet scratched by a previous attempt at repolishing using ordinary methods. Crown angles 40°, pavilion angles 40°.

Gem grade occasionally obtained from old stocks of St. Johns Island material and, more recently, from deposits in the gem tract of Burma. Crystals as large as 400 carats from the latter locality have been brought to the United States. Also abundant as small grains and nodular masses from Peridot Mesa in Arizona, and elsewhere in this state and in New Mexico.

PETALITE

G. 2.39–2.46   **HM** 6–6.5   **HL** 7–7.5   **R.I.** 1.5–1.52

Colorless fragments from massive material; crystals rare. Transparent; brittle but tough. One perfect cleavage, difficult to develop. Not heat sensitive. Grinds slowly but smoothly, some directional differences noted. Polish on Lucite with cerium oxide or on tin with Linde A. Crown angles 40°–50°, pavilion angles 43°.

Facet grade from Mineral Lease 80, Londonderry, West Australia, and from South West Africa. Some of the latter is a pink mas-

sive material which makes attractive cabochons.

PHENAKITE

G. 2.95–2.97   **HM** 7.5–8   **HL** same   **R.I.** 1.65–1.67

Colorless, glassy, flat crystals, seldom over 1 inch in size. Often flawed, seldom allowing stones larger than a carat or two to be cut. Tough, not heat sensitive. Possesses a good cleavage but started with difficulty. Grind normally. Polish using a thick paste of Linde A on tin, almost dry, or 6400 diamond dust on tin. Polishes slowly. Crown angles 40°, pavilion angles 40°.

Most cuttable material from Brazil, but some small gems are cut from material obtained in the Pikes Peak region of Colorado. Many years ago cuttable phenakite was found in the Uralian emerald mines of Russia.

PHOSPHOPHYLLITE

G. 3.08   **HM** 3–3.5   **HL** 5   **R.I.** 1.6–1.61

Hitherto known only in the form of small, pale blue-green crystals from a locality in Germany, this exceedingly rare phosphate mineral has recently been discovered in Bolivia in flawless transparent crystals over an inch in length. Broken fragments have been faceted and produce lovely gems. Despite the low hardness given for the German material, it is obvious in treating the larger crystals from Bolivia that the textbook values are much too low. Brittle; inclined to split along a perfect cleavage plane but otherwise, fairly tough. Slightly heat sensitive but can be dopped using stick shellac. Grind on diamond/copper lap. Large facets glaze when ground on 400 grit lead lap. Polishes easily with Linde A on tin or wax. Crown angles 40°, pavilion angles 40°.

PIEDMONTITE

As cherry red compact masses yielding attractive cabochon or slab material. Difficult to prevent undercutting because the rock in which it occurs generally contains quartz and other minerals of differing hardnesses. Treat by careful wet sanding followed by polishing on leather with tin oxide or Linde A. Flat sections should be lapped with 1200 grit followed by polishing on pitch or wood.

POLLUCITE

G. 2.9–2.94   **HM** 6.5   **HL** 7   **R.I.** 1.52–1.525

Colorless to white in massive forms, also gray, yellowish, or pinkish. Often contains numerous small inclusions resembling balls or spikes of white color. Quite brittle, not heat sensitive. Polishes well on Lucite with cerium oxide. Crown angles 40°–50°, pavilion angles 43°. Found in clear pieces at several Maine localities and more recently in Connecticut. Very rare.

PREHNITE

G. 2.8–2.9   **HM** 6–6.5   **HL** same   **R.I.** 1.61–1.65

Mainly in rounded masses conforming in shape to the cavities in which it occurs; also as vein fillings. Green to yellowish-green. Translucent to almost transparent. Tough in thick sections but splits readily along fibers. Cuts and grinds easily; polishes with Linde A on tin or leather. For faceted stones, crown angles 40°, pavilion angles 40°.

Good prehnite is common but superior cabochon and facet material is scarce. Very fine from Paterson, New Jersey. Highly translucent greenish-yellow suitable for faceted gems from Scotland. Also from South Africa, France, Germany, and Nova Scotia.

PROUSTITE

G. 5.57   **HM** 2–2.5   **HL** same   **R.I.** 2.79–3.08

An extremely soft ore of silver occasionally cut into exceedingly beautiful faceted gems possessing deep rich red color and peculiar semi-metallic luster. The difficulty of procuring suitable rough almost matches that of cutting. Small preforms can be carefully dopped with stick shellac but it is safer to use cold cement. Sawing is difficult. The saw blade clogs and cutting is stopped with normal diamond sawing techniques. A thin silicon carbide slitting disk rotated by a hand-held rotary tool should be used to make nicks on all sides of the rough and the piece broken apart. Preform on a well-trued grinding wheel and cut facets on a freshly charged diamond/copper lap. A freshly charged 400 grit lead lap will also cut facets. Polishing is rapid and smooth using Linde A on wax but very fine scratches frequently develop. Because of its high refractive index, pavilion facets are cut as low as 30° without much loss of brilliance. This is recommended to make the gem appear sufficiently pale in color. Crown angles 30°–40°, pavilion angles 37°–40°.

Common in a number of European localities, also several in Mexico, the United States and Canada but facet material confined to splendid large crystals from Chanarcillo, Atacama, Chile.

PSILOMELANE

A black banded hard material has lately come upon the market from an unspecified source in Mexico and purports to be "psilomelane," a manganese mineral. Microscopic observations on polished material, plus specific gravity and refractive index determinations, show it to be chalcedony heavily impregnated with a black mineral which may or may not be psilomelane. Due to the content of chalcedony, the material reacts in much the same manner but is liable to undercut where bands are heavily impregnated with the black mineral. Treatment is the same as for jaspilite as described under Quartz.

PYRITE

G. 5.02   **HM** 6–6.5   **HL** 5

Pyrite is abundant, particularly in ore deposits, but solid material suitable for cabochons or faceted gems is not easy to obtain. Most specimens are internally flawed, admixed with other sulfide minerals, or penetrated by many cracks which cause pieces to fall apart when subjected to any shock. Very brittle and quite heat sensitive; also sensitive to the shock

of grinding and sawing. Large pieces for cabochons should be very slowly elevated to temperature when dopping. Grind and preform
on well-trued 220 or 400 wheels. Grinding and
lapping are messy because of black staining.
Sanding and lapping always leave many small
pits which are removed with difficulty in
polishing. Final sand with a thick paste of
1200 silicon carbide on a leather wheel. Polish
with Linde A on leather. For faceting, use 400
grit on lead to obtain a finish smooth enough
for polishing. Polish with a thick paste of
Linde A on wood or wax. In Germany, pyrite
is polished on felt or flannel using magnesium
oxide.

Localities for pyrite are too numerous to
list and almost any mineral dealer can supply
large pieces inexpensively.

QUARTZ

Crystalline Varieties

Rock crystal—colorless, transparent.
Amethyst—purple, transparent.
Citrine—yellow, transparent.
Smoky Quartz—brown to black, transparent
  to opaque.
Rose Quartz—translucent, seldom trans-
  parent.
Green Quartz—pale green, transparent.
Catseye and Tigereye—fibrous inclusions
  give silky luster; green, yellow, gray,
  red, etc.
Rutilated Quartz—inclusions of rutile.
Tourmalinated Quartz—inclusions of tour-
  maline.
Dumortierite Quartz—inclusions of du-
  mortierite.
Aventurine Quartz—flat inclusions give
  spangled effect, in various colors.
Prase—minute inclusions of amphibole;
  dark green.

Cryptocrystalline Varieties

Chalcedony—gray, blue, white, translucent
  to rarely transparent; contains no pronounced pattern or color which sets it
  apart.
Carnelian—reddish or orangish chalcedony.

Sard—brownish chalcedony.
Chrysoprase—bright yellow-green chalcedony.
Plasma—dull dark green chalcedony.
Agate—chalcedony in various layers, bands,
  colors, patterns, mosses, tubes, etc.
Onyx—straight-banded   chalcedony   in
  strongly contrasting colors.
Sardonyx—same, except that sard or carnelian are included in the layers.
Jasper—very impure chalcedony, usually
  containing considerable earthy or clayey
  material. Generally distinguished from
  agate as any variety which is opaque.
Petrified Wood, coral, bone, etc.—organic
  remains replaced by chalcedony, agate,
  or jasper.

G. 2.65–2.66 for crystalline material; impure forms such
as jasper may be higher.
HM 7   HL same but often apparently higher for cryptocrystalline varieties because of toughness.
R.I. 1.54–1.55

Crystalline forms often brittle, cryptocrystalline forms may be exceedingly tough. Not
heat sensitive to ordinary temperatures; ame-
thysts are turned a bright reddish-brown color
or, more rarely, pale green, by heating to high
temperature. No cleavages but slight differences in hardness noted in crystals, depending
on direction. Twinned crystals common in
amethyst; hence troublesome because good
polishing directions alternate with poor ones.
All quartz is ordinarily polished with cerium
oxide on felt, wood, or leather, but cheaper
agents such as tripoli and levigated alumina
are also used. Undercutting types, of which
tigereye is a prime offender, are best polished
on leather with Linde A. Facet material is
usually finished on Lucite with cerium oxide
but Linde A on tin is also good. For faceting
amethyst, change polishing direction to avoid
development of a "rippled" finish or scratches
due to twinning. Crown angles 40°–50°, pavilion angles 43°.

ROCK CRYSTAL

Clear and colorless; the most common and
widespread of all varieties. Fine material from
Hot Springs, Arkansas; also Brazil.

AMETHYST

From very pale, almost worthless material to deep rich purple. Present commercial supply from Brazil, but small amounts from Mexico and the Four Peaks region of Arizona. Sold according to color and quality, best material is "Siberian" followed by "Uruguay" and "Bahia." Richer colors are rare and expensive. Rough seldom large enough to cut gems in excess of 40 carats. Most shows color zoning; orient rough so edges of zones do not show on table of finished gem. Common flaws are veils of bubbles, color zones, and small inclusions. Rough is deceptive and should be examined in immersion fluid.

CITRINE

Pale to rich yellow; color grays off with admixture of smoky bands, which are frequently present. Dark, rich reddish-brown produced by heat treatment of some amethyst. Citrine often occurs in pieces large enough to cut gems of several hundred carats. Principally from Brazil; also Madagascar.

SMOKY QUARTZ

Morion is a black variety; *cairngorm* a deep, somewhat citrine-colored variety originally from Scotland. Material ranges from very pale to rich brown. Dark colors suitable only for small stones; those with medium hue best adapted for color and brilliancy in finished gem; very pale effective in gems of 20 to 40 carats. Fine material in all sizes and colors from Brazil; also Madagascar.

ROSE QUARTZ

Richly colored rose quartz rare. Brazilian material sometimes displays strong catseye or star effects.

GREEN QUARTZ

Pale green Brazilian quartz is amethyst from one mine which, when heated, turns green. The largest gems are about 20 carats.

CATSEYE AND TIGEREYE

Silky luster due to many closely packed fibers representing another mineral which was replaced or permeated by the quartz. Fine quartz catseyes have come only from Ceylon but, rarely, straight-grained tigereye from Africa also produces excellent gems. Best is somewhat translucent, indicating a high degree of silicification. Brown material usually of better quality than blue or green because alteration into quartz has proceeded further. Tigereye seldom exceeds 2 inches across the chatoyant direction. Sand to a very fine finish and polish with Linde A or chrome oxide on leather, although cerium oxide on felt will do.

RUTILATED QUARTZ

Highly prized for the many bright sparkling needles of golden rutile which flash in all directions within a matrix of clear quartz. Attractive in large cabochons or cabinet specimens but may also be faceted in tablet form. Mainly from Brazil but fine specimens also from North Carolina.

TOURMALINATED QUARTZ, ETC.

A large number of other minerals besides rutile are found in rock crystal, among them tourmaline, in fine or coarse needles; actinolite; hornblende; etc. If present in quantity, a handsome stone can be cut from any of these.

DUMORTIERITE QUARTZ

Granular quartz filled with minute inclusions of dumortierite; cut to take advantage of the blue and purple shades. Blue and pink dumortierite is found in Nevada; fine blue and white-speckled material from Guadalcazar, San Luis Potosi, Mexico; blue material also in California and Arizona.

AVENTURINE QUARTZ

Characteristic spangled effect from many small flat crystals of mica lying more or less parallel to each other. Best is a compact fine green variety from India; a paler green from Brazil is known. Yellow or honey-colored once from Russia but now unavailable.

PRASE

Dark grayish-green crystalline quartz in which many inclusions of a green mineral, such as amphibole, have made it nearly opaque. It is unattractive and seldom used.

CHALCEDONY

Chalcedony and its varieties are very tough forms of quartz in which individual crystals are so small that they defy detection by the most powerful microscopes. Chalcedony is widespread but mostly dull and not as eagerly sought as some of its interesting varieties. Fine blue material is prized but seldom found in good quality.

CARNELIAN

Best is bright orangey-red and typical of the kind produced in India. Natives heat ordinary material causing it to take on its lovely color. Fine carnelian from Brazil along with ordinary gray chalcedony. Many pieces that look carnelianized on the outside are gray inside. Sometimes this color can be improved by slabbing and heating on the stove, using an asbestos lined can as an oven. Keep the flame on low for about an hour to drive off all moisture; then turn to medium and allow the stones to reach a high temperature. Cooling must also be gradual.

CHRYSOPRASE AND CHRYSOCOLLA

Bright yellow-green chalcedony stained by a nickel mineral. Once in large quantities from Silesia in Germany but none being mined today. Fine material from California, Brazil, and Australia. Troublesome to polish; its peculiar structure leads to undercutting unless polished on leather. Heat gently for dopping or the delicate color will be driven off. Chrysocolla quartz is bright blue chalcedony stained by fine inclusions of chrysocolla. It is treated in the same way as chrysoprase.

AGATE

Varieties are endless; it is banded, spotted, patchy, or may have inclusions which resemble trees, ferns, or seaweed. Many names have been given to the varieties but the following are fairly standard:

Banded—concentric narrow bands of contrasting color.

Fortification—bands which make angular turns, somewhat like the outline of an old-style fortress.

Eye—banded agate cut at a low angle across a humplike projection, thus creating circular bands of contrasting hue; often improved by judicious dyeing.

Iris—any agate or chalcedony in which polished thin sections held to a strong light show a brilliant display of rainbow colors (see Figure 81).

Ruin—broken bits of banded agate cemented together with more agate; rare.

Moss Agate—clear agate with mosslike inclusions; with the properly shaped mossy markings, other names may be given, such as "tree," "fern," etc.

Sagenitic—containing many fine needles of another mineral or the cavities left by them.

Plume—moss type in which inclusions look like billowing ostrich feathers.

Flower—moss agate in which varicolored inclusions resemble a group of blossoms.

JASPER

A highly impure chalcedonic quartz found in many more geological situations than agate. A large variety of patterns are known, some of which follow:

Orbicular—showing round spots or circular patterns in contrasting colors.

Ribbon, Striped, or Banded—coarse bands of contrasting color.

Moss—containing dendritic patterns.

Egyptian—brownish color found in the desert areas of Egypt and showing complicated darker brown stainings which create "scenes"; rare.

Jaspilite—hematite and jasper in thin bands; found in the iron ore regions of Minnesota.

More troublesome in polishing than chalcedony; many varieties are earthy and porous, and others, such as jaspilite, contain difficult-to-polish hematite. Wet the jasper and discard pieces with high water absorption. Difficult jaspers polish better on leather with Linde A than on the standard felt with cerium oxide.

Petrified Wood, Coral, etc.

When buried in the ground, some vegetable and animal remains are replaced by mineral substances, commonly calcite or chalcedony. Perfectly preserved specimens of wood are abundant in central Washington and other states of the West.

RHODIZITE

In cuttable crystals only from Madagascar. No information available regarding cutting characteristics. Exceedingly rare.

RHODOCHROSITE

G. 3.45–3.6   **HM** 3.5–4.5   **HL** same   **R.I.** 1.6–1.8

Gem rough rose-red to pink, sometimes in light shades. Glassy luster in crystals; fibrous or satiny in massive varieties. Transparent to translucent. Three directions of easy cleavage similar to calcite; brittle; weak. Heat sensitive but not unduly so. Crystals small, mostly flawed. Massive material banded in deep pink to pale pink layers.

Must be handled with care to avoid shock. Grind cabochons and facet preforms only on fine wheels. Sanding rapidly deforms cabochons because of slightly different hardnesses in various bands. Polish cabochons on leather using Linde A or tin oxide. Pre-polish faceted stones on tin with Linde A, finish on wax with Linde A. Takes excellent polish. Crown angles 40°, pavilion angles 40°.

Cabochon material from Argentina; facet-grade crystals and cleavages from various mines in Colorado.

RHODONITE

G. 3.5–3.68   **HM** 5.5–6.5   **HL** same   **R.I.** 1.71–1.75

Massive; rarely in distinct crystals. Various shades of pink or light red. One perfect cleavage contributes to the well-known undercutting tendencies of this mineral. Single crystals extremely sensitive to shock and must be sawed with the greatest delicacy. Difficult to preform; much care required to prevent cleavages from developing. Fine grained massive types very tough; coarsely granular very weak, often breaking apart in the fingers. Not heat sensitive. Often veined with black or brown. Deep color material takes a better polish.

Prolonged sanding on 400 grit wet-sanding cloth with a copious flow of water is required to lay groundwork for a fine polish. An additional treatment using 1200 grit on leather is effective in eliminating small pits which are difficult to remove during polishing. Polish with Linde A on leather; felt gives only a dull gloss. Chrome oxide is objectionable because of staining. Faceted stones are polished on tin with Linde A. Crown angles 40°, pavilion angles 40°.

Facet grade rhodonite is found in some of the small granules of massive ore at Franklin, New Jersey; also in splendid crystals of a brownish-red color from Broken Hill, New South Wales; small clear crystals from Langbanshyttten, Vermland, Sweden. The New South Wales crystals are largest but will only yield stones up to several carats. Massive rhodonite is common in many places in the United States.

RUTILE

G. 4.18–4.25   **HM** 6–6.5   **HL** 6.5–7   **R.I.** 2.6–2.9

Natural rutile suitable for faceting occurs only in dark red crystals. Synthetic material is regularly available from lapidary supply houses either in preforms, boule sections, or in full boules which may weigh several hundred carats. Rutile is tough and insensitive to heat. Grinding proceeds much more slowly than the Mohs hardness indicates and this reluctance to abrade is noted also in sawing, where blades seem to glaze and cut very slowly. Both natural and synthetic material tend to develop numerous small pits in certain crystal directions and it is necessary to check lapping frequently to see if such pits are appearing. If so, the lapping direction should be changed immediately, preferably before the facet is fully cut. If pits are allowed to remain, much material must be polished away before they disappear. The chances are that the facet will then be larger than the others and consequently all will have to be re-cut and repolished. Methods for polishing vary. A thick paste of Linde A on tin is used by some; others claim that a superlative polish is achieved only on a very smooth tin lap with a very thin mixture of Linde A and water. As with lapping, it is often necessary to change polishing direction in order to find the one which gives the fastest and smoothest polish. Facet angles are immaterial in natural material, which is too dark to be brilliant, however, in the case of synthetic material, 30° to 40° crown angles and 37° to 40° pavilion angles will provide satisfactory brilliance. Important in achieving good results is the need to orient rough properly to avoid the strong doubling of back facets due to double refraction. In this respect it is helpful to polish a face on rough and to observe the appearance of a pencil mark on the back. Twist the rough until a direction is noted where the pencil mark appears to be single rather than double; imagine that the table facet will be at right angles to this line of sight and cut the rough accordingly.

SAMARSKITE

Masses of black material are often found in pegmatites and may be cut into faceted gems, though such have nothing to commend them except their curious nature. Insensitive to heat but brittle. Laps scratchily on dia-mond-copper laps, but a better finish is obtained on lead charged with 400 silicon carbide grit. Polish with thick paste of Linde A on deeply-scored tin lap.

SCAPOLITE

G. 2.61–2.70   **HM** 6.5   **HL** 6–7   **R.I.** 1.55–1.56

Transparent to translucent. Yellow in various shades, colorless, pink, gray, white, and violet blue. Not heat sensitive. Differences in hardness depending on crystal direction. Two cleavages but not harmful to cutting. Brittle. Facet rough sometimes quite large. All types polish with cerium oxide on felt or cerium

oxide on lucite. For faceted stones, crown angles 40°–50°, pavilion angles 43°.

Yellow facet-quality material from Mada-gascar and Brazil. Colorless, gray, pink, and violet blue from gravels of Mogok District, Burma, sometimes providing very fine, sharp catseyes; the pink especially fine.

SCHEELITE

G. 5.9–6.1   **HM** 4.5–5   **HL** 5–5.5   **R.I.** 1.92–1.93

Transparent to translucent. Brittle; cleavages present but not troublesome. Not sensitive to heat. Pre-polish on tin with Linde A; finish on wax lap with the same. Seldom polishes perfectly and edges of facets tend to chip. Crown angles 40°, pavilion angles 40°.

Fine, colorless facet-grade crystals from Kern County, California; exceptional facet-grade yellow to yellow-orange crystals from Utah, Arizona, and Mexico.

SCORZALITE

Treat in the same manner as lazulite.

SERPENTINE

G. 2.5–2.6   **HM** 2.25–4   **HL** 4–4.5   **R.I.** 1.49–1.57

Invariably found in finely granular masses, sometimes in enormous quantities, lending itself to use as building stone. *Verde antique* is oily green mottled with white veinlets of calcite. *Precious serpentine* designates kinds which are lighter in color, more compact and translucent, and hence capable of being cut and polished for jewelry or carved into small objects. *Bowenite* is an indefinite name applied to pale-green varieties, supposedly somewhat harder than ordinary kinds. *Williamsite* is a rich bluish-green, highly translucent variety found with chromium ores; the unusual color is attributed to small amounts of this element. *Satelite* is a fibrous kind affording distinct catseyes; excellent catseyes are also observed in other fibrous types of precious serpentine.

Soft and easily carved, but considerable

care must be taken to achieve a good polish. In sawing, water is the preferred coolant because oil is absorbed readily and is difficult to remove. Grinding must proceed with care, as impurities are frequent and alter hardness characteristics appreciably. Tough; not heat sensitive. Polishes best on almost-dry leather using Linde A, but chrome oxide does almost as well. Undercutting is to be expected but can be prevented by careful sanding on 400 grit cloth using large quantities of water.

Exceptionally clear fragments can be faceted using Linde A on tin, followed by Linde A on wax. Crown angles 40°–50°; pavilion angles 43°.

Very widespread. Reddish, brownish, and mottled types quarried at the Lizard, a promontory near the western tip of Cornwall, England. Green varieties from various localities in Ireland. Verde antique comes from Greece, Italy, and Egypt and, in recent times, from quarries near Roxbury and Cavendish, Vermont. Fine-grained, light-colored varieties bearing a strong resemblance to certain kinds of jadeite are quarried and carved in China and sold to the uninformed as "Soochow Jade." Precious serpentine is found in many places in the United States, for example: fine yellow and yellow green at Montville, New Jersey, williamsite at the Line Pits Chrome Mines, near Rock Springs, Maryland, and also in California near Indian Creek, north of Happy Camp, Siskiyou County. Satelite is found in this state east of Lindsay, Tulare County. New Mexico is famed for *ricolite*, a variety with strongly pronounced banding in many colors.

SHATTUCKITE

G. 3.8 or less   **HM** 3.5–4   **HL** 3.5

Rare copper mineral; in compact fibrous masses in copper mines of Arizona. Deep blue color. Dopping, grinding, sanding normal; polish with tin oxide or Linde A on leather; polishes on felt but undercuts, especially if masses are contaminated with other minerals, as is frequently the case.

SILICON CARBIDE

G. 3.17   **HM** 9.5   **HL** same   **R.I.** 2.65–2.7

Clear crystals sometimes cut into small brilliant gems. Colors range from dead black and opaque to deep blue-green and even yellow-brown. Most gems are small due to the fact that spongy crystal masses recovered from commercial electric ovens yield only very thin crystals. Sawed on regular faceting saws and preformed slowly but surely on silicon carbide wheels. Cuts readily on copper-diamond laps but is inclined to be scratchy and to wear laps excessively unless they are well-charged. Polished with 6400 diamond grit on tin, copper or typemetal. Deeply colored gems should be cut shallow with crown angles no more than 30° and pavilion angles from 30° to 35°. Paler material is cut with crown angles of 35° and pavilion angles of 37°–40°.

SIMPSONITE

G. 5.92–6.27   **HM** ?   **HL** 7.5–8   **R.I.** 2.06

Excessively rare; in facet grade only from Tabba Tabba, Australia. Bright orange-yellow. It is unfortunate that this mineral is so rare since it has all the qualifications for an excellent gemstone. Not heat sensitive. Hard and tough. Cuts slowly on diamond-copper lap; polishes slowly but surely with Linde A on tin. Crown angles 30°–40°, pavilion angles 37°–40°.

SINHALITE

G. 3.46–3.52   **HM** 6.5   **HL** 7   **R.I.** 1.68–1.70

In view of the lapidary behavior of sinhalite as compared to peridot, which gemstone it was for many years thought to be, it is surprising that no one suspected that it was not peridot. Unlike peridot which grinds and laps so easily, sinhalite reacts more like tourmaline, grinding away with the peculiar, somewhat "gritty" feel of harder and more brittle minerals. Sinhalite is easy to facet and handles well in all stages of treatment. Not heat sensitive. Polishes with difficulty using cerium on Lucite but readily with Linde A on tin. Crown angles 40°, pavilion angles 40°.

Pale brown to dark brown; from Ceylon.

SMARAGDITE

(Edenite)

A green, massive, amphibolite from Cullakenee Corundum Mine, Clay County, North Carolina. Contains red corundum nodules making a fine color contrast. Differences in hardness between the matrix and the corundum, however, make preparation of smooth cabochons almost impossible. A similar material containing bright red corundum crystals in a matrix of vivid green granular zoisite is known from Africa but suffers from similar polishing difficulties.

SMITHSONITE

G. 4.30–4.45   **HM** 4–4.5   **HL** 5   **R.I.** 1.62–1.85

Rarely colorless and transparent; mostly massive compact in green, blue, yellow, white. Fracture smooth granular in fine-grained massive forms; tends to separate along layers of growth. Three cleavages in facet grade but not troublesome. Fairly insensitive to heat. Rough ranges from thin incrustations to masses which may weigh many pounds. Slices parallel to layers to growth inclined to be more intense in color.

Usually cut cabochon and polished on felt with tin oxide. Linde A produces a superior finish when used on leather. Because of pitting, as individual fibers are broken out during sanding, it pays to finish sanding with 1200 grit on leather before polishing. Facet material is very scarce but may be cut and polished without too much difficulty despite the presence of cleavages. Cutting is accomplished on a lead lap using 400 silicon carbide grit; polish on tin using thick tin oxide or Linde A mixtures. If scratches occur, repolish on wax with either of the agents mentioned. Crown angles 40°, pavilion angles 40°.

Splendid massive smithsonite of bright green-blue color from Kelly district in New

Mexico; bright yellow material from Sardinia, and Laurium, Greece, and from Arkansas; deep green from Tsumeb, South West Africa. The last is probably the finest smithsonite ever found. Pale yellow facet grade crystals from Broken Hill, New South Wales.

SODALITE

G. 2.2–2.4   **HM** 5.5–6   **HL** same   **R.I.** 1.48

Massive, deep blue, solid in hue or streaked with veins of other minerals. Translucent to, rarely, transparent. Somewhat greasy luster, breaks with irregular fracture. Fairly brittle. Not heat sensitive. Rough sometimes in very large masses. Polishes perfectly on felt with cerium oxide, or on Lucite with the same agent in the case of faceted gems. These are sometimes obtainable in very small sizes from exceptionally clear Canadian material. Facet angles, crown 40°–50°, pavilion 43°.

Primarily from the Princess Quarry, Ontario; also from Ice River near Kicking Horse Pass, British Columbia. Very fine from Kishingarh, India; also from Cerro Sapo, Ayopaya, Bolivia, and, lately, Brazil.

SPHALERITE

G. 3.91–4.1   **HM** 3.5–4.0   **HL** same   **R.I.** 2.37

Greasy yellow, orange, brown, brownish red, green. Transparent, often banded in other colors and often with inclusions. Six directions of perfect cleavage but not troublesome. Fairly brittle. Not heat sensitive. Rough seldom yields clear pieces greater than about 1 inch in size.

Grinds quickly and smoothly on 1200 lap. Pre-polish using Linde A on tin. Observe facets closely, immediately change direction if pitting occurs. Finish polishing on wax with Linde A. Crown angles 30°–40°, pavilion angles 37°–40°. Attractive cabochons are cut from material unsuited to faceting. Polish on leather with Linde A.

Fine facet grade from Picos de Europa, Santander, Spain, in golden colors; green and yellow-green from Cananea, Sonora, Mexico. Small ruby-red cuttable crystals from Tiffin,

Ohio. Rare, almost colorless, material from Franklin, New Jersey yields splendid gems. Also from Montana and Utah.

SPHENE

(Titanite)

G. 3.45–3.56   **HM** 5–5.5   **HL** same   **R.I.** 1.9–2.03

In transparent yellow, green, brownish-green, brown or dark brown crystals of characteristic bladed form, so thin that it is difficult to obtain finished gems of over one or two carats. However, recently discovered deposits near Pino Solo, Baja California Norte, Mexico, provide crystals which sometimes exceed ½ inch in thickness and furnish faceted gems up to 10 carats or more. Crystals are often twinned and color-zoned parallel to twin boundaries with paler colors in exterior zones. Remarkably insensitive to heat; requires red heat to crack small fragments. Brown sphenes heat treat to reddish-brown or orangish-brown; fragments must be heated red hot for a considerable number of minutes to effect the change; faster changes occur with higher temperatures. Tough. Cuts more rapidly in certain directions than others. Polishes easily on tin with Linde A but is inclined to furrow. Crown angles 30°–40°, pavilion angles 37°–40°.

Facet material from sources other than Mexico is very scarce; classic yellow-green from various Alpine deposits; dark brown from Ontario is sometimes heat-treatable and makes very small but acceptable gems.

SPINEL

G. 3.58–3.64   **HM** 8   **HL** 7.5   **R.I.** 1.71–1.74

All colors, but seldom pure or clear. Transparent; often with small inclusions. Tough; not heat sensitive. Takes a fine easy polish on tin with Linde A. Crown angles 40°, pavilion angles 40°. Synthetic spinel is treated in the same manner.

Major source of gem cutting rough from gravels of Ceylon; also Siam and Burma. Fine rough seldom available in the United States.

SPODUMENE

Gem Varieties

Hiddenite—bluish-green.
Kunzite—lilac, violet, and pink.
Also colorless; pale yellow; greenish-yellow; pale yellowish-green.

G. 3.13–3.2   **HM** 6.5–7   **HL** 6.5–8   **R.I.** 1.65–1.68

Transparent to translucent. Glassy luster. Two directions of perfect and easy cleavage. Somewhat heat sensitive. Crystals under strain shatter if left partially completed; complete stones in one session if possible. Rough for cabochons in coarse silky masses; facet-grade material characteristically deeply etched and pitted. Hiddenite rare and always small.

Difficult to cut but easy to polish. Preforms best on a coarse well-trued 100 wheel; avoid sawing if possible; if not, blade should be thin and freshly charged. Feed slowly. Nick all the way around first with sharp edge of grinding wheel, then saw through. Grinds very slowly in directions across crystal ends. If diamond lap is used, it should be freshly charged. Facets are best cut using 400 silicon carbide grit on a lead lap. Polish with Linde A on tin. Crown angles 40°, pavilion angles 40°. Make girdle generous. Table across end of crystal gives best color.

Cabochons of fibrous material provide fair eye. These are ground normally and polished on leather with Linde A.

Facet material (kunzite) from San Diego County, California, often rich in color; also from Brazil. Hiddenite only from Stony Point, North Carolina; green material in paler shades from Brazil. Madagascar and Brazil provide various colors of spodumene, yellow and colorless among others.

Cabochon spodumene providing weak catseyes from Lower Pit, Plumbago Mt., Newry, Maine; pink massive material with eye effect from several places in Massachusetts.

STAUROLITE

Rarely faceted from small fragments provided by slender crystals associated with blue kyanite in the paragonite schists of the St. Gotthard region of Switzerland.

STIBIOTANTALITE

G. 6.3–6.9   **HM** 5.5   **HL** same   **R.I.** 2.37–2.46

Clear places in small tabular crystals from the Himalaya Mine in San Diego County, California, provide faceted gems seldom over a carat in weight. Somewhat heat sensitive, dop cautiously. Laps easily and smoothly, polishes well on tin with Linde A. Differences noted in speed of grinding, direction parallel to the broad face of the crystal being softer than other directions. Crown angles 30°–40°, pavilion angles 37°–40°; cut shallow because of dark color and high refractive index.

STICHTITE

Lilac to purple veinlets sometimes handsomely mottling serpentine and providing attractive cabochons or polished flats. The treatment is the same as for serpentine.

STRONTIUM TITANATE

G. 5.13   **HM** 6.5   **HL** 6   **R.I.** 2.4–2.42

Beautiful new synthetic gem material produced in boules of several hundred carats weight by Verneuil process. Boules are not sold for lapidary purposes except to concerns authorized to facet the material into gems. Colorless, remarkably heat resistant, soft but fairly tough; lacks the double refraction which is so objectionable in synthetic rutile. Processes easily to polishing where it tends to scratch on tin laps despite greatest care. It polishes on wax using Linde A. Crown angles 30°–40°, pavilion angles 37°–40°.

TAAFEITE

G. 3.6   **HM** 8   **HL** ?   **R.I.** 1.72

Few specimens in cut form are known and nothing is known about its lapidary treatment. However, since it has been cut by native lapidaries in Ceylon along with spinels and tourmalines, it is assumed that it will react favor-

ably to similar treatment. Crown angles 40°, pavilion angles 40°.

TEKTITE

G. 2.3–2.5   **HM** 5.5   **HL** 5.5   **R.I.** 1.48–1.5

Tektite is a catch-all name for natural glasses which are found on the earth's surface, with no obvious connection to geological formations in the vicinity. Many authorities consider them to be celestial in origin. Like glass in their reaction to cutting; brittle; heat sensitive; polish with cerium oxide on felt or Lucite, etc. Crown angles 40°–50°, pavilion angles 43°.

Green, transparent, from Bohemia (Moldavite); variety of colors from southern Australia and Tasmania; also from other islands in the southeast Pacific. Black tektites found in Texas and dark green specimens in Georgia. Most tektites are extremely dull after cutting due to inclusions, swirl marks, and low refractive index. They should not be cut as a rule because of their considerable scientific value.

THAUMASITE

G. 1.877   **HM** 3.5   **HL** 3

Compact white weakly chatoyant masses in cavities in pillow basalts. Soft but able to be cut into cabochons, beads, and flats. Grinds and sands quickly. Polish with tin oxide on felt, or Linde A on leather. Colored agents are to be avoided because they will stain.

Suitable material from basalt quarries in New Jersey and at Centerville, Virginia.

THOMSONITE

G. 2.3–2.4   **HM** 5–5.5   **HL** 4.5–5

Nodular material composed of radiated masses of thousands of microscopic needles. Common only on the beaches near Grand Marais, Minnesota. Also on Isle Royale at various places. Fine specimens make beautiful cabochons. *Lintonite*, a compact and translucent variety, is found in the same situations; however, it is dull green and has little to offer as a gem.

Thomsonite cuts quickly due to softness and often has hard spots which make stones lopsided unless care is taken. Pattern is near the surface and excessive grinding may remove it. Polish on felt with cerium oxide.

TOPAZ

Gem Varieties

Golden Topaz—pale yellow.
Imperial Topaz—deep orangey yellow.
Also colorless, blue, rarely brown, purple, red, pale green.

G. 3.4–3.6   **HM** 8   **HL** 7.5   **R.I.** 1.63–1.64

Transparent to translucent crystals or rolled pebbles, sometimes very large. Often flawed with veils, cracks, and cleavage planes. Blue frequently zoned in color. Orange stones heat treat to pink. One perfect cleavage difficult to start but avoid placing on any facet. Tough; not heat sensitive.

Saws, grinds, and laps readily. Small gems polish on tin with thick paste of Linde A, allowing lap to run almost dry. Large facets troublesome; diamond lap leaves deep scores which take much time to eliminate. Lap very large table facet by hand, finishing with 1200 grit. Examine against light at a low angle to observe scratches; if present, relap until perfectly smooth. Finish large facets with 400 grit on lead or 600 grit on iron. Polish on deeply scored tin lap; smooth laps will not remove enough material to eliminate fine pits left after lapping. Cabochons are finish sanded with 1200 grit on leather and polished with Linde A on leather. Crown angles 40°, pavilion angles 40°.

Almost all commercial topaz from Brazil; most is colorless to pale blue; fine blue rare. Deep blue sometimes substituted for aquamarine. Large blue topaz crystals from alluvial deposits in Texas, occasionally cutting gems over 100 carats. Large fine blue and sherry crystals from Pike's Peak region of Colorado; sherry fades to colorless if kept in light. Russian sources unproductive.

TOURMALINE

Gem Varieties

Rubellite—red.
Indicolite—blue.
Pink, various shades of green, brown, and, rarely, colorless (achroite) or yellow. Sometimes crystals banded in various colors.

G. 3–3.2   **HM** 7–7.5   **HL** 7   **R.I.** 1.62–1.64

Ordinarily in long striated crystals. Strong color change depending on direction; best through sides of crystal for blue and green; pink and red best through ends. Orient preforms accordingly. Transparent; often flawed, sometimes with many fine tubes and then yielding excellent catseyes. Brittle. Somewhat heat sensitive.

Grinds quickly but tends to chip on rough wheel. Polishes well on tin with Linde A, and, for cabochons, on leather with Linde A or chrome oxide. Avoid overheating. Catseye material porous and sealing off tubes is required. Large facets scratch readily and it is necessary to change polishing direction. Large tables polish best on wooden lap. Crown angles 40°, pavilion angles 40°. Cut dark colors shallower.

Commercial rough primarily from Brazil; also Madagascar and Mozambique. Only commercial source in the United States is the Himalaya Mine in San Diego County, California. Also from Ceylon, chiefly in dull green or brown.

TREMOLITE

G. 2.9–3.2   **HM** 5–6   **HL** same   **R.I.** 1.6–1.62

Crude crystals; also massive. Fibrous varieties make fair catseyes. Transparent; often minutely shattered because of several highly perfect, easily started cleavages. Dark grayish-green, bluish-gray-green. Not heat sensitive. Extremely fragile.

Use very slow feed in sawing, to prevent fraying. Preform and shape cabochons "with the grain," using a fine grinding wheel and fine sander. Polish on felt with cerium or tin oxide. Use 1200 copper lap only for cutting facets and polish on Lucite with tin or cerium oxide, tin preferred. Much difference in hardness and ease of polish according to direction. Crown angles 40°, pavilion angles 40°.

Fine lilac-pink facet material in small transparent grains from St. Lawrence County, New York (*hexagonite*). Gray, green, and blue from Ontario, also fine catseye material.

TURQUOIS

G. 2.6–2.83   **HM** 5–6   **HL** 5–5.5

Opaque to slightly translucent on thin edges. Best color intense pale blue; as shades of green appear, value decreases. Chalky appearance in rough except finest grades which are waxy in luster on fracture surfaces. Not brittle. Somewhat heat sensitive, particularly Persian material. Due to porosity, avoid sawing with oily coolants; plain water preferable. Handles without difficulty. Polish with Linde A on leather; chrome oxide also polishes but may stain.

Rough from many places in western United States. Persian material seldom available commercially.

ULEXITE

G. 1.955   **HM** 2–2.5   **HL** 2   **R.I.** 1.49–1.53

Compact fibrous forms strongly chatoyant, providing showy pure white catseyes and spheres. Seam sections, when polished across fiber ends, reflect images from one side to the other causing this kind of ulexite to be called "television stone." Very heat sensitive; soft and brittle. Avoid dopping. Shape stones cautiously on very smooth-running 220 wheel. Television stone types are sawed across fibers but great care must be taken to prevent splitting. Polish with tin oxide or Linde A on felt or leather; cross-sections are polished on a strip of cloth or leather with the same agents. Alters upon surface, becoming coated with white powder, requiring repolishing.

Only from deposits in the borate district of Southern California.

VARISCITE

G. 2.2–2.5   **HM** 4.5   **HL** 3–5

Nodules often sliced through and polished as flat display specimens. Exceptionally hard and pure pieces afford excellent cabochons of vivid yellow-green color. Seldom pure and often penetrated by veinlets of other minerals of varying hardness. Difficult to prepare into cabochons of uniform curvature. Dark material harder, taking a better polish; paler material softer and more porous. Somewhat heat sensitive. Sand cautiously to avoid deforming cabochons. Polishes easily on leather with Linde A; also with cerium or tin oxide on felt. Finish flats with 1200 grit; polish on wood, wax, pitch, or laps covered with Pellon.

Gem material from localities in Utah and Nevada; colorful complete nodules, often very beautiful because of veinlets of other minerals in contrasting hues, from Fairfield, Utah.

VERDITE

G. 2.82–2.96   **HM** 3   **HL** 3

Massive, fine grained, opaque serpentine rock. Fairly tough. Not heat sensitive. Rough in large sizes. Grinds quickly, workable with steel tools. Polishes with Linde A on leather.

Only from near Nord Kaap in the Barberton District, South Africa.

VIVIANITE

Extremely easy cleavage causes rough to fall apart at slightest shock. The author has been completely unsuccessful in faceting this material. However, if preforms can be made, and the stone successfully dopped and ground, it can be polished with Linde A on wax. Fine, dark blue-green vivianite crystals suitable for faceting from Bolivia and Idaho.

WILLEMITE

G. 3.89–4.18   **HM** 5.5   **HL** 5.5   **R.I.** 1.69–1.72

Transparent to translucent. Green, yellow-green, reddish-brown, orange. Somewhat brittle. Not heat sensitive. Handles easily in grinding and polishing. Linde A on tin, or cerium oxide on Lucite will polish. Crown angles 40°, pavilion angles 40°. Sometimes massive material polished into cabochons, spheres, and ornamental objects. Only from zinc mines of Franklin, New Jersey, area.

WITHERITE

G. 4.27–4.35   **HM** 3–3.75   **HL** same   **R.I.** 1.53–1.68

Translucent, yellowish, brownish-yellow, fine grained massive. Sometimes translucent enough to facet. Tough. Not heat sensitive. Grinds easily and facets well. Use 1200 lap only. Polishes with scratching on normal laps; pre-polish on tin with Linde A and finish on wax. Crown angles 40°, pavilion angles 40°.

From Minerva Mine, Hardin County, Kentucky, in translucent pale yellowish masses; also from Lockport, New York.

WOLLASTONITE

G. 2.8–2.9   **HM** 4.5–5   **HL** 4

Fibrous material sometimes compact enough to polish. Pure white or very pale yellow to pink hues. Soft; easily ground away. Polish with Linde A on leather.

WULFENITE

G. 6.7–7.0   **HM** 2.75–3   **HL** same   **R.I.** 2.30–2.40

Transparent flattish orange-yellow to orangey-red crystals. Brittle; somewhat heat sensitive. Bright luster. Cleavages are not troublesome. Must be handled with care. Inspect cutting of facets frequently to avoid pitting. Prepolish on very smooth tin lap with Linde A; use wax lap for final polish with tin oxide. Crown angles 30°–40°, pavilion angles 37°–40°.

In fine transparent crystals from various mines in Arizona.

ZINCITE

G. 5.43–5.7   **HM** 4–4.5   **HL** 5   **R.I.** 2.01–2.03

Facet grade, transparent, deep orange-red material only from Franklin, New Jersey. Usu-

ally very small fragments; gems over ⅛ inch across rare. One good cleavage but not troublesome. Brittle, rather weak. Not heat sensitive. Grinds scratchily to smoothly depending on direction. Polish on tin with Linde A. Tends to scratch requiring changes in polishing direction. Crown angles 30°–40°, pavilion angles 37°–40°. Polished surfaces tarnish after several months but luster can be restored by light rubbing with tissue paper.

ZIRCON

Gem Varieties

Hyacinth or Jacinth—reddish brown.
Jargoon—smoky yellow.
Red; pale yellow; golden yellow; green; greenish blue; blue; and colorless.

G. 3.95–4.72   **HM** 7.5   **HL** 7.5–8   **R.I.** 1.79–1.99

In rolled crystals. Transparent. Brittle but tough. Not heat sensitive. Rough seldom large, but stones up to 50 carats have been cut.

Difficult to saw, tends to clog blade. Grinds easily in pre-forming but shows striking variations in hardness in cutting. Polishes easily but slowly on tin with Linde A. Crown angles 40°, pavilion angles 40°.

Blue and colorless varieties obtained by heat treatment of brownish or reddish stones; a piece of rough held in a pair of forceps over a gas flame and heated to glowing white heat shows decided change of color within a matter of minutes. The rough will not crack.

Rough mainly from Ceylon and Indochina; rarely from Kimberley Diamond Mine, and New South Wales. Australian material is sometimes very good but not large. Occasionally as small, clear, red areas in tips of large crystals from Renfrew County, Ontario.

ZOISITE

G. 3.12   **HM** 6–6.5   **HL** 4.0–4.5

Massive, bright-pink material is known as "thulite". Somewhat porous; undercuts; tends to gloss rather than polish. Very careful fine sanding on 400 cloth wet is required to give a finish which will polish well. A copious flow of water is necessary to give mild abrasive action. Polish on leather with Linde A or tin oxide; do not use chrome oxide.

Finest material from Trondheim, Norway, also good material from several localities in the United States.

Appendix 1—Mechanical Tables

TABLE OF RPM VERSUS PULLEY DIAMETER
Rpm Obtained by Using Various Pulley Combinations

Motor Pulley Size in Inches, 1,725 Rpm Motor	Arbor Pulley Sizes, in Inches														
	2	2¼	2½	2¾	3	3½	4	5	6	7	8	9	10	11	12
2	1,725	1,485	1,305	1,170	1,050	880	755	590	485	410	355	315	280	255	230
2¼	2,000	1,725	1,515	1,350	1,220	930	875	685	560	475	415	365	325	295	270
2½	2,280	1,960	1,725	1,540	1,390	1,160	1,000	780	640	540	470	415	370	335	310
2¾	2,550	2,200	1,935	1,725	1,560	1,300	1,120	875	715	610	530	465	415	380	345
3	2,815	2,440	2,140	1,910	1,725	1,440	1,240	970	795	675	585	515	460	420	380
3½	3,380	2,910	2,560	2,280	2,060	1,725	1,480	1,160	950	805	700	615	550	500	455
4	3,940	3,390	2,980	2,660	2,400	2,000	1,725	1,350	1,105	935	815	720	645	580	530
5	5,040	4,350	3,820	3,400	3,085	2,570	2,210	1,725	1,415	1,200	1,140	920	825	745	680

Note: The above table assumes that a ⅜ inch vee belt is used with the top of the belt flush with the top of the pulley. If the belt extends above the top, the effective diameter of each pulley will be increased and vice versa.

TABLE OF RIM SPEEDS FOR SAWS AND WHEELS

Diameter in Inches	To obtain the following rim speeds, in feet per minute:									
	1,000	2,000	3,000	4,000	5,000	6,000	7,000	8,000	9,000	10,000
	These revolutions per minute will be needed:									
1	3,820	7,640	11,460	15,280	19,100	22,920	26,740	30,560	34,375	38,200
2	1,910	3,820	5,730	7,640	9,550	11,460	13,340	15,280	17,190	19,100
3	1,275	2,550	3,820	5,095	6,370	7,640	8,915	10,190	11,460	12,730
4	955	1,910	2,865	3,820	4,775	5,730	6,685	7,640	8,595	9,550
6	635	1,275	1,910	2,550	3,185	3,820	4,455	5,095	5,730	6,365
8	475	955	1,430	1,910	2,385	2,865	3,340	3,820	4,295	4,775
10	380	765	1,145	1,530	1,910	2,290	2,675	3,055	3,440	3,820
12	320	635	955	1,275	1,590	1,910	2,230	2,545	2,865	3,185
14	275	545	820	1,090	1,365	1,635	1,910	2,185	2,455	2,730
16	240	475	715	955	1,195	1,430	1,670	1,910	2,150	2,385
18	210	425	635	850	1,060	1,275	1,485	1,700	1,910	2,120
20	190	380	575	765	955	1,145	1,335	1,530	1,720	1,910
24	160	320	475	635	795	955	1,115	1,275	1,435	1,590
30	125	255	380	510	635	765	890	1,020	1,145	1,275

Example: If a rim speed of 4,000 rpm is required for a 10-inch saw blade, look down the 4,000 column above and pick off 1,530 rpm opposite the number 10. Now look in the previous table and select any number reasonably close to 1,530 rpm; above and to the side will be given the pulley combinations that will deliver a rim speed of approximately 4,000 rpm.

Appendix 2—Weights and Measures Useful to the Gem Cutter

Carat: the unit of weight used for gemstones.

One gram equals . . . . 5 carats
One ounce avoir. equals . . 28.35 grams
One ounce avoir. equals . . 141.75 carats
One pound equals . . . . 453.60 grams
One kilogram equals . . . . . 1,000 grams
One kilogram equals . . . . . 2.203 pounds

Grain: the unit of weight used for pearls.

One grain equals . . . . ¼ carat

Troy weight: the weight used for precious metals.

24 grains equal . . . . 1 pennyweight

20 pennyweights equal . . . . 1 ounce
12 ounces equal . . . . 1 pound
One pound avoir. equals . . 14.58 ounces troy

Millimeter: used to give dimensions of gemstones.

One millimeter equals . . . . about 25.3 millimeters
One inch equals . . . . about ⅟₂₅ inch

ABBREVIATIONS

Carat—ct.	Grain—gn.	Ounces—oz.
Pound—lb.	Pennyweight—dwt.	
Millimeter—mm.	Avoirdupois—avoir.	

Appendix 3—Tables of Angles for Faceted Gems

The angles given below will produce satisfactory results in clear, well-polished facet material. As refractive indices rise, it is possible to cut gems somewhat shallower in relation to their width without destroying brilliance. This is reflected in the tables. Specific settings for certain gemstones are not attempted, and indeed it is doubtful if the exact settings advocated by some writers can be supported, inasmuch as there is so much disagreement among them. The author tabulated fourteen gemstones for which angles were given by four writers; in only *four* cases out of fourteen did they agree!

Gemstones falling with the following refractive index ranges may be cut within the crown and pavilion angles as shown. The general rule of thumb is that when the index rises, the angles may be decreased; when the index falls, the angles are increased.

GEMSTONE ANGLES BY REFRACTIVE INDEX RANGE

Refractive Index	Crown Angles	Pavilion Angles
1.40 to 1.60	40° to 50°	43°
1.60 to 2.00	40°	40°
2.00 to 2.50	30° to 40°	37° to 40°

A complete alphabetical list of gemstones with recommended ranges of angles is given below.

CROWN AND PAVILION ANGLES FOR GEMSTONES

Note: Angles are for main facets only in the case of brilliants; for step cuts they are for the facets at the apex of the pavilion and the middle facets on the crown.

Gemstone	Crown Angles	Pavilion Angles
Actinolite	40°	40°
Amber	40° to 50°	43°
Amblygonite	40°	40°
Analcime	40° to 50°	43°
Andalusite	40°	40°
Anglesite	40°	40°
Anhydrite	40° to 50°	43°
Apatite	40°	40°
Apophyllite	40° to 50°	43°
Aragonite	40°	40°
Augelite	40° to 50°	43°
Axinite	40°	40°
Azurite	40°	40°
Barite	40°	40°
Benitoite	40°	40°
Beryl	40° to 50°	43°
Beryllonite	40° to 50°	43°
Boracite	40°	40°
Brazilianite	40°	40°
Calcite	40° to 50°	43°
Cassiterite	30° to 40°	37° to 40°
Celestite	40°	40°
Cerussite	40°	40°
Chondrodite	40°	40°
Chrysoberyl	40°	40°
Cinnabar	30° to 40°	37° to 40°
Clinozoisite	40°	40°
Colemanite	40°	40°
Corundum	40°	40°
Crocoite	30° to 40°	37° to 40°
Cuprite	30° to 40°	37° to 40°
Danburite	40°	40°
Datolite	40°	40°
Diopside	40°	40°
Dioptase	40°	40°
Enstatite	40°	40°
Epidote	40°	40°
Euclase	40°	40°
Feldspar	40° to 50°	43°
Fibrolite	40°	40°
Fluorite	40° to 50°	43°
Garnet	40°	40°
Glass	40° to 50°	43°
Hambergite	40°	40°
Hodgkinsonite	40°	40°
Idocrase	40°	40°
Iolite	40° to 50°	43°
Kornerupine	40°	40°

CROWN AND PAVILION ANGLES FOR GEMSTONES (*Cont.*)

Gemstone	Crown Angles	Pavilion Angles
Kyanite	40°	40°
Leucite	40° to 50°	43°
Magnesite	40°	40°
Microlite	30° to 40°	37° to 40°
Natrolite	40° to 50°	43°
Obsidian	40° to 50°	43°
Opal	40° to 50°	43°
Periclase	40°	40°
Peridot	40°	40°
Petalite	40° to 50°	43°
Phenakite	40°	40°
Phosphophyllite	40°	40°
Pollucite	40° to 50°	43°
Prehnite	40°	40°
Proustite	30° to 40°	37° to 40°
Quartz	40° to 50°	43°
Rhodizite	40°	40°
Rhodochrosite	40°	40°
Rhodonite	40°	40°
Rutile	30° to 40°	37° to 40°
Scapolite	40° to 50°	43°
Scheelite	40°	40°
Serpentine	40° to 50°	43°
Silicon carbide	30° to 40°	37° to 40°
Simpsonite	30° to 40°	37° to 40°
Sinhalite	40°	40°
Smithsonite	40°	40°
Sodalite	40° to 50°	43°
Sphalerite	30° to 40°	37° to 40°
Sphene	30° to 40°	37° to 40°
Spinel	40°	40°
Spodumene	40°	40°
Stibiotantalite	30° to 40°	37° to 40°
Strontium titanate	30° to 40°	37° to 40°
Taafeite	40°	40°
Tektite	40° to 50°	43°
Topaz	40°	40°
Tourmaline	40°	40°
Tremolite	40°	40°
Willemite	40°	40°
Witherite	40°	40°
Wulfenite	30° to 40°	37° to 40°
Zincite	30° to 40°	37° to 40°
Zircon	40°	40°

Appendix 4—Magazines and Books

The following publications are useful to those wishing to keep abreast of current developments or to study the earth sciences further. Some of the books are out of print and are difficult to obtain because of keen competition for them. Inquire for rates to the magazines concerned.

MAGAZINES

Earth Science. Box 1357, Chicago, Ill., bimonthly. General earth sciences; includes mineralogy, paleontology, collecting and lapidary work.

Desert Magazine—Palm Desert, California. Interesting and detailed field trip articles in desert areas of southwestern United States and Mexico; also brief lapidary articles.

Gemmologist. N.A.G. Press, Ltd., Finwell House, 26 Finsbury Square, London, E.C.2., England; monthly, Agent for North America: George H. Marcher, 5250 Broadway Terrace, Oakland 18, Calif. Interesting and informative articles, many of value by recognized gemological authorities.

Gems and Gemology. Quarterly journal of the Gemological Institute of America, 11940 San Vicente Blvd., Los Angeles 49, Calif. Excellent and authoritative; includes book reviews, popular articles, and reports of trade laboratories.

Gems and Minerals. P.O. Box 687, Mentone, Calif.; monthly. Popular with amateurs; includes field trips, club and society news, practical articles on mineralogy and paleontology; heavy emphasis on lapidary work.

Journal of Gemmology. Quarterly journal of the Gemmological Association of Great Britain, Saint Dunstan's House, Carey Lane, London, E.C.2., England. Authoritative articles, association news, book reviews, and abstracts of articles in other journals.

Lapidary Journal. P.O. Box 518, Del Mar, Calif., monthly. Devoted exclusively to lapidary work, gem collecting and jewelry making. April issue is called the "Rockhound Buyers Guide" and is encyclopedic in scope. All issues contain numerous authoritative and interesting articles on every aspect of gems and gemology.

Mineralogist. P.O. Box 808, Mentone, Calif.; bimonthly. Covers all aspects of the earth sciences but greatest stress is laid upon minerology.

Rocks and Minerals. Box 29, Peekskill, N.Y.; bimonthly. Covers all aspects of the earth sciences with greatest emphasis on mineralogy and paleontology. Also articles on lapidary work, jewelry making, and others of interest to craftsmen and collectors.

BOOKS

ANDERSON, B. W.—*Gem Testing.* 6th ed., London: Heywood & Co., Ltd., 1958. Authoritative treatment on practical gemology and gem testing by a leading scientist in the field.

BAUER, M.—*Edelsteinkunde* (in German). Leipzig: Tauchnitz, 1909. Out of print. Classic work on precious stones and gemology. An English language edition by L. J. Spencer is also out of print and copies extremely expensive when obtainable.

ENGLISH, G. L. & D. E. JENSEN.—*Getting Acquainted with Minerals.* Revised edition. New York:

McGraw-Hill, 1958. Excellent for beginners in mineral collecting.

EPPLER, A.—*Die Schmuck- und Edelsteine* (in German). Stuttgart: Felix Krais Verlag, 1912. Out of print. Excellent work in which many lapidary processes used in German cutting centers are explained.

FISCHER, W.—*Praktische Edelsteinkunde* (in German). Ketturg Ruhr: Verlag Gustav Feller-Nottuln, 1953. A work on gemology containing much information on lapidary techniques and equipment used in Germany.

FORD, W. E.—*A Textbook of Mineralogy*. 4th ed., New York: John Wiley & Sons, 1932. Standard college text but of great value as a reference for beginners.

GRODZINSKI, P.—*Diamond Technology*. London: N.A.G. Press, Ltd., 1953. Exhaustive treatise on lapidary techniques for all gemstones in addition to diamond.

GUBELIN, E. J.—*Inclusions as a Means of Gemstone Identification*. Los Angeles: Gemological Association of America, 1953. Helpful to the student of gemology.

HOLTZAPFFEL, J. J.—*Turning and Mechanical Manipulation*. Vol. III. London: Holtzapffel & Co., 1864. Out of print. All volumes of this set are valuable to the lapidary but Volume III is most useful.

HURLBUT, C. S.—*Minerals and How to Study Them*. New York: John Wiley & Sons, 1952. A fine beginning text.

JENKINS, L. & B. MILLS—*The Art of Making Mosaics*. Princeton, N.J.: D. Van Nostrand Co., 1957. Valuable information directly applicable to the efforts of lapidary workers.

KRAUS, E. H. & C. B. SLAWSON—*Gems and Gem Materials*. New York: McGraw-Hill, 1947. Interesting popular treatment.

MAIER, W.—*Brillanten und Perlen* (in German). Stuttgart: E. Schweizerbartsche Verlag, 1949. The most thorough study available on the optics and theories of cutting gems for maximum brilliance.

von NEUMANN, R.—*The Design and Creation of Jewelry*. Philadelphia: Chilton, 1961. Excellent, thorough and clearly illustrated text with stress on modern designs and techniques.

PARSONS, C. J. & E. J. SOUKUP—*Gem Materials Data Book*. Mentone, California: Gemac Corp., 1957. Convenient compilation of gemstone data useful to the cutter as well as the gemologist.

————— *Gems and Gemology*. Mentone, California: Gemac Corp., 1961. Excellent gemological textbook designed specifically for the beginner.

QUICK, L. & H. LEIPER—*How to Cut and Polish Gemstones*. Philadelphia: Chilton Co., 1959. Inspiring treatment richly illustrated with photographs and drawings.

SHIPLEY, R. M.—*Dictionary of Gems and Gemology*. Los Angeles: Gemological Institute of America. Names all gems and gives brief technical data on many of them.

SHAW, L. E.—*Faceting*. Newark, New Jersey: privately published by the author. 1961. A fine small book, interestingly and clearly written; contains many valuable hints.

SINKANKAS, J.—*Gemstones of North America*. Princeton, New Jersey: D. Van Nostrand Co., 1959. Comprehensive descriptions; over 2,000 localities for gemstones.

————— *Gemstones and Minerals—How and Where to Find Them*. Princeton, New Jersey: D. Van Nostrand Co., 1961. Explains how minerals and gemstones form, where they form, and how to prospect for them. Also chapters on collecting, cleaning of specimens, and marketing.

SMITH, G. F. H.—*Gemstones*. 13th ed., revised by F. C. Phillips. London: Methuen & Co., Ltd., 1958. The standard authority on gemstones in the English language.

SOUKUP, E. J.—*Facet Cutters Handbook*. Mentone, California: Gemac Corp., 1959. Small booklet containing much information and cutting diagrams.

SPERISEN, F. J.—*The Art of the Lapidary*. 2nd ed. Milwaukee: Bruce Publishing Co., 1961. Excellent and detailed work on gem cutting, with much useful information on cutting and polishing or ornamental objects.

VICTOR, E. V. & L. M.—*Gem Tumbling*. 8th ed. Spokane, Washington: Victor Agate Shop, 1961. Small booklet clearly explaining the practice of tumbling.

WEBSTER, R.—*The Gemmologist's Compendium*. London: N.A.G. Press, Ltd. Outstanding compilation of gemstone data; invaluable to students and cutters as a ready reference.

Index

INDEX